THE JUDGMENT OF CULTURE

Legal systems do not operate in isolation but in complex cultural contexts.

This original and thought-provoking volume considers how cultural assumptions are built into American legal decision-making, drawing on a series of case studies to demonstrate the range of ways courts express their understanding of human nature, social relationships, and the sense of orderliness that cultural schemes purport to offer. Unpacking issues such as native heritage, male circumcision, and natural law, Rosen provides fresh insight into socio-legal studies, drawing on his extensive experience as both an anthropologist and a law professional to provide a unique perspective on the important issue of law and cultural practice.

The Judgment of Culture will make informative reading for students and scholars of anthropology, law, and related subjects across the social sciences.

Lawrence Rosen is the William N. Cromwell Professor Emeritus of Anthropology at Princeton University, USA, and Adjunct Professor of Law at Columbia Law School, USA. As an anthropologist he has worked on Arab social life and Islamic law; as a legal scholar he has worked on the rights of indigenous peoples and American socio-legal issues. He is a member of the bar of the State of North Carolina and the U.S. Supreme Court.

THE JUDGMENT OF CULTURE

Cultural Assumptions in American Law

Lawrence Rosen

Routledge
Taylor & Francis Group

LONDON AND NEW YORK

First published 2018
by Routledge
2 Park Square, Milton Park, Abingdon, Oxon OX14 4RN

and by Routledge
711 Third Avenue, New York, NY 10017

Routledge is an imprint of the Taylor & Francis Group, an informa business

British Library Cataloguing-in-Publication Data
A catalogue record for this book is available from the British Library

Library of Congress Cataloging-in-Publication Data
A catalog record has been requested for this book

ISBN: 978-1-138-23778-0 (hbk)
ISBN: 978-1-138-23779-7 (pbk)
ISBN: 978-1-315-29899-3 (ebk)

Typeset in Bembo
by codeMantra

For
Terry MacTaggart and Carol Zanca
colleagues and friends

CONTENTS

ILLUSTRATIONS

ACKNOWLEDGMENTS

Many of the issues considered in this book have a long history of thinking and re-thinking, and were I to acknowledge all those who have shared in their development the list would be inordinately long. For support, however, I wish to thank the School for Advanced Research, Santa Fe for the William Y. and Nettie K. Adams Fellowship in the History of Anthropology, the Stanford University Center for Advanced Study in the Behavioral Sciences for appointing me as a Mellon Fellow, the University of Arizona School of Anthropology for hosting me as a Residential Scholar during their centennial year, and my colleagues and students at Princeton University and Columbia Law School. I have also benefited from the comments by attendees at my University of Oxford Socio-Legal Studies Annual Lecture and as a Phi Beta Kappa Lecturer, as well as at talks I have presented at the University of Geneva and the law schools at the University of California, Berkeley, the University of Michigan, New York University, and Duke University. A special note of thanks is due to Thérèse de Vet and J. Stephen Lansing for the gracious loan of their Tucson home where portions of this book were written and to Matt Birkhold for many insights he added to the various topics raised here. Jeremiah D. LaMontagne was enormously helpful with the illustrations. The Native American Rights Fund allowed me to spend a summer as a legal intern when I was in law school, a privilege whose intellectual rewards I have gratefully reaped over the course of many years.

Sections of some of the chapters in this volume appeared previously and are reprinted by agreement with the original publishers: "Metaphor and the Narration of Native Intellectual Production," Michael Hanne and Robert Weisberg, eds., Metaphor and Narrative in the Law, New York: Cambridge University Press, 2017; "Natural Law, Religion, and the Jurisprudence of the US Supreme Court," in Franz von Benda-Beckman, et al., eds., Religion in Disputes, London: Palgrave Macmillan, 2013, pp. 183–200; "Anthropological Perspectives on the

Abolition of Marriage," in Anita Bernstein, ed., Marriage Proposals: Questioning a Legal Status, New York: New York University Press, 2006, pp. 147–70; and "The Anthropologist as Expert Witness," American Anthropologist, vol. 79, no. 3 (September 1977), pp. 555–78.

The book is dedicated to my friends and colleagues Terry MacTaggart and Carol Zanca who have had to put up with my ramblings, on land and at sea, only to be punished for their forbearance and good humor with yet more musings by a grateful author.

INTRODUCTION

"Left at large as we are…."

[To Judge Learned Hand from Justice Felix Frankfurter. December 6, 1947. Supreme Court of the United States:] *Dear B, I await with an eagerness bordering on impatience the full text of your opinion in the* Repouille *case. Apart from all the questions that arise in connection with mercy killing, my interest is aroused by the psychological-judicial problem that confronted you, namely to what extent may a judge assume that his own notions of right moral standards are those of the community? But if it is his job—as you and I believe it to be—to divine what may rightly be deemed the standards of the community, by what process is he to make that divination? How and whether should he look for disclosures of the community's mores?*[1]

★ ★ ★

In 1947, a case came before the Federal Court of Appeals for the First Circuit in Boston. Sitting on the three-judge panel were two cousins with the stentorian names of Learned and Augustus Hand; the third judge was Jerome Frank, a no less redoubtable and articulate figure.[2] The case before them involved a resident foreign national, Louis Repouille, who was seeking American citizenship. The statute required that eligible candidates must be "of good moral character." The problem was that Repouille had killed his terribly malformed thirteen-year-old son almost five years earlier. The jury had convicted him of manslaughter in the second degree with a recommendation of "utmost clemency." The district court trial judge placed Repouille on probation for a period that, by the time the naturalization issue came up, had already expired. The question, therefore, was whether a so-called mercy killing is "immoral" and thus renders a person ineligible for citizenship. Perhaps more to the point, since the American legal system does not permit judges to implement their own moral sensibilities, where exactly were the members of the court supposed to go to determine what constitutes good moral character? (Figure I.1)

FIGURE I.1 Louis Repouille in custody for killing child.
Source: Acme Newspictures, October 12, 1939; photo owned by author.

Writing for the two-man majority, Learned Hand appeared stymied. In his youth a very religious man who later became an agnostic, Hand—who was at once a politically active Progressive, a strong proponent of judicial restraint, and often described as the most influential judge who never sat on the Supreme Court—expressed his uncertainty, if not indeed his anguish, in the following terms (Figure I.2):

[O]ften questions will arise to which the answer is not ascertainable.... Indeed, in the case at bar itself the answer is not wholly certain; for we all know that there are great numbers of people of the most unimpeachable virtue, who think it morally justifiable to put an end to a life so inexorably destined to be a… brutish existence, lower indeed than all but the lowest forms of sentient life….Left at large as we are, without means of verifying our conclusion, and without authority to substitute our individual beliefs, the outcome must needs be tentative; and not much is gained by discussion. We can say no more than that, quite independently of what may be the current moral feeling as to legally administered euthanasia, we feel reasonably secure in holding that only a minority of virtuous persons would deem the practice morally justifiable, while it remains in private hands, even when the provocation is as overwhelming as it was in this instance.[3]

The majority found Repouille currently ineligible for citizenship but noted that all he need do is wait a short while, after which the manslaughter conviction would be too old to be relevant to a new application for citizenship.

Judge Frank dissented. Famous as a legal realist and head of the Securities and Exchange Commission in the years leading up to World War II, Frank's first book argued that judges were motivated by their personal psychological orientations while to the last he emphasized the fallibility and uncertainties present in the legal process.[4] In his dissent, Frank argued that *Repouille* should be remanded to the trial court for additional fact-finding using a somewhat different standard (Figure I.3):

FIGURE I.2 Judge Learned Hand.
Source: Phillippe Halsman/Magnum Photos.

FIGURE I.3 Judge Jerome Frank (1939).
Source: Harris & Ewing Collection, Prints and Photographs Division, Library of Congress, Washington, D.C., ref. #: LC-DIG-hec-26352; public domain.

> I incline to think that the correct statutory test (the test Congress intended) is the attitude of our ethical leaders. That attitude would not be too difficult to learn; indeed, my colleagues indicate that they think such leaders would agree with the district judge. But the precedents in this circuit constrain us to be guided by contemporary public opinion about which, cloistered as judges are, we have but vague notions. (One recalls Gibbon's remark that usually a person who talks of "the opinion of the world at large" is really referring to "the few people with whom I happened to converse.") The judge should give the petitioner and the government the opportunity to bring to the judge's attention reliable information on the subject, which he may supplement in any appropriate way.
>
> *(Repouille v. United States: 154)*

Where, then, would each of these judges have sent us to determine good moral character? Hand dismisses certain indicators, such as whether what was done was against the law.[5] After all, he suggests, were not the Abolitionists, in their opposition to slavery, acting morally though illegally? He also mentions the use of polls, but seems unsure of their appropriateness. Even Frank feels somewhat uncomfortable relying on studies of public opinion—which may account for his preferring the views of 'ethical leaders'—saying of the information the trial court on remand might adduce: "Of course, we cannot thus expect to attain certainty, for certainty on such a subject as public opinion is unattainable."[6] Hand even seems to reject the standard that was set for interpreting the statute in an earlier decision by his own court, i.e., whether "'the moral feelings, now prevalent generally in this country' would 'be outraged' by the conduct in question: that is, whether it conformed to 'the generally accepted moral conventions current at the time'."[7] And yet, in his own way each judge does feel somewhat "left at large" even as they are all quite prepared to import, one way or another, some of the cultural standards of their time and place.[8]

It could, of course, simply be that, for all their handwringing or obfuscation, judges are either doing whatever they want or that, like anyone else faced with uncertainties, they rely on the things they have learned from and shared with others like themselves. Judge Richard Posner (2016), for example, says that judges (including U.S. Supreme Court justices) are "inevitably" influenced by their political beliefs. Indeed, he and his fellow judges are so affected by their own upbringing, career experience, and religious background that they are often "impervious to evidence." He points to the role of a judge's religion, specifically noting that notwithstanding the death of Justice Antonin Scalia in 2016 there are still several ardent Catholics on the Supreme Court. Reminiscent of the dilemma posed for Hand and Frank (but with his characteristic self-assurance), Posner concludes that for judges such personal background features (which he calls "priors")

> tug them this way or that, and the tug may be decisive. That is inevitable, and bowing to the inevitable is not misconduct, however much it deviates from the 'official'—the self-protective 'the law made me do it'—conception of judicial decision-making.

Unusual as it is for a prominent judge to spell out matters in this fashion, Posner's concept of a judge's 'priors' remains rather generalized, and he does not address the question of how distinctively cultural concepts might play into specific decisions.

And it is this question—how do such cultural assumptions appear in American law—with which we will be concerned. Like Hand and Frank, though, utter precision is not to be expected and perhaps not even to be desired. It is not just that in so vast and diverse a country and so wide a range of judges and fact perceptions that a high degree of cultural uniformity is unlikely to be found, but that it is in the nature of things for there to be a multiplicity of means and contexts in which cultural concepts may be employed. By taking a case-study approach it may, however, be possible to triangulate in on a limited range of modes and situations in which such concepts do indeed appear to flesh out legal decisions, concepts that for all their open-endedness may be indispensable to and revelatory of much that transpires in the formation and articulation of legal decisions.

That the way courts go about incorporating cultural concepts is vital not just to their work but to public discussion and acceptance of critical issues should need little emphasis. Judicial phrases—'clear and present danger,' 'the right to be let alone,' 'a level playing field'—resonate well beyond the precincts of the court. Judge Irving R. Kaufman has said of the U.S. Supreme Court that its only armor is the cloak of public trust and its sole ammunition the collective hopes of society. But its shield and sword depend more on the instrument of language than on force, and the language employed is itself so deeply embedded in the available repertoire of recognizable cultural concepts as to be inseparable from them. Ideas of human nature, risk, familial life, individual responsibility, and mental capacities may certainly change over time, but the interaction of court and society at the juncture of shared conceptualizations is integral to the nature of the contest and its results.

Indeed, from the perspective in anthropology that I share, culture is that set of categorizations by which a people orient themselves with sufficient predictability toward one another and their environs so as to create a sense of the world as orderly, obvious, and natural. Such categories may be open-textured, just as the capacity to create such categories may be integral to the way our species evolved, and we may owe to this feature above all others our ability to adapt to changing circumstances.[9] Law, then, is no different than other domains of life in that it is not hermetically sealed within its own categories (any more than are religion, the marketplace, or the home), and by contributing to and deriving from multiple domains of a society's life the law gives to its distinctive imagination a vivid sense of reality. The task of this volume is to render visible some of the areas and means by which this process operates in a variety of legal contexts.

The strategy will be one of addressing a series of case studies—in the sense of legal cases and the concerns faced in the incorporation of cultural ideas in specific examples. In doing so I partake of a penchant, as an anthropologist, for the particular, and, as a lawyer, for contending stories as a useful way of revealing the actualities of bringing culture into law. To get the flavor of some of the ways cultural assumptions play into legal decisions, though, a few brief examples may help set the stage for the more extended instances that will then be discussed in the individual chapters.

Do you believe that when people are dying they tell the truth? Or that they do so at moments of great excitement, as when they identify the vehicle that has just struck a loved one? The rules of evidence in the United States generally do not permit second-hand testimony but do allow various exceptions, including statements made in extremis.[10] To some the rationale for this exception is, in the one case, that facing one's maker the dying person is prone to tell the truth, while an alternative explanation claims that it takes more time to formulate a lie than fear of imminent death allows. The latter conception of time and truth also grants an exception to the introduction of hearsay testimony when, close to the moment of a crime's commission, a suspect remains silent when accused of the crime, it being permissible to then introduce his silence as evidence of his having accepted as true the other's accusation. If the Federal Rules of Evidence that include this and other forms of 'excited utterances' as exceptions to the hearsay rule are, as the statute says, to be understood according to the principles of the common law "as they may be interpreted by the courts of the United States in the light of reason and experience," in what ways are reason and experience grounded on the judges' reading of cultural norms?[11]

Or, to choose another example, how does one go about assessing another's character? As we have seen in *Repouille* this can be central to an immigration issue, but it can also be crucial for jurors trying to determine if a witness is being truthful or for a judge trying to decide on an appropriate sentence.[12] My American students say they focus on 'body language'—whether the person appears uncomfortable and edgy—while my Chinese students say they look at the way the person eats—whether greedy or sharing. In a somewhat similar vein, what exactly would Justice Potter Stewart be drawing upon when he said, in a Supreme Court case on pornography, that he did not know what hard core pornography is but that "I know it when I see it"?[13] What assumptions go into barring polygamous unions once same-sex marriages are permitted? Or what cultural concept of shaming is at work when a judge pleads in open court with pharmaceutical executives to notify women still in danger of being harmed by their company's contraceptive device and the judge is found to have acted improperly?[14] Clearly, in these and similar situations, legal propositions are dependent on and derived from a set of assumptions about time, human nature, truth, and mortality. Without understanding those sources and interconnections, the rules—whatever else there is to be said for them—would be as meaningless to their adherents as would another culture's views of the probative value of oracles or witchcraft accusations.

Similar questions arise in numerous other legal contexts. What assumptions about a witness's credibility figure into deciding whether to permit a woman wearing a full face veil to testify in court (Lubet 2007), or whether someone who is blind or deaf should be qualified to serve as a juror?[15] How do judges describe relationships in family law cases, and what proclivities of human nature do they assume are universal in deciding such intimate matters?[16] If we allow husbands and wives—like congregants to their clergymen, patients to their doctors, and clients to their lawyers—the privilege of barring testimony by their spouse under certain circumstances, what are we assuming about the nature of truth, confidence, and the vulnerabilities of these relationships?[17] When U.S. Supreme Court Justice Anthony Kennedy characterizes those who are not married as lonely,[18] when Justice Antonin Scalia validates an all-male military school's discrimination against female cadets in part because integration would undermine the school's "Code of a Gentleman"—which contains such provisions as "A Gentleman does not hail a lady from a club window" and "does not mention names exactly as he avoids the mention of what things cost" (*United States v. Virginia* 1996: 602)—what images of society and gendered roles is each assuming? What is the actual content and source that judges would apply when they speak of 'dignity,' the 'traditions and conscience of our people,' or that the law should not sanction acts that are 'against good morals' (*contra bonos mores*)? What does it mean for a judge in an auto accident case to say that criminal negligence requires "that the carelessness must be such that its seriousness would be apparent to anyone who shares the community's sense of right and wrong" (*People v. Conway*), and how does a judge know—whether in a tort case or under a 'community standards' rule for determining pornography—where 'the community' is and what is in its mind? Similarly, one may ask what is our cultural notion of risk, such that just compensation may be paid, or free will, such that a contract may be invalidated if 'freedom of choice' is absent?[19] What do we assume about the nature of bargaining when, under the Uniform Commercial Code, particular terms may be deemed 'unconscionable'?[20]

In each of these examples—and those to follow throughout this book—no circumscribed theory of the relation of cultural propositions and the law will be propounded, no singular answer to styles of approach will be suggested for the whole of the American legal system.[21] Rather the aim, as is appropriate to many issues in the human sciences, is not so much to achieve an analytic goal as a synoptic one, not a universal theory of cause and effect but an understanding of a wide range of instances through which, like a gem turned in the light, we see the facets, the reflections, the interactions that enliven and describe the diverse roles of culture in the law. As William James said, "a large acquaintance with particulars makes us wiser than the possession of abstract formulas, however deep." To garner such a synoptic view of the role of culture in the law one must (to borrow a phrase) open wide 'the bounds of relevance,' remain mindful of the contingent nature of each case, and attend carefully to the language by which every instance is defined and appraised.

For example, in the opening chapter on the cultural defense plea we will see that the courts tend to regard culture not as a feature of a collectivity but as an attribute of the individual, rather like the personal choice of wardrobe or favored cuisine. To claim 'my culture made me do it' seems profoundly un-American. In so individualistic a nation as the United States refusing to view collective culture as a basis for personal excuse may seem unsurprising. But when people from other cultures come before the court, an inherent contradiction is almost unavoidable—that one wants to know about their situated background yet not use it as a formal defense to a criminal charge or the decisive element in a civil suit. As a test case of the ways in which culture slips into legal decision-making, one could hardly have a more provocative example than the specific cases in which we will see the cultural defense or its functional equivalent at work.

If culture is in some sense problematic, why not turn to the professionals, the experts who are supposed to understand the subject? Why not let them be the ones to bring cultural factors before the court and instruct the trier of fact in their proper relevance? In Chapter 2, we will look at my own profession—that of anthropology—and the ways in which the uses of its expertise have, in fact, played out over the course of time. Whether cases involving native peoples' land claims, race-related legislation, or matters of family law, anthropologists have appeared in a wide range of law suits, and the experience of informing the court has had the reciprocal effect of leading to decisions based on their expertise and reconsideration of the anthropologists' own theories as they have had to answer the distinctive questions posed by the proceedings.

If culture is the set of categories by which a group of people creates and organizes experience so as to orient actions toward one another, then surely the proliferation of these categories across numerous domains of social life—religious, political, economic, familial—gives those nested sets of categories the appearance of being both immanent and natural. And metaphor constitutes a—if not *the*—preeminent vehicle for stitching those domains together. To see how powerful metaphor is in law and the crucial role it plays in the process of bringing culture into legal decision-making, we will look at the specific instance of intellectual production by native peoples. We may be so used to thinking uncritically that the issue is one of intellectual *property*, or even *heritage*, that we may fail to appreciate the implications of choosing one metaphor over another. But when we consider some of the analogies that native peoples themselves apply, we have the opportunity to realize that what seems commonsensical to one culture and its legal system could come out quite differently if other metaphors are employed.

But perhaps culture is not what should be considered at all. Maybe there are natural propositions that transcend culture—transcend *any particular* culture. Commonly put under the heading of 'natural law' (or, at other times, 'natural rights'), this source of law is not supposed to constitute a basis for decisions before American courts. Yet, as a cultural notion in its own right, it does slip in, sometimes under other rubrics, sometimes through the orientation of a given judge. Focusing on the U.S. Supreme Court, Chapter 4 will survey the uses of natural law by that highest forum and consider in what ways the religious, cultural, and philosophical views of some of its justices may constitute a vehicle for importing cultural concepts of a very distinctive sort into their decisions.

Custom may be one of the more direct ways in which cultural practices are brought into the law. The example I want to use for this purpose may seem curious. What do you understand when a car coming toward you flashes its headlights? Is it that the driver wants you to go ahead, that he is asserting his right of way, that he is warning you of something, or even that he is engaged in a protest or celebration? Starting with a comparable practice that has developed at a traffic roundabout near my own university—a practice that is directly opposed to the law and the signage—I want to ask how custom shows up in the law and, indeed, how it is addressed by courts when it is in play. The cases that fall within this ambit—including important commercial considerations—will afford a chance to see how, even when not formally part of a court's purview, custom may intrude as the court seeks to fill in the facts and standards without which its judgments may seem to their adherents to make no sense.

What's wrong with incest may seem a question only a fool would ask. Everyone knows it is wrong, dangerous, just plain bad—what is there not to understand?

But if one begins to unpack the rationales and surveys the changing bounds of this taboo, the issue becomes far more problematic than it may seem at first glance. By considering the range of familial forms that have developed, the implications of new reproductive technologies, and the comparative instances that test claims of universal application, the example of incest will afford a way into seeing how developing social practices may challenge once-prevalent cultural assumptions and reveal much about the law's uncertain approach to cultural norms.

Is male circumcision child abuse? The answer at one level must surely be, yes. An infant, totally incapable of choice, is being subjected to removal of a portion of his body. Certainly, that must qualify as abuse if anything does. And yet this procedure—the most common operation performed in the United States—is quite legal. How have the courts addressed this issue, and how have they imported culture into their decisions, particularly when the rationales for this practice have changed over the course of time? Here, too, we have the opportunity to ask how concepts like cultural integrity, identity, belief in medical science, and parental versus state rights form part of a cultural paradigm, and how the law addresses their import.

If custom somehow goes beyond the individual and at times holds that individual to a standard not of his or her own making, and if at other times we press the concept of culture into an individual attribute because we do not, especially in the law, have a way of addressing collectivities, are there instances in which the courts are nevertheless prepared to consider communities as possessing rights or interests separate and distinct from those of the individual or the state? Here, what I shall call 'the romance of community' that is present in numerous domains of American culture comes up against the law's emphasis on individuals and state or federal institutions. Using as our key instance the case of the Amish who did not want to send their children to school beyond the eighth grade we will see how the U.S. Supreme Court, relying greatly on the testimony of an anthropologist at the trial level, allows the community a place in the legal analysis. It will be an example that, in a sense, rounds out nicely the ways in which culture makes its way into the law and vice versa.

While the concentration in this book is on the United States, as an anthropologist, I cannot resist the urge to make comparisons to other cultures, and as a lawyer I cannot resist the temptation to suggest solutions to what I see as continuing legal problems. I do not do so in all instances: The concentration on American law, as in the discussion of natural law and the Supreme Court, remains focused on only that nation's highest legal institution, while in other instances—for example the question of male circumcision—I remain, so far as policy is concerned, frankly indecisive. Indeed, as concerns such moments of indecision I take as my guiding avatar the character Lucy in the Peanuts cartoon who, while holding forth in her psychoanalytic booth, answers Charlie's question about what is wrong with him by saying that he is ugly and stupid and his mommy dresses him funny, and then, asked by Charlie what he should do about it, responds, 'I don't offer solutions, I am just here to point out what the problems are.' Many of the issues raised here have troubled philosophers and divines for ages. Here too I can only say that while many theologians may insist that 'ought' mirrors 'is' and some philosophers that 'is' should be 'ought,' like many of my fellow social scientists I am too much the relativist to rely on supposed universals. William Blake may have overstated it when he said "To Generalize is to be an Idiot. To Particularize is [Alone] the Distinction of Merit." But I do favor the particular for getting at the interconnected details and appreciating that over-inclusive explanations may defeat recognition of the distinctive.

At the end of the day, this volume is, then, an invitation to consider the issues rather than an offer of a theory of everything legal and cultural, and as such its aim is to foster an opening to issues opponents too often simplify and proponents too often constrict. I hope the examples that follow will help encourage those who identify with Lucy to think further about the problems and for those who identify with Charlie to see that, for all our failings, culture and law, for better *and* for worse, are there to help us understand the problems—and then to muddle through.

Notes

1 Quoted in Jordan (2013: 278–79). Justice Frankfurter, following the practice of the judge's own family, addressed Hand as B from his full name, Billings Peck Learned Hand.

2 Hand dealt with a number of cases in which good moral character was at issue: see Gerald Gunther (2010: 542–46). Hand tried to develop a concept of 'common conscience' in these cases but bridled at the legislature requiring him to make such decisions at all. He also did not like leaving matters to the jury, which in at least one case had sentenced a man to life imprisonment for euthanasia. See Gunther (2010: 545).

3 *Repouille v. United States* (1947: 153). Gunther (1994: 633) states:

> Hand reached this rare conclusion only after extensive discussion with his colleagues. Having at first been prepared to admit Repouille to citizenship, relying mainly on the jury's obvious compassion—'Not only does the law at times fail to keep pace with current morals; but current morals at times may make the law morally inadequate'—he found this impulse was not shared by his colleagues Gus Hand and Jerome Frank.

Indeed, Hand also seemed to be sympathetic to the dilemma jurors faced in determining where the truth lies when the character of a criminal defendant is at issue: "With only the rough and ready tests supplied by their experience of life, the jurors were to look into the workings of another's mind, and discover its capacities and disabilities, its urges and inhibitions, in moments of intense excitement" (*People v. Zacowitz*).

4 Frank's picture appeared on the cover of *Time* magazine's issue of March 11, 1940. Frank's first book (1931) was written after six months of personal psychoanalysis; his later work (1949) was written around the time of the Repouille case and stressed the role that partisanship and imperfect procedures play in the trial process.

5 In *United States ex rel. Iorio v. Day* (p. 921), Hand, ruling in 1929 that a violation of prohibition laws was not an act of "moral turpitude" warranting deportation, first articulated his "common conscience" test for such cases: "While we must not, indeed, substitute our personal notions as the standard, it is impossible to decide at all without some estimate, necessarily based on conjecture, as to what people generally feel."

In *Schmidt v. United States*, where he held that extra-marital sex did not constitute an act of moral turpitude, Hand dismissed "anything so tenebrous and impalpable as the common conscience." For an assessment of the good moral character requirement that is still incorporated in American statutory law, as applied in the post-9/11 world, see Chin and Hassan (2015).

6 *Repouille v. United States* (Frank dissenting, note 4). In their correspondence Judge Hand and Justice Frankfurter ridiculed Judge Frank's suggestion that courts should rely on the opinion of ethical leaders.

> [To Felix Frankfurter, December 9, 1947. Judge Learned Hand's Chambers.] "F. F.: I am enclosing a copy of our opinion in the *Repouille* case. I suppose I should have realized that it would get a good deal of publicity and be thoroughly misunderstood. Perhaps this has been accentuated by Jerry's [Judge Jerome Frank's] to me *outré* dissent. I assume that he expected the district judge, *sua sponte*, to call the Cardinal Bishop Gilbert, an orthodox and a liberal rabbi, Reinhold Niebuhr, the head of the Ethical Culture Society, and Edmund Wilson to be all crossexamined ending in a 'survey.' Oh, Jesus! I don't know how we are supposed to deal with such cases except by the best guess we have…"

> [To Learned Hand from Felix Frankfurter. December 11, 1947. Supreme Court of the United States.] "Dear B.: Your opinion in the *Repouille* case is a shining example of 'form' as part of 'substance.' The way you state the elements of the problem makes persuasive—to me inevitable—the conclusion. It really is fantastic to assume that the kind of confused ethical judgements you would get from Jerry's imagined panel of experts would be a dependable basis for a judicial judgment on such an issue as you had before you."

> *(quoted in Jordan 2013: 279–80. See the fuller quote at Gunther 1994: 632)*

(Jordan leaves out of her quotation from Hand's letter to Frankfurter the phrase "Oh, Jesus!" which is included in the quote as rendered by Gunther 2010: 544.) In a case involving the same statute decided by the Supreme Court a few years later, Justice Jackson, citing Hand, picked up on the phrasing the latter had used to express his dilemma: "How should we ascertain the moral sentiments of masses of persons on any better basis than a guess!" (quoted from Jackson's dissent in *Jordan v. De George*, 341 U.S. 223 (1951) in Gunther 1994: 630).

7 *United States v. Francioso*. See also Hand's opinion in *United States ex rel. Iorio v. Day*. Direct inquiries into moral conduct may arise in other contexts, such as the employment terms of a teacher, judge, professional athlete, or entertainer. Courts, looking very much to cultural standards, have not found such character clauses too vague to enforce. For another example, see Dubler (2006).

8 One study (Danziger et al., 2011) even claims that whether and at what time a judge has a snack affects his or her decision.

9 For the theory involved in this view of culture, see Geertz (1973: 33–86). A wonderful contemporary American example of unusual categorizing is mentioned in Case (2005: 1130–31), in which a West Point cadet says that "meat taken in action always tastes better than food captured at the grocery" because the cow is betrayed by the man who nurtures but then slaughters it, whereas "deer is meat that has never been lied to."

10 See, e.g., *Commonwealth of Pennsylvania v. Brown*, particularly the thoughtful dissent by Justice Musmano about the assumptions that go into regarding a dying declaration as similar to an oath in its probative value. See also, Liang (1998).

11 As for an excited utterance being less likely to involve lying, a county sheriff in the hard-scrabble coal mining region of Virginia explained his support for Donald J. Trump saying: "He talks before he thinks, so he doesn't have time to think up something and lie to you" (Davis and Ballhaus 2016: A12).

12 See, e.g., Yankah (2004); and, for the British situation, Spenser (2006).
13 *Jacobellis v. Ohio* (1964: 197). On the rationality of Stewart's statement, see Gewirtz (1996).
14 See Mokhiber (1988: 149–63); Engelmayer and Wagman (1985: 227–63).
15 See *United States v. Watson* (it is within the discretion of the trial court to determine if there is a basis for excluding a deaf or blind person from serving on the jury).
16 "What views of human nature inform family law?... A family law that fears that people are naturally depraved must differ from one that hopes they are naturally virtuous" (Schneider 1985: 1057–58).
17 See, e.g., *United States v. Tsinnijinnie* (1979: 1039) (disallowing privilege in a case of an excited utterance heard by a spouse: "Experience demonstrates that the potential benefits of the marital privilege are often more imaginary than real.")
18 *Obergefell v. Hodges* ("Marriage responds to the universal fear that a lonely person might call out only to find no one there.... [Same-sex couples'] hope is not to be condemned to live in loneliness"). Observers noted, however, that two of the Kennedy's female colleagues, Justices Sotomayor and Kagan, have chosen to remain single. See, Cobb (2015).
19 On risk perception and the relevance of its cultural foundations for tort law, see Wilson (2011). On freedom of choice and contract, see, e.g., the language in *Kugler v. Romain*.
20 Useful comparative sources on the concept of unconscionability include Angelo and Ellinger (1979), Beatson (1981), and Bridwell (2003).
21 Other examples and a more extensive theory of culture are discussed in Rosen (2008).

References

Angelo, A. H. and E. P. Ellinger 1979, "Unconscionable Contracts," *Otago Law Review*, vol. 4, pp. 300–39.

Beatson, J. 1981, "Unconscionability: Placebo or Pill?" *Oxford Journal of Legal Studies*, vol. 1, no. 3, pp. 426–31.

Bridwell, Philip 2003, "The Philosophical Dimensions of the Doctrine of Unconscionability," *University of Chicago Law Review*, vol. 70, pp. 1513–32.

Case, Mary Anne 2005, "Pets or Meat?" *Chicago-Kent Law Review*, vol. 80, pp. 1129–50.

Chin, Jennifer and Zeenat Hassan 2015, "As Respected as a Citizen of Old Rome: Assessing Good Moral Character in the Age of National Security," *University of California Irvine Law Review*, vol. 5, pp. 945–72.

Cobb, Michael 2015, "The Supreme Court's Lonely Hearts Club," *New York Times*, June 30.

Danziger, Shai, Jonathan Levav, and Liora Avnaim-Pesso 2011, "Extraneous Factors in Judicial Decisions," *PNAS (Proceedings of the National Academy of Sciences)*, vol. 108, no. 17, April 26, pp. 6889–92.

Davis, Bob and Rebecca Ballhaus 2016, "The Place That Wants Donald Trump Most," *Wall Street Journal*, April 18, p. A1.

Dubler, Ariela R. 2006, "Immoral Purposes: Marriage and the Genus of Illicit Sex," *Yale Law Journal*, vol. 115, pp. 756–812.

Engelmayer, Sheldon and Robert Wagman 1985, *Lord's Justice: One Judge's Battle to Expose the Deadly Dalkon Shield I.U.D.*, New York: Anchor Press/Doubleday.

Frank, Jerome 1931, *Law and the Modern Mind*, New York: Brentano's.

——— 1949, *Courts on Trial: Myth and Reality in American Justice*, Princeton: Princeton University Press.

Geertz, Clifford 1973, *The Interpretation of Cultures*, New York: Basic Books.

Gewirtz, Paul 1996, "On 'I Know It When I See It,'" *Yale Law Journal*, vol. 105, 1023–47.

Gunther, Gerald 1994, *Learned Hand: The Man and the Judge*, New York: Alfred A. Knopf.

——— 2010, *Learned Hand: The Man and the Judge*, 2nd edn., Oxford: Oxford University Press.

Jordan, Constance, ed. 2013, *Reason and Imagination: The Selected Correspondence of Learned Hand*, Oxford: Oxford University Press.

Liang, Bryan A. 1998, "Shortcuts to 'Truth': The Legal Methodology of Dying Declarations," *American Criminal Law Review*, vol. 35, pp. 229–77.

Lubet, Steven 2007, "Veiled Truth," *The American Lawyer*, March 1.

Mokhiber, Russell 1988, *Crime and Violence*, San Francisco: Sierra Club Books.

Posner, Richard A. 2016, "The Supreme Court is a Political Court: Republicans' Actions are Proof," *Washington Post*, March 9.

Rosen, Lawrence 2008, *Law as Culture: An Invitation*, Princeton: Princeton University Press.

Schneider, Carl E. 1985, "The Next Step: Definition, Generalization, and Theory in American Family Law," *University of Michigan Journal of Law Reform*, vol. 18, pp. 1039–59.

Spenser, John R. 2006, *Evidence of Bad Character*, Oxford: Hart Publishing.

Wilson, Molly J. Walker 2011, "Cultural Understandings of Risk and the Tyranny of the Experts," *Oregon Law Review*, vol. 90, pp. 113–89.

Yankah, Ekow N. 2004, "Good Guys and Bad Guys: Punishing Character, Equality and the Irrelevance of Moral Character to Criminal Punishment," *Cardozo Law Review*, vol. 25, pp. 1019–67.

Cases cited

Commonwealth of Pennsylvania v. Brown, 388 Pa. 613, 131 A.2d 367 (1957).

Jacobellis v. Ohio, 378 U.S. 184 (1964).

Kugler v. Romain, 58 NJ 522, 279 A.2d 640, 652 (1971).

Obergefell v. Hodges, 576 U.S. ___ (2015).

People v. Conway, 6 N.Y.3d 869 (N.Y. Ct. of Appeals 2006).

People v. Zacowitz, 254 N.Y. 192, 172 N.E. 466 (N. Y. Ct. App. 1930).

Repouille v. United States, 165 F.2d 152 (2d Cir. 1947).

Schmidt v. United States, 177 F.2d 450 (2d Cir. 1949).

United States v. Francioso, 164 F.2d 163 (2nd Cir. 1947).

United States ex rel. Iorio v. Day, 34 F.2d 920 (2nd Cir. 1929).

United States v. Tsinnijinnie, 601 F.2d 1035 (9th Cir. 1979).

United States v. Virginia, 518 U.S. 515 (1996).

United States v. Watson, 483 F.3d 828 (D.C. Cir. 2007).

PART I
Bringing culture into the law

1

DEFENDING CULTURE

The cultural defense and the law's theory of culture

Over the years, I have had occasion to pose two questions to audiences comprised of judges and academics in both the U.S. and the UK. When I ask in regard to criminal law how many would like there to be a formal cultural defense, in which a plea is based on how one is expected to act in one's own culture, few if any hands are raised. When I ask how many think information about the culture of the accused should be allowed into evidence, virtually all of the hands go up. Similar responses are obtained when a civil case is proposed. In one sense, this may not be a contradiction, for many of those responding say they want to hear the cultural information either for purposes of understanding the acts involved or to gauge an appropriate outcome, even though introducing aspects of one's culture should not be treated in the same way as a self-defense or insanity plea.

In many respects, of course, keeping a person's culture out of consideration is impossible. As one American judge told me, "the moment I see the person has a particular accent or is clearly from a foreign culture how can I be expected not to let it rouse my curiosity?" And certainly, there are many ways for an attorney to slip in information about the party's cultural background even if no formal defense is permitted. Cultural background often figures in both criminal and civil proceedings. However, scholars rarely ask how American courts think about culture in these contexts. If a formal cultural defense is not favored yet cultural information is desired, how should such information be structured into the proceedings? How do courts conceptualize culture, and how may current theories of culture help us think about individual versus collective orientations? How, in this context, do courts approach issues of free will, internal cultural variation, and the proper role of experts?

In this chapter, we will review a number of cases that raise these and similar issues and consider not only how culture makes its way into judicial proceedings in this regard but how one might best manage its consideration absent a formal cultural defense.

The dilemma of the cultural defense

The cases themselves go a long way toward pointing up the dilemma.

In January 1985, Mrs. Fumiko Kimura tucked her four-year-old son under one arm, her six-month-old daughter under the other, and walked into the waters of the Pacific Ocean off a beach at Santa Monica, California.[1] By the time people nearby realized their difficulty both children had drowned. Mrs. Kimura was rescued. She told officials that she had recently learned that her husband had been having an affair with another woman and although the relationship had been concluded, she believed the appropriate way for a traditional Japanese woman like herself to eliminate the shame such an affair brings to the family is to engage in *oyako-shinju* (parent-child suicide). While the practice is punishable under Japanese law, the penalty, if any, is usually very light, the mother's act being seen as one of love and devotion: "The mother who commits suicide without taking her child with her is blamed as an *oni no yon a hito* (demon-like person)" (Iga 1986: 18). "According to one report, Kimura said of her rescuers: 'They must have been Caucasians, otherwise they would have let me die.'"[2] The state charged her with murder. A petition was quickly signed by over 4000 members of the Japanese-American community in Los Angeles stating that her action was understandable, especially for one who, though a resident in the U.S. for many years, spoke little English and was very traditional in orientation. By the time of her trial more than 25,000 people had called for her release, including the initial district attorney in the case. Eventually, Mrs. Kimura was allowed to plead guilty to two counts of voluntary manslaughter. She was sentenced to a year in prison but because she had been held in custody for more than that period she was immediately released and put on five years' probation. Although everyone agreed that her cultural background should not have been a relevant consideration, it is far from clear that it was in fact disregarded.[3]

A few months later, in Fresno, California, Kong Moua, a twenty-three-year-old Hmong tribesman from Laos, took Seng Xiong, a nineteen-year-old woman who was also a Laotian Hmong, from her workplace at a local community college. When she charged him with kidnapping and rape he countered that this was an act of traditional Laotian 'bride capture' and that the woman's protestations and his act of sex with her at the house of his relative was consonant with the next step in their engagement/betrothal process.[4] Judge Gomes permitted the cultural evidence to be heard and the defendant was allowed to plead guilty to a misdemeanor of false imprisonment for which he received a few months' sentence and a $1000 fine, most of which was paid to the victim as a form of reparation.[5]

In Alaska, at just about the same time, charges were being dismissed, following a four-day trial, against an Eskimo man charged with child sexual abuse. The court found that attempts at fondling the genitals of a twelve-year-old white boy at a birthday party attended by white and Eskimo children at the defendant's home were part of Eskimo cultural behavior when a young boy achieves manhood and that the actions of the defendant were devoid of any unlawful erotic intent.[6]

Cases such as these raise serious questions about the relevance of cultural background to the defense of a criminal charge.[7] Much of the discussion has centered on the use of cultural information to mitigate the penalties imposed, particularly where the incident involves an act of violence by a man against a woman that, even if permissible in his country of origin, is not acceptable in the United States. It can, however, be misleading to assume that these cases concern only mitigation or gender crimes: The full range of cases—many of which are not the subject of reported judgments—must be kept in mind as one analyzes the uses of cultural data in such instances.

Thus, one can point to a case in which a Haitian immigrant who killed a man he believed was working voodoo against him had the charge of murder reduced to manslaughter based, in part, on anthropological testimony; the trial of an Ethiopian man who was acquitted by a jury for wounding a woman he thought was an evil spirit (Renteln 2004: 39); the case of *New York v. Chen* (1988), in which a man killed his purportedly adulterous wife and was given a mild sentence based, in part, on the (often incorrectly reported) testimony of an anthropologist; the British case in which a judge mitigated the sentence of a gang of Somali Muslim girls who beat a non-Muslim because, he said, given the Islamic prohibition they were not used to drinking alcohol (Rayner 2011); or the appellate opinion in the case of a Puerto Rican youth who wished to show in mitigation that he would have been a social pariah in his community in Connecticut if he had not fired a gun, rather than run away (as the state law required), when threatened by a group of other Puerto Ricans (*State v. Rodriguez*). Cases may involve serious infractions, as when Middle Eastern parents have engaged in the 'honor killing' of a disobedient daughter (Abu-Odeh 2005a,b; Cohan 2010; Rose 2009; Wikan 2008),[8] or be dismissed as relatively trivial, as when a Danish mother visiting New York was subjected to a criminal charge for leaving her child outside where she could see her while the mother went into a cafe, as is common in Europe (Sullivan 1997; Weiser 1999), or be regarded as harmless infractions as when an Afghan man, following the custom of his native country, kissed the penis of his small child but was not convicted of child sexual abuse because the harm was deemed so slight as not to amount to a criminal act (*Maine v. Kargar*; Wanderer and Connors 1999).[9]

In civil cases, too, the issue of cultural understanding has played a role. For example, after an Iranian wife argued that it was the custom in their culture for the husband to hold the wife's property in trust for her, rather than to share equally in it, a court found that, while not accepting Iranian custom, a constructive trust existed such that the wife's pre-marital property would not have to be divided as required by the state divorce law. In another case, a Japanese man was permitted to have a condition of his employment contract read in by the court when he showed that Japanese custom precluded his asking specifically about the terms of a commission from his superiors.[10] Similarly, courts have looked to the secular elements of Muslim law and custom in deciding cases of child custody (*Nahavandi v. Nahavandi*),[11] bridewealth payment (*Odatalla v. Odatalla*), and—for the limited purposes of inheritance and workman's compensation—the interests of a polygamous spouse.[12]

While culture has frequently been employed as a defense, it should be noted that it has also been used as a prosecutorial tool. Thus in Britain prosecutors have charged some Muslims with 'honor killings' rather than simple manslaughter in order to get the higher penalties such a listed crime carries.[13] And in one amusing American case, a federal district attorney charged individuals who were going on trial for drug dealing with having attempted to kill the judge assigned their case by sending home to Haiti for a voodoo doll in the shape of the judge (Curriden 1989). No one seems to have told the prosecutors, however, that you cannot actually kill someone by poking needles in an effigy—but then no one seems to have told the defendants that, by the standards of their own culture, they should have known that voodoo does not work across water!

As one combs through the records, and attends to the anecdotes of colleagues involved in such cases, it appears that courts often do consider the cultural background of defendants, particularly immigrants (and sometimes tourists), even though the 'cultural defense' has received no formal acknowledgment in any American jurisdiction. Informal interviews with many American and British judges indicate almost all wish to hear about the parties' cultural background even though they do not favor a formal cultural defense.[14] Cultural stereotypes may be consciously employed in legal proceedings. Attorneys for Native Americans have told me that at times they have played on the court's stereotypes of Indian alcoholism to get drunkenness-related charges against their clients dismissed or reduced. In many instances, though, courts have flatly refused to consider evidence of the defendant's cultural background. For example, in the rape trial of an African-American, testimony was not allowed that purported to show that in the parties' cultural milieu people commonly shout at each other and hence the victim's loud response would not readily have been understood as a refusal to have sex with him (*People v. Rhines*). So, too, in *Nguyen v. State,* evidence of verbal abuse directed against the accused wife—evidence that may have supplied some context to her fears—was ruled inadmissible by the lower court judge. However, on appeal the Georgia Supreme Court ruled that in certain instances such cultural information might be relevant and admissible, although they did not support its introduction in this particular instance (see generally, Crockett 2005–6). Similarly, the New Jersey appellate court, in *S.D. v. M.J.R.*, ruled that it was an error for the lower court to regard a Muslim husband as not having the intent to commit marital rape simply because he thought Islam gave him the right of sexual access to his wife even without her consent, a cultural consideration the higher court said it "soundly rejects."

In other instances, courts have refused to allow anthropologists to testify as to the cultural background of a South Asian whose sensibilities about caste may have contributed to the nature of the provocation he said was offered (*People v. Poddar*;

Blum 1986), while other courts have refused to hear expert testimony on the cultural meaning of alcohol consumption among Native Americans.[15] The procedural standards of a criminal trial have also been applied to preclude culturally distinctive defendants from telling their stories in their own fashion, even when doing so would not necessarily contradict existing rules. For example, Zacarias Moussaoui, tried in connection with the events of 9/11, may have pled guilty, as Moroccans commonly do, so that he could then explain the reasons he believed his act to be justified. Moussaoui may also have disrupted the proceedings at moments because he could not address the jurors directly, and he may have appeared irrational when the court disallowed testimony that went to past actions and other 'irrelevant' factors that Moussaoui may have thought indispensable to his self-presentation.[16] Whether admitted or excluded, the issues raised by cultural evidence thus bring into focus both the theoretical problems posed for analysts and the practical issues that attend the use of such information.[17] Indeed, these cases question the ways in which culture is understood by the American legal system generally.

The most obvious political and legal difficulty posed by the prospect of a cultural defense is simply one of standardized law applicable to all versus the balkanization of the legal system that might result from allowing different defenses for people of different backgrounds. Within the broad ideology of assimilationist views many Americans regard cultural differences as inherently divisive, indeed as "a break in the social compact."[18] It is along these lines that Coleman (1996), for example, argues that in the interests of 'ordered liberty' the cultural defense must be denied. Others would permit it on the basis of 'fairness' (Sing 1999) or as a means of stressing that society as a whole has an interest in viewing difference as contributing to everyone's relationships rather than being the concern of a group or individual alone (Wade 2000: 48–49). Some commenters argue in favor of the defense because the preservation of cultural practices that lie within a range to which American law can afford to accommodate itself should be paramount (Renteln 2004) or because a party to whom a communicative bridge has not been adequately extended cannot receive a truly fair trial (Duff 1998). Others reflect either ambivalence or indecisiveness. Thus, Phillips (2007: 99) argues that paying too much attention to culture results in insupportable generalizations yet calls for a "more nuanced way" that would deal with both gender and class, without specifying how that might be accomplished.[19]

How, then, is one to balance the needs of uniformity and inclusiveness with an appropriate level of sensitivity to multicultural concerns? If, as Joseph Raz (1990) suggests, our theories of justice are more political than neutrally philosophical, and if, as Michael Walzer (1983) argues, we are entitled to do what is right *for us* (even if it does not have universal value), may we not apply our own standards in pursuit of the congruity of our own culture, notwithstanding the risk, as Coleman (1996) reminds us, of going against some of our liberal values?[20] But is it really fair to expect people to live up to the behavior of the dominant community when it means having to exercise choices that may jeopardize their own distinctive identity? What theory of free will and individual psychody-namics best suits the needs of legal decision-making when culture is taken into consideration? Is it proper to distinguish between justification and excuse in the criminal law—or indeed to limit severely the range of permissible excuses—if the foundation of the right to punish is the existence of moral blameworthiness, which may itself be inflected by cultural expectations? If we agree to mitigate our punishments for considerations of cultural background, why not do so be-cause of a socially deprived upbringing? And if we do not allow mitigation in such cases do we sacrifice to some image of cultural uniformity those who are in a weakened position to choose between the contexts of their existence? Nor can we ignore for a moment that a large proportion of the cases involve violence against women, and that it would be naïve to enter into decisions about crimes of violence if we do not take gender seriously into consideration.

On a more theoretical plane the cultural defense calls into question some of the basic ways in which the concept of culture is itself characterized and used in the social sciences.[21] Is it best to think of culture as a highly personalized feature, like mental state, such that analogies to its place in explaining behavior should be drawn from those applied in the insanity defense or a diagnostic manual's list of specific cultural forms of mental aberration (e.g., 'running amok,' a diagnosis limited to Malays)?[22] If instead we think of culture predominantly as a matter of shared symbols, conceptions, and orientations—the attributes of a group—are we also required to think of the individual's attachment to his or her own cul-ture in terms of shared responsibility, with all of its legal implications? Indeed, how uniform is any culture and who speaks for it? If, for example, the men and women of a given culture have rather different orientations, or endure different effects from, say, the male-dominated view of women's 'proper' roles and behav-ior, to whose view of the matter should preeminent legal attention be directed? And if we do allow the cultural defense in a more regularized way, how shall the concept of reasonableness be configured, and why should such a concept not serve to acquit a defendant altogether rather than just mitigate the offense?

At the core of all of these issues lies a view of culture, as portrayed in popular sentiment, embraced by legal institutions and encouraged by professional social science. Whatever might be argued for or against the formal adoption of a cul-tural defense, in the law it is this vision of culture itself that must be unpacked, examined, and perhaps subjected to measured reassessment by theoreticians and practitioners alike.

The implicit legal theory of culture

Provocation provides an excellent place to begin such a consideration. American law, in concert with its broader common law development and the Judeo-Christian emphasis on the formation of individual mental states, has long held that for most serious crimes the accused must be shown to have possessed the intent to commit the act involved: We simply do not believe it is fair to inflict unmitigated punishment on those who lack the capacity to intend their acts. And notwithstanding a multitude of hazy definitions, hairsplitting delineations, and outright exceptions (i.e., the limited use of strict liability offenses) this mental element has long remained central to our sense of legal culpability and fair play.

At the same time, Anglo-American law recognizes that human beings are vulnerable and may, at times, be prompted to unlawful responses by the provocative acts of another. If each person is not to set his or her own standard for acceptable levels of provocation some impersonal standard has had to be asserted by the courts, and it is here that one manifestation of the concept of culture may come into play. Generally speaking, courts have said that the reaction of the defendant must have been that of a 'reasonable' person, indeed a reasonable person in similar circumstances. Thus, people who take deadly offense at a personal slight, however susceptible they may have been to such an act or remark, must be judged against a more objective standard than their own felt sense of injury. Of course, the idea of provocation, though cast as a common human reaction, may itself be deeply suffused with cultural assumptions and may thus embrace what, in a particular culture, is both the expressed ideal of human behavior in various situations and an articulation of how a society is willing to limit its reaction to violence.[23] Where the matter becomes still more intriguing from a cultural point of view is if the defendant's response was not a personal one—as we tend to imagine it in Anglo-American culture—but a feature of an impersonal cultural standard. One of the domains in which the common law has tested the meaning and limits of culture's role in the question of provocation has concerned accusations of witchcraft in former colonial territories.

In a long line of cases, the British courts and their successors in sub-Saharan Africa, Australasia, and North America have been faced with instances in which an individual harmed another believing that potentially lethal witchcraft was being used against the accused or his close relatives. The courts have had to decide whether a reasonable person standard should be used and if so whether that reasonable person was to be, say, a native African who believed in witchcraft or the 'modern' man on the street in London or Nairobi. Although some courts tended to regard witchcraft as impossible—and hence a reasonable belief in its efficacy would be a non-sequitur—most came to adopt the idea that if the belief, though 'reasonable,' led to dangerous behavior the requisite intent to commit the forbidden act was clearly present (Dumin 2006; see also Dressler 2002; Gershiere 2006; Kanter 1995; Seidman 1966; Yeo 1987). Yet, as some commenters and jurists have pointed out, it is equally clear that it may be unjust to punish a person who cannot realistically choose to believe other than he or she does.[24] True, the state may compel alternative behavior, either by threat or actual punishment. And it is no less true that even if culture does not determine all of a person's actions it may be unfair for the state to pretend that defendants are entirely free in their choice of the conduct they believe to be appropriate. The dilemma is compounded by a moral and psychological model of free will and responsibility coupled with a political desire to cast all citizens in the same mold of socially acceptable conduct (Sommers 2012).

An interesting response to this conundrum is shown in the 1982 decision *R. v. Dincer* by an Australian court. A Turkish Muslim father was accused of killing his daughter when he learned of her sexual relationship with a young man. The court said that if the characteristics that led to the act by the accused are permanent rather than transitory in nature, thereby rendering him distinguishable from the ordinary man of the community, then the jury should be allowed to consider this factor in its deliberation. But though the court held that the features of this defendant's beliefs and background constituted just such characteristics that take him out of the run of the ordinary they held that evidence on such matters may not be introduced at trial, thus leaving the matter entirely up to the jury without any real information to guide them.

Although the Australian court may have tried to bring culture into formal consideration only to find itself blocked by existing rules of evidence, cases like this are particularly revealing for the way in which Anglo-American law has come to conceptualize culture. Two themes stand out in this regard. First, the state often creates a standard that, though its premises may be strained or tendentious, nevertheless professes to draw everyone together into an inclusive society. But even if this approach is politically and legally desirable, it is not without its costs. The harsh effects of the law's questionable premises concerning free will may be cloaked by an oracular jury or ameliorated at the penalty phase, but that does little to mask the questionable justice of holding a person to a standard of behavior that is contrary to a cultural premise to which that individual feels inextricably bound. Moreover as the witchcraft cases and others involving cultural background show, courts tend to treat culture not as an independent variable with qualities and implications of its own but as a feature of individual personality—a kind of agglutinative artifact that acts no differently on a person's total character makeup than appearance, sexual vulnerabilities, or upbringing. This calls for some balance between the individual, so conceived, and the social groups to which one belongs. In a striking, almost Tocquevillian, passage French anthropologist Hervé Varenne (1977: 206) has written that for Americans:

> There is a central difference between groups and individuals. For while groups gain substance through interaction, the individual is supposed to lose his substance in a group, and this group is supposed to gain substance by differentiating itself from other groups. Thus, while a small community has to be one-minded, the wider society has to become—logically and historically—diverse; that is, many-minded. Thus can we solve the paradox that what seems to some the most conformist nation in the world is also the most diverse. Furthermore, even though a group has natural aspects and the individual has cultural aspects, it is groups—communities—that are evidently cultural, and persons—individuals—who are natural. For individuals, however hard they may try, never lose their substance, and groups never gain any.

This treatment of cultural features as dispensable individual traits is equally apparent and troublesome when one considers the attendant issue of what it would mean if culture, like some personal characteristic, had to be enfolded within existing distinctions between justification and excuse.

In American law, an otherwise unlawful act is generally regarded as justified if it is thought to be warranted under the circumstances: To kill another in self-defense is thus morally acceptable and legally exculpatory. On the other hand an excused act is, broadly speaking, one for which the actor is not fully responsible. Thus to act under duress in the killing of another, or to do so because one is insane or thinks one is shooting at a target instead of a person means that one could not live up to the standard of behavior normally expected since something has intervened to affect the moral blameworthiness of this particular act. Justifications, then, may tend to relate more to standards by which we assess situations while excuses speak more to the composition of a particular personality. Arguing for a transactional analysis rather than one based on comparative harm, Horowitz (1986: 126) says: "Justification evolved precisely to exonerate defendants acting against recipients who posed an unlawful threat. Excuse evolved to exculpate defendants generally acting against recipients who did not pose an unlawful threat. It can only enlighten the analysis, then, to consider the active parties in the action, rather than the action alone."[25]

The line between justification and excuse is, in the eyes of many commenters, by no means exact.[26] Despite this imprecision—or, from the perspective of those who believe we must draw the line with clarity, because of it—in recent years there has been a marked increase in the range of excuses allowable in the law at the expense of justifications. Such a development may reflect decreased confidence in applying uniform standards of social behavior and the increased use of a medicalized model of persons that renders every influence a trait of character (see Fletcher 1984: 18–19; Horowitz 1986: 116–18). The rise of the battered wife syndrome, the post-traumatic rape shock syndrome, the abused child syndrome, and many others focus attention on the way circumstances may reveal an act that is otherwise reprehensible as a reaction born of confined choice. Others, like the so-called 'gay panic' defense, have arisen as homosexuality has been de-medicalized and thus shifted from a form of temporary insanity on the part of the perpetrator to a form of provocation.[27] As American culture has limited justification in order to preserve society from too unstandardized a view of permissible conduct, it has found itself permitting ever more elaborated excuses in order to accommodate the different life experiences and stresses of individual actors.

One result has been to squeeze culture out of formal legal consideration—either because if culture is deterministic it threatens the state's claim to specify and guide appropriate behavior through the criminal law or, if culture is as subject to free will as the choice of clothing or lifestyle, because people would be forced to choose between their cultural orientations and the risks posed by a powerful state bent on uniformity. That de facto, covert, and furtive efforts have allowed the cultural defense to slip into the law without formal acknowledgment points up the fact that it is easier to convert culture into a feature of personal psychic composition, particularly since the whole thrust of modern excuses has been to allow cultural features only if they can be equated, through medical or psychological analogues, to an aspect of one's personal psychodynamic. Put somewhat differently, courts have come to treat culture as a feature that inheres in the personality and, conversely, to treat culture not as an attribute of a group but, at most, as personality writ large. This attitude may also account in part for the tendency on the part of many to see the capacity of women to leave their culture if they do not agree with aspects of it as an appropriate criterion for deferring to that culture's illiberal elements, whereas critics argue that it is illusory to imagine that women in such circumstances can realistically be regarded as having a full range of choices to exit the culture in which they have been raised (see Okin 2002). For example, in the law suit that followed the devastating 1972 flood at Buffalo Creek, West Virginia, when a coal slurry dam collapsed destroying sixteen settlements, the court was prepared to allow evidence of a loss of community but only under the heading of "psychic impairment," thus further demonstrating the emphasis on individual psychological harm rather than culture as a collective attribute (see Erikson 1978; Stern 2008).

These approaches challenge some aspects of the classic analysis of intent and mens rea. For some (Kim 2006), cultural context should be admitted only for purposes of establishing one's state of mind. But, as Martin Golding (2002) and others have noted, this does not adequately address either the interests of groups or whether ignorance of the law or unwillingness to pay the price of one's sense of the orderliness of the world is really captured by putting matters solely in terms of intent. To the quip of one commenter on the *Kimura* case that in America the insanity defense *is* our cultural defense, one can interpose the proposition that bias toward majoritarian culture is either essential to the law or simply a way of continuing to stereotype minority groups who, in the absence of being able to bring culture in as evidence, do not have the opportunity afforded mainstream groups to have their values heard.[28] As we will see in more detail in a later chapter, when one notes, in this context, that the Amish have been permitted not to send their children to public school beyond the eighth grade because the community might thus be destroyed—an argument propounded, on questionably functionalistic assumptions, by the anthropologist whose testimony the Supreme Court, in *Wisconsin v. Yoder*, accepted as "uncontradicted"—we can readily see that it may only be a certain type of exception (the community that arguably lives up to some of our most idealized values) that gets to have its cultural argument heard at all. As Susan Kuo (2004: 1308) suggests, there is the danger that "the formal neutrality of the law conceals its innate bias"—that minority views are seen as subjective, whereas those of the majority are regarded as objective, and hence inherently superior.

Perhaps the strongest argument against allowing anything other than a 'neutral' analysis of intent is put forth by Doriane Coleman (2001: 982), who argues that cloaking cultural evidence as if it spoke to mens rea is "a disguised attempt to have the courts accept informally that which they could not and should not accept formally, an affirmative defense to immigrant crime that would undermine the native American culture's fealty to the uniform application of its criminal laws." Focusing in particular on the *Chen* case, Coleman does a disservice to her own arguments, however, by distorting and maligning the testimony offered by anthropologist Burton Pasternak. (She cites the statement by Volpp 1994: 70, namely that his testimony represented only "his own American fantasy," and she goes on to say that Pasternak's testimony "was likely a figment of that anthropologist's imagination"—without supplying any support for this casually unsubstantiated assertion. Coleman 2001: 990).[29] Accepting without question the Kantian notion of free will, and regarding any deviation from it as evidence of mental problems, Coleman (2001: 994, italics added) demonstrates the fallacy of her own position when she says that "the criminal law is properly wedded to the notion of free will, *even if it is in some instances a legal fiction.*"

Free will is not only shot through with cultural assumptions of our own, but if it does serve as a legal fiction, is that not reason enough for allowing evidence that may challenge the fiction? Is it not possible that people caught in an emotional moment may assert their cultural ideals with greater force than they might under less pressing circumstances, which makes it more complex than a simple case of free will or mental defect? (Who has not said "because I am your [mother, father], that's why!" or defended the reputation of one's country while traveling abroad more intensely than one feels it at home—and is that not relevant to understanding provocation, which may otherwise be reduced to a flawed mental state?) For Coleman (2001: 996) ultimately to claim that justice is only what the community demands reveals the ethnocentrism in her claimed neutrality. Simply pretending that mens rea is the complete and culturally unalloyed concept that alone stands against the slippery slope of information that could result in the dissolution of regularity in the criminal law only perpetuates received assumptions and closes the law to any consideration of concepts beyond those already inscribed. This kind of reductionism may suit some imagined efficiency or Platonic idea of 'ordered liberty,' but it comes at the price of freezing knowledge and perpetuating majority biases.

Indeed, the tendency in American culture to approach individuals in a somewhat reductionist fashion—to portray the whole person by a dominant feature—finds its expression in the law affecting cultural defenses. The law has long essentialized in its own way when, for example, it reduces culpable mental state to the specific intent to perform the act in question or when it allows jurors to assess credibility by demeanor on the witness stand rather than (a few exceptions aside) by more direct evidence of the person's overall character or past acts. An example is provided by the case of *People v. Wu*, in which a mother strangled her eleven-year-old son. The trial judge refused to instruct the jury, as requested by the defense, that it was her culturally based sense of being humiliated by her husband's rejection that led to the mother's act. She was found guilty of murder and sentenced to fifteen years to life. The appeals court reversed, instructing the lower court to allow an instruction based on the concept of excuse due to uncon-sciousness, i.e., the inability, due to the effect of her culture on her state of mind, to form the requisite intent. At the second trial, she was convicted of voluntary manslaughter and sentenced to eleven years imprisonment.[30]

While the *Wu* case is not necessarily typical, it does highlight the emphasis in American law on treating culture as an aspect of personal psychological composi-tion. The result is a kind of regulated common sense, a simultaneous skeletalization of the 'facts' (to make them 'workable') and fleshing out of the facts (through cul-tural assumptions that make them comprehensible) that is characteristic of the cul-ture of law—an approach that receives additional support by the way personhood is portrayed in advertising, religion, popular psychology, and ordinary gossip. The law thus acts on an 'as if' basis in ways that have resonances throughout the culture—holding people responsible where freedom of action is by no means entirely 'free,' assuming that consumers have choices when their options may be severely limited, or holding individuals to behavioral standards from which we fully expect they will and at times should depart. This emphasis on culture as an aspect of the person is a common ingredient in many of the analyses of the cultural defense (e.g., Kim 2006: n.131; Sing 1999: 1862; Zimbroff 2007: 1326), and, as we shall see, constitutes a somewhat different view of culture than is held by many anthropologists.

Put somewhat differently, we are dealing here with what Melissa Demian (2008) has called the "fictions of intention." Culture, she argues, is fallaciously employed as a vehicle for claiming access to people's inner states: It is used by some legal systems to convert an imagined occurrence into a legal capacity. It is, however, important to recall that no legal process can exactly replicate any claimed 'fact.' In court, one can only approximate what *might* have been, some-thing that should have been learned, for example, from such cases as the different readings of the infamous 1991 video-recorded beating by Los Angeles police of Rodney King.[31] Claims about the characteristics of a particular culture may, as Demian says, be contested by different members of the culture or those who study them, but the law's problem is always that it must give definite answers to that which commonly escapes utter certainty. Levels of proof and the parti-tioning of burdens of proof may ameliorate this uncertainty or indeed convert it to reality (you *are* guilty once pronounced guilty), but it is not an adequate complaint against the use of any cultural information in a legal proceeding that it cannot perfectly replicate something in the world.

Like other legal fictions, this view of culture and its use in the production of cultural evidence clearly has its limits. But this should not mean that we allow culture to disappear altogether, to duck the question of whether your culture can drive you crazy, to avoid the issue of whether an entire culture may be insane, or to leave us (as Demian says) with culture as no more reliable than a horo-scope. Demian is right to suggest that what we should not fail to ask is "when are intentions cultural?" even though, to the extent that the question is asked in Anglo-American jurisprudence, it is usually at the end of the proceeding, when sentencing is the only remaining issue.

There are, of course, those who argue that cultural background may so overwhelm an individual's choice of actions as to essentially nullify choice and hence responsibility. Thus in several cases in France involving female genital cutting, expert psychiatrists have appeared at trial arguing that the actions of individuals are controlled by a "group superego" that controls the actions of its members, thus equating tradition with an irresistible force leading to acts beyond the perpetrator's free will (see Winter 1994: 949–50). An extreme example of this problem is presented by the so-called 'rotten social background' defense. The argument here is that, owing to a person's 'deprived' circumstances, the individual was not able to conform his or her actions to what is socially accepted (Bazelon 1976: 388, 1988: 101–17; see generally, Alabama Civil Rights and Civil Liberties 2011; Delgado 1985; Jayaraman 2002; Villaran 2015). Thus in one case an African-American accused of murder argued that the racial epithet that provoked his rage arose from the impairment of his behavioral controls and was tantamount to an "abnormal condition of mind" (*Alexander v. Murdock*; Delgado 1985). On a more developmental level, in the 2015 trial of Dzhokhar Tsarnaev, the Boston marathon killer, the defense unsuccessfully argued that a teenager's brain is insufficiently developed, thus impairing his ability to form the requisite criminal intent.[32] Once again, however, the model used is that of psychology, of culture affecting, at worst, one's mental capacity to conform one's actions to conventional expectations. If any excuse is to be allowed it is because of personal impairment, not because, as a matter of social identity and inclusion, people may or may not be able to stand against those very cultural precepts by which the world makes sense to them.[33] In each instance, the dilemma of culture is largely transformed into a problem of individual psychic structure.

American law has, to some degree, attempted to face this dilemma by separating considerations of guilt from those of appropriate punishment. Even so the introduction of additional information at sentencing is not entirely unproblematic: "Typically, we have entertained our doubts at the sentencing phase of the criminal process, where the ultimate issue of responsibility is less prominently involved, and allowed our 'progressive' approach in that context to disguise from ourselves how little we have confronted the implications of our doubts at the trial stage, where responsibility is most directly involved" (Green 1995: 1917). The U.S. Supreme Court has acknowledged that in cases that carry the death penalty or mandatory life imprisonment for someone who was a juvenile at the time of the crime the defendant's 'background' should be taken into consideration. *Miller v. Alabama,* citing *Eddings v. Oklahoma* (1982: 116), thus held that in a death penalty case involving a juvenile the court must consider "background and mental and emotional level of a youthful defendant." Neither the *Miller* nor the *Eddings* court specifies what is included in "background" or whether it really is separable from the psychological makeup of the defendant. Thus in most cases where it has entered legal proceedings, culture is admitted not as a formal defense but as a factor to be taken into consideration at the sentencing stage. Here the distinction between motive and intent—itself hardly marked by a pristine line of demarcation—often becomes relevant.

In theory, the law is only concerned about whether the forbidden act was performed and whether one had the intent to commit such an act. But in sentencing, as well as by statute in some instances (e.g., the Mann Act, 18 USC §§ 2421–2424, barring interstate transportation of women for 'immoral purposes'), a person's motive (i.e., the reason the act was performed), which otherwise is usually regarded as irrelevant, now becomes germane. Many judges openly acknowledge their reliance on motivation. For example, Judge Denny Chin, who sat on the federal trial bench for sixteen years before being raised to the Court of Appeals for the Second Circuit, is cited as having told a reporter "that individuals with different levels of culpability should be treated differently...As always, he said, judges must also look at other factors, like a defendant's history, background and motivation" (Weiser 2011).

We are thus faced with an often-contradictory situation: Motive is disallowed except where it is allowed (e.g., in some so-called 'mercy killings,' like the *Repouille* case noted earlier). But motive is often comprehensible only in terms of a person's cultural context. For a number of years even when motive has entered considerations of sentencing the idea of an act being conduced by one's culture, rather than as a matter of personal motivation, never received clarity. Federal sentencing guidelines, to choose a particularly cogent example, mentioned features like education but not culture as a group phenomenon.[34] With Congressional vacillation on the subject and the subsequent move in *U.S. v. Booker* (2005) away from standardized guidelines in federal sentencing the earlier cases that never resolved the issue of whether culture could be used to increase or decrease a sentence have once again been rendered a matter of judicial discretion (see Martin 2007: 1316, 1321, and 1327–30).[35] It remains to be seen whether culture will find its way in through the side door of sentencing just as it has when the distinction between culture as evidence and culture as a defense has proven to be as porous as any distinction, say, between action and belief or justification and excuse.

Indeed, as we will suggest below, it would not be a great step for American courts to formally allow considerations of motive. In *State v. Raguseo*, for example, the Supreme Court of Connecticut, in its majority opinion, while favoring an objective test for determining the reasonableness of the circumstances perceived by someone in the defendant's situation as he believed those circumstances to be, nonetheless acknowledged that motive may assist in this determination. The dissent went farther, arguing for a combined objective/subjective test for determining extreme emotional disturbance, citing a New York high court case (*People v. Casassa*) to the effect that judges should attend to the "subjective, internal situation" without restricting the analysis only to a criterion of objective reasonableness (see also *People v. Liebman*).[36] Under this standard, one could well imagine that introducing culture, quite aside from avoiding the charade of pretending that it is otherwise being kept out, could easily be considered within the context of this dual test.

Solving for culture

American law, we have suggested, regards culture as an attribute of the person rather than of a group. Indeed, courts do not always treat culture as an aspect of the personhood of the accused alone: They may also look at the implications for other individuals, as for example, when the judge in *Chen* said the cultural repercussions of putting the defendant in jail for his children's marriages would be severe. To some extent, this emphasis on the individual is unsurprising. Ever since the Federalists won the day and America was not to be a congeries of confessional communities but a polity composed of individuals, on the one hand, and federal/state structures, on the other, the place for groups as distinct legal entities largely fell out of the political equation. Where even the corporation is analogized for some purposes to a person and associations have no inherent group rights there is no significant political space between the individual and the state. As we will see in greater detail in our final chapter, despite the American romance of community collectivities have been offered no real constitutional space. Unsurprisingly, then, culture is treated as part of that structure—often as some mystical element of nationhood ('the traditions and conscience of our people') or simply as an attribute of the individual.

But this is not quite the way many anthropologists see the matter. True, any theory of culture incorporates the notion that individuals must somehow attach themselves to their group's orientations, which are themselves not simply qualities of a person. But to those anthropologists who see culture as the preeminent attribute developed in our evolutionary history a rather different view obtains. Even before our current speciation, such a theory suggests, we developed the capacity to create the categories of our own experience and were thus destined to adapt to our own adaptations. Thought, far from existing in the 'secret grotto of the mind' became extrinsic, embraced in those symbols, concepts, and categories that appeared to their adherents to be as material as any physical form (Geertz 1973). And when a category suffuses multiple domains of life—kinship, economy, religion, politics, law—to the point that it seems both imminent and natural it appears to stand outside any individual who orients his or her life in its terms. Seen from this theoretical perspective, the approach of American law to culture as primarily an aspect of the individual rather than an attribute of the group seems crabbed and misdirected. Yet to operationalize this anthropological view in the law of crimes and torts seems to pose insurmountable problems. For if the view of culture as personal attribute appears an inelegant approach to the subject of culture generally how can one avoid the inexact fit and the discrepant results that will likely arise between a one-standard-fits-all law and a far more variable and collectivist vision of culture?

To this one might offer what many will regard as a characteristically American solution, namely a particular form of hypocrisy, i.e., not formalizing the cultural defense but allowing the trier of fact to hear the information that informs it. Indeed, in this instance, hypocrisy, far from being regarded as a vice, may rise to the status of a virtue. Indeed, acknowledging this hypocrisy may be no worse than the current situation where, as one commenter has put it: "Today, it seems like a lottery where, depending on which judge an immigrant defendant draws, the defendant has a chance of hitting the jackpot and being allowed to present a cultural defense" (Sikora 2001: 1714, n.122; see also Henry 2010). For if it is true that most Americans (like those in other common law jurisdictions) do not want a formal cultural defense but do want to hear about the parties' cultural background why not allow the common law process to sort out the utility of this background? This is not to romanticize the common law. It is not to argue, as some earlier scholars (e.g., Lon Fuller) suggested, that since the common law is logical and good is always logical the common law will always produce good and never evil. Rather it is to suggest that Edward Levi (1962) was right when he characterized the common law as a "moving system of categorizing concepts," a view that may accord quite nicely with the nature of culture as itself a system of just such categorizing processes and results.[37] The introduction of information about people's backgrounds may, in time, yield a more refined (or at least up-to-date) way of assessing persons and more sophisticated ideas of intention and responsibility, particularly if reasons must be given for considering in a regularized way that which is already sneaking in through the side door.

Nor is this to suggest that we should permit the state to hold the individual hostage to the dictates of the group. Quite the contrary, a key element of allowing cultural evidence would have to include a more systematic investigation (and likely confirmation) of the range of difference—and indeed choice—within any cultural group. Moreover, introducing such evidence may reinforce an assessment of the degree to which an individual did—or could—either separate him- or herself from the standards and categories of the available culture or realistically be expected to make changes in it.[38] Nor does it mean giving up a standard such as 'harm.' Studies of immigrants from the early twentieth century, to say nothing of more recent interviews with judges and social workers, clearly indicate that often when a court first hands out a punishment, even though mollified by cultural sensitivity, the message gets out in the subject community that this is not an acceptable practice in the host country or majority culture and will precipitate ordinary punishment levels if it persists (see Claghorn 1923; Fisher 1998: 1850, n.23; Moore 1999; Sellin 1938). As the British judge in a case involving a Nigerian mother who cut ritual scars in the face of her son put it: "You and others who come to this country must realize that our laws must be obeyed... It cannot be stressed too strongly that any further offenses of this kind in pursuance of tribal traditions in Nigeria or other parts of Africa... can only result in prosecution. Because this is a test case ... I am prepared to deal with you with the utmost leniency. But let no one else assume that they will be treated with mercy. Others have now been warned" (*R. v. Adesanya*, quoted in Hallevy 2010: 31, n.53). In other instances, courts have created culturally distinctive punishment regimes. For example, some Canadian courts, in dealing with native peoples, convene a traditional 'sentencing circle' in which tribal members work with the defendant and others to fashion a form of punishment appropriate to re-inclusion of the individual into the group. This may involve a form of temporary banishment intended to put the person in touch with the spirits and to appreciate the need for social involvement (see Mills 1998).[39] If, moreover, there is merit in the argument that the criminal law has not, as I was taught, historically developed only according to 'the Mikado principle' (that we 'make the punishment fit the crime') but has at least as often been characterized by the exact reverse ('Sentence first—verdict afterwards,' i.e., we create categories of crime to fit the punishments we think may be appropriate to the infraction), then allowing the courts to consider culture may result in the continuation, indeed the renewal, of this very process of category creation that is both vital to culture and the very manifestation of it.[40]

Moreover, one need not be an unrepentant legal realist to appreciate that we already allow culture to enter our proceedings in a variety of ways. Members of the dominant culture may be regarded as having committed 'normal' crimes— those that are readily comprehensible and culturally familiar (Sudnow 1965)— even if their personal actions are made to seem unrepresentative of our culture, whereas the culturally distinctive defendant is commonly made to seem normative to his or her own culture (Volpp 1994, 1996, 2000). The lawyer who makes immigrant clients appear as mere creatures of their culture may undermine any sense of individuality, but it may be just as misleading if the analogies applied to the defendants' acts render them so similar to the majority that they may only be regarded as an exception to normality (D'Hondt 2010). Indeed, minorities or immigrants are simultaneously made to conform to majority standards or lose all distinctiveness as they disappear into the maw of some overarching universality. This is, of course, a power play by the majority (or a segment of it) and a way of diminishing the threat of difference. But when it leads to the exclusion of evidence, alternative standards, or other ways of interpreting acts and utterances, the results are not always benign. American legal history is full of such instances— whether in deciding if an Indian or a Chinese is a 'person' (*Yick Wo v. Hopkins*), whether the black extended family is a 'single family' for zoning purposes (*Moore v. City of East Cleveland*), or whether women qualify for various professions or military roles. To assume that we have now purged ourselves of equivalent assumptions would be nothing short of rank hubris. Only by letting difference in have we countered a number of stereotypes in the past and only by doing so again may we contest their present-day counterparts.

But if we do allow more cultural testimony to be considered in court should we not set certain parameters for its introduction? As in other situations, if the 'test' is too generalized, it may provide little real guidance; if it is too specific it may cut off useful information and remedies. Alison Renteln's test, for example, consists of three elements: "1. Is the individual a member of the ethnic group? 2. Does the group have such a tradition? 3. Was the individual motivated by the tradition when he or she acted?" (Renteln 2010: 268).[41] This may only raise a host of other questions, as we have seen: who speaks for the culture, are cultures monolithic, when is a practice a 'tradition', etc. Alternatively, one can employ a very open-ended test and hope the experts can fill in the blanks. However, the experience of the insanity defense is perhaps worth recalling in this respect. When Judge Bazelon in *U.S. v. Durham* opened up the testimony about insanity to psychiatrists so they would not be constricted by the MacNaughten Rule's emphasis on distinguishing right from wrong and allowed the experts to speak to mental disease or defect, he not only went so far as to entertain the possibility of a 'rotten social background' defense but discovered that the experts still could not address the law's concerns ('is the person insane?') with black and white precision. The same could certainly happen with testimony about culture: No anthropologist can say that a person's culture makes him act in a certain way or whether individual and group orientations precisely coincide or diverge. The goal, however, is to increase the quality and the utility of relevant evidence, not to replace judicial decision-making with expert claims.

The cultural defense cases, therefore, offer both the legal system and social scientists a distinctive opportunity. The courts can use this issue to refine their approaches to such expertise—indeed to the use of experts generally—and the social scientists can test their theories against a set of circumstances that may result in the development of new and more sophisticated theories of their own. As we will see in greater detail in the following chapter, the involvement of anthropologists and ethnohistorians in the claims brought by Native American tribes before the Indian Claims Commission, for example, led to rethinking by Julian Steward and other scholars of the theories relating to the categories of tribe, band, and organized entities, the only units permitted by statute to bring a case before the Commission. While on its face greater involvement of anthropologists in the legal process may sound not only vague but easily denominated the "Anthropologists' Full Employment Act," it is with this dual possibility in mind that some of the following ways to operationalize the consideration of culture in the law might be considered:

- Experts appearing for both sides (together with any court-appointed expert) would be required to meet to sort out issues and the range of believable supporting material. Their goal would be to clarify issues and differences where they exist, without obscuring genuine theoretical and interpretive differences. Where this has been tried—as in Australia's so-called 'hot-tub' approach—it is not that disagreement among experts is resolved or even that expertise is made more compatible with questions asked by the law but that, in addition to clarifying terminology and sources, a good deal of extraneous matter is eliminated so that the court can decide if there is indeed something useful for them to learn from these experts (Edmond 2009; see also Civil Justice Council 2005).
- Experts would be expected to clearly articulate the concept and theory of culture they are using to assess evidence. The standard should be that noted by Nobel Laureate Richard P. Feynman (1999: 205): "Details that could

throw doubt on your interpretation must be given, if you know them. You must do the best you can—if you know anything at all wrong, or possibly wrong—to explain it." Again, if the result is that one is simply left with competing theories that appear to be of equal weight, so be it. But if, in the competition of theories, criteria develop for regarding one or another approach as either more explanatory or more helpful to the needs of the legal system it would be far better to organize these competing orientations up front than to leave them to the vicissitudes of a system that has largely ducked the issue.

- In a number of important cases where cultural matters have been introduced, only one side has presented an expert while the other side has either regarded the testimony as irrelevant or did not know how to counter it. Thus, as we shall see in greater detail later, in the Amish education case, the testimony of anthropologist John Hostetler was characterized by the U.S. Supreme Court as "uncontradicted," and in the *Chen* case no expert was offered by the state, perhaps provoking the outraged response of one prosecutor when he lost the case to claim that the expert testimony was just anthropological 'hocus-pocus.' Where courts do allow such testimony, therefore, every effort should be made to introduce equivalent expertise on the other side, whether by encouragement from the bench or the use of a court-appointed expert. Judges themselves are often eager to have such testimony: Whitman (2005: 24) cites the judge in the *Navahandi* case as admonishing one party by saying: "Can't you get an expert?" Expertise does not necessarily have to be professional: It may be offered by someone from the community. In the Canadian case of *R. v. Ly* (1996) the court allowed testimony by the chairman of the Vietnamese refugee association on the insult to the accused but limited the charge to the jury to the issue of actual provocation rather than whether an 'ordinary man' would lose control. If the common law's openness to new information is to continue to have a role to play in legal development no expert testimony the court treats as germane should be allowed to pass without a realistic, adequately funded opportunity to challenge it.

- Expert witnesses should be required to indicate the range of cultural variation of any given act and the basis on which they know of such a range. Here, the operative notion is that cultures are, by their very nature, neither uniform nor unalterable. If choices are available within the culture itself— if, to return to Unni Wikan's example, the father of a wayward daughter could, by the lights of his own culture, legitimately choose avoidance over violence—that is a factor the court has a right to know.[42]

- Information should be supplied about the party's embeddedness in his or her culture—including evidence as to whether the person is bilingual, bicultural, or otherwise involved in more than the home culture. Evidence should be forthcoming about the repercussions for this individual if he or she fails to conform to group expectations. Once again, it will be impossible to avoid assumptions about human nature and human decision-making. But if we are to be open to alternative conceptualizations, born, in some instances, by different cultural traditions, then simply applying the mainstream assumptions unquestioningly can hardly offer itself as a preferred approach in a system of common law that is supposed to consider the possibility of change from the ground up rather than only from the state down.

- The criterion for admissibility should not be whether the evidence goes to the issue of mens rea alone: That legal category is itself too internally contradictory and dependent on cultural assumptions based on Western experience to constitute the end point of inquiry. Such a focus not only produces inconsistent results but also forces defense attorneys to rely on emotional stereotypes.[43] Moreover, as in the *Kargar* and *Krasniqi* cases, where the courts found sexual overtones to the conduct involving minors but no sexual intent, allowing the cultural evidence was vital to explaining the gap that existed between what was intended and what was done. Courts will still have to decide whether the evidence presented should affect penalties, but no artificial separation of guilt determination and sentencing should constrain the presentation of information helpful to the court. The same is true for motivation, which can be broadly considered rather than slipped in sideways as is presently the case.

- Where juries are involved, an appropriate instruction can be given on the use of cultural evidence. Thus in *Douangpangna v. Knowles* the California Appellate Court held that the trial judge erred in refusing to charge the jury that they could, but were not required to, consider the defendant's cultural background in determining mens rea. As we have suggested, the charge need not be limited to issues of mens rea, such that a similar instruction could be readily applied in all such cases without distorting the existing criteria for assessing guilt.[44]

- Lawyers need to be trained in the role that culture plays in the cases involving their clients. While medical schools in several states (e.g., California, New Jersey) now require cultural and linguistic competency training, no state bar or law school requires such preparation.[45] The subtle ways in which culture may play into legal issues—from the use of a heated coin by a Southeast Asian parent to treat a child's ailment to the demeanor of a witness who is thought by jurors to be unfeeling when, in conformity with his own cultural style, he is actually trying to demonstrate the self-control that never would have led him to commit such a crime—need to be appreciated if the standards of adequate representation are to be met.[46]

Applying the principles suggested here will not mechanically produce indisputable results to particular cases. But they will help to shape the development of general criteria. One could, therefore, imagine that Mrs. Kimura, applying these criteria, may properly be seen to have had a very limited capacity to act other than she did,[47] whereas Dong-Lu Chen and those engaged in 'honor' killings could have availed themselves of the alternatives their own cultures offered.[48]

Kargar may be seen as rightly decided since the harm was minimal, especially as it is most likely that the child involved would grow up to see his father's act as one of love rather than sexual predation, while Moua's act of bride capture could be regarded as culpable (particularly if the woman had not consented to the preliminary stages of their relationship) but not as full-scale rape (Evans-Pritchard and Renteln 1994; Thomson 1985). And, given his distinctive cultural background, accused terrorist Zacarias Moussaoui should have been allowed to tell his story in his own fashion, just as many others should (Rosen 2018). In each instance, hearing the evidence will help the court understand the nature of the act no less than the remedies that may prove most appropriate.

"Are violations of rights ever right?"[49]

As these proposals imply, the legal thrust of introducing cultural evidence is to understand very broadly the meaning of a party's act. Such evidence should not concern only the formation of intent, the determination of a final penalty, or be used to limit information about alternative customs. In a sense, the procedural aspects of introducing cultural evidence should follow more the path of family and juvenile court proceedings—or, for that matter, one of the primary purposes of most European proceedings, namely, deciding what it is that should be done about this particular person or relationship. Since American criminal law is mainly oriented toward the determination of guilt or innocence rather than an assessment of the whole person—hence the highly restrictive use of character evidence and the broad application of the hearsay rule—the present suggestion may seem to go against the grain of American jurisprudence. But if such evidence is slipping in regardless and if the courts are to continue to be open to change from below, a call for inclusion or rejection on the basis of actual judicial experience of some version of cultural evidence is neither a romantic vision of the common law nor a call for major procedural revision. Such an approach does not violate the right to be treated similarly if *anyone's* culture may be part of the relevant consideration.[50]

This would, then, be a call to allow courts to assess, on the basis of open and well-regulated experience, the background features of the parties with an eye to sorting out the relevant from the irrelevant, the policy-consistent with the policy-inconsistent. Connolly (2010: 202–15) argues not only that judges are capable of learning about others' cultures but that a number of procedural alterations in Australia and Canada, for example, have paved the way for such consideration. Included are permitting testimony in groups, offering culturally sensitive information to be given in private, and not relying on unfamiliar sources (e.g., survey maps in land disputes) when native peoples conceptualize relationships in very different terms. To allow such cultural background information at all is, of course, to acknowledge that cultural information is indeed useful and fair, even though one certainly does not have to go so far as to claim a right to the 'free exercise of culture' (equivalent to religion) an unbounded 'right of cultural integrity' or even to maintain that cultural evidence is admissible without any preconditions set by judicial relevance.[51] The very introduction of culture, whether by counsel or through experts, may, of course, be used to cloak the imposition of 'mainstream' or 'majority' culture. And it is certainly an aspect of sovereignty that a people should be able to apply many of their cultural standards within their own territory. But it is naïve to pretend that majority standards are not frequently at work. Nations may be entitled to a bias in favor of well-articulated values, but they are not entitled to pretend that those values and laws are either natural or imperturbable. If the bench and the jury have often served as vehicles for openness to a society's values then rethinking some of the rules of evidence as they relate to cultural information—a process that generally lies within the discretion of the courts—should also be open to revision.

To welcome testimony of culture, even if it is ultimately to withhold legitimizing some of its expressions, may seem little more than a proposal for increasing the battle of the experts. But it is also true that the encounter with courts—as, for example, in the proceedings of the Indian Claims Commission or appearance in race-related cases—has at times forced social scientists to revise their own theories of culture, and this may very well happen in the current context as well.[52] Openness to new concepts may be required of both the law and the disciplines. Through the interaction of law and cultural information social scientists may, for example, have to refine the notion of culture as *shared* symbols when a wide range of opinions about the content of a given culture is presented in court. It may even be necessary to rethink how humans keep alive our adaptive capacity—our category-creating capacity—at the level of individual choices and not collective or institutionalized ones. Disciplinary benefits aside, to defend culture in the courts is to defend a process by which the common law and cultural expression reinforce one another. Whether that will mean the development of better forums and tools for balancing pluralism with national unity or will produce a realization that the goals and concepts of the analyst simply do not yield a workable degree of legal certainty is impossible to predict. Since the process of hearing cultural information seems to be happening whether we like it or not, letting it play out with greater regularity seems consonant with the common law's characteristic mode of openness to change.

That there will remain a significant degree of ambiguity and ambivalence in the assessment of a person's background is only a hindrance to those who see the law as necessarily precise at every point. But it is possible to consider ambiguity not as a violation of orderly decision-making and predictability in the law but as a vehicle for recognizing that variation is as vital to the common law as it is to many other domains of life. As one anthropologist has noted: "[I]n human cultural repertoires there may actually be more domains which derive their salient semantic order from ambiguity and variation than there are domains whose orderliness reflects consensus and uniformity" (Harris 1968: 582; see also Levine 1985). Similarly, it may be said of law, as a former Secretary of State said of statesmanship, "It implies a willingness to manage nuance and to live with ambiguity. The practitioners of the art must learn to put the attainable in the service of the ultimate and accept the element of compromise inherent in the endeavor" (Kissinger 2011: 46). Or as Kenneth Burke (1969: xviii, original italics) said of the particular problem of determining motives: "what we want is *not terms that avoid ambiguity but terms that clearly reveal the strategic spots at which ambiguities necessarily arise.*"

The criminal law in particular will always appear imperfect. It cannot replicate events, unerringly penetrate to one's inner state, or identify and respond immediately to social change. But that is not to say, with Plato, that outsiders must be given separate consideration because "the foreigner is not surrounded by friends and companions, and stirs the compassion of gods and men that much more" (quoted in Kozin 2011: 40). To say that our concern is with what to do with someone found to have committed a forbidden act—and to say it while trying to fathom the uncertainties that may arise when the act itself is inseparable from the meaning someone attributes to it—is not to forsake any regularity or equality in the law. Nor is it to dismiss out of hand claims that, as a matter of human rights, one is entitled to at least offer evidence of one's culture when tried in a jurisdiction foreign to one's own background (see Brelvi 1990; Hassan 1982). Rather it is to acknowledge honestly that our curiosity about another's cultural context is part and parcel of the way we do in fact try to understand others and their actions in our ordinary lives. Allowing not a cultural defense but the admission of cultural evidence, at the guilt determination as well as sentencing phase of a trial, will need to have limits in the same way limits exist for every other form of evidence. But to assume in advance that such evidence will betray either equality or efficiency is too weak an argument to preclude the potential benefits of comprehending what has been done and what we must do about it. If the common law means anything, it should mean that openness to such issues should not be foreclosed in the name of perpetuating momentarily dominant cultural assumptions and their attendant application in the law.

Notes

1 For a picture of Mrs. Kimura and her children, see Schnabel (2013).
2 For additional details see Weatherall (1986). On suicide in Japan, including that of a mother in Kimura's circumstances, see generally MacFarquhar (2013).
3 In the 1980s, parent-child suicides reportedly occurred as often as once a day in Japan (McCaslin 1985). In 2005 child-parent suicide was reported to have occurred in 19 cases, involving a total of 30 deaths. Of the 30 deaths, 12 were children under three years of age, a total of 24 being children killed by their mothers. The number of cases increased to 65 and 64 in 2006 and 2007 (Ministry of Health 2009). It is also noteworthy that in *Kimura* the prosecutor was eager to find a way to reduce the charge and avoid a trial, saying: "I want a good psychiatric report that we can hang our hat on" (McCaslin 1985). See especially, Dolan (1985). I am grateful to Kazuko Suzuki for data on parent-child suicide in Japan. See also Bryant (1990) and Kawanishi (1990). Compare *Kimura* to the 2002 case of Narinder Virk who tried to kill her two children after learning her husband planned to divorce her. She was found guilty of attempted murder but insane at the time of the crime and sent for an indeterminate

period to a mental hospital over the objection of many South Asians who believed her act was that of an uneducated countrywoman in a strange land (Piccalo 2000; Woo 1989, 2004: 296).

4 See, for an account of each side's story, Evans-Pritchard and Renteln (1994).

5 The courts in California can order the defendant to pay restitution directly to the victim in addition to a fine to the state. Cal. Pen. Code § 1202.4. See generally, http://www.cdcr.ca.gov/victim_services/docs/Restitution_Guide.pdf (accessed January 5, 2017). In this case the court reportedly inquired of the girl's family what the appropriate sum would be in their culture for the harm done an unmarried woman through inappropriate 'bride-capture' and took that information into consideration in fashioning the sum granted the victim. On the Hmong and American law, see generally Beger (2001) and (Ly 2001).

6 *Compare* Toomey (1985) *with* Booth (1993). In the case of a recent Albanian immigrant (*Krasniqi v. Dallas City Child Protective Services*), an American court concluded that the defendant's fondling of his four-year-old daughter in public was a normal practice in his native land (as a film from his home country shown the court purported to demonstrate), thus leading the judge to state that the man "was indeed unaware of his offense" (cited in Kozin 2011: 42). See also Renteln (2004: 59).

7 See generally, Ramirez (2007) and (2009), Sams (1986), and Appiah (2015).

8 See also the case of a Greek father in Florida who in 1974 was acquitted of the murder of his daughter's rapist partly on the grounds that no Greek father could be expected to wait for the police (cited in Rose 2009). See Krošlák (2016). See generally, Foblets and Yassari (2013).

9 For a similar case involving a mother from the Dominican Republic living in Maine who was also charged with inappropriately kissing her child's genitals, see *Maine v. Ramirez*, as discussed in Ramirez (2009). See also Kihara (2006) and Malpass (1999: 153). On corporal punishment and the cultural defense, see Lansford (2010) and Renteln (2010). For the argument that the cultural defense should not constitute justification for child abuse, see Shasburger (2013).

10 In *Rogers v. American Airlines*, the court dismissed the claim of an African-American employee who wore corn-row braids in violation of the then-existing airline's dress code, saying that this was not an immutable feature but one that could be changed. On the assimilationist bias in many such cases, see Yoshino (2007). See also Kim (2011) on employment cases. For the use of culture in assessing the commercial regulation of culturally distinctive enterprises, see Bell (2007–8). Anthropologists also figure prominently in a number of immigration cases: See Holden (2011), Koptiuch (1996). For tort cases involving cultural claims, see Donald and Brooks (2009).

11 For the argument favoring consideration of culture in child custody determinations, see Mabry (2009–10). See also *In re Marriage of Gambia* 2006 (mother's need to teach biracial child of African-American culture may be considered in child custody determination), and *Marsden v. Koop* 2010 (court may consider culture in best interests determination of custody of enrolled Indian child). Several American states, including Minnesota and Connecticut, mandate consideration of culture in custody cases.

12 See Estin (2004: 565). But see *Ali v. Ali* 1994: 262 (court refuses to honor Gazan custody order against American-born Muslim mother since Muslim law on the subject is a "mechanical formula" that is "undeniably arbitrary and capricious"). For other cases see Demian (2008), Donovan and Garth (2007), Fournier (2002), Kutty (2014), Moore (1995, 2002, 2005), Renteln (2004), and Whitman (2005). Legal and political approaches have varied widely. A German court (immediately overruled) stirred protest by rejecting a Muslim woman's petition for divorce on grounds of spousal abuse, saying that Quranic law permitted the husband to beat his wife (Landler 2007). Britain has allowed religious arbitration since 2007 but Ontario, which had permitted it to Jewish and Christian courts, barred all use of religion in arbitration as a result of protests against employing Islamic law in such proceedings (Freeze 2005). On allowing some recognition of polygamy, see Alexandre (2007).

13 Personal communication from Prof. Gabriele Marranci. For another example of what might be called 'the cultural offense' used against the relatively powerless by a dominant government, see Briggs and Mantini-Briggs (2000). For plaintiff use of culture as offense, see Glass-O'Shea (2009).

14 A limited survey conducted among Canadian judges showed that most would allow social science information in briefs and oral arguments but do not feel that they can rely on such information sufficiently to base their decisions on it (Williams 1996: 201). The argument for a formal defense, with adequate notice that it will be offered, is made by Renteln (2004), and in the special case of Native Americans by Dearth 2010–11. See also, for Native Americans, Kozin (2011). For comparisons see, Foblets and Renteln (2009). For an indication that the actual use of cultural defenses is inadequately studied, as well as for an empirical attempt to address it in the Israeli courts, see Tomer-Fishman (2010).

15 See also *People v. Aphaylath* (evidence of culture shock to Laotian who stabbed his wife not allowed). In *People v. Odinga* the court refused to allow testimony concerning the fear a black defendant accused of killing a policeman would experience given the history of racial oppression, whereas in *People v. Aliwoli* the court allowed the prosecution to introduce evidence that black Muslims commonly characterize white police as devils. See generally, Persaud (2012). In another case, a practitioner of Winti, an Afro-Surinamese religion, said he committed armed robbery for the money he needed to visit his dying grandmother. If he was unable to say goodbye, he claimed, her spirit would not forgive him and would forever haunt him. The court rejected his argument. See also Van Broeck (2001: 22–23).

16 See the discussion of this trial in Rosen (2018). See generally, Donahue (2007) and Moussaoui (2003). The presentation of oneself and one's understanding of the 'facts' may be common to many witnesses and litigants, but it may be exaggerated in the case of those who come from minority or foreign cultures. See Conley and O'Barr (1990). Language may play a key role here: see Eades (2000) and Gibeaut (1999).

17 See generally, Kay Levine (2003) and Hoeffel (2006).

18 See generally, Greenhouse (2011). See also Chiu (1994).

19 For an application of cultural analysis to the field of conflict of laws, see Riles (2008).

20 Raz (1994) (arguing against "conservative nostalgia" for the preservation of "pure exotic cultures").

21 Some commenters and courts rely on very outdated social science concepts in this regard. See, e.g., DePalma (2009: 10–11). The cultural defense also tests other legal approaches, including the concept of legal pluralism. See Sharafi (2008).

22 On amok, see *Hawaii v. Ganal*. The DSM-IV (American Psychiatric Association 1994) listed a number of such cultural ailments that could bear on a culture-based insanity defense (Parzen 2003). The most recent edition of the Manual, DSM-5 (American Psychiatric Association 2010, 2013), adds a number of other syndromes, such as 'panic disorder,' said to be manifested by some Hispanics. See generally, Hinton and Good (2009). See also Davis (2016).

23 See, e.g., the study of provocation and murder in Houston, Texas by Lundsgaarde (1981). See also Kesselring (2016).

24 British law has undergone recent changes. After the court in *R. v Smith* left it to juries to decide the moral structure of the provocation defense several appellate courts held that the standard of self-control must be objective (Macklem and Gardner 2001; Phillips 2003). Changes may have been further stimulated as a result of the controversial suggestion by the Archbishop of Canterbury (2008) that in some instances Islamic law should be allowed to govern relations among Muslims in Britain. The Coroners and Justice Act 2009 (effective October 4, 2010), Ch. 25, §§ 54–56 enshrines the objective standard, although case law may still have to flesh out the meaning of such phrases as a "qualifying trigger" event and "a justifiable sense of being seriously wronged." Sometimes the statutory ambiguity is purposeful: "The critical element in the Model [Penal] Code formulation is the clause requiring that reasonableness be

assessed 'from the viewpoint of a person in the actor's situation.' The word 'situation' is designedly ambiguous" (American Law Institute 1980). On the merits of ambiguity in the law, see Shiffrin (2010).

25 On the distinction between acts and reasonable persons in the analysis of justification and excuses, see Baron (2005) and Hurd (1999). On justification and cultural defense, see E. Chiu 2006. See also Tadros (2001); Vuoso (1987); Westin (2006).

26 *Compare* Greenawalt (1986) *with* Fletcher (1984). Though he thought he could keep excuse and justification distinct, J. L. Austin (1956–57) points to some of the difficulties when he writes: "It is arguable that we do not use the terms justification and excuse as carefully as we might; a miscellany of even less clear terms, such as 'extenuation', 'palliation', 'mitigation', hovers uneasily between partial justification and partial excuse; and when we plead, say, provocation, there is genuine uncertainty or ambiguity as to what we mean—is *he* partly responsible, because he roused a violent impulse or passion in me, so that it wasn't truly or merely me acting 'of my own accord' (excuse)? Or is it rather that, he having done me such injury, I was entitled to retaliate (justification)?" The relation of justification to excuse has been the subject of extended discussion. Among the useful sources on these issues are Greenawalt (1984), Corrado (1992), Christopher (1994), Duff (2004), Berman (2003), and Baron (2014).

27 See Chen (2000–1); Dumin (2006). For a critique of all such excuses, see Dershowitz (1995).

28 On Kimura's alleged insanity, see Goel (2004); Reddy (2002). See generally, Hamilton (2009). The reporter who originally covered the case reports: "She returned to Japan to undergo therapy and I have no idea what happened to her after that" (Schnabel 2013).

29 Coleman (2001: 1001, n.43) goes even further: "It appears that the anthropological evidence presented by the defense in Chen was at least anachronistic, or perhaps even fraudulent." The citations then offered provide no foundation for this slanderous remark. Among those who, like Coleman and Volpp, misstate Pasternak's testimony are Sikora (2001: 1696), Sing (1999: 1876), and Phillips (2007: 75–76). Renteln (1993: 480–81), however, gets it right. What Pasternak said was that normally in the defendant's home area in China if a man threatens an allegedly adulterous wife others intervene, acknowledging the husband's sense of injury, so that it is very rare for any violence to occur. Absent such a support community in New York, Chen's need for others to validate his feelings was not forthcoming and no one was there to prevent him from taking his show of violation to its ultimate conclusion. Whether he thought the absence of intervenors required or licensed his violence is not clear from the record.

30 The case is reported in Kataoka (1992) and discussed in Cohen and Bledsoe (2002).

31 See, Rodney King Video Beating (1991).

32 See, The Expert Institute (2015). Testimony was also offered by Princeton Professor Michael Reynolds to the effect that in Chechen culture a younger brother like Dzokhar would have had to defer to the direction of his elder brother, hence any penalty should be mitigated. Reynolds' testimony was the subject of withering cross-examination. Reilly and Martin (2015).

33 For arguments based on this 'cultural cognition hypothesis'—that culture disposes one to view facts in a given way—and the implications for criminal cases, see Kahan (2007).

34 On the consideration of culture in sentencing, see Neff (2003).

35 In *United States v. Tomono* the trial court allowed a downward departure from the sentencing guidelines for a Japanese man who illegally imported turtles, citing as the basis the man's culture, not his national origins. On Appeal the Eleventh Circuit reversed but left open the possibility that culture might be relevant in some instances. For this and related cases, see Nafziger (2010: 54–61).

36 On the limited use of motive, see also the arguments in Hessick (2006), and Tribe (1993).

37 For an excellent example of Levi's concept applied, with important theoretical implications, in an African context, see Fallers (1969). On the capacity of common law systems to reach 'reasonable accommodations,' see Santoro (2009).

38 See Wikan (2008) for the example of a Muslim father who could perhaps have opted for shunning his daughter rather than preserving his 'honor' through killing her. See also Okin (2002).

39 In other cases in the U.S., tribal banishment has proven to be either a hoax or a vehicle for disenrolling members of one faction by another. Such banishment was not, for example, allowed to displace state-imposed punishment in the case of *Washington v. Roberts and Guthrie* (reversing as an abuse of power the lower court's suspension of punishment during the course of a tribally imposed period of wilderness isolation for the defendants). See also, Hamilton (2009: 7–23). Cases involving the cultural background of Australian aborigines are also very instructive: See *Regina v. Muddarubba*, unpublished opinion, Australia (1956), in Goldstein (1974). See also Misner (1986). An Australian judge even ordered a convicted aborigine to be released from jail if he does not understand the point of his punishment (Australia 1969).

40 See *Brown v. United States* (the categories of provocation have changed over time and should be subject to greater input by juries). See also, Black (1983).

41 For her application of the same test in the international context, see Renteln (2011); see also Loeb (2005); Torry (1999). For a critique of Renteln's proposal, see the review of her book by Howes (2005). For another set of proposals on how to include culture in the legal proceedings, see Malpass (1999: 158–60).

42 For an example of a situation where the women affected contested the culture to which they were being subjected, see O'Cinneide (2009: 151). See generally Sunder (2001).

43 Referring particularly to *Kimura*, Woo (2004: 298) has written: "[B]ecause of the pivotal role of intent within the Western judicial framework, it is not surprising maternal filicides are framed by defense attorneys in terms of emotionality, irrationality, or a psychological instability that would rule out intent."

44 The disputed charge read: "You have received evidence of defendant's cultural background and the relationship of his culture to his mental state. You may, but are not required, to consider that evidence in determining the presence or absence of the essential mental states of the crimes defined in these instructions, or in determining any other issue in this case." In this instance, the appellate court held that failure to include this charge was harmless error since much of the evidence of the defendant's belief that the victim had worked black magic against him had actually been allowed. *Douangpangna v. Knowles*, reported in Dix and Sharlot (2008: 801–2).

45 On the medical school example compared to legal education, see Wong (2012: 1460–62). On cultural competence generally, see Symposium 2012.

46 Thus, in *Kwan Fai Mak v. Blodgett* (1992: 618, n.5), the Court of Appeals for the Ninth Circuit affirmed the reversal of a Chinese man's conviction for murder in part because the lawyer did not introduce expert testimony showing that the defendant's apparently emotionless demeanor "did not necessarily indicate disinterest or coldness, but was consistent with cultural expectations of Chinese males." See Renteln and Valladares (2009: 195). In *Siripongs v. Calderon* an anthropologist sought to testify on the retrial of a man from Thailand convicted of murder that given the defendant's cultural background any show of emotion that may have affected the jury's view of him would have been culturally inappropriate. To be free of any emotional display could, it was argued, be easily misinterpreted by non-Buddhists. See Nafziger (2010: 56–60). A similar fictional example is given in Gutterson (1995: 154–55), where an innocent Japanese-American on trial for murder "sat upright in the hope that his desperate composure might reflect the shape of his soul....Now, looking at himself, scrutinizing his face, he saw that he appeared defiant instead." A similar bias was evident in the reporting about Veteran Affairs Secretary Shinseki's testimony before Congress: see Shear and Weisman (2014).

47 What options a person has vary a great deal with the facts in each case: "Alison Matsumoto also suggests that Japanese women have other options for dealing with promiscuous husbands that involve community sanctions. Kimura, however, did not have personal or material resources to exercise these options. She was structurally constrained in many ways. At thirty-two years old, she had lived in the US for about sixteen years at the time of this incident. Yet she was remarkably insulated from mainstream society. She did not drive, although she lived in the Los Angeles area, and she had few interests and friends outside her family. As a mother, she obsessed over her children, and as a wife waited up each night to bathe her husband's feet upon his return home from work" (Woo 2004: 294).

48 It should be remembered that the judge in *Chen* did state that "culture was never an excuse"—a statement some commenters regard as contradicted by his other assertions (Sing 1999: 1845). For another 'honor killing' in the U.S., see Georgy (1994).

49 The phrase is borrowed from Applbaum (1998).

50 Arguments have been made, too, that emotion has a role to play in judicial decision-making: Even Judge Richard Posner has suggested such relevance (Masur 2008). If emotion can be in service of reason, then surely greater balanced knowledge of cultural background may also be valuable. See Marony (2011). For an argument that expert testimony should open the way for multiple ways of thinking through a legal issue, see Taslitz (1998).

51 See, e.g., Sager (2000). For the argument that majorities have the right to protect their culture, see Orgad (2016).

52 See Chapter 2 below. For the view that almost all social scientists should be barred as expert witnesses, see Wilson (1997).

References

Abu-Odeh, Lama 2005a, "Crimes of Honor: Overview," in Suad Joseph, ed., *Encyclopedia of Women and Islamic Cultures*, vol. 2. Boston: Brill, p. 221.

——— 2005b, "Honor: Feminist Approaches to." *Id.*, pp. 225–27.

Ahmad, Muneer I. 2007, "Interpreting Communities: Lawyering across Language Difference," *UCLA Law Review*, vol. 54, p. 999.

Alabama Civil Rights and Civil Liberties Law Review 2011, "'Rotten Social Background' 25 Years Later: Should the Criminal Law Recognize a Defense of Severe Environmental Deprivation?" *Alabama Civil Rights and Civil Liberties Law Review*, vol. 2, pp. 1–173.

Alexandre, Michele 2007, "Lessons from Islamic Polygamy: A Case for Expanding the American Concept of Surviving Spouse So As to Include de facto Polygamous Spouses," *Washington & Lee Law Review*, vol. 64, pp. 1461–81.

American Law Institute 1980, *Model Penal Code and Commentaries*, Comment to § 210.3 at 62–63.

American Psychiatric Association 1994, *DSM-IV (Diagnostic and Statistical Manual of Mental Disorders)*, Fourth Edition. ("Appendix I: Outline for Cultural Formulation and Glossary of Culture-Bound Syndromes," pp. 843–49). Washington: American Psychiatric Association.

——— 2010, DSM-V Anxiety, OC Spectrum, Posttraumatic, and Dissociative Disorder Work Group, *Panic Disorder: A Review of DSM-IV Panic Disorder and Proposals for DSM-V.* Washington: American Psychiatric Association.

——— 2013, *DSM-V: Diagnostic and Statistical Manual of Mental Disorders*, Washington: American Psychiatric Publishing.

Anonymous 1974, "Discharge for Mother in Tribal Cuts Case," *The Times* [London], July 17, p. 4.

Appiah, Ama N., ed. 2015, *Cultural Issues in Criminal Defense*, 4th edition, Huntington, NY: Juris Publishing, Inc.

Applbaum, Arthur Isak 1998, "Are Violations of Rights Ever Right?" *Ethics*, vol. 108, pp. 340–66.

Archbishop of Canterbury 2008, "Full Text of Archbishop's Lecture—Civil and Religious Law in England: A Religious Perspective," *The Times* [London] *Online*, February 8. http://rowanwilliams.archbishopofcanterbury.org/articles.php/1137/archbishops-lecture-civil-and-religious-law-in-england-a-religious-perspective (accessed January 5, 2017).

Austin, J. L. 1956–57, "A Plea for Excuses," *Proceedings of the Aristotelian Society*, vol. 57, pp. 1–30, reprinted in J. L. Austin, *Philosophical Papers*, J. O. Urmson and G. J. Warnock, eds., Oxford: Oxford University Press, 1961, pp. 123–52.

Australia 1969, "Australia Asks Aborigine to Adjust to Jail Term," *Washington Post*, October 5.

Baron, Marcia 2005, "Justifications and Excuses," *Ohio State Journal of Criminal Law*, vol. 2, pp. 386–406.

——— 2014, "Culpability, Excuse, and the 'Ill Will' Condition," *Aristotelian Society Supplementary Volume*, vol. 88, no. 1, pp. 91–109.

Bazelon, David L. 1976, "The Morality of the Criminal Law," *Southern California Law Review*, vol. 49, pp. 385–405.

——— 1988, *Questioning Authority: Justice and Criminal Law*, New York: Alfred A. Knopf.

Beger, Randall R. and Jeremy Hein 2001, "Immigrants, Culture, and American Courts: A Typology of Legal Strategies and Issues in Cases Involving Vietnamese and Hmong Litigants," *Criminal Justice Review*, vol. 26, pp. 38–61.

Beirne, Piers 1983, "Cultural Relativism and Comparative Criminology," *Contemporary Crises*, vol. 7, pp. 371–91.

Bell, Monica C. 2007–8, "The Braiding Cases, Cultural Deference, and the Inadequate Protection of Black Women Consumers," *Yale Journal of Law and Feminism,* vol. 19, pp. 125–53.

Berman, Mitchell N. 2003, "Justification and Excuse, Law and Morality," *Duke Law Journal*, vol. 53, pp. 1–77.

Black, Donald 1983, "Crime as Social Control," *American Sociological Review,* vol. 48, no. 1, pp. 34–45.

Blum, Deborah 1986, *Bad Karma: A True Story of Obsession and Murder*, New York: Atheneum.

Booth, Michael 1993, "Culture Clash Cited in Alleged Illegal Touching," *Trenton* [NJ] *Times*, 22 July, p. A2.

Brelvi, Farah Sultana 1997, "'News of the Weird': Specious Normativity and the Problem of the Cultural Defense," *Columbia Human Rights Law Review*, vol. 28, pp. 657–83.

Briggs, Charles L. and Clara Mantini-Briggs 2000, "'Bad Mothers' and the Threat to Civil Society: Race, Cultural Reasoning, and the Institutionalization of Social Inequality in a Venezuelan Infanticide Trial," *Law and Social Inquiry*, vol. 25, no. 2, pp. 299–354.

Bryant, Tamie 1990, "Oya-Ko Shinju: Death at the Center of the Heart," *UCLA Pacific Basin Law Journal,* vol. 8, pp. 1–31.

Burke, Kenneth 1969, *A Grammar of Motives*. Berkley: University of California Press.

Chen, Christina Pei-Lin 2000–2001, "Provocation's Privileged Desire: The Provocation Doctrine, 'Homosexual Panic,' and the Non-Violent Unwanted Sexual Advance Defense," *Cornell Journal of Law and Public Policy,* vol. 10, pp. 196–235.

Chiu, Daina C. 1994, "The Cultural Defense: Beyond Exclusion, Assimilation, and Guilty Liberalism," *California Law Review,* vol. 82, pp. 1053–124.

Chiu, Elaine M. 2006, "Culture as Justification, Not Excuse," *American Criminal Law Review*, vol. 43, pp. 1317–74.

Christopher, Russell L. 1994, "Mistake of Fact in the Objective Theory of Justification: Do Two Rights Make Two Wrongs Make Two Rights," *Journal of Criminal Law and Criminology*, vol. 85, no. 2, pp. 295–332.

Civil Justice Council, Ministry of Justice, United Kingdom 2005, "Protocol for the Instruction of Experts to give Evidence in Civil Claims," www.justice.gov.uk/courts/procedure-rules/civil/contents/form_section_images/practice_directions/pd35_pdf_eps/pd35_prot.pdf (accessed January 5, 2017).

Claghorn, Kate Holladay 1923, *The Immigrant's Day in Court*, New York: Harper & Brothers Publishers.

Cohan, John Alan 2010, "Honor Killings and the Cultural Defense," *California Western International Law Journal,* vol. 40, pp. 177–252.

Cohen, Jane Marlow and Caroline Bledsoe 2002, "Immigrants, Agency, and Allegiance: Some Notes from Anthropology and from Law," in Richard Shweder, Martha Minow, and Hazel Rose Marcus, eds., *Engaging Cultural Differences: The Multicultural Challenge in Liberal Democracies*, New York: Russell Sage Foundation, pp. 99–127.

Coleman, Doriane Lambelet 1996, "Individualizing Justice through Multiculturalism: The Liberals' Dilemma," *Columbia Law Review,* vol. 96, pp. 1093–167.

——— 2001, "Culture, Cloaked in *Mens Rea*," *South Atlantic Quarterly*, vol. 100, no. 4, pp. 981–1004.

Conley, John M. and William M. O'Barr 1990, *Rules versus Relationships: The Ethnography of Legal Discourse.* Chicago: University of Chicago Press.

Connolly, Anthony J. 2010, *Cultural Difference on Trial: The Nature and Limits of Judicial Understanding.* Farnham, U.K.: Ashgate.

Coroners and Justice Act (2009), United Kingdom, www.legislation.gov.uk/ukpga/2009/25/contents (accessed January 5, 2017).

Corrado, Michael 1992, "Notes on the Structure of a Theory of Excuses," *Journal of Criminal Law and Criminology*, vol. 82, no. 3, pp. 465–97.

Crockett, Hannah Yi 2005–2006, "Cultural Defenses in Georgia: Cultural Pluralism and Justice—Can Georgia Have Both?" *Georgia State University Law Review,* vol. 22, pp. 665–88.

Curriden, Mark 1989, "Voodoo Attempt? Two Face Charges in Failed Death Hex of Judge," *American Bar Association Journal,* vol. 75, pp. 48.

D'Amato, Anthony 1995, "Should Groups Have Rights?" in his *International Law and Political Reality, Collected Papers, Volume One*, The Hague: Kluwer Law International, pp. 309–22.

Davis, Alexa 2016, "In Defense of Cultural 'Insanity': Using Insanity as a Proxy for Culture in Criminal Cases," 49 *Journal of Law and Social Problems* 387–415.

Dearth, Megan H. 2010–11, "Defending the 'Indefensible': Replacing Ethnocentrism with a Native American Cultural Defense," *American Indian Law Review,* vol. 35, pp. 621–60.

Delgado, Richard 1985, "'Rotten Social Background': Should the Criminal Law Recognize a Defense of Severe Environmental Deprivation?" *Law and Inequality*, vol. 3, pp. 9–92.

Demian, Melissa 2008, "Fictions of Intention in the 'Cultural Defense'," *American Anthropologist*, vol. 110, pp. 432–42.

DePalma, Aahren R. 2009, "I Couldn't Help Myself—My Culture Made Me Do It: The Use of Cultural Evidence in the Heat of Passion Defense," *Chicana/o-Latina/o Law Review*, vol. 28, pp. 1–18.

Dershowitz, Alan M. 1995, *The Abuse Excuse: And Other Cop-Outs, Sob Stories, and Evasions of Responsibility*, Boston: Back Bay Books.

D'Hondt, Sigurd 2010, "The Cultural Defense as Courtroom Drama: The Enactment of Identity, Sameness, and Difference in Criminal Trial Discourse," *Law & Social Inquiry*, vol. 35, pp. 67–98.

Dix, George E. and M. Michael Sharlot 2008, *Criminal Law*, 6th edn., St. Paul: Thomson/West.

Dolan, Maura 1985, "Two Cultures Clash over Act of Despair: Mother Facing Charges in Ceremonial Drowning," *Los Angeles Times*, February 24.

Donahue, Katherine C. 2007, *Slave of Allah: Zacarias Moussaoui vs. the USA*. London: Pluto Press.

Donald, Bernice Bouie and Brennan Tyler Brooks 2009, "Culture as a Factor in Determining Tort Damages," *Judicature*, vol. 92, no. 5, pp. 220–23.

Donovan, James M. and John Stuart Garth 2007, "Delimiting the Cultural Defense," *Quinnipiac Law Review*, vol. 26, pp. 109–46.

Dressler, Joshua. 2002, "Why Keep the Provocation Defense? Some Reflections on a Difficult Subject," *Minnesota Law Review*, vol. 86, pp. 959–1002.

Duff, R. A. 1998, "Law, Language and Community: Some Preconditions of Criminal Liability," *Oxford Journal of Legal Studies*, vol. 18, no. 2, pp. 189–206.

——— 2004, "Rethinking Justifications," *Tulsa Law Review*, vol. 39, pp. 829–50.

Dumin, Jennifer 2006, "Superstition-Based Injustice in Africa and the United States: The Use of Provocation as a Defense for Killing Witches and Homosexuals," *Wisconsin Women's Law Journal*, vol. 21, pp. 145–73.

Eades, Diana 2000, "*I Don't Think It's an Answer to the Question*: Silencing Aboriginal Witnesses in Court," *Language in Society*, vol. 29, pp. 161–95.

Edmond, Gary 2009, "Merton and the Hot Tub: Scientific Conventions and Expert Evidence in Australian Civil Procedure," *Law & Contemporary Problems*, vol. 72, pp. 159–89.

Erikson, Kai 1978, *Everything in Its Path: Destruction of Community in the Buffalo Creek Flood*, New York: Simon & Schuster.

Estin, Ann Laquer 2004, "Embracing Tradition: Pluralism in American Family Law," 63 *Maryland Law Review* 540–604.

——— 2008, *The Multi-Cultural Family*, Aldershot: Ashgate.

Evans-Pritchard, Deirdre and Alison Dundes Renteln 1994, "The Interpretation and Distortion of Culture: A Hmong 'Marriage by Capture' Case in Fresno, California," 4 *Southern California. Interdisciplinary Law Journal* 1–48.

Fallers, Lloyd A. 1969, *Law Without Precedent*. Chicago: University of Chicago Press.

Feynman, Richard P. 1999, "Cargo Cult Science," in his *The Pleasure of Finding Things Out*, New York: Penguin, pp. 205–216.

Fisher, Michael 1998, "The Human Rights Implications of a 'Cultural Defense' as an Excuse for Criminal Behavior," *Southern California Interdisciplinary Law Journal*, vol. 6, pp. 663–702.

Fletcher, George P. 1984, "Rights and Excuses," *Criminal Justice Ethics*, vol. 3, pp. 17–27.

Foblets, Marie-Claire and Alison Dundes Renteln, eds. 2009, *Multicultural Jurisprudence: Comparative Perspectives on the Cultural Defense*, Oxford: Hart Publishing.

Foblets, Marie-Claire and Najma Yassari, eds. 2013, *Approches Juridiques de la Diversité Culturelle*, Leiden: Brill.

Fontein, Joost 2014, "'She Appeared to be in Some Kind of Trance': Anthropology and the Question of Unknowability in a Criminal Trial," *Hau: Journal of Ethnographic Theory*, vol. 4, no. 1, pp. 75–103.

Fournier, Pascale 2002, "The Ghettoisation of Differences in Canada: 'Rape by Culture' and the Danger of a 'Cultural Defence' in Criminal Law Trials," *Manitoba Law Journal*, 29, pp. 81–119.

Freeze, Colin and Karen Howlett 2005, "McGuinty Government Rules Out Use of Sharia Law," *Globe and Mail* (Toronto), September 12.

Geertz, Clifford 1973, *The Interpretation of Cultures*. New York: Basic Books.

Georgy, Michael 1994, "Fugitive in Jordan Describes Slaying of Wife in New Jersey," *New York Times*, July 25, p. A1.

Gershiere, Peter 2006, "Witchcraft and the Limits of the Law," in Jean Comaroff and John L. Comaroff, eds., *Law and Disorder in the Postcolony*, Chicago: University of Chicago Press, pp. 219–46.

Gibeaut, John 1999, "Troubling Translations: Cultural Defense Tactic Raises Issues of Fairness," *American Bar Association Journal,* vol. 85, pp. 93.

Glass-O'Shea, Brooke 2009, "The Cultural Offense: How Plaintiffs Use Cultural Claims in U.S. Courts," *The Journal of Law in Society,* vol. 10, pp. 56–98.

Goel, Rashmi 2004, "Can I Call Kimura Crazy? Ethical Tensions in the Cultural Defense," *Seattle Journal for Social Justice*, vol. 3, pp. 443–64.

Golding, Martin P. 2002, "The Cultural Defense," *Ratio Juris*, vol. 15, no. 2, pp. 146–58.

Goldstein, Joseph, Alan Dershowitz, and Richard D. Schwartz, *Criminal Law*, 2nd edn., 1974.

Green, Thomas A. 1995, "Freedom and Criminal Responsibility in the Age of Pound: An Essay on Criminal Justice," 93 *Michigan Law Review* 1915–2053.

Greenawalt, Kent 1984, "The Perplexing Border of Justification and Excuse," *Columbia Law Review,* vol. 84, pp. 1897–1927.

——— 1986, "Distinguishing Justifications from Excuses," *Law and Contemporary Problems,* vol. 49, pp. 89–126.

Greenhouse, Carol J. 2011, *The Paradox of Relevance*. Philadelphia: University of Pennsylvania Press.

Gutterson, David 1995, *Snow Falling on Cedars*. New York: Vintage.

Hallevy, Gabriel 2010, "Culture Crimes against Women," *Social Science Research Network*, February 10. http://papers.ssrn.com/sol3/papers.cfm?abstract_id=1564098 (accessed January 5, 2017).

Hamilton, Jennifer A. 2009, *Indigeneity in the Courtroom*, New York: Routledge.

Harris, Marvin 1968, *The Rise of Anthropological Theory*, New York: Thomas Y. Crowell.

Hassan, Farooq 1982, "The Right to be Different: An Exploratory Proposal for the Creation of a New Human Right," *Loyola of Los Angeles International and Comparative Law Journal,* vol. 5, pp. 67–99.

Henry, Samantha 2010, "Immigrants' Lawyers Using Culture as Crime Defense," *Yahoo News*, December 8.

Hessick, Carissa Byrne 2006, "Motive's Role in Criminal Punishment," *Southern California Law Review*, vol. 80, pp. 89–149.

Hinton, Devon E. and Byron J. Good, eds. 2009, *Culture and Panic Disorder*. Stanford: Stanford University Press.

Hoeffel, Janet C. 2006, "Deconstructing the Cultural Evidence Debate," *University of Florida Journal of Law and Public Policy*, vol. 17, pp. 303–46.

Holden, Livia, ed. 2011, *Cultural Expertise and Litigation*, New York: Routledge.

Horowitz, Donald L. 1986, "Justification and Excuses in the Program of the Criminal Law," *Law and Contemporary Problems*, vol. 49, pp. 109–26.

Howes, David 2005, "Review of Renteln 'The Cultural Defense'," *McGill Law Journal*, vol. 50, pp. 999–1006.

Hurd, Heidi M. 1999, "Justification and Excuse, Wrongdoing and Culpability," *Notre Dame Law Review,* vol. 74, pp. 1551–74.

Iga, M. 1986, *The Thorn in the Chrysanthemum: Suicide and Economic Stress in Japan,* Berkeley: University of California Press.

Jayaraman, Mythri A. 2002, "Rotten Social Background Revisited," *Capital Defense Journal,* vol. 14, no. 2, pp. 327–44. http://scholarlycommons.law.wlu.edu/wlucdj/vol14/iss2/6 (accessed January 5, 2017).

Kadish, Sanford H. 1987, *Blame and Punishment: Essays in the Criminal Law,* New York: Macmillan Pub. Co.

Kahan, Dan M. 2007, "The Cognitively Illiberal State," *Stanford Law Review,* vol. 60, pp. 115–54.

Kanter, Andrew M. 1995, "The Yenaldlooshi in Court and the Killing of a Witch: The Case for an Indian Cultural Defense," *Southern California Interdisciplinary Law Journal,* vol. 4, pp. 411–54.

Kataoka, Mike 1992, "Indio Woman Who Strangled Son Sentenced to 11 Years in Prison," *Press-Enterprise* [Riverside, CA], October 31, p. B1.

Kawanishi, Yuko 1990, "Japanese Mother-Child Suicide: The Psychological and Sociological Implications of the *Kimura* Case," *Pacific Basin Law Journal,* vol. 8, pp. 32–46.

Kesselring, Krista J. 2016, "No Greater Provocation? Adultery and the Mitigation of Murder in English Law," *Law & History Review,* vol. 34, pp. 199–225.

Kihara, David 2006, "Mother Pleads Guilty," *Las Vegas Review-Journal,* January 4, p. 1B.

Kim, Andrew Tae-Hyun 2011, "Culture Matters: Cultural Differences in the Reporting of Employment Discrimination Claims," *William and Mary Bill of Rights Journal,* vol. 20, pp. 405–55.

Kim, Nancy S. 2006, "Blameworthiness, Intent, and Cultural Dissonance: The Unequal Treatment of Cultural Defense Defendants," *University of Florida Journal of Law and Public Policy,* vol. 17, pp. 199–229.

Kissinger, Henry A. 2011, "Mr. X (review of John Lewis Gaddis, *George F. Kennan, An American Life*)," *New York Times Book Review,* November 13, pp. 1ff.

Koptiuch, Kristin 1996, "'Cultural Defense' and Criminological Displacements: Gender, Race, and (Trans)Nation in the Legal Surveillance of U.S. Diaspora Asians," in Smadar Lavie and Ted Swedenburg, eds., *Displacement, Diaspora, and Geographies of Identity,* Durham: Duke University Press, pp. 215–33.

Kozin, Alexander V. 2011, "Native American Identity and the Limits of Cultural Defense," *Law Critique,* vol. 22, pp. 39–57.

Krafka, Carol, et al. 2002, "Judge and Attorney Experiences, Practices, and Concerns Regarding Expert Testimony in Federal Civil Trials," *Psychology, Public Policy, and Law,* vol. 8, pp. 309–32.

Krošlák, Daniel 2016, "Honor Killings and Cultural Defense," New York Law School, Research Papers Series. http://ssrn.com/abstract=1422503 (accessed January 5, 2017).

Kuo, Susan S. 2004, "Culture Clash: Teaching Cultural Defenses in the Criminal Law Classroom," *Saint Louis University Law Journal,* vol. 48, pp. 1297–1312.

Kutty, Faisal 2014, "'Islamic Law' in US Courts: Judicial Jihad or Constitutional Imperative?" 41 *Pepperdine Law Review* 1059–90.

Landler, Mark 2007, "Germany Cites Koran in Rejecting Divorce," *New York Times,* March 22.

Lansford, Jennifer E. 2010, "The Special Problem of Cultural Differences in Effects of Corporal Punishment," *Law and Contemporary Problems,* vol. 73, pp. 89–106.

LaRue, Lewis H. and David S. Caudill 2004, "A Non-Romantic View of Expert Testimony," *Seton Hall Law Review,* vol. 35, pp. 1–45.

Lee, Cynthia 2007, "Cultural Convergence: Interest Convergence Theory Meets the Cultural Defense," *Arizona Law Review*, vol. 49, pp. 911–59.

Levi, Edward H. 1962, *An Introduction to Legal Reasoning*, rev. edn., Chicago: University of Chicago Press.

Levine, Donald N. 1985, *The Flight from Ambiguity*, Chicago: University of Chicago Press.

Levine, Kay L. 2003, "Negotiating the Boundaries of Crime and Culture: A Sociological Perspective on Cultural Defense Strategies," *Law & Social Inquiry*, vol. 28, pp. 39–85.

Loeb, Elizabeth 2005, "Book review of *The Cultural Defense* by Alison Renteln," *Anthropological Quarterly*, vol. 78, pp. 297–302.

Lundsgaarde, Henry P. 1981, *Murder in Space City: A Cultural Analysis of Houston Homicide Patterns*, New York: Oxford University Press.

Ly, Choua 2001, "The Conflict between Law and Culture: The Case of the Hmong in America," 2001 *Wisconsin Law Review* 471–99.

Mabry, Cynthia R. 2009–10, "The Browning of America—Multicultural and Bicultural Families in Conflict: Making Culture a Customary Factor for Consideration in Child Custody Disputes," *Washington and Lee Journal of Civil Rights and Social Justice*, vol. 16, pp. 413–43.

McCaslin, Megan 1985, "A 'Cultural Defense' at Issue in Trial," *Philadelphia Inquirer*, September 1.

MacFarquhar, Larissa 2013, "Last Call: A Buddhist Monk Confronts Japan's Suicide Culture," *The New Yorker*, June 24.

Macklem, Timothy and John Gardner 2001, "Provocation and Pluralism," *The Modern Law Review*, vol. 64, pp. 815–30.

Magnarella, Paul 1991, "Justice in a Culturally Pluralistic Society: The Cultural Defense on Trial," *The Journal of Ethnic Studies*, vol. 19, pp. 65–84.

Maguigan, Holly 1995, "Cultural Evidence and Male Violence: Are Feminist and Multiculturalist Reformers on a Collision Course in Criminal Courts?" *New York University Law Review*, vol. 70, pp. 36–99.

Malpass, Roy S. 1999, "Subjective Culture and the Law," in John Adamopoulos and Yashihisa Kashima, eds., *Social Psychology and Cultural Context*, New York: Sage Publications, pp. 151–60.

Marony, Terry A. 2011, "The Persistent Cultural Script of Judicial Dispassion," 99 *California Law Review* 629–81.

Martin, Elizabeth 2007, "All Men Are (or Should Be) Created Equal: An Argument against the Use of the Cultural Defense in a Post-*Booker* World," 15 *William and Mary Bill of Rights Journal* 1305–31.

Matsumoto, Alison 1995, "A Place for Consideration of Culture in the American Criminal Justice System: Japanese Law and the Kimura Case," 4 *Detroit Journal of International Law* 507–38.

Masur, Jonathan 2008, "How Judges Think: A Conversation with Judge Richard Posner," *The Record Online* (University of Chicago Law School Alumni Magazine), Spring. www.law.uchicago.edu/alumni/magazine/spring08/posnerhowjudgesthink (accessed January 5, 2017).

Mills, P. Dawn 1998, "The Myth of Swan: The Case of *Regina v. Taylor*," *The Canadian Journal of Native Studies*, vol. 18, no. 2, pp. 255–70.

Ministry of Health, Labour and Welfare, Japan 2009, "Kodomo gyakutai ni yoru shibo jirei nado no kensho kekka nado nit suite, Dai 5ji hokoku, Heisei 21 nen 7 gatsu" (Verification on Death Cases of Child Abuse, the 5th Report, July 2009). www.mhlw.go.jp/bunya/kodomo/dv37/dl/01.pdf (accessed January 5, 2017).

Misner, Robert L. 1986, "The Awkward Case of Henry Gibson," 1986 *Arizona State Law Review* 691–725.

Moore, Joanne I., ed. 1999, *Immigrants in Court*, Seattle: University of Washington Press.

Moore, Kathleen M. 1995, *Al-Mughtaribun: American Law and the Transformation of Muslim Life in America*, Albany: State University of New York Press.

———— 2002, "Representation of Islam in the Language of Law: Some Recent U.S. Cases," in Yvonne Yazbeck Haddad, ed., *Muslims in the West: From Sojourners to Citizens*, Oxford: Oxford University Press, pp. 187–204.

———— 2005, "Law: Cultural Defense," in Suad Joseph, ed., *Encyclopedia of Women and Islamic Cultures*, vol. 2, Leiden: Brill, pp. 411–13.

Moussaoui, Abd Samad (with Florence Bouquillat) 2003, *Zacarias, My Brother: The Making of a Terrorist*, New York: Seven Stories Press.

Nafziger, James A. R., Robert Kirkwood Paterson, and Alison Dundes Renteln 2010, *Cultural Law*, New York: Cambridge University Press.

Neff, Kelly M. 2003, "Removing the Blinders in Federal Sentencing: Cultural Difference as a Proper Departure Ground," 78 *Chicago-Kent Law Review* 445–78.

O'Cinneide, Colm 2009, "'A Million Mutinies Now': Why Claims of Cultural Uniqueness Cannot be Used to Justify Violations of Basic Human Rights," in Dawn Oliver, ed., *Justice, Legality, and the Rule of Law: Lessons from the Pitcairn Prosecutions*, Oxford: Oxford University Press, pp. 131–56.

Okin, Susan Moller 2002, "'Mistresses of their Own Destiny': Group Rights, Gender, and Realistic Rights of Exit," *Ethics*, vol. 112 (January), pp. 205–30.

Orgad, Liav 2016, *The Cultural Defense of Nations: A Liberal Theory of Majority Rights*, Oxford: Oxford University Press.

Parzen, Micah David 2003, "Toward a Culture-Bound Syndrome-Based Insanity Defense?" *Culture, Medicine, and Psychiatry*, vol. 27, pp. 131–53.

Persaud, Shiv Narayan 2012, "Is Color Blind Justice Also Culturally Blind? The Cultural Blindness in Justice," *Berkeley Journal of African-American Law and Policy*, vol. 14, pp. 23–64.

Phillips, Anne 2003, "When Culture Means Gender: Issues of Cultural Defence in the English Courts," 66 *The Modern Law Review* 510–31.

———— 2007 *Multiculturalism without Culture*, Princeton: Princeton University Press.

Piccalo, Gina 2000, "Attorneys to Cite Similar Incident in Drowning Case Defense," *Los Angeles Times*, February 17.

Poulter, Sebastian 1975, "Foreign Customs and the English Criminal Law," *The International and Comparative Law Quarterly*, vol. 24, pp. 136–40.

Ramirez, Linda Friedman 2007, *Cultural Issues in Criminal Defense*, 2nd edn. Huntington, NY: Juris Publishing Inc.

———— 2009, "The Virtues of the Cultural Defense," *Judicature*, vol. 92, no. 5, pp. 207ff.

Ramirez, Rafael L. 1999, *What it Means to be a Man: Reflections on Puerto Rican Masculinity*, New Brunswick: Rutgers University Press.

Rayner, Gordon 2011, "Mercy for the Drunk Muslim Girl Gang who Attacked Woman," *The Telegraph* [London], December 7.

Raz, Joseph 1990, "Facing Diversity: The Case of Epistemic Abstinence," *Philosophy and Public Affairs*, vol. 19, pp. 3–46.

———— 1994, "Multiculturalism: A Liberal Perspective," in his *Ethics in the Public Domain*, Oxford: Clarendon Press, pp. 170–91.

Reddy, Sita 2002, "Temporarily Insane: Pathologizing Cultural Difference in American Criminal Courts," *Sociology of Health and Illness*, vol. 24, pp. 667–87.

Reilly, Adam and Phillip Martin 2015, "At the Tsarnaev Trial: It's Cultural Identity versus Personal Responsibility," *WGBH News*, May 11. http://wgbhnews.org/post/tsarnaev-trial-its-cultural-identity-versus-personal-responsibility (accessed January 5, 2017).

Renteln, Alison Dundes 2004, *The Cultural Defense*, Oxford: Oxford University Press.

——— 2010, "Corporal Punishment and the Cultural Defense," *Law and Contemporary Problems*, vol. 73, pp. 253–79.

——— 2011, "Cultural Defenses in International Criminal Tribunals: A Preliminary Consideration of the Issues," *Southwestern Journal of International Law*, vol. 18, pp. 267–85.

Renteln, Alison Dundes and Rene Valladares 2009, "The Importance of Culture for the Justice System," *Judicature*, vol. 92, pp. 194–95.

Riles, Annelise 2008, "Cultural Conflicts," *Law and Contemporary Problems*, vol. 71, pp. 273–308.

Roberts, Dorothy E. 1999, "Why Culture Matters to Law: The Difference Politics Makes," in Austin Sarat and Thomas R. Kearns, eds., *Cultural Pluralism, Identity Politics, and the Law*, Ann Arbor: The University of Michigan Press, pp. 85–110.

Rodney King Video Beating 1991, www.youtube.com/watch?v=sb1WywIpUtY (accessed January 5, 2017).

Rose, Jacqueline 2009, "A Piece of White Silk," *London Review of Books*, vol. 31, November 9, pp. 5–8.

Rosen, Lawrence 2018, *Islam and the Rule of Justice*, Chicago: University of Chicago Press.

Sager, Lawrence G. 2000, "The Free Exercise of Culture: Some Doubts and Distinctions," *Daedalus*, vol. 129, no. 4, pp. 193–209.

Sams, Julia P. 1986, "The Availability of the 'Cultural Defense' as an Excuse for Criminal Behavior," *Georgia Journal of International and Comparative Law*, vol. 16, pp. 335–54.

Santoro, Emilio 2009, "'Ha da passa'a 'a nutta': Reasonable Accommodation, a Tool for Defending Coexistence Based on Respect for Rights in a Pluralist Society," in *Institutional Accommodation and the Citizen: Legal and Political Interaction in a Pluralist Society*, Strasbourg: Council of Europe Publishing.

Schnabel, Tom 2013, "A Buddhist Monk Confronts Japan's Suicide Culture," August 20. http://tomschnabel.com/tag/japanese-views-on-suicide/ (accessed January 5, 2017).

Seidman, Robert B. 1966, "Mens Rea and the Reasonable African: The Pre-Scientific World-View and Mistake of Fact," *International and Comparative Law Quarterly*, vol. 15, pp. 1135–64.

Sellin, Thorsten 1938, *Culture Conflict and Crime*, Washington, DC: Social Science Research Council.

Sharafi, Mitra 2008, "Justice in Many Rooms since Galanter: De-Romanticizing Legal Pluralism through the Cultural Defense," *Law and Contemporary Problems*, vol. 71, pp. 139–46.

Shasburger, R. Lee, Jr. 2013, "The Best Interest of the Child? The Cultural Defense as Justification for Child Abuse," *Pace International Law Review*, vol. 25, pp. 161–208.

Shear, Michael D. and Jonathan Weisman 2014, "V.A. Accusations Aggravate Woes of White House," *New York Times*, May 20.

Shiffrin, Seana Valentine 2010, "Inducing Moral Deliberation: On the Occasional Virtues of Fog," *Harvard Law Review*, vol. 123, pp. 1214–46.

Sikora, Damian W. 2001, "Differing Cultures, Differing Culpabilities: A Sensible Alternative: Using Cultural Circumstances as a Mitigating Factor in Sentencing," *Ohio State Law Journal*, vol. 62, pp. 1695–1728.

Sing, James J. 1999, "Culture as Sameness: Toward a Synthetic View of Provocation and Culture in the Criminal Law," *Yale Law Journal*, vol. 108, pp. 1845–84.

Sommers, Tamler 2012, *Relative Justice: Cultural Diversity, Free Will, and Moral Responsibility*, Princeton: Princeton University Press.

Stern, Gerald M. 2008, *The Buffalo Creek Disaster: How the Survivors of One of the Worst Disasters in Coal-Mining History Brought Suit against the Coal Company—and Won*, revised edition, New York: Vintage.

Sudnow, David 1965, "Normal Crimes: Sociological Features of the Penal Code in a Public Defender Office," *Social Problems*, vol. 12, no. 3, pp. 255–76.

Sullivan, John 1997, "Charges against Danish Mother are Dropped," *New York Times*, May 17.

Sunder, Madhavi 2001, "Cultural Dissent," 54 *Stanford Law Review* 495–567.

Symposium 2008, "On the Reasonable Person in Criminal Law," 11 *New Criminal Law Review* 1–171.

Symposium 2009, "The Nature, Structure, and Function of Heat of Passion/Provocation as a Criminal Defense," *University of Michigan Journal of Law Reform*, vol. 43, pp. 1–244.

Symposium 2012, "Cultural Competency," *University of Memphis Law Review*, vol. 42, no. 4.

Tadros, Victor 2001, "The Character of Excuse," 21 *Oxford Journal of Legal Studies* 495–519.

Taslitz, Andrew E. 1998, "Abuse Excuses and the Logic and Politics of Expert Relevance," *Hastings Law Journal*, vol. 49, pp. 1039–68.

The Expert Institute 2015, "Expert Witness Testimony in the Boston Bombing Trial," May 27. www.theexpertinstitute.com/expert-witness-testimony-in-the-boston-bombing-trial/ (accessed January 5, 2017).

Thomson, Mark. 1985, "The Cultural Defense," *Student Lawyer*, vol. 14, pp. 25–27.

Tomer-Fishman, Tamar 2010, "'Cultural Defense,' 'Cultural Offense,' or No Culture at All? An Empirical Examination of Israeli Judicial Decisions in Cultural Conflict Criminal Cases and of the Factors Affecting Them," *Journal of Criminal Law and Criminology*, vol. 100, pp. 475–521.

Toomey, Sheila 1985, "Eskimo Erotica: Traditional-Conduct Plea Wins Sex-Charge Acquittal," *National Law Journal*, February 4, p. 6.

Torry, William I. 1999, "Multicultural Jurisprudence and the Cultural Defense," *Journal of Legal Pluralism and Unofficial Law*, vol. 44, pp. 127–61.

———— 2000, "Culture and Individual Responsibility: Touchstones of the Cultural Defense," *Human Organization*, vol. 59, pp. 58–71.

Tribe, Laurence H. 1993, "The Mystery of Motive, Private and Public: Some Notes Inspired by the Problems of Hate Crime and Animal Sacrifice," *The Supreme Court Review 1993*, Chicago: University of Chicago Press, pp. 1–36.

Uniacke, Suzanne 2007, "Emotional Excuses," *Law and Philosophy*, vol. 26, pp. 95–117.

United Kingdom, Ministry of Justice 2005, *Civil Procedure Rules, Practice Direction—Experts and Assessors*. www.justice.gov.uk/courts/procedure-rules/civil/rules/part35/pd_part35 (accessed January 5, 2017).

Van Broeck, Jeroen 2001, "Cultural Defence and Culturally Motivated Crimes," *European Journal of Crime, Criminal Law and Criminal Justice*, vol. 9, pp. 1–32.

Varenne, Hervé 1977, *Americans Together: Structured Diversity in a Midwestern Town*, New York: Teachers' College Press.

Villaran, Sierra 2015, "Narratives of Cultural Collision and Racial Oppression: How to Reconcile Theories of Cultural Defense and Rotten Social Background Defense to

Best Serve Criminal Defendants," *University of Southern California Law Review*, vol. 88, pp. 1239–68.

Volpp, Leti 1994, "(Mis)Identifying Culture: Asian Women and the 'Cultural Defense'," *Harvard Women's Law Journal*, vol. 17, pp. 57–101.

—— 1996, "Talking 'Culture': Gender, Race, Nation, and the Politics of Multiculturalism," *Columbia Law Review*, vol. 96, pp. 1573–1617.

—— 2000, "Blaming Culture for Bad Behavior," *Yale Journal of Law and the Humanities*, vol. 12, pp. 89–116.

Vuoso, George 1987, "Background, Responsibility, and Excuse," *Yale Law Journal*, vol. 96, pp. 1661–86.

Wade, Peter, ed. 2000, *The Right to Difference is a Fundamental Human Right*, Manchester: Department of Anthropology, University of Manchester.

Walzer, Michael 1983, *Spheres of Justice: A Defense of Pluralism and Equality*, New York: Basic Books.

Wanderer, Nancy A. and Catherine R. Connors 1999, "Culture and Crime: *Kargar* and the Existing Framework for a Cultural Defense," *Buffalo Law Review*, vol. 47, pp. 829–74.

Weatherall, William 1986, "The Trial of Fumiko Kimura." www.yoshabunko.com/suicide/Kimura_trial.html (accessed January 5, 2017).

Weiser, Benjamin 1999, "Danish Mother's Claim of False Arrest is Rejected," *New York Times*, December 15.

—— 2011, "A Judge's Education, One Sentence at a Time," *New York Times*, October 9, p. NJ1.

Westen, Peter 2006, "An Attitudinal Theory of Excuse," *Law and Philosophy*, vol. 25, pp. 289–375.

Whitman, Sylvia 2005, "Whose Place to Decide? Islamic Family Law Issues in American Courts," Unpublished paper presented at AMSS 34th Annual Conference, September 30–October 2. www.amss.net/pdfs/34/finalpapers/SylviaChoate Whitman.pdf (accessed July 3, 2011).

Wikan, Unni 2008, *In Honor of Fadime: Murder and Shame*, rev. edn. (Anna Paterson, trans.), Chicago: University of Chicago Press.

Williams, R. James 1996, "Grasping a Thorny Baton... A Trial Judge Looks at Judicial Notice and Courts' Acquisition of Social Science," *Canadian Family Law Quarterly*, vol. 14, pp. 179–232.

Wilson, James Q. 1997, "Keep Social-Science 'Experts' Out of the Courtroom," *The Chronicle of Higher Education*, June 6, section: Opinion, p. A52.

Winter, Bronwyn 1994, "Women, the Law, and Cultural Relativism in France: The Case of Excision," *Signs*, vol. 19, pp. 939–74.

Wong, Annette 2012, "Note. A Matter of Competence: Lawyers, Courts, and Failing to Translate Linguistic and Cultural Differences," *Southern California Review of Law and Social Justice*, vol. 21, pp. 431–65.

Woo, Deborah 1989, "The People v. Fumiko Kimura: But Which People?" *International Journal of the Sociology of Law*, vol. 17, pp. 403–28.

—— 2004, "Cultural 'Anomalies' and the Cultural Defense: Towards an Integrated Theory of Homicide and Suicide," *International Journal of the Sociology of Law*, vol. 32, pp. 279–302.

Yarnall, Megan A. 2009, "Comment. Dueling Scientific Experts: Is Australia's Hot Tub Method a Viable Solution for the American Judiciary?" *Oregon Law Review*, vol. 88, pp. 311–40.

Yeo, Stanley Meng Heong 1987, "Ethnicity and the Objective Test in Provocation," *Melbourne University Law Review,* vol. 16, pp. 67–82.

Yoshino, Kenji 2007, *Covering: The Hidden Assault on Our Civil Rights*, New York: Random House.

Zimbroff, Jennifer 2007, "Cultural Differences in Perceptions of and Responses to Sexual Harassment," *Duke Journal of Gender Law and Policy,* vol. 14, pp. 1311–41.

Cases cited

Ali v. Ali, 652 A.2d 253 (N.J. Super. Ch. 1994).

Brown v. United States, 584 A.2d 537 (D. C. App. 1990).

Bui v. State, 717 So.2d 6 (Ala. Crim. App. 1998).

Chase v. United States, 468 F.2d 141 (7th Cir. 1972).

Dang Vang v. Vang Xiong X. Toyed, 944 F.2d 476 (9th Cir. 1991).

Eddings v. Oklahoma, 455 U.S. 104 (1982).

Green v. Regina, 148 ALR 659 (High Ct. of Australia 1997).

Hawaii v. Ganal, 917 P.2d 370 (Haw. 1996).

Inmates of the Nebraska Penal and Correctional Complex v. Greenholtz, 567 F.2d 1368 (8th Cir. 1977).

In re Marriage of Gambia, 855 N.E.2d 847 (Ill. Ct. App. 2006).

Krasniqi v. Dallas City Protective Services, 809 S.W. 2d 927 (TX Ct. of App. 1991).

Kwan Fai Mak v. Blodgett, 970 F.2d 614 (9th Cir. 1992), *cert. denied* 507 U.S. 951 (1993).

Maine v. Ramirez, 2005 WL 3678032 (Me. Super. Ct. 2005).

Marsden v. Koop, 2010 ND 196, 789 N.W.2d. 531 (ND 2010).

Masuda v. Kawasaki Dockyard Co., 328 F.2d 662 (2d Cir. 1964).

Miller v. Alabama, 567 U.S. ___, 132 S. Ct. 2455 (2012).

Mohamed v. Knott, [1968] 2 All E.R. Q.B.D.

Moore v. City of East Cleveland, 431 U.S. 494 (1977).

Mull v. United States. 402 F.2d 571 (9th Cir. 1968).

Nahavandi v. Nahavandi, Superior Court of New Jersey Chancery Division – Family Part, Middlesex County, Docket No. FM-12-2237-97 [cited in Whitman 2005].

New York v. Chen, No. 87-7774 (N.Y. Sup. Ct. 1988).

Nguyen v. State, 505 S.E.2d 846 (Ga. Ct. App. 1998), *aff'd.* 271 Ga. 475, 520 S.E.2d 907 (1999).

Odatalla v. Odatalla, 810 A.2d 93 (N.J. Super. Ch. 2002).

People v. Aliwoli, 606 N.E.2d 347 (Ill. App. Ct. 1992).

People v. Aphaylath, 499 N.Y.S.2d 823 (A.D. 4 Dept. 1986).

People v. Casassa, 49 N.Y.2d 688,427 N.Y.S. 2d 769, 404 N.E.2d 1310 (Ct. of App. N.Y. 1980), *cert. denied*, 449 U.S. 842, 101 S. Ct. 122, 66 L.Ed2d 50 (1980).

People v. Dong Lu Chen, No. 87-7774 (N.Y. Sup. Ct., Dec. 2, 1988).

People v. Douangpangna, No. C03136, Cal. App., Third Dist., October 11, 2000 (unreported), appealed as *Douangpangna v. Knowles*, No CN S-01-0764

GEB JFM P (E. D. Cal. April 5, 2007), 2007 WL 1040967 (magistrate's opinion), *adopted* 2007 WL 1521069 (E.D. Cal. 2007) [cited in Dix & Sharlot 2008: 801–2].

People v. Estep, 583 P.2d 927 (CO. S.Ct. 1978).

People v. Kimura, No. A-091133 (Super. Ct. LA County, April 24, 1985).

People v. Kong Pheng Moua, (Super. Ct. Fresno County, February 7, 1985).

People v. Liebman, 179 App. Div.2d 245, 583 N.Y.S.2d 234 (1992).

People v. Odinga, 143 A.D.2d 202 (N.Y. App. Div. 1988).

People v. Poddar, 26 Cal. App.3d 438, 103 Cal. Rptr. 84 (Cal. Ct. App. 1972).

People v. Rhines, 131 Cal. App.3d 498 (Cal. Ct. App. 1982).

People v. Wu, 235 Cal. App.3d 614, 286 Cal. Rptr. 868 (1991)

R. v. Adesanya, unreported (1974); J, [1999] 2 F.C.R. 345, [1999] 2 F.L.R. 678, [1999] Fam. Law 543; [noted in Poulter 1975].

R. v. Bibi, The Weekly Law Reports 1193, October 17, 1980 (C.A.).

R. v. Dincer, [1983] Victorian Reports (Supreme Court of Victoria, Australia), vol. 1 (1983) 461.

R. v. Ly, Alberta Ct. of App. (1996), 193 A.R. 149, 135 W.A.C. 149 [1996], A.J. No. 1089 (QL).

R. v. Smith, [2001] 1 AC 146.

Rogers v. American Airlines, 527 F. Supp. 229 (S.D.N.Y. 1981).

S.D. v. M.J.R., 415 N.J. Super. 417, 2 A.3d 412 (NJ Super. Ct., App. Div. 2010).

Siripongs v. Calderon, 133 F. 3d 732 (9th Cir. 1997).

State v. Curbello-Rodriguez, 351 N.W.2d 758 (Wis. App. 1984).

State of Maine v. Mohammad Kargar, 679 A.2d 81; 1996 ME. LEXIS 162; 68 A.L.R. 5th 751 (Supreme Judicial Court of Maine 1996).

State v. Raguseo, 225 Conn. 114, 622 A.2d 519 (Conn. 1993).

State v. Rodriguez, 25 Conn. Sup 350, 204 A.2d 37 (Review Div. of Conn. Superior Ct. 1964).

Thomas v. Norris, [1992] 2 CNLR 139 (B.C.S.C.).

United States v. Alexander and Murdock, 471 F.2d 923 (D.C. Cir. 1972).

United States v. Booker, 543 U.S. 220 (2005).

United States v. Durham, 214 F.2d 862 (D.C. Cir. 1954).

United States v. Guzman, 236 F.3d 830 (7th Cir. 2001).

United States v. Ruiz-Alonso, 397 F.3d 815 (9th Cir. 2005).

United States v. Tomono. 143 F.3d 1401 (11th Cir. 1998).

United States v. Yu, 954 F.2d 951 (3d Cir. 1992).

Van Meter v. State. 743 P.2d 385 (Alaska Ct. App. 1987).

Washington v. Roberts and Guthrie, 77 Wash. App. 679–87 (WA. Ct. of App. 1995).

Wisconsin v. Yoder, 405 U.S. 205, 92 S.Ct. 1526, 32 L.Ed.2d 15 (1972).

Yick Wo. V. Hopkins, 118 U.S. 356 (1886).

2

LEAVE IT TO THE EXPERTS?

The anthropologist as expert witness

'Lies, damned lies, and statistics.' We all recognize Benjamin Disraeli's famous aphorism. The problem is that he is almost always misquoted. What he actually bemoaned were 'Lies, damned lies, and experts.' *For even in the early days of the industrial revolution, experts could be found on all sides of an issue. To some this was evidence of their venality or self-importance; to others it was a circumstance the more to be pitied. A* Saturday Review *article from January 1862 noted: "It is a fact that in all matters which require to be investigated through the evidence of expert witnesses, the same remarkable discrepancies show themselves. Hardly a single patent case is ever tried in which men of the highest scientific eminence do not appear to contradict one another....[I]n short, judges and lawyers are rapidly coming to the conclusion that skilled testimony, which ought to be the most decisive and convincing of them all, is of all the most suspicious and unsatisfactory."[1] Others were more sympathetic. An article in* Blackwood's Edinburgh Magazine *remarked: "A pitiable specimen is that poor man of science, pilloried up in the witness box, and pelted by the flippant ignorance of his examiner! What a contrast between the different caution of the true knowledge, and the bold assurance, the chuckling confidence, the vain-glorious self-satisfaction, and mock triumphant delight of his questioner!"[2]*

Perhaps no field of inquiry has been unrepresented in American courtroom proceedings, and many of the issues raised by the presence of experts in these fields are broadly shared: background theories that may innocently color one's interpretations, the law's need to answer an issue of guilt or liability more definitively than the expert's knowledge allows, conveying to judges and jurors who are not themselves experts the information they need to decide among those who are. Procedural problems get merged into common assessments of expert knowledge—and indeed the cultural role of the expert—such that much more comes into play than the information advanced.

In the present chapter, we will concentrate on expert witnesses drawn from my own discipline, anthropology. Such witnesses constitute an intriguing example, because their evidence is not of the sort that is subject to some of the criteria, say, of forensic or medical science, yet is still offered for its probative value. Sometimes the information lies far beyond the ken of the trier of fact, as, for example, in the customs of a distant people; sometimes it lies so close to home that jurors and judges imagine themselves to be experts on the subject. In each instance, we can see the courts trying to meld their own cultural assumptions with those being presented by a qualified expert. The result is not always pretty, but it does reveal a good deal about how common cultural notions and specialized assertions may interact as a court of law tries to comprehend the very nature of culture and its relevance to the case at hand.

The problematic nature of social science testimony

As scholars and teachers, governmental advisers, and agency bureaucrats, anthropologists play a number of different roles in American society. Each role entails certain intellectual and moral issues, but there are few roles that confront conscientious anthropologists with more serious scholarly and ethical problems than those posed by their appearance in legal proceedings as expert witnesses. Drawing on specialized knowledge and ostensibly attuned to a professional superego that demands an impartial analysis of the data, the expert witness is brought, usually by one of the adversary parties, into a proceeding whose form and goals often appear foreign, if not overtly antithetical, to scholarly capacities and purposes. Although awareness of the experiences of other expert witnesses may be limited, and visions of legal proceedings drawn more from television and films than professional knowledge, the expert witness will doubtless be aware that American courts have made frequent reference to sociological data and that an expert's testimony may prove significant to the outcome of the case. Regardless of personal affinity to the position argued by the employing party, the anthropologist may not understand how expert testimony fits together with judicial reasoning and legal precedent, how judges, lawyers, and jurors may view their testimony, and precisely how the court's investigation of the facts articulates with the forms of knowledge the anthropologist possesses.

The general use of experts in American courts is familiar to almost everyone.[3] The prosecution or defense, or the parties to a civil proceeding, may call expert witnesses to the stand to testify on anything from the findings of a ballistics test, the medical condition of an accident victim, or the tracks left by an automobile tire. The use of expert psychiatrists in cases involving the insanity defense or competence to stand trial is also widely known. Sociologists have been called as expert witnesses in cases involving the custody of children of mixed racial parentage (Rose 1956: 210), the relationship between race and the application of the death penalty (Wolfgang 1974), the relevance of statistical analysis (Fienberg 1989), and the impact on minorities of segregated schooling (Levin 1975, Sanders et al. 1981–2). Linguists have testified on the readability of a back-pay agreement in a dispute involving minority employees (*Rodgers v. United States Steel Corp.*), and the role of language in cases involving perjury, defamation, rape, and the interpretation of contractual clauses.[4] Ethnohistorians have appeared in cases involving the oral history of native peoples and the relevance for group identity of material culture.[5] Archaeologists have testified in a wide variety of forensic cases, as well as to water rights and the length of occupation of a given site (Ferguson 2014). Sociologists and social psychologists have applied their studies of social indicators in trademark disputes (Barksdale 1957), issues of sexual identity, and determinations of parental fitness. In addition to actual testimony, courts and attorneys have frequently cited the work of social scientists in their decisions and briefs (Rosen 1972).

The range of cases in which anthropologists have testified, or been prepared to testify, is practically as broad as the discipline itself. Already in 1925, in *United States v. Cartozian*, Franz Boas appeared as an expert witness on behalf of an applicant for immigration from Armenia, testifying that he was white. Anthropologists have been involved in the impact of public works projects on ethnic communities (Aswad 1974), the social repercussions of severe facial injuries (Macgregor 1973), the effect of decisions made by the Department of Defense on the people of Enewetak Atoll (Kiste 1976), and the meaning of the term 'cousin' in a rich man's will.[6] Anthropologists have also been involved in environmental disputes, especially in the formulation of environmental impact statements under a law that instructs federal agencies to "utilize a systematic, interdisciplinary approach which will insure the integrated use of the natural and social sciences and the environmental design arts in planning and in decision-making which may have an impact on man's environment."[7] Anthropologists have also testified in cases concerning racial segregation, miscegenation laws, and child custody as well as cases bearing on the nature of religious communities, the cultural background of criminal defendants, migrants' claims for political asylum, and (as we shall see in Chapter Nine) the right of Amish parents not to send their children to public school beyond the eighth grade.[8] They have also played a prominent role in cases involving indigenous peoples in a wide array of countries. In suits brought during the tenure of the Indian Claims Commission, anthropologists testified as to the nature of aboriginal land titles, the structure and identification of social groupings, and the comprehension by Indians of treaties signed with the federal government. In non-claims cases, they have testified as to the practice of Indian peyotism, the nature and consequences of acculturation, and the religious significance of Indian burials, sacred sites, and cultural artifacts.

In all of these cases common problems of relevancy, form, and ethics almost always arise, problems that have been at the heart of expert involvement throughout the history of the common law. The role of such experts is deeply entwined with the development of the jury system. Even when bench trials are involved, many of the rules governing expert testimony, as well as many of the difficulties posed for it, are associated with the emergence of this distinctive institution of legal fact-finding.[9] The early English jury was a very different institution than its contemporary successor. In the 12–14th c., juries consisted of groups of neighbors who were already acquainted with the facts of a case or regarded as capable of discovering them. In a sense, jurors in this period were as much witnesses as judges of the facts: They brought facts to the court rather than receiving them there. In some cases, particularly those involving disputes among tradesmen or other specialists, the jury was drawn from people with expertise in the matter. Occasionally, the court itself summoned an expert to supply information on a given topic. In these instances, the information was probably furnished directly to the court, rather than to the jury, and the judge was apparently left to decide whether and how the jurors should be informed of the testimony (Hand 1901: 41–42; Rosenthal 1935: 408). It was only in the 16th c., as the jury was transformed from a panel of co-residents or colleagues to a group of uninformed arbiters who, instead of bringing their own knowledge of the facts to bear on a case, waited for evidence to be presented to them in court, that experts were brought in by the contending parties to give testimony.

Special rules have also developed concerning the presentation of expert testimony. Whereas ordinary witnesses were increasingly barred from expressing their own opinions on many issues, various jurisdictions created an exception for the expert witness. Although different courts follow significantly different rules, most contemporary American courts permit the judge to exercise substantial discretion in deciding the propriety and qualifications of proffered expert witnesses.[10] As we will see, the standards for admitting expert testimony have changed in recent years, although many commenters contend that the rules still remain somewhat muddled. Overwhelmingly, experts are hired by each side: Already in 1991 a study showed that 86% of civil trials involved expert testimony, with an average of four experts per trial. Although several jurisdictions, including the federal courts, have encouraged the use of court-appointed experts that practice remains relatively rare in the United States.

A number of persistent questions thus arise concerning the use of expert witnesses generally and anthropologists in particular. The first set of problems concerns the adequacy, context, and form of presentation of anthropological evidence in an adversary proceeding. Does the mere fact that one holds a doctorate in anthropology qualify one as an expert in all aspects of the discipline or one of its subdivisions? In what sense is the anthropologist's testimony adequate to the interpretation of a highly specific issue that often turns on prospective consequences? Is it true for anthropologists—as most psychiatrists and some sociologists argue for their disciplines—that the kinds of questions they are capable of addressing are not the same as those posed to the court, and that their evidence is therefore either inappropriate for or distorted by involvement in a legal proceeding? If anthropologists study the everyday orientations of their subjects, do they challenge or play into the cultural assumptions jurors and judges bring to the proceedings? What is the expert's relation to the attorney and clients, and how have anthropologists viewed the process of cross-examination and introduction of a contending expert's testimony? In the courtroom setting, as well as in the presentation of depositions and supporting documents, what evidentiary standards do anthropologists appear to set for themselves, and how do the forms of argument used in these situations compare to those employed when writing for a scholarly or popular audience? What relationships exist between the 'facts' to which anthropologists testify and the theories that inform those facts, and how sensitive are the courts and lawyers to anthropologists' unstated theoretical biases?[11] Indeed, might the expert have an undue impact on the jury, particularly if he or she is an appealing witness?[12]

A second set of questions revolves around the mutual effect that courts and anthropologists have had on one another. How have anthropologists' own concepts been affected by the experience of such litigation, and how has expert testimony shaped judicial thought? Having participated in such proceedings, will the anthropologist be so concerned with the possible legal significance of his or her work that future scholarly investigations will be altered in some fashion?

Finally, serious questions are raised about anthropologists' conceptions of their role in such proceedings, and how the courts and the profession may contribute to appropriate reforms in the present system. Are anthropologists really the providers of crucial information from which judgments are actually derived, or are they merely important personages whose presence in court is useful for rationalizing judgments that are founded on other, perhaps judicially less palatable, bases?[13] How, if at all, should anthropology as a profession approach the ethical implications of expert testimony? What reforms might appear most useful given the experience of anthropologists and others as participants in the judicial process?

In order to explore these questions, a series of cases will be analyzed in which anthropologists have been involved as expert witnesses. In each example, the aim is to sharpen understanding of the issues presented and to show that while no incontrovertible answers exist for the questions posed, this fact alone justifies neither an attitude of utter relativism nor the professional *amour-propre* to which both anthropologists and lawyers may fall prey.

Anthropological testimony and racial discrimination

JUSTICE FRANKFURTER: … [W]e are here in a domain which I do not yet regard as science in the sense of mathematical certainty. This is all opinion evidence.

MR. GREENBERG: That is true, Your Honor.

JUSTICE FRANKFURTER: I do not mean that I disrespect it. I simply know its character. It can be a very different thing from, as I say, things that are weighed and measured and are fungible. We are dealing here with very subtle things, very subtle testimony.[14]

In the years leading up to the 1954 *Brown v. Board of Education* decision, in which the U.S. Supreme Court ruled that segregated education was inherently unequal, lawyers for the black litigants placed considerable stress on the writings and testimony of social scientists. As part of their strategy, lawyers for the National Association for the Advancement of Colored People (NAACP) sought to use social science testimony to strengthen their argument that discriminatory classifications are unconstitutional if, among other things, they are lacking in any rational justification (United States Supreme Court 1949). The NAACP was well aware of the implicit psychological and sociological ideas that suffused the 'separate but equal' doctrine announced in the Court's 1896 decision in *Plessy v. Ferguson*. They knew, too, that at least since the introduction of the Brandeis Brief, with its frequent citation of social and economic indicators, the Court had become familiar with sociological data.[15] It was not, however, until the desegregation cases arose that social science testimony took so central a place in constitutional litigation.

Four years before the *Brown* decision, the Supreme Court was called on to decide whether the education afforded whites at the University of Texas Law School and that afforded blacks at a separate state institution could be supported under the separate but equal doctrine. The case, *Sweatt v. Painter*, was unusual in that at the trial level NAACP lawyers called as a witness one of the leading anthropologists of the day, Robert Redfield. Redfield was, in many respects, an ideal choice. Trained as a lawyer before coming into anthropology, and possessing years of experience in integrated education as Dean of the Social Sciences at the University of Chicago, "Redfield proved a brilliant witness whose every word suggested a cool, considered judgment with great authority behind it."[16] The thrust of Redfield's testimony dealt less with specific anthropological studies of the composition and character of the races than with the social consequences of segregated education and the possible repercussions of court-ordered integration. His testimony was intended to support the argument that if legislators sought to give a rational, constitutional basis to racial discrimination they would find nothing in the experience of social science to support their position (Redfield 1963: 165–68). The following excerpts indicate something of the force and direction of the anthropologist's direct testimony, as conducted by the NAACP's Thurgood (later U.S. Supreme Court Associate Justice) Marshall, and the cross-examination by counsel for the State of Texas, Price Daniel.

[On direct examination by Mr. Thurgood Marshall:]

Q: Dr. Redfield, are there any recognizable differences as between Negro and white students on the question of their intellectual capacity?

MR. DANIEL: Your Honor, we object to that. That would be a conclusion on the part of the witness. It covers all Negro students and all white students. It isn't limited to any particular study or subject or even show what it is based on.

THE COURT: I suppose his qualifications he has testified to would qualify him to draw his conclusions.

A: We got something of a lesson there. We who have been working in the field in which we began with a rather general presumption among our common educators that inherent differences in intellectual ability of capacity to learn existed between Negroes and whites, and have slowly, but I think very convincingly, been compelled to come to the opposite conclusion, in the course of long history, special research in the field.

Q: ... [W]hat is your opinion as to the effect of segregated education...?

A: ... [I]t prevents the student from the full, effective and economical coming to understand[ing of] the nature and capacity of the group from which he is segregated.... It is my view that education goes forward more favorably if the community of student, scholar and teacher is fairly representative of the whole community.... [S]egregation... accentuates imagined differences between Negroes and whites. These false assumptions... are given an appearance of reality by the formal act of physical separation.

[Cross-examination by Mr. Price Daniel:]

Q: Do you think the [segregation] laws should be changed tomorrow?

A: I think that segregation is a matter of legal regulation. Such a law can be changed quickly.

Q: Do you think it has anything to do with the social standing in the community?

A: Segregation itself is a matter of law, and that law can be changed at once...

Q: ... [D]o you recognize or agree with the school of thought, that regardless of the ultimate objective concerning segregation, that if it is to be changed in southern communities... it must be done over a long period of time...?

A: That contention, I do not think, will be my opinion on the matter scientifically.

Q: Does that represent, scientifically, a school of thought on that, in your science, in the matter?

A: There are some that feel that way.

Q: Yes, sir. You are acquainted with the history of the carpetbagger days in the Civil War?

A: I feel better acquainted with it today, sir, than anybody.

Q: Dr. Redfield, let me get you clearly on that. You are not talking about your own trip down here, are you, to Texas? You say you are acquainted with it today?

A: It just drifted into my mind.

Q: Doctor, are you acquainted with the Encyclopedia Britannica, the publication by that name?

A: I have a set. I don't look at it very often.

Q: You are from the University of Chicago?

A: Yes.

Q: Is that publication now published under the auspices of that University?

A: Yes, sir; and it badly needs rewriting.

Q: It is published under the auspices of your University?

A: Yes.

Q: Have you read the article therein on education, and segregation of the races in American schools?

A: If I have I don't remember it.

Q: You don't remember it. Have you written any articles for the Encyclopedia Britannica?

A: No, we are just beginning a revision of anthropological articles, and it seems there has to be a very drastic change.

Q: Could you give us some of the authorities that you think we would be justified in taking as authorities on the subject you have testified to us about? Have you written any books on the subject?

A: Not with respect to the American Negro. I have written on the general subject with respect to other racial groups. Franz Boes [sic: Boas], Ruth Benedict, Ashely Montague [sic: Ashley Montagu], Otto Klineberg. Is that enough?

Q: Give us one more.

A: I will make it a good one. Then, Dr. Leslie White.

Q: Do all of these scientists have the same, share your ideas as to segregation?

A: I don't know.

Q: But on your conclusion as to education, you told me there were authorities in the field who disagreed with your conclusion?

A: I think not.

Q: Maybe I am speaking about the gradual change.

A: I don't know who I could cite for that.

Q: That is all.[17]

Redfield's testimony was an early and important basis for the contention that no rational foundation for segregation could be found in the social science literature.[18] Ultimately, in the *Sweatt* case, the Supreme Court avoided the implication of Redfield's argument that separate education is inherently unequal, and simply found that the facilities provided by the segregated law schools of Texas were not, in fact, equivalent. But Redfield's testimony was also read into the record of *Briggs v. Elliott*, a South Carolina case that was joined before the Supreme Court with *Brown*, and to which Marshall made frequent reference in his briefs and oral argument. By then, a number of social scientists, most notably the psychologist Kenneth B. Clark, had testified in the various desegregation cases.[19] Indeed, it was the famous doll test of Kenneth Clark and his wife Mamie Phipps Clark that fueled the greatest controversy, their claim that black children preferred white dolls over ones that looked like themselves being used to suggest that the psychological harm done by segregation had an adverse effect even on the youngest of children. Kenneth Clark and a number of other scholars, Redfield among them, were also signatories to the statement by social scientists that formed an Appendix to the Appellant's Brief in *Brown* (Chein 1955) (Figure 2.1).

When the desegregation cases came before the Supreme Court, the Justices, especially Mr. Justice Frankfurter, pressed counsel on the relevance and implications of the sociological data. Through his questioning, Frankfurter asserted the Court's right to read, as well as hear, what social scientists had to say (Friedman 1969: 63), and responded to the argument by counsel for the states that there was no social science support for the segregationist argument by saying: "But the testimony of a witness is subject to intrinsic limitations and qualifications and illuminations. The mere fact that a man is not contradicted does not mean that what he says is so" (Friedman 1969: 172). Expressing the common concern of the Court, Frankfurter probed for the perceived consequences of an order

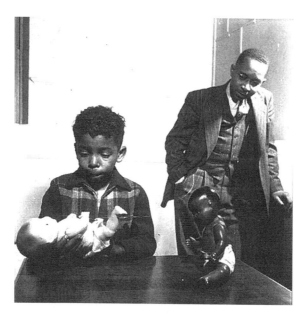

FIGURE 2.1   Kenneth Clark conducting Doll Test (1947).
Source: Gordon Parks, photographer; public domain.

striking down the 'separate but equal' doctrine, and responded favorably when the NAACP stuck to its constitutional argument that if the states could supply no scientific or other basis for their racial classifications, blacks should not have to bear the demonstrated burdens of this discrimination (Friedman 1969: 44–45). The Court also let pass the remarks of John W. Davis, arguing for the states, that "much of that which is handed around under the name of social science is an effort on the part of the scientist to rationalize his own preconceptions. They find usually, in my limited observation, what they go out to find."[20]

When the Court handed down its unanimous decision in *Brown* (1954: 494) it adopted the finding that segregated education does indeed have "a detrimental effect upon the colored children," that "the policy of separating the races is usually interpreted as denoting the inferiority of the negro group," and that "a sense of inferiority affects the motivation of a child to learn." The Court then formally repudiated the implicit psychology of the 'separate but equal' doctrine and supplied a footnote reference to the writings of Kenneth Clark, Isador Chein, Gunnar Myrdal, and other social scientists to support their assertion that the harm of segregation "is amply supported by modern authority."[21]

The Court's decision, and particularly its footnote reference to social science, sparked great controversy. Some Southern Congressmen labeled the social scientists as "Commies" and "foreigners" (Garfinkle 1959: 37; Rosen 1972: 173–75), and Senator James Eastland of Mississippi sought to undercut the constitutional basis of the decision by introducing a Senate Resolution that began: "Whereas this decision was based solely and alone on psychological, sociological and anthropological considerations...."[22] More responsible commenters were also concerned that the Court had indeed relied more on sociology than law in its decision and that some of the social science findings used were inadequate (Berger 1957: 475; Cahn 1955; van den Haag 1959–60). The social scientists whose material was cited defended the relevance and quality of their findings (Clark 1953, 1959–60, 1969: xxxi-1), and over the years numerous commenters have attempted to assess the merits of each side's contentions (Balkin 2001; Garfinkel 1959; Kluger 1976: 355–56; Rosen 1972: 182–96).

Throughout this controversy, the precise importance of the social science testimony to the Court's decision has remained elusive. Chief Justice Earl Warren said the Court cited the testimony simply to counter the argument in *Plessy* that the harm of discrimination was a figment of the Negro's imagination (Kluger 1976: 706). Court of Appeals Judge John Wisdom (1975: 142) wrote: "The social science evidence was the kind of support a court likes to find in a record to lend factual and scientific aura to a result sustainable by other, purely abstract and sometimes formalistically legal, considerations, but dictated by the moral necessity of changing social attitudes." And one of the NAACP lawyers has asserted that the testimony aided in the general awareness of the adverse effects of segregation, and that if the sociological data were inadequate, the defendants had ample opportunity to demonstrate this during cross-examination.[23] Whether, as the NAACP argued, the demonstration of segregation's effects was at "the heart of our case" (Friedman 1969: 18) or was simply the only mechanism available for attacking directly the legal issues surrounding racial discrimination, a close reading of the history of the desegregation cases shows that the arguments of Redfield and others not only preempted the pseudo-scientific assertions of the segregationists but supported, and perhaps even compelled, acceptance of the argument that segregation was without constitutional justification.

The desegregation cases are not the only legal actions concerning race in which anthropological evidence has been employed. Physical anthropologists have appeared in cases involving mixed racial marriages (Maslow 1959–60: 245), and numerous citations were made to anthropological works in *Loving v. Virginia*, the 1967 case in which the Supreme Court struck down anti-miscegenation laws as unconstitutional.[24] Other anthropologists have testified about racial classifications in the case of an East Indian who claimed to have been dismissed from his job as a result of racial discrimination. In that case the Court, obviously confused as to how anthropologists might once have classified some dark-skinned persons as Caucasian, but now relied more on blood group data, simply told the jury to ignore the expert testimony and determine the "race" of the plaintiff on the basis of their own perceptions and common sense.[25] Whether race is in any sense an appropriate biological category or an entirely socio-historical construct has also exercised considerable thought in more recent years.

Each of these cases raises serious issues about the adequacy, impact, and appropriate presentation of social science findings. In the desegregation cases, such data and interpretations contributed to a result that was consonant with both the professional and personal positions adopted by the majority of anthropologists at the time. However, agreement on interpretations and the suitability of anthropological knowledge is not invariably so clear. When such knowledge stems mainly from theoretical orientations and is directed toward prospective consequences, the difficulties inherent in expert testimony become more sharply posed.

The battle of the experts

In many cases, anthropologists have appeared on the side of only one of the parties in the case. Quite often, however, anthropologists appear on opposite sides of a case, and one is confronted with what to some is the rather unseemly—and to others the thoroughly delightful—spectacle of two anthropologists, with varying degrees of experience in such proceedings, being delivered up to the tender mercies of the adversary system. In most instances, legitimate differences of interpretation exist, equally competent and honest experts bringing their separate perspectives to bear on the legal questions posed.[26]

An example of such a clash of experts occurred in the case of the Mashpee Indians. In 1976–77, following a series of failed negotiations, the tribe brought suit against the town of Mashpee, Massachusetts, to gain control of some 11,000 acres on Cape Cod worth thirty million dollars, lands they argued that were assured them by an early treaty. In the process, the Mashpee called to the stand several historians and anthropologists, among them William Sturtevant and Jack Campisi, to testify to their continuing identity as an Indian tribe, while the opposition relied on the presentations made by a combination of anthropological and historical testimony, mainly from Francis G. Hutchins and Jeanne Guillemin.[27] At issue was whether the Mashpee claimants had been continuously identified as an Indian grouping. Indeed, when the case was submitted for decision, the jurors were instructed to return a special verdict, that is, to give answers to a series of specific questions, with the court determining what direction those answers pointed to in formulating a final judgment. The Indians' experts stated that, notwithstanding their conversion to Christianity, loss of their native language, and use of Western clothing, the Mashpee still regarded themselves as a Native American group. However, after a forty-day trial, the jury, asked whether the Mashpee were or were not so identified at specific moments in their history, returned a mixed set of answers leading the court to conclude that the Mashpee were not continuously identifiable as Indians.

Of particular interest for our purposes is the testimony by the anthropologists and historians on each side. Those appearing for the Mashpee concentrated on self-identification, and maintained that acculturation is not an all-or-nothing proposition, i.e., that just as one might be bilingual, one might be bicultural. Thus, they implied, one could be identified with a tribe and be part of the broader American culture without inherent contradiction. The trial court relied on the early twentieth century definition of a tribe from *Montoya v. United States*

(1901: 266; cited in *Mashpee* 1979: 582): "By a 'tribe' we understand a body of Indians of the same or similar race, united in a community under one leadership or government, and inhabiting a particular though sometimes ill-defined territory...." In sustaining the lower court decision, the appellate court upheld the charge to the jury that used this definition, though with some apparent reluctance.[28]

The experts' views of tribes, no doubt influenced by the requirements of the statute and the experience of colleagues in other Indian claims cases, did not, however, draw on certain theories of tribal organization that might have stressed cultural representations more than structural features. A number of anthropologists have also argued that tribal organization emerges and recedes in response to state structures, thus appearing to lack constancy, when in fact, tribal organization might be regarded as remaining latent but capable of responding to surrounding political and economic circumstances that might call for its being brought back into operation. Alternatively, the experts might have stressed that what is key to tribal organization is a deep sense of ambivalence to power, such that leaders are put up for particular purposes but not held out as permanent spokesmen, that tribes are characterized by no one being able to claim moral superiority over any other, and that—far from the common usage of the term to suggest highly bounded and exclusive membership—tribes (as Robert Lowie and others noted long ago) are highly porous, adopt numerous outsiders, and freely borrow one another's practices, thus surviving by being highly adaptable and occasionally disguised or invisible.[29] Yet none of these interpretations was offered, whatever their effect on the jury might have been to the outcome of the case. Thus we have yet another problem that may be encountered with expert testimony, namely that it may not fully represent views in the field. When that may be true, however, is it best to point the finger of blame at the adversarial system, the court's own lack of expertise in the field, or the failure of those responsible for financing the system to insure that all possible viewpoints could be brought before the trier of fact?

For many reasons, then, appearance as an expert witness has been a troubling experience for a number of anthropologists, and many of them have given rather agonized accounts of their involvement. Feldman (1980: 255) summarizes the feelings of many: "Once involved in a legal dispute, the anthropologist faces numerous decisions at every juncture. When the process is completed, no mistakes will be as painful to live with, or as harmful to the legal process, as compromising one's research standards or misrepresenting disciplinary limitations in discovering and interpreting data. If one becomes emotionally involved in trying to 'win' the case subtle psychological pressures build which can make winning the case more important than being an anthropologist."[30] I, too, have been peripherally involved in several such cases affecting American Indians and experienced similar concerns. During the summer following my second year in law school, while working with an American Indian litigation group, I was asked to prepare the cross-examination of expert anthropologists appearing as witnesses against our clients in several important cases. One of these was the case of *United States v. State of Washington*. The case was among several suits brought over the preceding decade involving the fishing rights of Indians along the Northwest Coast. Basically, the State of Washington argued that the Indians were subject to all state conservation laws and fishing regulations when netting salmon off their reservations. The federal government, as trustee of the Indians' rights, argued that the treaty provisions permitting Indians to fish at all their "usual and accustomed" sites are such that the Indians are exempt from state control even when fishing at sites that are no longer part of reservation lands and in a manner forbidden to non-natives.

One of the arguments put forth in support of the state's case was that the Indians of northwestern Washington State had become so acculturated to American life that their tribes effectively ceased to exist. Since the original treaty rights were granted to the tribes as organized bodies, and since the organization of these groups had been fundamentally altered by contact with whites, the present litigants were not, the state argued, entitled to the rights accorded the pre-existing tribes. In furtherance of this general line of argument, the state presented the testimony of an expert anthropologist. He noted that by the 1850s, when the treaties in question were signed, the Indians had been so decimated by disease that they could no longer be regarded as solidary units, even if some of the groups had at one time possessed an overall political structure.[31] On the question of Indian acculturation he testified as follows:

Q: What do you mean when you use the term "culture" or "native culture"?
A: Having an historical ethnological orientation, I tend to think in terms of culture rather than in terms of society. I will give a very simple definition of culture: That is totality of learned behavior, the kind of behavior that we learn rather than the behavior that is part of our biological heritage. A "native culture" is the learned behavior of a given group of people, especially that behavior that sets them off from other groups.
Q: Is there a native culture in Western Washington today?
A: At least among groups I have investigated, acculturation has proceeded pretty far. Western Washington Indians wear western clothes, use modern technology, speak English, share in Western religious traditions, are United States citizens, and, generally speaking, look at the world through Western-European eyes. The amount of "Indianness" varies from group to group and certainly between young and old. I wonder how many Western Washington Indians under 21 today really speak native languages.[32]

Clearly, this testimony presented substantial difficulties. To argue that the region was characterized by "village autonomy and... no tribal structure" seemed to ignore the whole concept of acephalous organization, the existence of inter-village ties, and the situational nature of group alliances and leadership in the region.[33] I was troubled by the expert's definition of culture as the "totality of learned behavior," his consequent assertion that the Indians had taken on the culture of the whites, and that the Indians had come to see the world through Western eyes. Wasn't this behavioristic theory of culture regarded as outdated by most anthropologists?[34] Didn't we know that different meanings might be attributed to similar symbolic forms, and that students of the region had found that "in spite of an almost complete replacement of material goods and century-long conflict between white and native beliefs and practices, basic features of native social organization remain" (Suttles 1963: 516)? Is it not possible for people to be bicultural, as well as bilingual, and is 'acculturation' capable of scientific measurement?

As I prepared our attorney for his appearance in the case, my sense of resolve in the wisdom of our own arguments grew. Yet at some point along the way I found myself asking how I, who had no field experience in the area, could be so sure that our own interpretations were correct. We had the detailed testimony of a highly qualified expert appearing for our side, and most of the anthropological arguments in the case could probably have been rendered secondary to purely legal issues. Moreover, I knew that while some of the opposing expert's assertions were subject to attack, the federal court would not be unmindful of the fact that Washington State courts had earlier relied on such testimony when they referred to Indians as similar to Irish- or Italian-Americans in their adoption of American culture. In fact, the state's highest court had once suggested that perhaps the 'special privileges' accorded the Indians were so excessive as to violate the constitutional prohibition against granting any citizens titles of nobility! But even in the face of these absurdities, how could I be so sure that we were right? Like other anthropologists involved in the process, I found myself prepping our lawyer with greater certainty of anthropological assertions than I might have used in a scholarly context.[35] As I read through the ethnographic literature, I could not get a simple yes or no answer as to whether the groups involved should somehow be characterized as 'acculturated.' I appreciated that for anthropologists, as for many other expert witnesses, the categories of law or judicial reasoning were not always very appropriate to scholarly inquiry. Classifications that courts might regard as conclusory, social scientists might see as shorthand formulations, general glosses, or purposely ambiguous rubrics covering details that cannot be summed up as categorical responses to certain kinds of questions. As an anthropologist, I was less certain that I was right about many of the arguments I was, as a then lawyer-to-be, encouraging our counsel to make.[36]

I could, of course, have rationalized it all by saying that the final determination was for the court and that I was just helping to bring out additional facts, but I found this line of reasoning no more comforting in myself than in the system at large. To say that there are simply different interpretations of social life and history and that I was just engaging in their formulation was equally unsatisfying. This was no mere academic debate, but a legal proceeding, the results of which the Indians would have to live with for years to come. I was pleased that the court eventually found in favor of the Indians and declared that the anthropological testimony on our side was more credible (*United States v. State of Washington* 1974: 350). Nevertheless, I began to look at other situations in which anthropological testimony had been used in courts, and wondered what effects such testimony might have, not only on the courts but on subsequent scholarly work.

The reciprocal effects of anthropological testimony

For several decades, anthropologists figured prominently in the proceedings before the Indian Claims Commission, and that experience is well worth recalling. Established in 1946, the Commission was authorized to hear Indian claims against the U.S. government, including those based on treaties, or the harm done by less than "fair and honorable dealings" with the Indians.[37] Under the statute, only a "tribe, band, or identifiable group" was permitted to file suit (Indian Claims Commission 1963). Moreover, in most cases, the plaintiffs were unable to show that an organized group, as opposed to a collection of individuals, was involved, without demonstrating that the group exclusively occupied a definite territory for a long period of time. From the inception of the Commission, the testimony of anthropologists was central to these determinations. In many instances, sharply differing interpretations were given by the experts involved. Julian Steward (1955: 298) related one such case:

> An important difference between witnesses concerning the nature of acculturation can be illustrated by the Northern Paiute case. Omer C. Stewart, witness for the Plaintiffs, assumed that territorial 'bands' and 'chiefs' mentioned by recent informants and by certain early observers were aboriginal features which continued to exist long after White occupation of the area. I, representing the Government, interpreted the same evidence as indicating that after horses were acquired predatory groups developed and lasted only during a brief phase of acculturation, when the native economy was changed by the presence of livestock and other foods that could be acquired through raiding. These bands had limited cohesion and transient membership, and they operated under 'chiefs' whose function was to lead these forays. None of these functions had an aboriginal basis. The Northern Paiute case also illustrated the hopeless inadequacy of using 'nation,' 'tribe,' 'band' and 'chief' to convey any precise meaning.

The legal meaning of such terms as 'tribe' and 'band' was so debatable to many anthropologists that, as one writer put it: "When the ethnologist is asked whether a group in question is a fragment of a tribe he is not certain what is intended by these terms" (Lurie 1955: 370). Yet the need to formulate more discriminating categories may have helped some scholars to rethink the categories they applied in their studies. Thus, Julian Steward (1955: 295) implied that his own distinction between different kinds of bands—patrilineal hunting bands, composite hunting bands, and predatory bands—was further spurred by his involvement in Claims Commission proceedings. Similarly, the question of Indian concepts and practices of property ownership sharpened Steward's (1955: 293–94) conclusion that: "The plain fact is that anthropology has failed to come to grips with this crucially important problem of 'property' in detail and concreteness."

The experience of anthropologists offering testimony to the Indian Claims Commission marked the real beginning of anthropological expert testimony in the United States, and the subsequent impact on the use of such testimony by the courts has been significant. Involvement in Claims Commission proceedings not only served to educate many anthropologists in the nature of expert testimony, but gave many in the legal profession their first experience with the use and relevance of anthropological knowledge. Proceedings before the Commission provided support for a great deal of basic research in ethnography and ethnohistory, and also provided scholars with "the opportunity and necessity for reappraisal of long accepted technical and ethnological approaches and consequent reaffirmation or abandonment of each of these" (Ray 1955: 287). Such proceedings also placed the anthropologist in a curious role because, as Steward (1955: 300–301) noted: "He himself becomes 'evidence' in that his testimony is based to an incalculable extent upon his theory (explicit or implicit), his experiences among the people, his travels over the territory." Anthropologists have also been involved, in more recent years, in cases arising under the Federal Acknowledgement Process, which allows previously unrecognized Indian groups to gain federal tribal status, and cases connected with the Indian Child Welfare Act, which gives jurisdiction to tribes to determine custody of off-reservation Indian children who have a connection to the tribe.[38]

Whatever their impact on developing judicial concepts and doctrine, and whatever the merits of alternative modes of presenting their data to a legal proceeding, it is clear that participation in legal cases has had a reciprocal effect on anthropological thinking. A series of unrelated cases in which anthropologists have sought to apply their concept of culture to various legal cases illustrates this point even more sharply.

The cultural argument

Anthropologists are frequently called on to explain to a court of law certain aspects of the culture of those who have sought their help as expert witnesses. The cases, both civil and criminal, present problems of interpreting to the court the language and concepts of the party involved, and the relation between the legal issues posed and the relevance of anthropological findings. Working closely with counsel, anthropologists have also been instrumental in formulating highly creative arguments that may influence the course and result of a case.

Consider, for example, the case of *United States v. Diaz*. The defendant was charged with removing an Apache ceremonial mask from its resting place in a cave on the Indian reservation, in violation of a federal criminal statute forbidding interference with any "object of antiquity" situated on government controlled lands. Since the mask was only a few years old the defendant argued that it was not protected by the statute. The government, however, brought to the stand an anthropologist, Keith Basso, who testified that the mask was simply the most recent material vehicle for the perpetuation of a traditional ceremony, and that the "object of antiquity" to be preserved was the ancient ritual of which the mask was an indispensable part. The trial court accepted the argument and decided in favor of the Indians. However, the appellate court reversed this decision, stating that if a recently made artifact could qualify as an "object of antiquity" a person would be unable to know in advance which of his actions might subject him to a criminal penalty. Accordingly, the court held, the statute itself was unconstitutionally vague.[39]

Similar cultural arguments have been made by several anthropologists involved in litigation surrounding the use of peyote by American Indians. Anthropologists have not only appeared in court to explain the relation between peyote and the beliefs of the members of the Native American Church; they have also made their views known to legislators working on the problem (La Barre 1951). In several cases, the courts have found that Indian peyotism was immune from governmental interference (*Native American Church v. Navajo Tribal Council*; *People v. Woody*); in other instances, special statutes have been passed to protect these religious practices (*Employment Division of Oregon v. Smith*). Anthropological data have played a similar role in cases involving snake-handling cults (*State ex rel. Swann v. Pack*).

As we saw in the previous chapter, difficult issues are also raised by attempts to argue that the social and cultural backgrounds of defendants are relevant considerations in a criminal proceeding. Some American courts have recognized that cultural factors may affect the ability of a person to form the intent necessary for criminal culpability or to control and direct his or her actions in an acceptable fashion (*Washington v. United States*). Various arguments have been put forth for a social defense similar to the insanity defense. As one commenter (Halleck 1967: 211) put it: "[T]he person whose criminal behavior is primarily engendered by poverty or persecution may be motivated by forces which are just as powerful and unrelenting as those which motivate the emotionally disturbed offender." Several scholars (Shuman 1973: 853–55; Walker 1969: 288–90) have argued for the introduction to the law of a concept of "social incapacitation" based on social background; others recommend that if extraneous social conditions—ghetto upbringing, a history of discrimination, etc.—are the proximate cause of a defendant's violent acts, the jury should be instructed that it could find the defendant guilty of a less serious offense than that charged (Rafalko 1967: 96–97). Others have argued in favor of a defense of 'black rage,' i.e., that highly charged and provocative language used to minorities constitutes a basis for self-defense or mitigation at trial.[40] Even when not used in the guilt determination phase of a criminal trial, data on social background are often considered by courts in determining an appropriate sentence.[41]

Whatever the merits of these approaches, the proffered testimony of anthropologists on the social background of criminal defendants has only intermittently been permitted by the courts. Recall, for example, that in *People v. Poddar* the court refused to allow an anthropologist to testify on the direct consequences of the cultural background of a student from India charged with the murder of a University of California co-ed who had rejected him. There, as we saw, the court said that the social scientist could testify on the cross-cultural aspects of the case, but that the testimony could not be directed toward the issue of diminished capacity, since only a psychiatrist would be competent to testify on that point.[42] A similar case arose in *Chase v. United States* (1972: 149), in which a group of antiwar protestors who destroyed draft files argued that, insofar as they could not conform their actions to accepted standards and could not distinguish right from wrong in the same way as others in American society, they should be able to avail themselves of a defense of "cultural insanity." In this case the court refused to allow an anthropologist to testify about the cultural relativity of insanity. In the court's words: "Defendants' proffered definition of insanity, whatever its anthropological or sociological validity, is not determinative of the issue of criminal responsibility." In some situations and other countries, however, anthropological data have had a significant impact on the outcome of murder trials involving 'arctic hysteria,' witchcraft murders, and the defense of provocation (Goldstein 1974: 985–98; Milner 1966). In each instance, though, the question remains whether the present forms of bringing expert testimony into legal proceedings are the most effective way of incorporating that evidence, or whether significant reforms might better serve the overall goals of adjudication.

Analyzing and reforming expert testimony

Like many other kinds of expert witnesses, social scientists who have appeared in legal proceedings have been deeply troubled by the ethical implications of their work, and alienated by some aspects of American trial procedure and tactics (Rose 1956; Wolfgang 1974). Some have been concerned that testimony, say, for one indigenous group may act to the detriment of another group; others worry that words used by scholars may mean something quite different in the law. T. J. Ferguson (2014: 251) provides an example that could be replicated in all of the discipline's subdivisions:

> In a legal setting words don't always mean what they mean in anthropological discourse. For example, archaeologists generally use the term 'abandonment' to denote that sites are no longer inhabited. In legal discourse, however, that means that all rights and claims to property have been relinquished, without vesting ownership in another person and with no intention of reclaiming rights in the future....The term 'abandonment' is thus problematical because many tribes have ancestral sites that are no

longer inhabited, but those tribes still claim ownership or rights to these ancestral places.

(Ferguson 2014: 251)

Many judges, lawyers, and legal scholars have also been critical of existing relations between expert testimony and the adversary system, and numerous suggestions have been made to reform the rules of evidence and procedure. Jurisdictions have the power to establish their own regulations, and attempts to adopt uniform rules of expert testimony have not succeeded.[43] For decades, the basic approach of the federal courts was that articulated in the *Frye* case, which stated that if such evidence was generally accepted within the field, it might be heard by the court. While the test had little effect on anthropological testimony, the Federal Rules of Evidence were changed in 1975 and, more importantly, interpreted in the 1993 *Daubert* case which, together with several later cases, no longer required adherence to the 'general acceptance' standard, and left it to the trial judge to "ensure that any and all scientific testimony or evidence admitted is not only relevant, but reliable."[44] The court offered some guidance by indicating that the evidence should be susceptible to and already tested, that peer review should already have been involved, that rates of error should have been considered, and that the theory or evidence should still have gained some general acceptance in the field.

Cultural anthropology remains in limbo under this standard, with questions left unanswered as to whether it is properly regarded as a 'science,' whether its theories are ever capable of 'testing,' whether 'general acceptance' is even possible in such a field, and how familiar judges and lawyers are with science or social science.[45] So far, the *Daubert Rule* does not appear to have dramatically impacted anthropological testimony, though in the absence of many cases appealed on the basis of such testimony, most of our knowledge of anthropologists' experience in court is only anecdotal. Nevertheless, it may be useful for the profession to consider what standards of evidence should be regarded as appropriate for expert testimony, and to formulate approaches that judges, in their wide discretion on this matter, could adopt in their courtrooms. In time, these standards might also influence the development of formal legislation. The following discussion therefore analyzes several aspects of the process of expert testimony as it applies to anthropologists, and suggests certain reforms that could be made in the present system.

Adversary and court-appointed experts

Perhaps the most troubling aspect of American legal procedures encountered by expert witnesses centers around the nature and rationale of the adversary system. Law, it has been said, is not history: One cannot hope to recapitulate on trial, the precise occurrences on which a legal case is based. Therefore, the argument continues, one must rely on the parties who have a vested interest in the outcome to present a neutral court with evidence they consider necessary to their case, while the law must determine whether the relevant proofs offered achieve an appropriate level of persuasion. But it remains true, as Judge Frankel (1975: 1036) remarked years ago, that "we know that many of the rules and devices of adversary litigation as we conduct it are not geared for, but are often aptly suited to defeat, the development of the truth." Despite their recognition of legitimate differences of interpretation, scholars appearing as expert witnesses often feel that courts should place less emphasis on trial gamesmanship and more on a sincere search for truth—even that truth which is not fully understood or unchanging.

A frequent suggestion made in this regard is that the law should rely mainly on court-appointed experts rather than experts presented by contending parties. This, it is argued, would have the advantage of decreasing the expert's tendency to be an advocate for one side and would increase the scientific stature of the offered testimony. For some years, several New York courts effectively utilized 'neutral' medical experts chosen by local professional societies, and similar processes have been used in various European systems (Menin 1961; Travis 1974). Section 706 of the revised Federal Rules of Evidence also permits court appointment of experts, a power courts have possessed for many years, though rarely exercised (Sink 1956). Critics of the exclusive use of court-appointed experts point out that such a procedure would not lessen bias since the expert would represent only that individual's point of view or that of a single school of thought, and the testimony would be cloaked with a false air of neutrality (Diamond 1965; Levy 1961). Similar failings have been noted by others studying the use of appointed experts in France, Germany, and Italy (Ploscowe 1935; Schroeder 1961). Whether court-appointed experts would, as one lawyer (Griffin 1961) contends, be less prone to mislead than adversary experts and whether they seldom represent schools of thought that are widely divergent are doubtful propositions in light of some of the cases reviewed. However, as will be discussed below, appropriate standards of professional conduct might alleviate these problems. For the moment, the question is not whether court-appointed experts should ever be used, but under what circumstances and in what ways they might best be presented. Optimism for reform in the use of court-appointed experts in the American version of the adversarial system is, however, in short supply. Law professor Samuel R. Gross (1991: 1231), noting that expert testimony has always resisted reform, suggests that proposals for using court-appointed experts is a feckless pursuit: "This is barren ground. In our system of litigation, virtually all resources and incentives are adversarial. Giving judges the option to disregard this reality is predictably ineffective; they know better."

Many commenters have long been struck with the irony that, as Samuel Butler put it, "the public do not know enough to be experts, yet know enough to decide between them." Recent studies suggest that jurors are often confused by the conflicting testimony of experts even though they are the ones called upon to choose among them (Koehler 2016). Confronted with this seeming anomaly, Judge Learned Hand (1901: 55), at the turn of the twentieth century, said that what juries need is "a deliverance to them by some assisting judicial body of those general truths, applicable to the issue, which they may treat as final and decisive."

Recalling early English practice, Hand suggested the use of a board of experts whose findings would be presented as evidence to a jury that could ignore it only at the risk of having the court dismiss their verdict as unsupported by the evidence (Hand 1901: 56–57). Hand's proposal never received support, but less categorical suggestions warrant closer attention. Court-appointed masters have long been used in complex commercial litigation. Where the evidence to be presented appears complicated, technical, or inadequate, the court may appoint a master to help with its finding of the facts. The use of masters has basically been limited to nonjury trials, but their use could be extended to any case involving social data. In such instances, they would primarily serve to simplify and hasten the trial by narrowing the issues involved, educating the court on extrinsic social facts, and investigating and reporting on matters to be considered on trial (Beuscher 1941; Note 1948; Silberman 1975a,b). This information could be used at the discretion of the courts in addition to that supplied by adversary witnesses. Counsel on both sides would, of course, retain the right to cross-examine the court-appointed experts. Another suggestion is that a public agency be created that would act as a depository for social and technological data. "Its mission would be to receive and catalogue social impact studies that qualify for judicial attention. The criteria for determining whether a study qualifies for approval would not be agreement or disagreement with its content or recommendations, but only a finding that its design and methods fall within the range of accepted standards of scientific inquiry. These standards would be akin to 'standard accounting principles' in financial practice" (Rosenberg 1976; see also Note 1948). Proponents of this approach do not, however, indicate how and by whom accepted standards of inquiry are to be applied in as interpretive a field as social science research.

Whenever one of the parties to a case indicates that social science data constitute an essential element of the evidence to be presented—and particularly when only one side intends to bring an expert anthropologist to the stand—the court should perhaps consider the appointment of its own expert or master. It has been argued that the Federal Rules of Civil Procedure wisely leave disclosure of the expert's official status to the judge's discretion, and refrain from requiring disclosure of his fee.[46] However, it might be more advisable for the court to indicate to the jury that the witness has been chosen, rather like a consulting physician, to give a second opinion on the issues, and that his status and payment in no way imply that he is more believable than experts presented by the adversary parties. Like all witnesses, the expert would be subject to full cross-examination by both sides after the presentation of the relevant findings.

At various times it has also been suggested that a list be formulated of experts eligible to be appointed by the court. But the use of such a standing panel of experts holds the risk of encouraging the development of an exclusive guild resistant to new approaches. This is particularly true if it is left to a professional association to choose the roster of experts (Travis 1974; Wigmore 1914). It would perhaps be wiser to encourage professional associations to prepare lists of all those persons—whether or not they belong to the association—who voluntarily ask to have their names placed on the roster of available expert witnesses. It would then remain the court's task to choose its own expert. The lists would aid courts and lawyers, who often do not know how to seek such expertise, in much the same way that lists of doctors and lawyers are made available to the residents of a community. No association should seek to certify or otherwise restrict access to the lists. They could, however, apprise those listed of the recommended standards of professional conduct adopted by their colleagues. These standards might include a recommendation that whenever an anthropologist consents to work on a case, he or she should have an agreement with the attorneys that the court and opposing counsel will be apprised of the existence of such lists in the event that either chooses to seek additional expert witnesses.

Another issue concerning the impartiality of adversary witnesses is raised by the use of experts' contingent fees. Bar association rules have generally not permitted lawyers to pay fees to experts contingent on the outcome of the case. However, in 1976, a federal court in New York invalidated a bar association disciplinary rule to this effect. Such a rule, said the court, means that less affluent or indigent litigants do not have an opportunity equal to that of wealthier litigants to have a full hearing of their case. One cannot automatically assume, the court continued, that experts will bias their testimony because they have been hired on a contingent fee basis; a blanket rule barring such fees, the court held, is too irrational to withstand constitutional inspection (*Person v. Association of the Bar of the City of New York*). However, the decision was overruled on appeal, thus reinstating the rule against expert contingent fees.

Pretrial procedures

Once experts have been chosen, whether by the contending parties or the court, there are several pretrial procedures that, its proponents claim, could increase the quality and efficiency of the legal process. For many years legal scholars and anthropologists with experience as expert witnesses have suggested that some form of pretrial conference be held in which all of the experts, representatives of the parties, and perhaps the presiding judge would be involved (Lurie 1955: 360; Manners 1956; Ordover 1974b; Travis 1974; Wigmore 1914). The purpose would be to narrow factual issues, to allow the experts to confront one another directly and discuss the nature of their findings and opinions, and to permit the experts themselves to consider whether they wish to prepare a joint report to be filed with the court.[47] Provided that counsel have agreed to such a conference, the attorneys should be barred from preventing the preparation of a joint statement of expert findings for presentation at the trial. The advantage to the lawyers of such a conference is that they would be able to prepare more fully for their respective cross-examinations. Moreover, counsel could be required to raise at that time all objections to the proffered testimony. These objections could be ruled on by the court prior to trial. This would not only speed the trial, but lessen the interruptions and grandstanding by lawyers when the case is heard. At the very least, there should be full discovery of all expert testimony well in advance of trial (Friedenthal 1962). Following the lead of several jurisdictions, written reports—and even written depositions of pretrial direct testimony similar to that which will be repeated in court—would have to be made available to both sides and the court. Anthropologists should be encouraged by the recommended standards of professional conduct to insist that these reports or records of testimony include statements of experience, methods, data limitations, and theoretical foundations. A bibliography of works relied on should also be attached. Like the pretrial conference, this would afford anthropologists the opportunity to tell their full story, to consider each other's assertions, and to provide lawyers and judges with a better understanding of the nature of anthropological knowledge. The most organized of these reform efforts is the Australian model known colloquially as the 'hot tub' approach. It incorporates many of the features noted above but has still been criticized for benefitting the parties rather than the court, not reducing contentiousness, and sometimes increasing costs.[48]

It is true that limiting the testimony of experts may mask genuine differences of method and interpretation. Not only is science at times 'acrimonious,' as one legal scholar notes, but, as another argues, in having to adapt their testimony to the criteria of credibility that suits lawyers and judges, the experts may, individually or collectively, distort their presentations.[49] Indeed, many lawyers do not wish to present an expert who is neutral. As a former president of the American Bar Association said (Shepherd 1973, 21–22): "Many people are convinced that the expert who really persuades a jury is the independent, objective, nonarticulate type…. I disagree. I would go into a lawsuit with an objective, uncommitted, independent expert about as willingly as I would occupy a foxhole with a couple of non-combatant soldiers. If you find the expert you choose is independent and not firmly committed to your theory of the case, be cautious about putting him on the stand. You cannot be sure of his answers on cross-examination. When I put an expert on the stand, he is going to know which side we are on." Nevertheless, some version of Australia's 'hot tub' approach may produce more coherent testimony, even when it remains the subject of dispute, and, as Mnookin says, it is also "more interesting than neutral experts."[50]

The presentation of expert testimony

Usually, the testimony of an expert witness is conducted orally in open court, first through the direct examination by the attorney who has called the witness, and then through cross-examination by opposing counsel. Expert witnesses have frequently cited, as one of the more annoying and demeaning aspects of their appearance in court, the challenge to their professional credentials by the cross-examining attorney. Cases could, however, be cited in which an ethnomusicologist testified in a child custody case, or a social scientist with a degree in "World Cultures" testified on the archaeological record of a California Indian tribe. Where a challenge to credentials is aimed at putting the witness in a defensive position or leading the witness to make more categorical assertions than might otherwise be made, it is incumbent on the court and the lawyers to gauge their response accordingly. It is, however, the primary responsibility of anthropologists to determine, when first approached, whether their knowledge is truly appropriate to the issue, and to refuse to participate whenever they feel that their studies and experience are not specifically applicable to the case. Beyond this, anthropologists must recognize that litigants have every right to question the basis of experts' assertions.

Who brings out relevant information is also an issue where expert testimony is involved. The judge may choose to ask questions of the witness but in American courtrooms judges usually keep such questions to a minimum. One problem with a question-and-answer format is that it may interfere with the full explication of the scholar's findings and opinions, and may stifle the need to explain why qualified and limited assertions appropriate to much social scientific knowledge are nonetheless informative and important. It has been wisely suggested that experts be permitted to present their testimony in narrative form or to read from the stand all or part of the testimony entered in the record (Diamond and Louiselle 1965; Ordover 1974a,b). If court procedures do not explicitly provide for such narrative testimony, the expert might, during preparation with counsel, require that ample opportunity be given on direct testimony to provide a full explanation of assertions before being turned over for cross-examination.

Moreover, the expert must utilize the opportunity to phrase testimony in terms that are no more definite than the data permit. As Marvin Wolfgang (1974: 245) has said: "Conditional clauses should be employed despite the fact that they are more vulnerable to cross-examination. Such words and phrases as 'may,' 'probable,' 'other things being equal,' 'holding constant certain variables,' and 'associated' rather than 'cause' are important verbal accouterments of the probabilistic language of science, and should not be neglected when presenting evidence in court." There should also be an understanding with counsel that witnesses will be able to explain in their own terms the research methods, forms of reasoning, data limitations, and contrary viewpoints surrounding their testimony.[51] As we have seen in several of the cases reviewed, neither opposing counsel nor the court can be relied on to be aware of these factors or to explore them adequately.

Finally, it is a common complaint of expert witnesses that they are asked questions that tend to distort or misconstrue the thrust of their testimony (Wolf 1976: 112–13; Wolfgang 1974). Before leaving the stand, the court should ask the witness whether the points raised have been adequately conveyed and whether the expert would like to make any final comments. This would afford the expert witness an opportunity to summarize the testimony offered without interfering with the right of counsel to present alternative interpretations in their closing remarks. Wherever practicable, it might also be advantageous for the court to request that contending experts be brought to the stand soon after one another so that the judge or jury will have the earlier testimony fresh in mind.

The role of professional associations

More than a century ago, Lee M. Friedman (1910: 252), in a discussion of the reform of expert testimony, wrote: "The remedy is not in the enactment of any new statute. No act of the legislature will make witnesses learned or honest. The reform must come from the professions themselves." Kenneth B. Clark (1953: 9–10), whose research and testimony played such a notable role in the desegregation cases, also called for the establishment by professional societies of safeguards against the abuse of their position by social science expert witnesses. And Judge Frankel (1975: 1057–59) suggested that the ethical standards governing lawyers should not only command loyalty to and zeal for the client, but a positive obligation to aid in the search for truth. Each of these assertions poses difficulties, while highlighting the roles that professional associations can take in restructuring expert testimony.

It is undoubtedly valuable for anthropological associations to formulate standards that will help guide those serving as expert witnesses. These standards should, however, be posed as recommendations rather than as requirements, and should carry no sanctions of any sort. By contrast, Anthony Kenny (1983: 215) argues that instead of allowing courts to determine whether a nascent discipline is or is not a science, "a register should be set up of such disciplines, and those claiming to have developed a new science should seek admission to the register," somewhat along the lines of applying for a patent, the matter being "decided not by a judge or barrister in haste, but by experts in adjacent disciplines at leisure." Some ethical issues confronting expert witnesses are already covered by existing ethical codes and practices. Thus, the question of what should be done if one's pre-testimony research runs counter to the interests of those who have commissioned it has been the subject of several iterations in the American Anthropological Association's code of ethics.[52] More specific standards of good practice have been noted above. The point to be stressed here is simply this: As recommended and non-sanctioned standards develop, and as anthropologists begin to share with one another their experiences in courtroom situations, it is possible to have a substantial influence on changing legal procedures and on the ways in which social science will be used in legal proceedings. Without exaggerating their own importance to the final decisions, anthropologists, using their professional associations, can formulate guidelines that will aid their own constituents as well as other social scientists and members of the legal profession.

Coping with uncertainty

A divergence in viewpoints often stems from the different theoretical positions with which any expert operates. Moreover, it is perfectly possible that more than one theory can explain the same phenomenon even if there is broad agreement on the 'facts.' Science is part of culture, not something that stands outside of it. The scientist appearing in cases as an expert witness is often placed in an awkward position twice over. First, the study he or she follows may yield less positive assertions than those required for a legal decision, and, secondly, the assumptions and orientations that are on offer—including the claims to professed expertise itself—may remain obscured and inarticulate. In the past (and still in some other legal systems) experts have been barred from testifying to that which the court believes any ordinary person could know or from testifying in so conclusory a fashion as to trench on the ultimate issues that only the trier of fact may address. While such limitations are now largely gone from American legal procedure they have, to a considerable extent, been replaced by the court's discretion in admitting or rejecting information counsel may seek to introduce through an expert. To some commenters, this is especially dangerous since it is important not only to hear different viewpoints but, in the particular case of a social scientist, to allow the expert to testify even to the emotional aspects of the information in question—indeed, to engage the judge or jury in a dialogue more than an adversarial confrontation (Abrams 2010; Taslitz 1998). Research suggests that jurors construct a running narrative based on the story that counsel is telling them. Thus decision-making is based not on waiting until all the evidence has been introduced, but on the same sort of cumulative and linear narration that carries truth in our religious life and character assessment (Finkel 2001; Taslitz 1999). So long as the legal system itself is based on the proposition that truth emerges from adversity, and that science is about truth and not workable interpretations, the value of experts and the structuring of their role in court will doubtless remain as ambivalent as is our contemporary attitude towards the many kinds of experts who populate our lives. Jennifer L. Mnookin (2008: 611) notes that while full solutions may not be forthcoming, the dilemmas of the adversarial presentation of expert testimony can nevertheless be clarified. Approaches to expert testimony, she says, will always be "imperfect, conceptually unsatisfying, and awkward....[T]hose who believe that we might ever fully resolve—rather than imperfectly manage—the deep structural tensions surrounding both partisanship and epistemic competence that permeate the use of scientific evidence within our legal system are almost certainly destined for disappointment."

The frequency with which anthropologists appear as expert witnesses is likely to increase in the coming years as they become more involved in asylum, environmental, familial, and minority-related cases. All of the subfields of anthropology have been represented in such proceedings, but the lack of communication within and beyond anthropology has inhibited the recognition of common problems and the development of potential reforms.

Whether anthropological testimony is central to a legal decision or serves to point out the inadequacy of causal assumptions underlying public policies, often anthropology can both aid and benefit from appropriate involvement in the legal process. At other times, of course, involving 'experts' may either be pointless window-dressing or may not be the best conduit for bringing information to the court's attention. It is hard to forget that Carl Sandburg once remarked that "an expert is just a damned fool a long ways from home," or Frank McKinney

Hubbard's definition of a liar as "an expert witness on the side of the Prosecution, or any witness called by the Defense." Perhaps anthropologists and other experts appearing in the courtroom can avoid these characterizations by understanding the roles that their colleagues have played in similar proceedings, thinking carefully in advance about the nature and form of their contribution to legal cases, and understanding—as scholars—the concepts and assumptions judges and juries bring to the proceedings.

Notes

1 Golan (2004: 104–5), quoting from Editorial, "Expert Witnesses," *Saturday Review* (January 11, 1862), pp. 32–33.
2 *Id.*: 105, quoting from *Blackwood's Edinburgh Magazine*, No. 96 (September 1864), p. 284.
3 On the problems posed by using experts in court, see generally Mnookin (2008).
4 See generally, Tiersma and Solan (2012), Solan (2015), Shuy (2010), Gumperz (1983: 163–95) (expert testimony in perjury case). Anthropological findings have also been vital to an understanding of witness credibility: see Conley and O'Barr (2005).
5 On the role of oral evidence in cases involving Canadian first nations, for example, see Ray (2012, 2016) and Miller (2011).
6 The latter example is based on a personal communication from Ashley Montagu, who testified in a dispute over the will of a member of the Duke family in the 1950s.
7 National Environmental Policy Act 1970. See also Catalano (1975).
8 See Good (2006) and Good (2008). On the Amish and similar instances, see Donovan and Anderson (2003: 99–105). But see *United States v. Curnew* (anthropologist not allowed to testify as to the social and cultural identity of Canadian Indian deported from U.S. in alleged violation of law requiring Attorney General's consent when American Indian is involved).
9 It is said that the foundation for expert testimony was "laid by Lord Mansfield in *Folkes v. Chadd* (1782) 3 Doug. 157 and was well laid: the opinion of scientific men upon proven facts may be given by men of science within their own science" (Lawton, L. J., [1975] Q.B. 834,841, quoted in Kenny 1983: 199).
10 For comparisons to the practices of other common law countries, see Freckelton (1985).
11 See, e.g., Peyrot and Burns (2001), Jassanoff (1992), and Jassanoff (1996).
12 See generally, Bernstein (2015).
13 See, Wilson (2011: 173–78).
14 Oral argument in *Gebhart v. Belton*, which was combined with *Brown*, quoted in Friedman (1969: 172–3).
15 Rosen (1972). On the originality and impact of the Brandeis brief, see Bernstein, (2011).
16 Kluger (1976: 264).
17 *Sweatt v. Painter, Briefs and Records*, pp. 192–5, 198, 203, 204–5. For additional excerpts of social science testimony in the cases surrounding *Brown*, see Kluger (1976: 493–4, 501–4, and 421–2).
18 For other examples of social science testimony in the cases leading up to the *Brown* decision, see Clark (1953: 7–9).
19 For the background and context of Clark's work, see Hentoff (1982).
20 Friedman (1969: 59).
21 *Brown* (1954: 494). In the literature this famous note is usually referred to by its original numbering as footnote 11.
22 Greenberg (1956: 965). On the impact of the case for social science funding, see Price (2016: 57–60).
23 Greenberg (1956); see also Clark (1969: xxxvi).

24 See, e.g., Kurland and Casper (1975a): 784–5, 874–86, 942–3, 958, and 987–91. See also Kurland and Casper (1975b).

25 Edward Jay, personal communication.

26 Cases of this type raise major ethical and scholarly issues for the anthropologists involved. See, e.g., Lurie (1956), Manners (1956), and Steward (1955). Without being specific, Kenneth Clark (1953: 10) had called on professional organizations to set up some sort of method that "will prevent social scientists from being haunted by the spectacle which has long bedeviled the field of psychiatry—two or more psychiatrists offering with equal certainty contradictory testimony concerning the sanity of a given defendant."

27 See generally, Brodeur (1985), Campisi (1993), Carrillo (1995), Kulikowski (1980), Torres and Milun (1990), Hutchins (1979). Guillemin's archives are housed at the Harvard Law School: http://oasis.lib.harvard.edu/oasis/deliver/~law00166 (accessed January 5, 2017).

28 *Mashpee Tribe* (1979: 587–8). In 2007 the tribe gained federal recognition; in 2008 they reached an agreement with the town, under which they received some lands in exchange for renouncing claims to other town lands.

29 See Rosen (2002: 39–55) and Rosen (2016).

30 For additional examples of anthropologists' experiences as expert witnesses see Valverde (1996), Freckelton (1985), Fontein (2014); the sardonic essay by Wuffle (1984), Loftus (1986), Mertz (1994), Jones (2015), Rodriguez (2014), Rodriguez (2015), Cohen and Trask (2015), Krafka (2002), LaRue and Caudill (2004), Steward (1955), and the interviews at McGranahan and Redeker-Hepner (2015).

31 *United States v. State of Washington*, Transcript of Testimony, 1973: 13, 30–31.

32 *Id.*: 1973: 22.

33 On these and other features, see Sahlins (1968: 21).

34 See, e.g., Singer (1968: 540).

35 Others have had similar reactions: "In my own experience as a witness I have often felt compelled to be definite….Not wanting to undermine the case for which I was testifying, and having the impression that for lawyers, social science basically means positivistic knowledge, I have often given my answers a much more definite epistemological status than I would do in teaching a class" (Valverde 1996: 208).

36 On the limitations of anthropological testimony, see Steward (1955: 299–302). A Canadian family law judge worries that experts are accepted too easily and that their information may not be of high quality at times (Williams 1996: 187, and 94).

37 See Lurie (1957). See generally, Rosenthal (1990). For an excellent study of the uses of anthropology and history in the Claims Commission and comparable forums in Australia, Canada, New Zealand, and South Africa, see Ray (2016).

38 On the recent history of federal recognition, see, e.g., Miller (2003) and Klopotek (2011). On the statute proper, see Federal Acknowledgement of Indian Tribes (2015). On expert testimony under the Indian Child Welfare Act, see Kouri (2004–2005), and Wothe (2012).

39 *United States v. Diaz*. The subsequent history of the Act is summarized by the court in *U.S. v. Corrow* (1997: note 12).

40 See, e.g., Godoy (2015) on the position of one public defender's office in such a murder trial. See generally, Grier and Cobbs (1992), and Harris (1999). *Compare* Coop 1995 (such testimony is not relevant) *with* Sneirson (1995: 2263–88) (allow limited use of such testimony).

41 *State v. Rodriguez* (1964: 38). Indeed, much of anthropological testimony often enters primarily at sentencing. For the Australian situation, see Freckelton (1985: 362).

42 *People v. Poddar* (1972: 88). See generally, Blum (1986). Poddar was, however, not actually from an untouchable caste, as the appellate court states. After his conviction was overturned on the grounds that the jury was inadequately instructed, the state chose not to retry him and he was allowed to return to India. The case took on additional fame when, in *Tarasoff v. Regents of the University of California*, the university

was held liable for failure by its health services to notify the deceased that threats had been made by Poddar against the young woman's life.

43 As far back as the 1930s, such uniform rules have been debated. The Uniform Expert Testimony Act, approved by the National Conference of Commissioners on Uniform State Laws at their 47th annual conference in 1937 is analyzed at "The Uniform Expert Testimony Act," 1938. A Model Expert Testimony Act has, like other such model acts, influenced a number of jurisdictions, and the Federal Rules of Evidence (§§702–706) have also been quite influential. For information on various state rules, see the National Clearinghouse for Science 2015. See, by comparison, Travis (1974); Williams (1996); Imwinkelried (1991); and Ward (2006).

44 *Daubert v. Merrell Dow Pharmaceuticals* (1993: 589). For a comparison of *Daubert* to the Canadian experience, see Williams (1996: 189). On the approach of courts in Australia addressing aborigine claims, see Ray (2016: 125–6).

45 On the criteria for qualifying as a science, see, e.g., Kenny (1983: 206–7): "However much we may be convinced of the merits of the Anglo-Saxon judicial system, the courtroom is not the best place, and the adversarial procedure is not the right method, to decide what is and what is not a science." See also Crump (2003). It has been argued that, with less than ten percent of law students having majored in subjects that require significant familiarity with math or science, "[t]he average lawyer is not only ignorant of science, he or she has an affirmative aversion to it" (Faigman 1999: xi).

46 The Federal Rules of Civil Procedure 1972, §26(a)(2)(b) requires an advance report by the expert so the other side may prepare its rebuttal. The report has to include: (1) a complete statement of all opinions to be expressed, and the basis or reasons for them, and (2) the data or other information considered by the witness in forming his or her opinion. See also Travis (1974: 520). For a website that suggests ways a lawyer should prepare an expert for court, see Flax (2013).

47 In Great Britain, in civil cases, experts are under the control of the court, with a single expert required in many cases, and cooperation among the experts encouraged, in part, by requiring them to sign a statement to the effect that their duty is to the court, rather than those who hired them. See Zuckerman (2006).

48 For a critique of the approach, see Edmond (2009). See also, Yarnall (2009).

49 See, for this latter point, Noll (2006).

50 Monookin (2008). See also, Liptak (2008).

51 On the expert's relation to the attorney, and general suggestions to lawyers and experts on the conduct of expert testimony, see Louisell (1955); and Rose (1956).

52 The 1973 code read: "An anthropologist should undertake no secret research or any research whose results cannot be freely derived and publicly reported." American Anthropological Association 1973, Section 3[a]. The present Principles of Professional Responsibility, dated November 1, 2012, eliminated the 'free publication' standard, citing various situations in which full disclosure may be harmful to the people studied. See http://ethics.americananthro.org/category/statement/ (accessed January 5, 2017). See generally, Wolfgang (1974: 243).

Several courts have held that in certain circumstances, the research findings of a scholar who is not a party to the case are entitled to confidential status, and a court may not require the scholar to testify or produce research interviews. *Richards of Rockford, Inc. v. Pacific Gas and Electric Co.* See also Washington Star (1976), Nejelski (1976), and Knerr (1982). In the case of *In Re Cusumano* the federal appeals court held that "Academicians engaged in pre-publication research should be accorded protection commensurate to that which the law provides for journalists.... Just as a journalist, stripped of sources, would write fewer, less incisive articles, an academician, stripped of sources, would be able to provide fewer, less cogent analyses." See generally Shelling (2000). *Compare* the decision of the U.S. First Circuit Court of Appeals described in Jaschik (2012) *with* the decision upholding researcher confidentiality by the Province of Quebec, Canada Superior Court, January 21, 2014. See also, Haney-Caron (2015).

References

Abrams, Kathryn and Hila Keren 2010, "Who's Afraid of Law and the Emotions?" *Minnesota Law Review*, vol. 94, pp. 1997–2074.

American Anthropological Association 1973, *Professional Ethics: Statements and Procedures of the American Anthropological Association*, Washington: American Anthropological Association.

Aswad, Barbara C. 1974, "The Southeast Dearborn Arab Community Struggles for Survival Against Urban 'Renewal'," in Barbara C. Aswad, ed., *Arabic Speaking Communities in American Cities*, New York: Center for Migration Studies of New York, pp. 53–83.

Balkin, Jack M., ed. 2001, Introduction to *What Brown v. Board of Education Should Have Said*, New York: New York University Press.

Barksdale, Hiram C. 1957, *The Use of Survey Research Findings as Legal Evidence*, Pleasantville, New York: Printers' Ink Books.

Berger, Morroe 1957, "Desegregation, Law and Social Science," *Commentary*, vol. 23, pp. 471–77.

Bernstein, David E. 2011, "Brandeis Brief Myths," *The Green Bag*, 2nd, vol. 15, pp. 9–15.

Bernstein, Hon. Mark I. 2015, "Jury Evaluation of Expert Testimony under the Federal Rules," *Drexel Law Review*, vol. 7, pp. 239–307.

Beuscher, J. H. 1941, "The Use of Experts by the Courts," *Harvard Law Review*, vol. 54, pp. 1105–27.

Blum, Deborah 1986. *Bad Karma: A True Story of Obsession and Murder*, New York: Atheneum.

Brodeur, Paul 1985, *Restitution: The Land Claims of the Mashpee, Passamaquoddy, and Penobscot Indians of New England*, Boston: Northeast University Press.

Cahn, Edmond 1955, "Jurisprudence," *New York University Law Review*, vol. 30, pp. 150–69.

Camper, Paul M. and Elizabeth F. Loftis [Loftus] 1985, "The Role of Psychologists as Expert Witnesses in the Courtroom: No More Daniels in the Lions Den," *Law and Psychology Review*, vol. 9, no. 1, pp. 1–13.

Campisi, Jack 1993, *The Mashpee Indians: Tribe on Trial*, Syracuse: Syracuse University Press.

Carrillo, Joe 1955, "Identity as Idiom: Mashpee Reconsidered," *Indiana Law Review*, vol. 28, pp. 511–47.

Catalano, Ralph, Steven J. Simmons, and Daniel Stokols 1975, "Adding Social Science Knowledge to Environmental Decision Making," *Natural Resources Lawyer*, vol. 8, pp. 41–59.

Chein, Isador, et al. 1955, "Appendix to Appellants' Briefs: Statements by Social Scientists," *Social Problems*, vol. 2, pp. 227–35.

Clark, Kenneth B. 1953, "The Social Scientist as an Expert Witness in Civil Rights Litigation," *Social Problems*, vol. 1, pp. 5–10.

——— 1959–1960, "The Desegregation Cases: Criticism of the Social Scientist's Role," *Villanova Law Review*, vol. 5, pp. 224–40.

——— 1969, "The Social Scientists, the Brown Decision, and Contemporary Confusion," in Leon Friedman, ed., *Argument: The Oral Argument before the Supreme Court in Brown v. Board of Education of Topeka, 1952–1955.* New York: Chelsea House, pp. xxxi–1.

Cohen, Jeffrey H. and Lexine Trask 2015, "Guilt, Innocence, Informant." www.academia.edu/11608838/Guilt_Innocence_Informant (accessed January 5, 2017).

Conley, John M. and William M. O'Barr 2005, *Just Words: Law, Language, and Power*, Chicago, IL: University of Chicago Press.

Coop, Kimberley M. 1995, "Note, Black Rage: The Illegitimacy of a Criminal Defense," *John Marshall Law Review*, vol. 29, pp. 205–38.

Crump, David 2003, "The Trouble with *Daubert-Kumho*: Reconsidering the Supreme Court's Philosophy of Science," *Missouri Law Review*, vol. 68, pp. 1–42.

Diamond, Bernard L. and David W. Louisell 1965, "The Psychiatrist as an Expert Witness: Some Ruminations and Speculations," *Michigan Law Review*, vol. 63, pp. 1335–54.

Donovan, James M. and H. Edwin Anderson, III 2003, *Anthropology and Law*, New York: Berghahn.

Edmond, Gary 2009, "Merton and the Hot Tub: Scientific Conventions and Expert Evidence in Australian Civil Procedure," *Law and Contemporary Problems*, vol. 72, pp. 159–89.

Faigman, David L. 1999, *Legal Alchemy: The Use and Misuses of Science in the Law*, New York: W. H. Freeman.

Federal Acknowledgement of Indian Tribes 2015, 25 CFR Part 83.

Federal Rules of Civil Procedure 1972, *United States Code Annotated, Title 28*, Rule 26(b)(4), St. Paul: West.

Federal Rules of Evidence 1975, *United States Code Annotated, Title 28*, St. Paul: West.

Feldman Kerry D. 1980, "Ethnohistory and the Anthropologist as Expert Witness in Legal Disputes: A Southwestern Alaska Case," *Journal of Anthropological Research*, vol. 36, no. 2, pp. 245–57.

Ferguson, T. J. 2014, "Archaeologists as Activists, Advocates, and Expert Witnesses," in Sonia Atalay, et al., eds., *Transforming Archaeology: Activist Practices and Prospects*, Walnut Creek, CA: Left Coast Press, pp. 239–53.

Fienberg, Stephen E., ed. 1989, *The Evolving Role of Statistical Assessment as Evidence in Court*, New York: Springer-Verlag.

Finkel, Norman J. 2001, *Commonsense Justice: Jurors' Notions of the Law*, Cambridge: Harvard University Press.

Flax, Ryan, 2013, "The Top 14 Testimony Tips for Litigators and Expert Witnesses." www.a2lc.com/blog/bid/65179/The-Top-14-Testimony-Tips-for-Litigators-and-Expert-Witnesses (accessed January 5, 2017).

Fontein, Joost 2014, "'She Appeared to be in Some Kind of Trance': The Question of Unknowability in a Criminal Trial," *Hau: Journal of Ethnographic Theory*, vol. 4, no. 1, pp. 75–103.

Frankel, Marvin E. 1975, "The Search for Truth—An Umpireal View," *University of Pennsylvania Law Review*, vol. 123, pp. 1031–59.

Freckelton, Ian 1985, "The Anthropologist on Trial," *Melbourne University Law Review*, vol. 15, 360–86.

Friedenthal, Jack H. 1962, "Discovery and Use of an Adverse Party's Expert Information," *Stanford Law Review*, vol. 14, pp. 455–88.

Friedman, Lee M. 1910, "Expert Testimony, Its Abuses and Reformation," *Yale Law Journal*, vol. 19, pp. 247–57.

Friedman, Leon, ed. 1969, *Argument: The Oral Argument before the Supreme Court in Brown v. Board of Education of Topeka, 1952–1955*, New York: Chelsea House.

Garfinkel, Herbert 1959, "Social Science Evidence and the School Segregation Cases," *Journal of Politics*, vol. 21, pp. 37–59.

Godoy, Jorge 2015, "The Black Rage Defense and the Death Penalty." www.guerrillalaw.com/deathpenalty.html (accessed January 5, 2017).

Golan, Tal 2004, *Laws of Men and Laws of Nature: The History of Scientific Expert Testimony in England and America*, Cambridge: Harvard University Press.

Goldstein, Joseph, Alan M. Dershowitz, and Richard D. Schwartz 1974, *Criminal Law: Theory and Practice*, New York: Free Press.

Good, Anthony 2006, *Anthropology and Expertise in the Asylum Courts*, London: Routledge-Cavendish.

——— 2008, "Cultural Evidence in Courts of Law," *Journal of the Royal Anthropological Institute*, vol. 14, issue supplement S1, pp. s47–s60.

Greenberg, Jack 1956, "Social Scientists Take the Stand," *Michigan Law Review*, vol. 54, pp. 953–70.

Grier, William H. and Price M. Cobbs 1992, *Black Rage*, 2nd edn. New York: Basic Books.

Griffin, F. Hastings, Jr. 1961, "Impartial Medical Testimony: A Trial Lawyer in Favor," *Temple Law Quarterly*, vol. 34, pp. 402–15.

Gross, Samuel 1991, "Expert Evidence," *Wisconsin Law Review,* vol. 1991: pp. 1113–1232.

Gumperz, John 1983, *Language and Social Identity*, 2nd edn. Cambridge: Cambridge University Press.

Halleck, Seymour L. 1967, *Psychiatry and the Dilemmas of Crime*, New York: Harper and Row.

Hand, Learned 1901, "Historical and Practical Considerations Regarding Expert Testimony," *Harvard Law Review*, vol. 15, pp. 40–58 (reprinted from 21 *Albany Medical Annals*, vol. 21, pp. 599ff., November 1900).

Haney-Caron, Emily, Naomi E. S. Goldstein, and David DeMatteo 2015, "Safe from Subpoena? The Importance of Certificates of Confidentiality to the Viability and Ethics of Research," *Akron Law Review*, vol. 48, pp. 349–82.

Harris, Paul 1999, *Black Rage Confronts the Law*, New York: New York University Press.

Hentoff, Nat 1982, "The Integrationist," *The New Yorker*, August 23, pp. 37–73.

Hostetler, John A. 1968, *Amish Society*, Baltimore: Johns Hopkins Press.

——— 1970, Transcript of Testimony in Wisconsin v. Yoder. Wisconsin Circuit Court, Green County, Wisconsin. Mimeograph.

——— 1972, Dr. John A. Hostetler. Temple University News Release.

Hutchins, Francis G. 1979, *Mashpee: The Story of Cape Cod's Indian Town*, Brookline, MA: Amarta Press.

Imwinkelried, Edward J. 1991, "A Comparativist Critique of the Interface between Hearsay and Expert Opinion in American Evidence Laws," *Boston College Law Review*, vol. 33, pp. 1–35.

Indian Child Welfare Act 1978, 25 U.S.C. §§1901–1963.

Indian Claims Commission 1963, *United States Code Annotated, Title 25*, Section 70, St. Paul: West.

Jaschik, Scott 2012, "Confidentiality Right Rejected," *Inside Higher Ed*, July 9. www.insidehighered.com/news/2012/07/09/appeals-court-rejects-researchers-bid-protect-oral-history-confidentiality (accessed January 5, 2017).

Jassanoff, Sheila 1992, "What Judges Should Know about the Sociology of Science," *Jurimetrics*, vol. 32, no. 3, pp. 345–59.

——— 1996, "Research Subpoenas and the Sociology of Knowledge," *Law and Contemporary Problems*, vol. 59, pp. 95–118.

Jones, Barbara 2015, Official Website. www.barbarajoans.com/anthropology/notes-from-an-expert-witness/ (accessed January 5, 2017).

Kenny, Anthony 1983, "The Expert in Court," *Law Quarterly Review*, vol. 99, pp. 197–216.

Kiste, Robert C. 1976, "The People of Enewetak Atoll versus the U.S. Department of Defense," in Michael A. Rynkiewich and James P. Spradley, eds., *Ethics and Anthropology: Dilemmas in Fieldwork*, New York: Wiley, pp. 61–80.

Klopotek, Brian 2011, *Recognition Odysseys: Indigeneity, Race, and Federal Recognition Policy in Three Louisiana Indian Communities*, Durham: Duke University Press.

Kluger, Richard 1976, *Simple Justice: The History of Brown v. Board of Education and Black America's Struggle for Equality*, New York: Knopf.

Knerr, Charles R. Jr. 1982, "What to Do before and after the Subpoena of Data Arrives," in Joan E. Sieber, ed., *The Ethics of Social Research*, New York: Springer-Verlag, 1982, pp. 191–206.

Koehler, Derek J. 2016, "Can Journalistic 'False Balance' Distort Public Perception of Consensus in Expert Opinion?" *Journal of Experimental Psychology: Applied*, vol. 22, no. 1, (March), pp. 24–38.

Kouri, Paul David 2004–2005, "Note. The 'Qualified Expert Witness' Requirements of the Indian Child Welfare Act. (In re M.J.J., J.P.L., & J.P.G., 69 P.3d 1226, Okla. Ct. App. 2003)," *American Indian Law Review*, pp. 403–19.

Krafka, Carol et al. 2002, "Judge and Attorney Experiences, Practices, and Concerns Regarding Expert Testimony in Federal Civil Trials," *Psychology, Public Policy, and Law*, vol. 8, pp. 309–32.

Kulikowski, James M. 1980, "Mashpee Revisited," *American Indian Journal*, vol. 6, no. 11, pp. 18–20.

Kurland, Philip B., and Gerhard Casper, eds. 1975a, *Landmark Briefs and Arguments of the Supreme Court of the United States: Constitutional Law, Vol. 64*. Arlington, Virginia: University Publications of America, pp. 687–1007.

———— 1975b, *Landmark Briefs and Arguments of the Supreme Court of the United States: Constitutional Law. Vol. 71*. Arlington, Virginia: University Publications of America, pp. 803–26.

La Barre, Weston, et al. 1951, "Statement on Peyote," *Science*, vol. 114, pp. 582–83.

LaRue, Lewis H. and David S. Caudill 2004, "A Non-Romantic View of Expert Testimony," *Seton Hall Law Review*, vol. 35, pp. 1–45.

Levin, Betsy and Willis D. Hawley, eds. 1975, "The Courts, Social Science, and School Desegregation," *Law and Contemporary Problems*, vol. 39, pp. 1–432.

Levy, Elwood S. 1961, "Impartial Expert Testimony-Revisited," *Temple Law Quarterly*, vol. 34, pp. 416–51.

Liptak, Adam 2008, "In U.S., Expert Witnesses are Partisan," *New York Times*, August 12.

Loftus, Elizabeth F. 1986, "Ten Years in the Life of an Expert Witness," *Law and Human Behavior*, vol. 10, no. 3, pp. 241–63.

Louisell, David W. 1955, "The Psychologist in Today's Legal World," *Minnesota Law Review*, vol. 39, pp. 235–72.

Lurie, Nancy Oestreich 1955, "Problems, Opportunities, and Recommendations," *Ethnohistory*, vol. 2, pp. 357–75.

———— 1956, "A Reply to: 'The Land Claims Cases: Anthropologists in Conflict,'" *Ethnohistory*, vol. 3, pp. 72–81.

———— 1957, "The Indian Claims Commission Act," *The Annals of the American Academy of Political and Social Science*, vol. 311, pp. 56–70.

McGranahan, Carole and Tricia Redeker-Hepner 2015, Expert Witnesses—Anthropology TV 2014. www.youtube.com/watch?v=UWPOl0Bvr20, March 4, 2015 (accessed January 5, 2017).

Macgregor, Frances Cooke 1973, "Traumatic Facial Injuries and the Law: Some Social, Psychological, and Economic Ramifications," *Trial Lawyers Quarterly*, vol. 9, pp. 50–53.

Manners, Robert A. 1956, "The Land Claims Cases: Anthropologists in Conflict," *Ethnohistory*, vol. 3, pp. 72–81.

Maslow, Will 1959–60, "How Social Scientists Can Shape Legal Processes," *Villanova Law Review*, vol. 5, pp. 241–46.

Menin, Henry and Gary Charles Leedes 1961, "The Present Status of the Impartial Medical Expert in Civil Litigation," *Temple Law Quarterly*, vol. 34, pp. 476–86.

Mertz, Douglas Kemp 1994, "The Role of the Anthropologist as an Expert Witness in Litigation." www.mertzlaw.com/Anthropolgist_as_Witness.html (accessed January 5, 2017).

Miller, Bruce Granville 2011, *Oral History on Trial: Recognizing Aboriginal Narratives in the Courts*, Vancouver: University of British Columbia Press.

Miller, Mark Edwin 2003, *Claiming Identity: The Five Tribes and the Politics of Federal Acknowledgment*, Norman: University of Oklahoma Press.

Milner, Alan 1966, "M'Naghten and the Witch Doctor: Psychiatry and Crime in Africa," *University of Pennsylvania Law Review*, vol. 114, pp. 1134–69.

Mnookin, Jennifer L., 2008, "Expert Evidence, Partisanship, and Epistemic Competence," *Brooklyn Law Review*, vol. 73, pp. 1009–33.

National Clearinghouse for Science, Technology & the Law 2015, "Rules of Evidence on Expert Testimony." www.ncstl.org/resources/702 (accessed January 5, 2017).

National Environmental Policy Act 1970, *United States Code Annotated, Title 42*, Sections 4331–35, St. Paul, MN: West.

Nejelski, Paul, ed. 1976, *Social Research in Conflict with Law and Ethics*, Cambridge, Massachusetts: Ballinger.

Noll, Gregor 2006, "Asylum Claims and the Translation of Culture into Politics," *Texas International Law Journal*, vol. 41, pp. 491–501.

Note 1948, "Social and Economic Facts-Appraisal of Suggested Techniques for Presenting Them to the Courts," 61 *Harvard Law Review* 692–702.

Ordover, Abraham P. 1974a, "Use of Written Direct Testimony in Jury Trials: A Proposal," *Hofstra Law Review*, vol. 2, pp. 67–95.

——— 1974b, "Expert Testimony: A Proposed Code for New York," *New York Law Forum*, vol. 19, pp. 809–31.

Peyrot, Mark and Stacy Lee Burns 2001, "Sociologists on Trial: Theoretical Competition and Juror Reasoning," *The American Sociologist*, vol. 32, no. 4, pp. 42–69.

Ploscowe, Morris 1935, "The Expert Witness in Criminal Cases in France, Germany, and Italy," *Law and Contemporary Problems*, vol. 2, pp. 504–9.

Price, David H. 2016, *Cold War Anthropology*, Durham: Duke University Press.

Province of Quebec, Canada Superior Court, January 21, 2014. www.caut.ca/docs/default-source/academic-freedom/jugemen_21janvier2014.pdf?sfvrsn=6 (accessed January 5, 2017).

Rafalko, Walter A. 1967, "Sociological Evidence as a Criminal Defense," *Criminal Law Quarterly*, vol. 10, pp. 77–98.

Ray, Arthur J. 2012, *Telling It to the Judge: Taking Native History to Court*, Montreal: McGill-Queens University Press.

——— 2016, *Aboriginal Rights Claims and the Making and Remaking of History*, Montreal: McGill-Queens University Press.

Ray, Verne F. 1955, "Anthropology and Indian Claims Litigation: Introduction," *Ethnohistory*, vol. 2, pp. 287–91.

Redfield, Robert 1963, *The Social Uses of Social Science: The Papers of Robert Redfield, Vol. 2*, Margaret Park Redfield, ed., Chicago: University of Chicago Press, pp. 163–68.

Rodriguez, Leila 2014, "A Cultural Anthropologist as Expert Witness: A Lesson in Asking and Answering the Right Questions," *Practicing Anthropologist*, vol. 36, no.3, pp. 6–10.

———— 2015, "The Epistemology of Expertise: Scientific Anthropology and Expert Witness Testimony in a Criminal Case," unpublished ms. www.uc.edu/news.NR.aspx?id=21378 (accessed May 1, 2015).

Rose, Arnold M. 1956, "The Social Scientist as an Expert Witness," *Minnesota Law Review*, vol. 40, pp. 205–18.

Rosen, Lawrence 2002, *The Culture of Islam*, Chicago: The University of Chicago Press.

———— 2016, "'Tribalism' Gets a Bum Rap," *Anthropology Today*, vol. 32, no. 5 (October), pp. 3–4.

Rosen, Paul L. 1972, *The Supreme Court and Social Science*, Urbana: University of Illinois Press.

Rosenberg, Maurice 1976, "Anything Legislatures Can Do, Courts Can Do Better?" *American Bar Association Journal*, vol. 62, pp. 587–90.

Rosenthal, Harvey D. 1990, *Their Day in Court: A History of the Indian Claims Commission*, New York: Garland Publishing.

Rosenthal, Lloyd L. 1935, "The Development of the Use of Expert Testimony," *Law and Contemporary Problems*, vol. 2, pp. 403–18.

Sahlins, Marshall D. 1968, *Tribesmen*, Englewood Cliffs: Prentice-Hall.

Sanders, Joseph, Betty Rankin-Widgeon, Debra Kalmuss, and Mark Chessler 1981–2, "The Relevance of 'Irrelevant' Testimony: Why Lawyers Use Social Science Experts in School Desegregation Cases," *Law and Society Review*, vol. 16, no. 3, pp. 403–28.

Schroeder, Horst 1961, "Problems Faced by the Impartial Expert Witness in Court: The Continental View," *Temple Law Quarterly*, vol. 34, pp. 378–85.

Shelling, Judith G. 2000, "A Scholar's Privilege: In Re Cusumano," *Jurimetrics*, vol. 40, no. 4, pp. 517–26.

Shepherd, John C. 1973, "Relations with the Expert Witness," in Grace W. Holmes, ed., *Experts in Litigation*, Ann Arbor, MI: Institute of Continuing Legal Education.

Shuman, S. I. 1973, "The Placebo Cure for Criminality," *Wayne Law Review*, vol. 19, pp. 847–72.

Shuy, Roger W. 2010, *The Language of Defamation*, Oxford: Oxford University Press.

Silberman, Linda J. 1975a, "Masters and Magistrates. Part 1: The English Model," *New York University Law Review*, 1070–118.

———— 1975b, "Masters and Magistrates. Part 2: The American Analogue," *New York University Law Review*, vol. 50, pp. 1297–1392.

Singer, Milton 1968, "The Concept of Culture," *International Encyclopedia of the Social Sciences. Vol. 3*, New York: Macmillan, pp. 527–43.

Sink, John M. 1956, "The Unused Power of a Federal Judge to Call His Own Expert Witness," *Southern California Law Review*, vol. 29, pp. 195–214.

Sneirson, Judd F. 1995, "Comment, Black Rage and the Criminal Law: A Principled Approach to a Polarized Debate," *University of Pennsylvania Law Review*, vol. 143, pp. 2251–88.

Solan, Lawrence et al., eds. 2015, *Speaking of Language and Law: Conversations on the Work of Peter Tiersma*, Oxford: Oxford University Press.

Steward, Julian H. 1955, "Theory and Application in Social Science," *Ethnohistory*, vol. 2, pp. 292–302.

Suttles, Wayne 1963, "The Persistence of Intervillage Ties among the Coast Salish," *Ethnology*, vol. 2, pp. 512–25.

Taslitz, Andrew E. 1998, "Abuse Excuses and the Logic and Politics of Expert Relevance," *Hastings Law Journal*, vol. 49, pp. 1039–68.

———— 1999, *Rape and the Culture of the Courtroom*, New York: New York University Press.

Tiersma, Peter and Lawrence Solan, eds. 2012, *Oxford Handbook of Language and Law*, Oxford: Oxford University Press.

Torres, Gerald and Kathryn Milun, 1990, "Translating *Yonnondio* by Precedent and Evidence: The Mashpee Indian Case," *Duke Law Journal*, vol. 1990, pp. 625–59.

Travis, William J. 1974, "Impartial Testimony under the Federal Rules of Evidence: A French Perspective," *International Lawyer*, vol. 8, pp. 492–522.

"The Uniform Expert Testimony Act" 1938, *Columbia Law Review*, vol. 38, pp. 369–75.

United States Supreme Court 1949, *Briefs and Records, Sweatt v. Painter*, Washington, DC: United States Supreme Court, pp. 189–208.

United States v. State of Washington 1973, Transcript of Testimony, United States District Court, Western District of Washington, mimeographed.

Valverde, Mariana 1996, "Social Facticity and the Law; A Social Expert's Eyewitness Account of Law," *Social & Legal Studies*, vol. 5, no. 2, pp. 201–17.

Van den Haag, Ernest 1959–60, "Social Science Testimony in Desegregation Cases—A Reply to Professor Kenneth Clark," *Villanova Law Review*, vol. 6, pp. 69–79.

Walker, Owen S. 1969, "Why Should Irresponsible Offenders be Excused?" *Journal of Philosophy*, vol. 66, pp. 279–90.

Ward, Tony 2006, "English Law's Epistemology of Expert Testimony," *Journal of Law and Society*, vol. 33, no. 4, pp. 572–95.

Washington Star 1976, "U.S. Court Shields Data of Scholar," *New York Times*, June 8.

Wigmore, John Henry 1914, "The Bill to Regulate Expert Testimony," *Illinois Law Review*, vol. 9, pp. 353–56.

Williams, Judge R. James (Jim) Williams 1996, "Grasping a Thorny Baton…A Trial Judge Looks at Judicial Notice and Courts' Acquisition of Social Science," *Canadian Family Law Quarterly*, vol. 14, pp. 179–232.

Wilson, Molly J. Walker 2011, "Cultural Understandings of Risk and the Tyranny of Experts," *Oregon Law Review*, vol. 90, pp. 113–90.

Wisdom, John Minor 1975, "Random Remarks on the Role of Social Sciences in the Judicial Decision-Making Process in School Desegregation Cases," *Law and Contemporary Problems*, vol. 39, pp. 135–49.

Wolf, Eleanor P. 1976, "Social Science and the Courts: The Detroit Schools Case," *The Public Interest*, vol. 42, pp. 102–20.

Wolfgang, Marvin E. 1974, "The Social Scientist in Court," *Journal of Criminal Law and Criminology*, vol. 65, pp. 239–47.

Wothe, Kacy 2012, "The Ambiguity of Culture as a Best Interests Factor: Finding Guidance in the Indian Child Welfare Act's Qualified Expert Witness," *Hamline Law Review*, vol. 35, pp. 729–76.

Wuffle, A. 1984, "A Wuffle's Advice to the Expert Witness," *PS: Political Science & Politics*, vol. 17, no. 1, pp. 60–61.

Yarnall, Megan A. 2009, "Comment. Dueling Scientific Experts: Is Australia's Hot Tub Method a Viable Solution for the American Judiciary?" *Oregon Law Review*, vol. 88, pp. 311–40.

Zuckerman, Adrian 2006, *Zuckerman on Civil Procedure: Principles of Practice*, 2nd edn. London: Sweet & Maxwell.

Cases cited

Briggs v. Elliot, 342 U.S. 350 (1952).

Brown v. Board of Education, 347 U.S. 483–96 (1954).

Chase v. United States, 468 F.2d 141–49 (7th Cir. 1972).

Daubert v. Merrell Dow Pharmaceuticals, 509 U.S. 579 (1993).

Employment Division of Oregon v. Smith, 494 U.S. 872 (1990).

Frye v. United States, 293 F. 1013 (1923).

Gebhart v. Belton, 33 Del. Ch. 144, 87 A.2d 862 (Del. Ch. 1952), *aff'd,* 91 A.2d 137 (Del. 1952).

In Re Cusumano, 162 F.3d 708 (1st Cir. 1998).

Mashpee Tribe v. New Sudbury Corp., 592 F.2d 575 (1st Cir. 1979).

Montoya v. United States, 180 U.S. 261 (1901).

Native American Church v. Navajo Tribal Council, 272 F.2d 131–35 (10 Cir. 1959).

Plessy v. Ferguson, 163 U.S. 537 (1896).

People v. Poddar, 103 Cal. Rptr. 84–93 (Cal. Ct. of App., 1st Dist, Div. 4 1972), *reversed* 10 Cal.3d 750, 518 P.2d 342 (1974).

People v. Woody, 61 Cal. 2d 716, 394 P.2d 813–22, 40 Cal. Rptr. 69 (1964).

Person v. Association of the Bar of the City of New York, 414 F. Supp.139–44 (E.D. N.Y. 1976).

Person v. Association of the Bar of the City of New York, 554 F.2d 534–9 (2nd Cir. 1977).

Richards of Rockford, Inc. v. Pacific Gas and Electric Co., 71 F. R. D. 388 (N. D. Cal. 1976).

Rodgers v. United States Steel Corp., 70 F. R. D. 639–48 (W.D. Pa. 1976).

State v. Rodriguez, 204 A.2d 37–38 (Conn. Super. Ct. 1964).

State ex rel. Swann v. Pack, 527 S.W. 2d 99–114 (Tenn. 1975), *cert. denied* 424 U.S. 954 (1976).

Sweatt v. Painter, 339 U.S. 629–36 (1950).

Tarasoff v. Regents of the University of California, 17 Cal.3d 425, 551 P.2d 334, 131 Cal. Rptr. 14 (Cal. 1976).

United States v. Cartozian, 6 F.2d 919 (D. Or. 1925).

United States v. Corrow, 119 F.3d 796 (10th Cir. 1997).

United States v. Curnew, 788 F.2d 1335 (8th Cir. 1986).

United States v. Diaz, 499 F.2d 113–5 (9th Cir. 1974).

United States v. State of Washington, 384 F. Supp. 312–423 (W.D. Wash. 1974).

Washington v. United States, 390 F.2d 444–62 (D.C Cir. 1967).

Wisconsin v. Yoder, 405 U.S. 205–49 (1972).

3

WHAT'S IT LIKE?

Native Americans and the ambivalence of legal metaphors

> "[Why is it] that we can so seldom declare what a thing is, except by saying it is something else?"
>
> —George Eliot, *The Mill on the Floss*

The year was 1926. The place was South Africa. The man's name was Raymond Dart. And he was about to make one of the great discoveries of twentieth-century science—though few people know about it. A box containing the skull of what his assistant offered as a new species of baboon arrived at Dart's home as he was dressing for a friend's wedding. Upon opening the box, Dart immediately knew this was no ancient baboon, but something far further along the line of development to modern humans. In the weeks to come, as he pains-takingly freed the fossil from the surrounding stone with his wife's knitting needles, Dart's labors revealed the braincase of a child—eventually known as the Taung Child—one of the earliest finds of an Australopithecine (Figure 3.1).

Dart soon drew two inferences from the discovery. Stone tools had been encountered in conjunction with several Australopithecine finds and Dart said that those tools went with these creatures. At the time, everyone in the discipline disagreed: You had to be fully human before you could produce such tools, they argued. It took several decades—until Willard Libby's Nobel Prize winning discovery of radiocarbon dating could confirm it—to establish that Dart was right, that tools were being produced 1–1.5 million years ago by these early hominins. But it was Dart's second inference that was so insightful. For he realized that we achieved the capacity for culture before, not after, we achieved our present speciation—indeed, that our ability to master toolmaking and other cultural forms contributed to our evo-lution into homo sapiens. *In short, having developed the capacity for culture, and having to adapt to our own adaptations, we humans (to borrow a phrase) really did make ourselves.*

In the following years, anthropologists built on Dart's inference as they developed a full-blown theory of culture consistent with the evolutionary record. Essentially, it argues, our

FIGURE 3.1 Raymond Dart and Taung child skull (1924).
Source: Courtesy of University of Witwatersrand Archives.

history is one of instinct being largely replaced by the capacity to create the categories of our own experience—what many anthropologists now mean by 'culture.' Whether it is in the array of possible kinship or political systems, modes of ecological exploitation or concepts of time and space, we are at base category-creating critters. Moreover, these conceptualizations, accomplishing much of the work that for other species is performed by instinct, are ramified across multiple domains to the point where they seem both immanent and natural. And it is metaphor that may constitute the preeminent vehicle by which these categories are spread and linked through the disparate realms of our lives. It is not just that we live by metaphors; it is that we cannot live as human beings without them.

Metaphors thus stitch together the disparate elements that form a particular cultural configuration. Originally meaning 'to carry over' or 'transfer,' it is therefore fitting that in modern Greek, metaphores should refer to a 'moving van,' a vehicle that brings elements of the familiar into the new. Through metaphors' crabwise mode of thought, the known and the unknown are as integrally linked in legal thought as among all other domains of life. It is for this reason that, when a particular part of a culture is under consideration—in this case the intellectual productions of native peoples—we should gravitate toward an analysis of the metaphors through which these artifacts and ideas are rendered comprehensible.

★ ★ ★

We are our metaphors. Whether a metaphor originates in just one domain—religion, law, folklore—its spread into other domains is vital to its cultural acceptance. Indeed, it may be argued, if human beings are most distinguishable for their evolved capacity to create the categories of their own experience as a vehicle for adapting to a shifting and uncertain world, and then proliferate those categories across multiple domains until they seem commonsensical, metaphor may be the primary instrument through which this integrative process is effected. Which metaphors are employed can make all the difference. To speak of the heart as a pump instead of a furnace, the eye as a receptor instead of a beacon, or the atom as the irreducible unit of matter rather than a miniature planetary system, can determine the very course of science, religion, and social relations. Indeed, the power of metaphor to capture what we take for the moment as reality is enormous. Does it not seem self-evident that money should be 'liquid,' or that an argument should be like a battle in which claims are 'indefensible,' 'shot down,' or 'demolished'?[1] Many of our culture's metaphors, of course, have overtones derived from sacred text: 'sour grapes,' 'salt of the earth,' 'drop in a bucket,' 'feet of clay,' 'filthy lucre,' 'skin of our teeth.' Religious metaphors also change with the times. As anthropologist Marshall Sahlins (1968: 96) amusingly notes:

> When we were pastoral nomads, the Lord was our shepherd. We were His flock, and He made us to lie down in green pastures, and led us beside the still waters.
>
> When we were serfs and nobles, the Lord was our king. Sat regnant on the throne of heaven, His shepherd's crook now a jeweled scepter; monarch of feudal monarchs, even to the Prince of Evil, His own contentious baron. But we were mostly peasants, and our comfort and justice no longer lay in the green pastures but in the land. And we would have it. We would inherit the earth.
>
> Finally we are businessmen—and the Lord is our accountant. He keeps a ledger on us all, enters there our good deeds in black and debits our sins in red. The Lord useth double-entry bookkeeping; He writeth a man down in fine columns. And when the Great Businessman closes our accounts, to those who show a profit He shall pay eternal dividends; but for those with a life ill spent—well, the Devil take the hindmost.

Indeed, the power of metaphor to capture what we take for the moment as reality is enormous. Politics and policies follow in the wake of our choice of metaphors. If what is required is a 'level playing field,' if welfare to those on the political left is a 'safety net' and to those on the right a 'hammock,'[2] if crime is seen as predation rather than a disease,[3] if thoughts exist in 'a marketplace of ideas'[4] and even a corporation is a 'person,' quite different legal protections may apply than if some other analogy is chosen. The sociological assumptions that inform the way we pursue scientific knowledge are no less affected by the choice of metaphor. If we see HIV/AIDS as a 'war' against an invading virus, our research may proceed quite differently than if we see it in terms of a lock and key; if we envision procreation not as a chemical process of stickiness but as the act of sperm forcing its way into the egg—itself rendered not just feminine but virginal and sacralized by calling several of its parts the 'corona' and 'vestments'—our religiously based view of human nature may appear as if it were a natural force. And if we call menstruation (as even recent medical texts have) 'the weeping of the womb,' and thus regard this process as a form of failure and loss, as opposed to theorizing that it is a cleansing of materials brought into the woman's body by men, is not our vision of gender differences in other domains of life significantly affected?[5]

How we think of property, production, and ownership are equally susceptible to the power of metaphor. Indeed, as Harry Kalven (1967: 38) said: "Competition among analogies is the essential circumstance of legal reasoning." The usual way lawyers in the common law tradition speak of property ownership is as a 'bundle of rights.' Even this may be conceptualized as rights I have vis-à-vis a given thing or as the distribution of rights among others and me as it concerns that thing. Either way, two features are immediately noticeable: the emphasis on the individual and the relative lack of emphasis on highly personalized reciprocal obligations that go beyond rights of alienation. For many, the image of property as a field of rights is also deeply entwined with moral precepts, whether phrased in terms of natural prerogatives and affinities, interpersonal duties, or God-given entitlements. Indeed, this cultural orientation is also naturalized, in the sense that any claim of ownership may then depend on separating the incomplete state of raw nature from the enhancement—indeed fulfillment—that is said to be the natural result of human endeavor.[6] The pervasive power of the property metaphor in American history is well represented by James Madison's assertion that he even had a property right in his reputation, his religion, and other personal matters.

But how well do the Western concepts and metaphors of property translate to the situation of native peoples, particularly when it concerns intangible productions of knowledge and artistic inspiration? Does a language of property and moral rights, of exclusive ownership or personal control translate adequately when the place of the individual, family, religious community, or tribe may occupy a very different conceptual space for native peoples? And when two, often conflicting, cultures are involved, which metaphors are most effective and fair?

When it comes to intellectual production and its legal protection, 'property' is surely the dominant metaphor, so much so that the phrase 'intellectual *property*' and its shorthand IP seem self-evident. But if one accepts the notion of ideas as property-like one may have to accept many attendant features as well. For if 'property' implies the exclusive power of alienation, it may be difficult to separate individual proprietary interests from the less tangible, but no less heartfelt, aspects of collective attachment. If, too, property implies that a material thing can be separated from the personhood of those identified with it, there may be no clear way of measuring and equating market value with spiritual, sentimental, or nationalistic value. Although it has never formed part of the common law, civil law countries recognize that certain objects may not enter into commerce (*res extra commercium*), including those objects that are vital to a particular religious or cultural group. In a sense, a similar notion has already been embraced in the Native American Graves Protection Act (NAGPRA) insofar as it requires the return to native groups of human remains and artifacts under certain conditions.[7] By analogizing cultural materials to this concept in civil and international law, one might argue that additional categories of native materials are beyond the scope of commercial trade. Indeed, as many Native Americans argue, if there was no legitimate title in the conqueror to begin with, how can it be transferable to another?

Whether some rights should extend beyond the sale of a work also depends on the metaphor one chooses. A number of Western countries, under such terms as *droit de suite*, acknowledge that an artist's interest is not entirely cut off by the work's sale, a portion of each resale being owed to the originator of the work or the artist's heirs.[8] In the U.S,. there is no comprehensive federal legislation on the practice nor has a case reached the Supreme Court addressing the continuing rights of the artist, California's law on the subject having been the subject of ongoing litigation. That statute, known as the California Resale Royalties Act (CRRA), requires a five percent payment to the artist upon each resale, but only if it occurs within the state.[9] The issue is placed entirely in terms of property and commerce, there being no direct reference by either the legislature or the courts to any 'moral' right or aspect of the artist's 'personality.'

Along with tangible, property-like conceptualizations, legal systems often institutionalize control of intangible products through laws of copyright, patent, and trademark. Although such regimes may work well when attached to national and international standards, they can be more problematic when an object or purpose does not fit neatly into categories generated from Western experience. The result is seen by many as a kind of colonization by the West of the concepts to be employed. For example, copyright is for a distinct and limited period of time. But if I create something, or if my group creates something, why should our control, like our group's culture, not be entitled to unlimited duration—or at least to our own conception of time—rather than a culturally different measure? Moreover, assigning control over something that holds meaning for an entire culture to an individual artist or producer may wholly displace communal interests.

After 'property,' the most common metaphor applied to native and non-native peoples is that of 'heritage.' Here the issue of collective interest comes more sharply to the fore. Defining and designating what shall count as part of a group's heritage is, of course, hardly self-evident, and the concept itself can lead to difficulties for native peoples in particular. An example from native religion and the law may be helpful here. At one time, American courts said that Native Americans could have access to their sacred sites off-reservation, provided they could show that the places were 'central and indispensable' to their religion. This left the courts to determine the natives' religion, with the odd result that having acknowledged one site and then asked about access to another, the courts responded by saying that they had just given the tribe their Vatican or their Temple Mount, as if the characteristics of a Western religion defined religion for all.[10] The risk, then, is that an outside source may be determining what the group involved means by its own heritage.

Nevertheless, since everyone can claim some heritage for their group, the concept does have the advantage of linking native peoples to a category non-natives employ for themselves, thus affording the broader protection of laws of general applicability, notwithstanding the highly interpretative aspect of their implementation. Embodied in international accords, such a foundational concept also has sparked an entire industry of experts and legal suits, all of which may, however, tend towards regularization of criteria that may or may not disadvantage those with less power or assets to contest their rights. Relying on the metaphor of 'heritage' may emphasize collective interests, but designating what shall count as part of a group's heritage is hardly self-evident, particularly if an outside source may be determining what the group involved means by its own heritage.

We also speak of the 'theft' or 'piracy' of intellectual productions. But what is an idea *like*? Is it like the air, free and unfenced, or (holding just to that analogy) is it like the air rights over a building that can in fact be commercialized, or the air around my head that I have a right not to have polluted with another's cigarette smoke? Should we envision the rights to intellectual products as being like a farmer entitled to reap what he sows?[11] Or should exclusive ownership be replaced by the idea that, like a crop not harvested, an object or idea belongs to whoever makes beneficial use of it? But does that mean that a tribal symbol forced or fallen into disuse may be appropriated by non-natives? Alternatively, we could see the use of another's cultural production as a violation of 'the commons' if one can only claim a certain level of usufructuary right, perfected by actual use, which must later pass to another in the community according to some system of distribution or rotation.[12]

We could, to vary the agricultural metaphor, imagine ideas and their production as being like a crop in an unfenced field. But if you think the seed came before the sower, a different moral sense may apply than if one attributes all rights to the planter. By that logic, if an artist builds on a traditional tribal design she may not have the right to sell it outside of the tribe. And like many patent laws, she might have to show that she has really added something new to the original object to perfect her legal control over it. Indeed, American patent law is based on an eighteenth-century image of the 'hero inventor' operating independent of all others, whereas the image of the laboratory-based 'team as hero' may help to link native peoples to existing laws by conceptualizing their productions, too, as collective entrepreneurship.[13] One question then would be: Who is really doing the inventing, the sowing, or is responsible for vitalizing the team? Or, to switch metaphors, is this a case of 'standing on the shoulders of giants' such that no addition could have existed without that which went before—which must at least be shared and attributed to the predecessor—if legal consequences of ownership are to flow from that analogy? The concept is hardly unknown even in the highly individualistic West. As Virginia Woolf, in *A Room of One's Own*, said: "Masterpieces are not single solitary births: they are the outcome of many years of thinking in common, of thinking by the body of the people, so the experience of the mass is behind the single voice."

Copyright, it must also be noted, protects a tangible form and its original expression, not the idea itself.[14] Patents garnering government approval must demonstrate a new, useful, and non-obvious process or technology. But when, in the case of native productions, is the line crossed to originality warranting a change in legal status? And what, if any, duty is owed whoever generated the original design? In the *Bulun Bulun* case, an Australian court held that the artist has a duty to protect the ritual knowledge he has been permitted to use in a bark painting, but it is not a duty that alone vests a financial interest in the tribe when the individual artist's work is used by a commercial textile manufacturer.[15] The court was not prepared to recognize communal title, but they did recognize that native law forms part of the 'factual matrix' that rendered the relation one of mutual trust and confidence, which, in this particular case, the artist was held to have fulfilled by stopping the textile from being manufactured.

Copyright is, of course, forward looking, but it is basically oriented towards the well-being of the proprietor alone and bars others' use of the work for a limited time. However, a very different concern arises for a number of indigenous peoples who see their work as oriented towards the group's future patrimony. Hunting, for example, may be a way of life that connects people to an environment and thus deserves protection. Whether it is the Makah hunting whales or the Hopi taking protected eagles—and whether it is by carving out exceptions to broader statutes for native peoples or making their cultures the objects of conservation—the focus on hunting as a form of cultural activity may, if we adopt a future-oriented metaphor, justify certain accommodations to indigenous peoples that individuated copyright precludes.

Perhaps one can at least draw the line at a false attribution. Thus a fabricated claim of connection to the Shinnecock by a non-Indian cigarette dealer precluded use of the tribal name by that proprietor. In some instances native peoples have been able to register a tribal insignia, even though exclusive protection is not assured. For example, ten petroglyphs have been registered in Canada by a Vancouver Island band, thus preventing unauthorized use by non-members. In other situations, however, matters may be considerably more fraught. For decades, Native American groups have objected to the use of names like *Redskins,* or half-time pageants like the dancing of the University of Illinois' Chief Illiniwek, regarded by the tribe as a sacred figure, with quite differential effect.[16]

Not only may there be spiritual and identity aspects to such uses of native names and images, but a form of collective slander may also be claimed. American law, as we shall see, does not favor actions for group libel, which many other countries permit. So, too, American law allows no defamation of the dead, but many indigenous groups do. The laws that tribes apply internally may reflect such a position, but may be difficult to apply beyond the territories over which they exercise some degree of sovereignty.[17] Sensitivity to other groups' cultural identifiers may, however, be justifiable on other grounds. Textiles and other motifs and designs are not only protectable for their exclusive economic value, but for their trivialization in out-of-context representations, as when something of a religious nature is used commercially.

Quite a different set of connotations may flow from thinking of indigenous productions as being like one's 'brainchild.' Sometimes put in organic terms (the product of a 'fruitful mind'), sometimes in the idiom of paternity, such metaphors in the past conveyed not a sense of perpetual ownership, but the right to continued acknowledgment and freedom from piracy. Thus Daniel Defoe in 1710 protested: "[A] book is the Author's Property, 'tis the Child of his Inventions, the Brat of his Brain." As Mark Rose notes, in the usages of the sixteenth to the seventeenth centuries, "the paternity metaphor is consonant with the emergence of the individual author in the patriarchal patronage society concerned with blood, lineage, and the dynastic principle that like engenders like."[18] Any intrusion may not only be a violation of a property right, but an assault on the person's very identity and self-regard. Many countries refer to this as a 'right to publicity,' or a 'right to personality.' It may be considered a property right, with all the legal protections (trespass, etc.) brought in by that analogy. Alternatively, intrusion into this right may be grouped under tort law, thus affording monetary remedies, or as an invasion of privacy, triggering issues of free speech and equitable remedies.[19]

Analogies based on personal identity can take many forms. A number of European countries phrase copyright as a 'moral right.' Moral rights were first recognized in France and Germany, before they were included in the Berne Convention for the Protection of Literary and Artistic Works in 1928. Article 6bis of the Berne Convention protects attribution and integrity, stating: "Independent of the author's economic rights, and even after the transfer of the said rights, the author shall have the right to claim authorship of the work and to object to any distortion, modification of, or other derogatory action in relation to the said work, which would be prejudicial to the author's honor or reputation." While the U.S. became a signatory to the Berne Convention in 1988, it still does not completely recognize moral rights as part of copyright law, but rather as part of other bodies of law, such as defamation or unfair competition. Indeed, in *Gilliam v. American Broadcasting* the Second Circuit Court of Appeals stated that moral rights are not part of American law, but they did use the Lanham Act to accomplish some of the same purposes that the European concept permits, namely recognition that one has the right not to have one's work distorted. If control is put in terms of moral rights, other implications besides those of compensable property invasion may follow, including those given legislative or judicial enforcement. In the UK, for example, moral claims may be made for property seized by the Nazis and now in public museums, a right that can survive the statutes of limitation. If museums are 'ethical guardians' the question arises whether indigenous tribes might also be so conceptualized.

There are other metaphors that relate to one's personal identity. The French speak of the 'right to control one's image,' while a number of other countries speak of a 'right to personality.'[20] In the U.S., The Visual Artists Rights Act (VARA) takes a somewhat more limited approach. It applies only to works of 'recognized stature' where there is some public interest, and allows an artist to bar attribution if (tracking the Berne language) such use would be "prejudicial to his or her honor or reputation" (VARA §106(a)(2). Indigenous peoples have somewhat similar ways of putting the matter. In the *Chilkat* case one Indian said of the tribe's Whale House artifacts: "The primary significance is knowing who you are. When you're selling an artifact you're not only getting rid of a piece of wood, you're getting rid of the music, the song, the dance, and the good, the bad and the ugly."[21] Commercial trademark commenters now speak of 'persona' as evoking an image that extends beyond the product proper to include an image that makes the trademark holder feel good about himself. If, say, the tipi symbol of a Kiowa design is seen as imbued with power that extends beyond its immediate referent—if, indeed, it incorporates the deeds and accomplishments no other man should be able to sing about or portray—one could analogize a right to that symbol's persona in the same way trademark law may protect an individual 'brand.' However, in this case the claim of exclusive control would be based on the 'medicine' or 'vision' that surrounds the production, rather than the object per se (Greene and Dresher 1994). As noted, unlike many European countries, U.S. law does not permit an action for group defamation. Yet if one were to extend the analogy of attacks upon one's culture as equivalent to holding one up to public shame or opprobrium—an action that clearly focuses on the collectivity as it affects the individual—cases that have previously failed to gain traction might command a legal basis.[22]

The term 'intellectual property' tends to place emphasis on the second part of that phrase, building analogies to other forms of real or intangible things. If, however, one focuses on the first word, other analogies may be suggested. For example, control over the presentation, rather than the title, to a native production may become the focus of concern. The question thus arises whether one can strip away the intellectual from the physical aspect of an artifact and fractionate the rights that attend that object just as one limits the use of land or intangible property by dividing the interests of the owner, the state, and other parties accordingly. Such an approach may have the merit of encouraging hybridity and the exchange of information across cultures, and may wean intellectual property law away from its emphasis on the property ownership element to the exclusion of the ideational and cultural value. Moreover if one emphasizes metaphors relating to the flow of information, the native originators may be regarded as legally cognizable stewards of the objects, the titleholders being analogized to trust beneficiaries who have a duty of care to the originators as well as to those to whom the objects are displayed.[23]

Finally, one could put matters in terms of human rights. The Covenant on Economic, Social and Cultural Rights is said to protect intellectual creations, and this might even be extended to such intangibles as folklore and songs. However, given the emphasis on persons rather than groups, one would have to interpret these artifacts as extending to collective and not just individual rights.[24] Many of the existing international accords, such as those promulgated through the World Intellectual Property Organization (WIPO) and those embodied in the United Nations Declaration on the Rights of Indigenous Peoples, are, however, in the nature of encouragement to negotiation or consideration, rather than enforceable regulations.[25]

The analogies discussed so far are drawn mainly from non-native legal regimes. But how do various native peoples analogize their own knowledge and products? There is a tendency to imagine that all indigenous groups are based on collective property holding. But ownership, in the sense of undivided control and the power of alienation, is hardly unknown to many indigenous peoples. An Australian aborigine may have an exclusive right to his song while a Melanesian may be far less concerned about its use by others than that its sale or transmission was conducted in an authorized way. Indeed, for the latter the sale or purchase may galvanize important social contacts while the benefits of demonstrating difference, which is vital to forming alliances, may be underscored by acquiring possession of the artifacts of others (Harrison 2000). From whom knowledge comes most recently may be more important than knowing who initiated it. Thus, while most Western metaphors center around the relation of the individual creator to the product, the approach of some indigenous groups may, by contrast, be thought of as concerned with the relations among people, the image being that of "a bundle of relationships, rather than a bundle of economic rights."[26] Similarly, the New Zealand Maori concept of *taonga* expresses the rights and obligations that span generations, and objects that are linked to this concept are not subject to being replaced by money or other objects in the ordinary course of exchange (Craig 2012). The dominant metaphor is thus one of kinship and mutuality. Indeed, some anthropologists would argue that a preeminent role of art is less as an expression of religious and aesthetic sentiments than as a vehicle to facilitate relationships, whether by demonstrating that persons can be substituted for the things portrayed, that art mediates individual and collective action, or that the contradictions posed by an art object promote creativity in social relationships no less than cosmological orientations. Andrew Gell (1998), for example, argues that things provoke attachments—that far from being passive, art is a form of instrumental action influencing the actions of others. Marilyn Strathern (1988) suggests that relations are substantially between persons and things, with the latter being substituted for the former in a number of instances. Clifford Geertz (1983: 99), taking a more cultural tack, argues against the structural-functional approach, "that is, that works of art are elaborate mechanisms for defining social relationships, sustaining social rules, and strengthening social values….The central connection between art and collective life does not lie on such an instrumental plane, it lies on a semiotic one….[Artists] materialize a way of experiencing, bring a particular cast of mind out into the world of objects, where men can look at it." [27]

Notwithstanding these interpretive differences, each theory recognizes that the emphasis on collective relationships often carries over to conceptions of time. When, for example, a Bamileke chief took office, he had his statue carved: "after his death, the statue was respected, but it was slowly eroded by the weather as his memory was eroded in the minds of the people" (Maquet 1979: 14). The intention of natural devolution would be violated were an outsider, then, to lay claim to the object. Clearly, native peoples are not the only ones for whom Western concepts may not fit. An analyst of Islamic cultures notes that it is often less the artist than the reception of his work that is important: "The author, or the artist, may still be recognized, but once the artistic product has been given to the ummah [the community of believers] as a whole, then that product is considered as the product of the Islamic milieu or worldview. This should not be regarded as the negation of the author; rather, the authorship is given to the ummah as a whole, and the center is not the author or artist, but in the Absolute upon which the piece is built" (Nasim 1998: 81). In each instance, the narrative of the intellectual product is not only wrapped up in the concept of the collective, but the extended metaphor, say, of natural decomposition is completely at odds with those of most Western stories that are aimed at the perpetuation of any artistic endeavor.

Indeed, to many indigenous peoples, culturally significant objects may be regarded as possessing life. For example, some Great Lakes Indian groups refer to their creations as living things, hence one approaches these objects—e.g., medicine bags, war clubs, drums, pipes—in relational terms. The Ojibwa greeting to such objects, for example, means "hello, all our relations." Similarly, in *United States v. Corrow* a Navajo anthropologist testified that the medicine bundles were living entities, as were the masks living gods. When seen as living things, objects may be regarded as travelling, and because they may not come back soon or ever, it may be acceptable to visit them even at a dominant population's museum. The museum at the University of British Columbia, for example, sets aside a room where native peoples can bring offerings of food to share with the ancestral spirits embodied in the objects housed there.

The relational implications of cultural objects can be very complex. Students of the culture of the Trobriand Islands have suggested that the transfer of such objects as axe blades may actually open up the possibility that expectable exchange may not prove to be reciprocal, and thus the seeming inalienability of an object may actually be outstripped by a discourse of possible relationships that go beyond the usual kin boundaries. What might be regarded as a threat to the stability of social ties may, then, operate as a test of existing relationships, an opening for new relationships, or a vehicle for keeping alive the adaptive capacity to form new ties wherever they may prove most efficacious. Under this view, boundaries are constantly being challenged, and an inappropriate regime of legal control—even one that emphasizes relationships over property-like alienation—risks freezing social flexibility in the name of cultural integrity or conservation. As Kimberlee Weatherall (2001: 227) notes: "The divisive potential of cultural integrity is a danger to be taken into account. The wise law-maker in this politically charged arena walks a tightrope between proper protection for minority interests, and accusations of apartheid and paternalism." Robert Lowie, among many anthropologists, long ago argued that borrowing was common among tribal groups and that the image of tribes as hermetically sealed entities is radically mistaken.[28]

While many legal protections may apply across native and non-native boundaries given their common situations, in many other instances the problems faced by native peoples may pose special problems. In addition to sacred symbols there are various cultural productions that hold special significance for the social and intellectual life of native groups, including music, dance, and folklore. When hip-hop duo OutKast used a Navajo sacred song, it caused outrage among the Indians, but unlike New Zealand, where there is protection for such songs, there is none in the U.S. short of obtaining a formal copyright. To take a case in point, in 2001 several Maori tribal groups threatened legal action against toymaker Lego for allegedly trademarking Maori words that the company was using in its Bionicle products. In response, a Lego spokesperson stated that only the term "Bionicle" had been trademarked, but after meeting with tribal representatives, the company did agree to change some, but not all, of the words involved.[29]

The use of native genetic material presents a particularly controversial situation.[30] The rule in U.S. law is that if a significant addition is made to a substance in the course of its extraction, a patent may be sought. The question then is what constitutes such an addition. If genetic material is taken from an Indian group and combined with extraneous material, is the result so changed as to be patentable? Native people fear that claims of tribal identity and membership may turn on the findings of such research. In one case, the Havasupai settled out of court with Arizona State University, whose researchers conducted studies of diabetes with tribal consent, but then used the findings for a study of schizophrenia that was not authorized by the tribe.[31]

Similar questions arise for the plants found in native territories, including those from which such medicines as aspirin, digitalis, and scopolamine have been derived (Yano 1993). Summarizing the findings of others, Hunter and Jones (2006–7: 4–5) note:

> A commonly accepted estimate in the literature indicates that a full 77% of all plant related pharmaceutical products, or roughly 25% of the entire pharmaceutical market contains significant elements of direct contribution from the appropriation of indigenous knowledge....Combining the indigenous contribution to pharmaceutical medicine with its traditional use world wide indicates that indigenous knowledge may be responsible for over 60% of medical treatment in developed nations and 85% in developing nations.

The result has been a number of disputes between native peoples and pharmaceutical companies, university researchers, and governmental agencies. The White Earth Ojibwa, for example, were involved in a long-running dispute with the University of Minnesota concerning the wild rice distinctive to their territory (Anders 2004). Various international conventions on 'genetic prospecting' do exist, but none is pointedly helpful for indigenous peoples.

Even recent expressions of ancient rituals may become the subject of legal suits. In the *Diaz* case, as noted in an earlier chapter, a trader in native artifacts took figurines used in a recent ritual from a cave on Indian land and put them up for sale. He was subsequently charged with violating the federal Antiquities

Act. He defended by saying that the objects were of recent vintage and thus did not qualify as antiquities. However, the court accepted the argument of an anthropologist that the object of antiquity to be protected was the ancient ritual of which the contemporary figures were but the most recent expression. In doing so, however, the court declared the statute itself void for vagueness inasmuch as one might not be able to tell in advance when one could be subjected to a criminal penalty if even a recent object could be a surrogate for an ancient ritual.[32]

Oral history also presents a special case for many native peoples. If we analogize it to written history we will get very different results and rules of admissibility than if it is equated to hearsay testimony. Courts have responded quite differently to accepting such testimony, and certain statutes governing the recognition of Indian groups (and hence their eligibility for programs and forms of sovereignty reserved to recognized groups) may turn on such evidence. In their land claims against other groups, for example, the Makushi Indians of Guyana have tried to show that their knowledge of plants and animals—as embodied in their folklore and traditions—demonstrates that they must have had at least partial dominion over certain lands where these organisms are found. However, when the tribe turned to photos in museum collections to show how they lived in peace with other tribes, the photos actually showed their use of war clubs, a fact that undercut their argument.[33]

As technologies change, so do the possibilities for building metaphorical extensions. In the field of software production, for example, the concept of an 'open source' license does not, in fact, mean the unconditional use by anyone of material developed by another. It requires that modifiers allow access to any changes they introduce. Moreover, suppliers usually find it more lucrative to charge for software service and support than for the actual software, so the financial incentives are not simply eliminated. One could imagine native productions being seen in the same fashion. Similarly, an analogy could be built from the area of trade secrets, thus treating native designs as proprietary by piggy-backing on the concept that prevails in much of non-native commercial law.[34]

When addressing indigenous rights, some foundational concepts may have to be recast. The basic question may simply be: What are we trying to protect? Is it "to preserve meaning and due honor for elements of cultural knowledge and to insure that these traditional universes, and their peoples, maintain their vitality… [or] to manage the degree and process by which parts of that cultural knowledge are shared with outsiders, and in some instances, to be justly compensated for it" (Kuruk 1999: 823)? The *Bulun* Equity Principle, that requires notification of the group affected, might keep firms from buying native designs, thus having a negative impact on the indigenous people economically, and may limit the communal interest to situations where there are clear tribal laws, where the products are of great social importance, or where the community is uniquely vulnerable in relation to its artists. But applying the *Bulun* principle may be inapplicable, say, to Navajo sand painting, given the U.S. courts' reluctance to allow tribes to reach out beyond willing tribal members, particularly if there are First Amendment problems of restricting artists' expressions (Matlon 2003–4). Indeed, who speaks for the entire group is not always straightforward, or whether group interests should trump those of an individual member.

Put differently, what exactly is the harm of 'cultural appropriation'? If the purpose is to allow groups to make collective decisions, then analogies based on group interests may be favored over analogies that stress intense individualism. Again, the cultural emphases are important to underscore. We may ask, for example: Are the names of indigenous artists really unknown, or purposely erased? Were their identities irrelevant in their time, or intentionally occluded to emphasize, like oral tradition, that the production bespeaks the values of an entire community?

Indeed, should we get rid of copyright and patents altogether? Goulven suggests a form of "equitable copyright" in which a group right would be cognizable, at least to hold matters steady while a longer term solution to respective interests is addressed.[35] Alternatively, should native groups have a right of first refusal for the purchase of an object that comes up for sale, or should certain sales be open only to those who, following purchase, agree to return the object to the native peoples?[36] Would it make greater sense to institute compulsory conciliation, arbitration, or mediation panels, rather than leaving these matters to courts of law? Or might one 'encourage' the use of such panels, in much the same way the Indian Gaming Act initially did—by mandating that if the other side refuses to engage in negotiation, the last offer placed on the table will have the force of law, a tactic that rapidly insured that states who were resisting engagement would negotiate compacts with tribes seeking to initiate gambling casinos?

In this regard, it may be necessary to jettison the numerous laws and declarations that lack sufficient specificity, protection, or enforcement. Some of the faults of these agreements are visible, for example, in The Indian Arts and Crafts Act,[37] which protects against claims of actual derivation from a given tribe. But Indian-inspired items (e.g., rugs), items made by one tribe mimicking the productions of another tribe (e.g., the Navajo fabrication of Hopi kachinas from a different kind of wood), and the difficulties of enforcement, have led some commenters to seriously criticize the law.[38] Sometimes a mix of litigation and negotiation has worked;[39] at other times, litigation having failed, using the embarrassment of bad publicity has resulted in effective settlements.[40] But in far too many instances the legislation presently in place, perhaps having been constructed on metaphors that perpetuate differences of power, has left much to be desired by way of clarity and equity in the field of indigenous intellectual rights.

In the law, the choice of metaphors and analogies can make all the difference. In the history of federal Indian law, for example, the early usage by the U.S. Supreme Court of terms like "domestic dependent nation," the relation of the U.S. to the tribes as being like that of "a guardian to a ward," and references to reservations as "schools" only exacerbated questions of sovereignty, trust relations, and the durability of treaty obligations. Indeed, the very narration of the past or characterization of the present may depend entirely on the metaphors employed in the telling. By our choice of one metaphor over another we may foreclose certain interpretations and consequences: To see the reservation as a 'school' may leave Indians perpetually infantilized, just as seeing matters in terms of 'a level playing field' may negate appropriate compensation for past harm. Alternatively, the same metaphor may carry a duty of education or preference in contracts or scholarships. Metaphors may be exclusive or mixed. John Gumperz reminds us that we can (and do) engage in 'metaphorical switching.' If, for example, we see hybridity as positive rather than weakening—and can think in such terms for all native matters—we can entertain multiple systems as not incommensurable possibilities. The danger, of course, is that when we cease questioning the dominant metaphor we may lose awareness of alternatives and take for granted the current vision as incontrovertible.

The choice and impact of a metaphor may, of course, be deeply entwined with the broader narrative style within which it operates. A story, biography, legal decision, or even a statute may, directly or indirectly, be an extended metaphor. In the present context, the analogy of intellectual products to 'property' is a perfect example of an extended metaphor that has taken on the aura of common sense. What form of narrative now carries our sense of individual and collective well-being? Do our intellectual products seem truer when their story is told as a voyage of discovery, rather than narrated as a tiny addition to a collective event envisioned as timeless? When courts choose an extended metaphor, does the entire decision, and the challenge posed to any dissent, not turn on how the narrative employs metaphors to convey and sustain its seemingly obvious result?

Conversely, the choice of metaphor may depend on the *style* of the narrative. In many societies, a truth may be claimed by a circular rather than linear form of telling, where chronological organization is displaced by a constant circling back to a central theme or the repeated iteration of a pattern.[41] So, if native peoples tell their story in a non-linear narrative style, yet are forced by the legal style of narrative into a directional, 'progressive' metaphor, the distortion to their sense of the natural order of things may be profound. The end result can be a clash of narrative styles that carry in their train the competition for a governing metaphor upon which collective life may depend.

Moreover, metaphors carry profound moral implications. To characterize the stranger as a guest because (as the Hebrew Bible says) we too were "strangers in a strange land," is a moral statement no less than a metaphorical one. If we think of museums as 'ethical guardians' why not envision the native peoples' control in these terms? If, to some native peoples, certain objects are seen as male or female and should not, therefore, be stored together, is it not a simple matter of respect to honor such beliefs? Indeed, as Joseph Raz (2001) has argued, if we have a duty to preserve the items to which *others* attach great importance should we not fractionate the concept of ownership and regard the intellectual productions of indigenous peoples as objects of mutual concern and control?

Surveying the alternative metaphors for native intellectual production and their implications for the stories that the law narrates through them, several conclusions can, therefore, be suggested: that a single governing metaphor (like intellectual *property*) neither suits all situations nor fairly addresses the differentials of power that render control over native resources contentious; that thinking in relational rather than possessory terms is far more common in other cultures, yet can still be comprehensible to non-native populations, thus forming a possible ground for shared approaches to particular classes of production; that the narrative style may drive the metaphor, rather than the other way around; and that given the relatively powerless position of many native groups, a version of affirmative action—perhaps in the form of various legal presumptions and rights of first refusal, perhaps under a principle of 'equitable copyright'—might (one can never resist a metaphor) level the playing field.

The crucial feature to recognize about native systems of cultural production is that, whatever their differences from dominant Western regimes, they are highly diverse, and no single metaphor may, therefore, fully capture their entire range. Just as some cultures may categorize foods by their taste and others by the way they feel in one's mouth, the intangible regimes of indigenous peoples run the gamut from control over the story being central to the Kiowa, to the song of an Aborigine being so central to his personal identity that it cannot be interfered with by any other. Even in the West, so categorizing a legal scholar as Sir William Blackstone (1979 [1765–1769]: Book II, Ch. II, 19) stumbled when trying to determine whether water is like land or, being "a moveable, wandering thing must of necessity continue common by the law of nature."

A uniform law of intellectual production is unlikely to suit all situations or to resolve all ambiguities, and a single governing metaphor can be as alluring as it can be dangerous. But as Richard Herz (1993: 713) argues: "Indeterminacy at the margin is an intrinsic characteristic of any balancing test in which competing values are weighed." It is ironic that the very imprecision of metaphors may also account for their strength in capturing the terms by which we can live with one another. As one commenter put it:

> The motive for metaphor… is thus not the *evasion* of the law's hard realities, but rather the *revelation* of two of the most basic of those realities: the inability of the law's language to encompass the world it would regulate; and the inescapable link between language and feeling in establishing the hold over opinion that distinguishes law from brute physical coercion.
>
> *(Grey 1991: 65, original italics)*

As competition for its defining metaphors continues to play a critical role in any culture, failure to attend to their implications can leave us with an inappropriately reified and truncated view of both law and culture. Metaphors invigorate, but they can also ensnare. As Justice Benjamin Cardozo said, "Metaphors are to be narrowly watched, for starting as devices to liberate thought they end often by enslaving it."[42] Particularly in the legal narratives of relatively powerless native peoples, we need to be sure to capture the situation in the metaphors, rather than allowing the metaphors to hold captive the situation.

Notes

1 On monetary metaphors, see Pasanek and Polillo (2013); on those relating to mind, see Pasanek (2015); on those in science, see Hallam (2000). See generally, Geary (2011) and Gibbs (2008).

2 Cammett (2014). In her endorsement of Donald Trump for president in January 2016, Gov. Sarah Palin used the same metaphor: "Tell me, is this conservative? GOP majorities handing over a blank check to fund Obamacare and Planned Parenthood and illegal immigration that competes for your jobs, and turning safety nets into hammocks…" http://www.buzzfeed.com/kyleblaine/so-uh-heres-the-full-text-of-sarah-palins-bizarre-trump-spee?utm_term=.fqwb5PV2q#.tfE1QO8Zv (accessed January 5, 2017).

3 Thibodeau (2009) ("When crime was compared to a virus, participants were more likely to suggest reforming the social environment of the infected community. When crime was compared to a predator, participants were more likely to suggest attacking the problem head on—hiring more police officers and building jails.")

4 See, Blasi (2004).

5 *Compare* Martin (1987), *with* Profet (1993).

6 On property metaphors, see Halper (1996).

7 See, Metzger (1996); Borelli and Lenzerini (2012); and a Canadian decision ordering the return from buyers of sacred objects belonging to the Catholic Church, as analyzed in Pelletier (1993). For the statute relating to the repatriation of Native American burials and artifacts see, Native American Graves Protection Act 2000.

8 See, e.g., Australia's Resale Royalty Right for Visual Artists Act 2009 ("Under the Scheme, artists receive five per cent of the sale price when eligible artworks are resold commercially for $1000 or more. Between 10 June 2010 and 15 May 2013, there have been 6801 eligible resales that have generated over $1.5 million in royalties for 610 artists."). http://arts.gov.au/visual-arts/resale-royalty-scheme (accessed January 5, 2017). This act is presently under review. On the experience of the British under a resale royalties law, see Grant (2014).

9 See also the initial and appellate decisions in Sam Francis Foundation v. Christie's. (Royalties Act violates the Commerce Clause when it attempts to gain royalties from transactions outside California between non-California parties.)

10 For an argument that the claim is not totally open-ended when Indians bring suit, for example, to gain access to sacred sites, see the dissenting opinion of Judge William A. Fletcher in *Navajo Nation v. United States Forest Service* (2009: 1098). See also Executive Order No. 13007 of May 24, 1996, which seeks, although with no real enforcement power, to accommodate access of Native Americans to off-reservation sacred sites.

11 See, generally, Loughlin (2006). See also, Scafidi (2005).

12 See, Loughlin (2006: 223–4).

13 See, Mays (1996: 264), Reich (1987), and Prasad (2015).

14 For a proposal that some legal protection should be afforded the generator of an idea who has not actually implemented it, see Bar-Gill and Parchomovsky (2005).

15 *Bulun Bulun v. R & T Textiles Pty Ltd.* For other cases of traditional design and commentary, see Weatherall (2001).

16 Two such instances resulted in agreements, following considerable legal and administrative wrangling. See, Cohen (2013). On the dispute over Crazy Horse beer, see Schilling (2012) and Newton (1997).

17 For the argument favoring tribal control in an environment of frequent theft of their intellectual productions, see Riley (2005).

18 Rose (1993: 39). See also, Strathern (2005: 58–61).

19 For other examples on control of one's name or image, see Madoff (2011).

20 For a survey of countries using this concept, see the listing in the article on "Personality Rights" in *Wikipedia*.

21 *Chilkat Indian Village v. Johnson*. The case was remanded to the tribal court where it was heard as *Chilkat Indian Village, IRA v. Johnson*.

22 So, for example, in the suit brought by the successors to Crazy Horse, their attempt to bar the use of his name on a brand of beer failed in the federal court. Schilling (2012) and Newton (1997).

23 See, Carpenter (2009), the discussion of their essay in Brown (2010), and the authors' response at Carpenter (2010). Kenney (2010–11: 546) also suggests that the parties may be analogized to co-authors of a copyrighted work, that the research aspect of such objects places them beyond the ordinary range of property analogies, and that such an image carries with it implications for cooperation and consultation not necessitated by ordinary property law.

24 A number of declarations have been issued by native peoples concerning their intellectual property. See the listings under the heading of "Indigenous Intellectual Property" at *Wikipedia*. On the collective interests of native peoples, see generally van Meijl (2009), and Forsyth (2012).

25 See, e.g., Center for International Environmental Law 2007. For similarly toothless conventions, see Hunter and Jones (2006–7) and Yano (1993). After reviewing Australia's laws, an attorney concluded: "Australia['s] need to enact much more than a voluntary Code of Conduct in respect of traditional culture is long overdue. The Courts can only do so much to extend the notions of statutory regimes to offer protection which is insufficient and which depends on the facts of a particular case. Australia needs to enact laws which acknowledge, respect and afford legal protection to traditional knowledge" (FAL Lawyers - Jenni Lightowlers 2013).

26 Daes (1997: s. 26). See also, Battaglia (1994). A more relational approach is not inconsistent with much of earlier Western approaches to copyright: See Alexander (1997) and Stern (2012a,b).

27 Andrew Gell (1998) argues that things provoke attachments—that far from being passive, art is a form of instrumental action influencing the actions of others. Marilyn Strathern (1988) suggests that relations are substantially between persons and things, with the latter being substituted for the former in a number of instances. Clifford Geertz (1983: 99), taking a more cultural tack, argues against the structural-functional approach, "that is, that works of art are elaborate mechanisms for defining social relationships, sustaining social rules, and strengthening social values….The central connection between art and collective life does not lie on such an instrumental plane, it lies on a semiotic one….[Artists] materialize a way of experiencing, bring a particular cast of mind out into the world of objects, where men can look at it."

28 "The divisive potential of cultural integrity is a danger to be taken into account. The wise law-maker in this politically charged arena walks a tightrope between proper protection for minority interests, and accusations of apartheid and paternalism" (Weatherall 2001: 227). Robert Lowie, among many anthropologists, long ago argued that borrowing was common among tribal groups and that the image of tribes as hermetically sealed entities is radically mistaken.

29 For an example relating to music, see Beeko (2011); For the Maori, see Williams (2013).

30 For an example of legislative and popular referendum action on bioprospecting in Costa Rica, see Pearson (2013). On the Australian experience, see Hunter and Jones (2006–7). See generally the essays in Brush and Stabinsky (1996).

31 Interview with Pilar N. Ossorio, a University of Wisconsin law professor who has served as an expert for the tribe, April 2005. See, Harmon (2010).

32 However, *United States v. Smyer*, interpreting The Antiquities Act of 1906, 16 U.S.C.A. §§ 431–433, found no vagueness in the statute as applied to objects that were 800–900 years old.

33 On the acceptance of oral history in Canadian First Nations cases, see Ray (2011).

34 For an example of this approach applied to an Alaskan case see, Schüssel (2012).
35 Cited in Weatherall (2001: 222).
36 For example, the Annenberg Foundation paid $530,000 at a Paris auction for twenty-four items they then returned to the Hopi (Cornu 2013; Nikic 2015; Sage 2013). Unlike the Hopi, the Navajo have been willing to purchase objects originally from their people at auction. Associated Press 2014. In other instances, collectors have refused to return objects to the native peoples, preferring a buyer at auction who they believe will better care for the items. See, e.g., Loke (1998). It is also important to remember that: "The market for illicit antiquities—of which indigenous cultural objects are a significant subset—is the third most profitable black market in the world behind drugs and arms" (Kenney 2011: 517).
37 Pub. L. No. 101–644, 104 Stat. 4664 (1990) was passed by unanimous voice vote in both houses of Congress on October 27, 1990.
38 See, e.g., Hapiuk (2001).
39 For the example of the return of the sacred Zuni war gods, see Suro (1990), and Ferguson (2000). For comparative examples from Africa and Latin America, see Nwauche (2015).
40 The Zia pueblo worked out an arrangement with Southwest Airlines that allowed the company to use one of the tribe's symbols: http://web.williams.edu/AnthSoc/native/newmexicoone.htm (accessed January 5, 2017). In other instances, however, the Zia have had to litigate the use of their sun sign: see Patton (2000) and Turner (2012).
41 Our sacred texts also use this style. See, e.g., Douglas (2001) and (2010).
42 *Berkey v. 3d Ave. Ry. Co.* (1926: 94). Criminal law and immigration law are two other domains in which the choice of metaphors can have a dramatic, potentially devastating, impact: see, e.g., Higinbotham (2014) and Cunningham-Parmeter (2011).

References

Alexander, Gregory S. 1997. *Commodity and Propriety: Competing Visions of Property in American Legal Thought, 1776–1970*, Chicago, IL: University of Chicago Press.

Anders, Jake et al. 2004, "Genetic Research on Wild Rice and Its Cultural Implications," May 6. www.d.umn.edu/~ande2927/Report.pdf (accessed January 5, 2017).

Associated Press, "Navajos Reclaim Sacred Mask at Auction" 2014, December 16. www.cbsnews.com/news/navajo-indians-buy-back-sacred-masks-in-france-auction/ (accessed January 5, 2017).

Bar-Gill, Oren and Gideon Parchomovsky 2005, "A Marketplace for Ideas?" *Texas Law Review*, vol. 84, pp. 395–431.

Battaglia, Debbora 1994, "Retaining Reality: Some Practical Problems with Objects as Property," *Man*, New Series, vol. 29, no. 3, pp. 631–44.

Beeko, E. Kwadwo Odame 2011, "The Dual-Relationship Concept of Right-Ownership in Akan Musical Tradition," *International Journal of Cultural Property*, vol. 18, no. 3, pp. 337–64.

Blackstone, William 1979 [1765–1769], *Commentaries on the Laws of England*, Chicago, IL: University of Chicago Press.

Blasi, Vincent 2004, "Holmes and the Marketplace of Ideas," *The Supreme Court Review, vol. 2004*, Chicago, IL: University of Chicago Press, pp. 1–46.

Borelli, Silvia and Federico Lenzerini, eds. 2012, *Cultural Diversity: New Developments in International Law*, The Hague: Martinus Nijhoff.

Brown, Michael F. 2010, "Culture, Property and Peoplehood," *International Journal of Cultural Property*, vol. 17, no. 3, pp. 569–79.

Brush, Stephen B. and Doreen Stabinsky, eds. 1996, *Valuing Local Knowledge: Indigenous People and Intellectual Property Rights*, Washington, DC: Island Press.

California Resale Royalties Act (CRRA) 1976, Cal. Civ. Code §986.

Cammett, Ann 2014, "Deadbeat Dads & Welfare Queens: How Metaphor Shapes Poverty Law," *Boston College Journal of Law and Social Justice*, vol. 34, pp. 233–65.

Carpenter, Kristen A., Sonia Katyal, and Angela Riley 2009, "In Defense of Property," *Yale Law Journal*, vol. 118, pp. 1022–5.

———— 2010, "Clarifying Cultural Property," *International Journal of Cultural Property*, vol. 17, no. 3, pp. 581–98.

Center for International Environmental Law 2007, "The Gap between Indigenous Peoples' Demands and WIPO's Framework on Traditional Knowledge," September. www.wipo.int/export/sites/www/tk/en/igc/ngo/ciel_gap.pdf (accessed January 5, 2017).

Cohen, Jodi S. 2013, "Chief Illiniwek Backer, University Reach Agreement on Mascot," *Chicago Tribune*, October 23.

Cornu, Marie 2013, "About Sacred Cultural Property: The Hopi Masks Case," *International Journal of Cultural Property*, vol. 20, no. 4, pp. 451–66.

Craig, Russell, Rawiri Taonui, and Susan Wild 2012, "The Concept of *Taonga* in Māori Culture: Insights for Accounting," *Accounting, Auditing and Accountability Journal*, vol. 25, no. 6, pp. 1025–47.

Cunningham-Parmeter, Keith 2011, "Alien Language: Immigration Metaphors and the Jurisprudence of Otherness," *Fordham Law Review*, vol. 79, pp. 1545–98.

Daes, Erica-Irene 1997, *Protection of the Heritage of Indigenous Peoples*, New York: United Nations.

Douglas, Mary 2001, *In the Wilderness: The Doctrine of Defilement in the Book of Numbers*, Oxford: Oxford University Press.

———— 2010, *Thinking in Circles: An Essay on Ring Composition*, New Haven: Yale University Press.

FAL Lawyers - Jenni Lightowlers 2013, "Australian Law Relating to Communal Indigenous Intellectual Property," *Lexology*, February 12. www.lexology.com/library/detail.aspx?g=073fdf42-e293-4566-bd7e-f93604e66ae1 (accessed January 5, 2017).

Ferguson, T. J., Roger Anyon, and Edmund J. Ladd 2000, "Repatriation at the Pueblo of Zuni: Diverse Solutions to Complex Problems," in Devon A. Mihesuah, ed., *Repatriation Reader*, Lincoln: University of Nebraska Press, pp. 239–65.

Forsyth, Miranda 2012, "Lifting the Lid on 'The Community': Who Has the Right to Control Access to Traditional Knowledge and Expressions of Culture?" *International Journal of Cultural Property*, vol. 19, no. 1, pp. 1–31.

Geary, James 2011, *I Is an Other: The Secret Life of Metaphor and How It Shapes the Way We See the World*, New York: Harper.

Geertz, Clifford 1983, *Local Knowledge*, New York: Basic Books.

Gell, Andrew 1998, *Art and Agency*, Oxford: Oxford University Press.

Gibbs, Raymond W. Jr. 2008, *The Cambridge Handbook of Metaphor and Thought*, Cambridge: Cambridge University Press.

Grant, Daniel 2014, "Artist Resale Royalties Haven't Hindered Art Trade or Helped Artists in the U.K.," *Huffington Post*, June 6.

Greene, Candace S. and Thomas D. Dresher 1994, "The Tipi with Battle Pictures: The Kiowa Tradition of Intangible Property Rights," *Trademark Reporter*, vol. 84, pp. 418–33.

Grey, Thomas C. 1991, *The Wallace Stevens Case: Law and the Practice of Poetry*, Cambridge, MA: Harvard University Press.

Hallam, Fernand 2000, *Metaphor and Analogy in the Sciences*, Dordrecht: Kluwer Academic Publishers.

Halper, Louise A. 1996, "Tropes of Anxiety and Desire: Metaphor and Metonymy in the Law of Takings," *Yale Journal of Law and the Humanities*, vol. 8, pp. 31–62.

Hapiuk, William J., Jr. 2001, "Of Kitsch and Kachinas: A Critical Analysis of the *Indian Arts and Crafts Act of 1990*," *Stanford Law Review*, vol. 53, pp. 1009–75.

Harmon, Amy 2010, "Indian Tribe Wins Fight to Limit Research of Its DNA," *New York Times*, April 21.

Harrison, Simon 2000, "From Prestige Goods to Legacies: Property and Objectification of Culture in Melanesia," *Comparative Studies in Society and History*, vol. 42, no. 3, pp. 662–79.

Herz, Richard 1993, "Legal Protection for Indigenous Cultures: Sacred Sites and Communal Rights," vol. 79, *Virginia Law Review*, pp. 691–716.

Higinbotham, Sarah 2014, "Bloodletting and Beasts: Metaphors of Legal Violence," *Wake Forest Law Review*, vol. 49, pp. 727–42.

Hunter, John and Chris Jones 2006–7, "Bioprospecting and Indigenous Knowledge in Australia: Implications of Valuing Indigenous Spiritual Knowledge," Bahá'í Library Online. http://bahai-library.com/hunter_jones_bioprospecting_australia (accessed January 5, 2017).

Kalven, Harry 1967, "Broadcasting, Public Policy and the First Amendment," *Journal of Law and Economics*, vol. 10, pp. 15–49.

Kuruk, Paul 1999, "Protecting Folklore under Modern Intellectual Property Regimes: A Reappraisal of the Tension between Individual and Communal Rights in Africa and United States," *American University Law Review*, vol. 48, pp. 769–849.

Loke, Margaret 1998, "Sacred and Secular Clash at Auction," *New York Times*, December 3.

Loughlin, Patricia 2006, "Pirates, Parasites, Reapers, Sowers, Fruits, Foxes…The Metaphors of Intellectual Property," *Sydney Law Review*, vol. 28, pp. 211–26.

Madoff, Ray D. 2011, "The New Grave Robbers," *New York Times*, March 27.

Maquet, Jacques 1979, *Introduction to Aesthetic Anthropology*, 2nd edition, Malibu, CA: Undena Publications.

Martin, Emily 1987, *The Woman in the Body: A Cultural Analysis of Reproduction*, New York: Beacon.

Matlon, Amina Para 2003–2004, "Safeguarding Native American Sacred Art by Partnering Tribal Law and Equity: An Exploratory Case Study Applying the *Bulun Bulun* Equity to Navajo Sandpainting," *Columbia Journal of Law and Arts*, vol. 27, pp. 211–47.

Mays, Thomas D., et al. 1996, "*Quid Pro Quo*: Alternatives for Equity and Conservation," in Stephen B. Brush and Doreen Stabinsky, eds., *Valuing Local Knowledge: Indigenous People and Intellectual Property Rights*, Washington, DC: Island Press, pp. 259–80.

Metzger, Oliver 1996, "Making the Doctrine of *Res Extra Commercium* Visible in United States Law," *Texas Law Review*, vol. 74, pp. 615–53.

Nasim, Omar W. 1998, "Toward an Islamic Aesthetic Theory," *The American Journal of Islamic Social Studies*, vol. 15, no. 1, pp. 71–90.

Native American Graves Protection Act (NAGPRA) 2000, 25 U.S.C. §§ 3001–3013.

Newton, Nell Jessup 1997, "Memory and Misrepresentation: Representing Crazy Horse in Tribal Court," in Bruce Ziff and Pratima V. Rao, eds., *Borrowed Power: Essays on Cultural Appropriation*, New Brunswick: Rutgers University Press, pp. 195–224.

Nikic, Samantha K. 2015, "Liberté, égalité, fraternité: The United Nations Declaration of the Rights of Indigenous Peoples Fails to Protect Hopi Katsinam from the Auction Block in France," *Brooklyn Journal of International Law*, vol. 41, pp. 407–38.

Nwauche, Enninyo S. 2015, "The Emerging Right to Communal Intellectual Property," 19 *Marquette Intellectual Property Law Review*, vol. 19, pp. 221–44.

Pasanek, Brad 2015, *Metaphors of Mind: An Eighteenth Century Dictionary*, Baltimore, MD: Johns Hopkins Press.

Pasanek, Brad and Simone Polillo, eds. 2013, *Beyond Liquidity: The Metaphor on Money in Financial Crisis*, London: Routledge.

Patton, Phil 2000, "Trademark Battle over Pueblo Sign," *New York Times*, January 13.

Pearson, Thomas W. 2013, "'Life is Not for Sale': Confronting Free Trade and Intellectual Property in Costa Rica," *American Anthropologist*, vol. 115, no. 1, pp. 58–71.

Pelletier, Benoît 1993, "The Case of the Treasures of L'Ange Gardien: An Overview," *International Journal of Cultural Property*, vol. 2, no. 2, pp. 371–82.

Prasad, Vinay 2015, "The Folly of Big Science Awards," *New York Times*, October 2.

Profet, Margie 1993, "Menstruation as a Defense Against Pathogens Transported by Sperm," *The Quarterly Review of Biology*, vol. 68, no. 3, pp. 335–86.

Ray, Arthur J. 2011, *Telling It to the Judge: Taking Native History to Court*, Montreal: McGill-Queen's University Press.

Raz, Joseph 2001, *Value, Respect and Attachment*, Cambridge: Cambridge University Press.

Reich, Robert B. 1987, "Entrepreneurship Reconsidered: The Team as Hero," *Harvard Business Review*, vol. 65, no. 3 (May/June), pp. 77–83.

Riley, Angela 2005, "Straight Stealing: Towards an Indigenous System of Cultural Protection," *Washington Law Review*, vol. 80, pp. 69–164.

Rose, Mark 1993, *Authors and Owners: The Invention of Copyright*, Cambridge, MA: Harvard University Press.

Sage, Alexandria 2013, "U.S. Foundation Buys Hopi Masks at Auction to Return to Tribe," Reuters, December 11. www.reuters.com/article/2013/12/11/us-france-auction-idUSBRE9B80QJ20131211 (accessed January 5, 2017).

Sahlins, Marshall D. 1968, *Tribesmen*, Englewood Cliffs, NJ: Prentice-Hall.

Scafidi, Susan 2005, *Who Owns Culture? Appropriation and Authenticity in American Law*, New Brunswick: Rutgers University Press.

Schilling, Vincent 2012, "Oglala Sioux Tribe's Alcohol Lawsuit Dismissed without Prejudice," *Indian Country*, October 3.

Schüssel, Stuart 2012, "Copyright Protection's Challenges and Alaska Natives' Cultural Property," *Alaska Law Review*, vol. 92, pp. 313–40.

Stern, Simon 2012a, "From Author's Right to Property Right," *University of Toronto Law Review*, vol. 62, pp. 30–91.

———— 2012b, "'Room for One More': The Metaphorics of Physical Space in the Eighteenth-Century Copyright Debate," *Law and Literature*, vol. 24, no. 2: 113–50.

Strathern, Marilyn 1988, *The Gender of the Gift: Problems with Women and Problems with Society in Melanesia*, Berkeley: University of California Press.

———— 2005, *Kinship, Law and the Unexpected*, Cambridge: Cambridge University Press.

Suro, Roberto 1990, "Zunis' Efforts to Regain Idols May Alter Views of Indian Art," *New York Times*, August 13, p. A13.

Thibodeau, Paul, James L. McClelland, and Lera Boroditsky 2009, "When a Metaphor May Not be a Victimless Crime: The Role of Metaphor in Social Policy." http://stanford.edu/~jlmcc/papers/ThibodeauMcCBoroditsky09CogSciProc.pdf (accessed January 5, 2017).

Turner, Stephanie B. 2012, "The Case of the Zia: Looking Beyond Trademark Law to Protect Sacred Symbols," *Chicago-Kent Journal of Intellectual Property*, vol. 11, no. 2, pp. 116–45.

Van Meijl, Toon 2009, "Special Issue: Pacific Discourses about Cultural Heritage and Its Protection," *International Journal of Cultural Property*, vol. 16, no. 3, pp. 221–370.

Visual Artists Rights Act (VARA) of 1990, 17 U. S. Code §106A.

Weatherall, Kimberlee 2001, "Culture, Autonomy and *Djulibinyamurr*: Individual and Community in the Construction of Rights to Traditional Designs," *The Modern Law Review*, vol. 64, pp. 215–42.

Williams, David V. 2013, "*Ko Aotearoa Tenei*: Law and Policy Affecting Maori Culture and Identity," *International Journal of Cultural Property*, vol. 20, no. 3, pp. 311–31.

Yano, Lester I. 1993, "Protection of the Ethnobiological Knowledge of Indigenous Peoples," *UCLA Law Review*, vol. 41, pp. 443–86.

Cases cited

Berkey v. 3d Ave. Ry. Co., 244 N.Y. 84 (1926).

Bulun Bulun v. R & T Textiles Pty Ltd., (Federal Court of Australia 1998), 157 A. L. R. 193.

Chilkat Indian Village v. Johnson, 870 F.2d 1469 (9th Cir. 1989).

Chilkat Indian Village, IRA v. Johnson, *Indian Law Reporter*, vol. 20, p. 6127 (Chilkat Tribal Court 1993).

Navajo Nation v. United States Forest Service, 535 F.3d 1058 (9th Cir. 2009).

Sam Francis Foundation v. Christie's, 860 F.Supp.2d 1117 (C.D. Cal. 2012), 784 F.3d 1320 (May 5, 2015), *cert denied* 136 S. Ct. 795 (January 11, 2016).

United States v. Corrow, 119 F.2d 796 (10th Cir. 1997).

United States v. Smyer, 596 F.2d 939 (10th Cir. 1979), *cert. denied* 444 U.S. 843 (1979).

PART II
Nature and the family

4

SHOULD WE JUST ABOLISH MARRIAGE?

The uses of anthropology in law and policy

To get married in the United States, you need to get a marriage license. But why not just take marriage private—get the state out of the business altogether?[1] After all, the state has not always been involved in authorizing marriage: that was largely the business of the church. And certainly removing marriage from state control would be consistent with the political position of libertarians and those conservatives who insist that the government is already too much involved in our personal lives. Covenants, contracts, and religious law could fill in for the state quite nicely.[2] Indeed, given the high rate at which couples are living together without benefit of marriage, and the fact that courts could deal with property and child custody issues quite apart from reading into a marriage certificate all sorts of implications, eliminating the state might not be so great a stretch as it might seem.

Were the legislatures to address the question, they would, of course, have to consider, among many other issues, the implications for the tax code, parental decision-making, and zoning regulations. Courts faced with the elimination of the state would have to address what may or may not be covered by contract, and what to read into a relationship for legal purposes. And this is where expert study of family life and broad cultural assumptions would undoubtedly come into play.

The present chapter considers how the law has made use of social science findings—here, mainly anthropological—as it constructs images of what families 'must' be like. If the results seem to undermine universals, or to give support to rampant relativism, does that mean that personal choice must necessarily displace state regularization? Even if one accepts that anthropological findings suggest few, if any, specific universals of family, kinship, marriage, and parental authority, is it not possible to claim that the members of a society are entitled to do what appears both authentic and right to them? Or does this mean that universal human rights are but a projection of Western values—which was the reason given by the American Anthropological Association for condemning the United Nations' Universal Declaration of Human Rights in the aftermath of the Second World War? To each of these questions, no definitive answer can be given. But in the process of considering how the law may rely on cultural studies, it may be possible to sharpen our understanding of the choices to be made and the implications they may entail.

★ ★ ★

Every discipline has its own conceit. And every discipline has attributed to it by others its presumed utility to the latter's own designs. The anthropological conceit is that it is the universal donor of academe: There is an anthropology of everything. And, perhaps as a sign of its success in promoting this conceit, other disciplines seem to think that there is almost always an anthropological perspective that can assist in the furtherance of their own claims. The resulting merger of conceits naturally has its benefits and its liabilities. Anthropologists get invited to everything, but like the too-traveled cousin or resident divine, often receive a respectful, if uncomprehending, nod at their end of the table from hosts who take the inclusion of these odd guests as proof of their own broad-mindedness. If, however, the anthropologists cannot reinforce the expectations of their host or, worse yet, undermine the universal claims or specific premises of the host, the anthropologists' contributions may be treated as proof of their marginal importance or boorish ingratitude.

Such is the case with almost all considerations of kinship. Seen as the natural domain of the anthropologist, issues of marriage, family form, and sexuality often prompt those coming from other disciplines to seek confirmation of their assumptions or all-inclusive claims through anthropology's own array of exotic instances. But if one understands that anthropology is not just a listing of curious traits and conventions, but a distinct set of approaches to seeking the linkages among a culture's diverse domains, the contribution of anthropology to discussions about kinship, sexuality, marriage, and the state may, perhaps, be placed on a more realistic and desirable footing. In this chapter I will, therefore, be trying to point out what anthropology can and cannot confirm in the perspectives taken by those who, in their roles in the judicial and policy-making organs of government, seek in anthropological material and theories support for their own working assumptions about marriage and the family. By surveying—admittedly, from my own perspective within the discipline—the limitations on our ability to corroborate certain views, we may, perhaps, see that assertions based on anthropology may not always be as supportive as some might wish them to be.[3] Properly seen, however, anthropological approaches may add in a far more theoretical than iterative pathway to discussions about the relation of marriage and family to the state.

Specifically, when issues are raised about marriage, family, and sexuality, questions often fall into several categories. Thus, to borrow the phrasings of several recent articles, one asks: Is marriage a necessary legal concept? Is kinship necessarily based on heterosexuality? Does family form matter? Do parents matter? What is 'marriage-like' like (Cossman and Ryder 2001)? The turn to anthropology prompts responses that may themselves be placed in several overlapping categories: the link, if any, between sexuality and kinship structures; the assessment of biology as a basis for such supposed universals as infant-parent bonding and the 'brute facts' of sexual dimorphism; the functions played by family forms, and the impact on these functions of alternative sexual orientations; the relation of marriage, however public or privatized, to the broader aspects of a culture; the cultural and political role of legitimization; and the problematic nature of political forms and their relation to conjugal life. Thus, as we move through the questions about marriage and its 'abolition,' we will, at each point, consider the uses being made of anthropological information and interpretations in an overall attempt to situate the claims to universality and function that often seek support from a discipline that has invested itself quite heavily in the comparative study of such matters.

Nature versus nurture

The debate over the respective importance of nature or social context has, in the course of American history, moved primarily from the domains of theology, racial discrimination, and educational policy to that of the legal status of sexuality and the family. The suitability of alternative forms of marriage and the family, the place of reproductive technology in the very idea of kinship, and the rationale for governmental involvement in the sexual lives of its citizens have become the new terrain for applying biological and anthropological information. The two predominant orientations of current debate center on questions of natural law and evolutionary biology.

To some, the issue is quite simple: like Lucretius, they believe that if you cast nature out the door, it will come flying back in through the window. Thus, the neo-natural law proponents, particularly those who draw their jurisprudential inspiration from religious sources, often argue, to use the phrasing of Mary Ann Glendon (1989: 146), that "underneath the mantle of equality [and freedom] that has been draped over the ongoing family, the state of nature flourishes." To these thinkers, common sense dictates that while marital and familial forms have obviously varied with time and place, there remain certain invariant 'facts'— that only women get pregnant, that conjugal relations occupy a unique place in the realm of human emotions, that children need recognizable and enduring parental attachments in order to develop healthy personalities, and that all of these are factors no stable system can afford to ignore. By contrast, the biologists, particularly the sociobiologists, see human nature as founded on a set of biological conditions that effectively constrain the range of possibilities human communities may create for themselves. Whether it is cast in terms of cognitive or psychological evolution, or the inseparability of biological forces from human behavior, the thrust is clearly toward seeing cultural practices as secondary to, indeed (at the analytic level said to be of greatest import) wholly dependent upon, the factors associated with the kind of biological animal that we are. Thus Edward O. Wilson (1998: 171), the dean of sociobiologists, asserts that genes "prescribe" the hereditary regularities in physical and mental development (epi-genetic rules) that "animate and channel the acquisition of culture," which, in turn "helps to determine which of the prescribing genes" survive and multiply so that these successful genes "alter" the epigenetic rules that "change the direction and effectiveness of the channels of cultural acquisition."[4] Whatever the merits of these arguments as philosophical positions, the occasional reliance on anthro-pology in each of these arguments is at least open to question.

Take first the uses of anthropology in the various natural law arguments. Working mostly from classical and Roman Catholic philosophers, contemporary proponents of a natural law approach see in the human situation a built-in dispo-sition to seek marital ties as a way of achieving the common good of two persons through their unity in both a biological (sexual) bond and the formation of new life. While such issues as same-sex marriage and adultery are, for most of these thinkers, violations of the goodness that flows from the unity of husband and wife, and while the question of non-procreative marriage is said to be finessed by claiming that such unions are not actively contrary to the possibility of unity, external support for natural law theories is difficult to come by. When 'exotic' instances are cited, it is usually for so broad a proposition as that every society has an incest taboo, or that 'families' exist everywhere—neither of which, inciden-tally, is quite true. The difficulties posed by particularly challenging examples are either dismissed as deviant (rather than statistical oddities) or, worse yet, as an invitation to rescue human nature or the human mind from the clutches of a misunderstood relativism "by placing morality beyond culture and knowledge beyond both" (Geertz 2000: 65).

Others, however, have sought 'natural' principles not in religious or philosoph-ical speculation and belief, but in those 'laws of nature' they see as manifest in hu-man sociality. In doing so they rely on ideas of the marketplace, sociobiology, or a mixture of the two. Thus Judge Richard Posner (1992: 85–110) can argue that, in a kind of free market of emotions, if the quest for companionate relationship cannot be found in heterosexual ties, it will be found elsewhere, and while the promptings of biology are not essential to the explanation of such relationships, at "later stages in the evolution of sexual morality," the marketplace—through employment opportunities outside the household, and the diminished advantages of marriage for economic well-being—adequately accounts for shifts in sexual practice and morality. Notwithstanding the disclaimers, the connection to socio-biology exists both in the inherent evolutionism of this account and in the claimed biological basis for the foundations of human sexuality. This approach (again with ritualistic disclaimers of biological determinism) is made more explicit, for exam-ple, by Richard Epstein, who asserts that "men and women are more comfortable in playing the roles that are congenial to their biological roles, and will find them-selves uneasy with powerful social [or legal] conventions that dictate a parity in social roles in courtship, marriage, and parenting."[5] Similarly, the assertion that women are more 'cooperative' than men (or even just perceived to be so) is taken to mean that women's need for relationship often leads them to settle for less than is acceptable to men, who can more readily treat particular relationships like any other 'inelastic' good they could do without (Rose 1994: 233–63).

Comparisons to other cultures enter these discussions in a characteristically limited and selective manner. Not only are instances of contrary power relations among men and women (or among various racial and ethnic groups) broadly ignored, but, as we shall see, certain fundamental premises of anthropology are reduced to simplistic assertions—for example, that the causal role of rational decision-making always follows along the lines first discerned in Western thought. The occasional nod at the 'exotic' is little more than that—a less than serious attempt to come to terms with alternative ways of constructing experience and the theoretically disruptive implications they pose. Thus, market rationality is regarded as a unitary phenomenon, the implications of socially constructed versus biologically grounded practices are left uninvestigated, and no larger social theory is produced in these purportedly 'theoretical' writings. Whether it is judges groping (with understandable difficulty) for some social science grounding or academic lawyers (with far less understandable difficulty) ignoring inconvenient examples, the result is a kind of potholing of anthropological information, rather than a concerted attempt to come to grips with it.

To see just how this plays out, let us allude briefly to the question of incest and the claims about infant-parent bonding, and, a bit more extensively to the challenge posed to the universality of marriage and kinship by the example of the Na of China. As we will see in greater detail in the following chapter, theories of incest come in several basic forms: genetic, natural revulsion, necessary alliance formation, and confusion of roles. Each has its particular varieties and attachments to grander theories—evolutionism, functionalism, and structuralism— and each has served as a basis for modern courts and legal scholars to justify both general and specific limitations on the right to marry. For example, some courts take a very sociologically functional view of the matter. Thus, the court in *State v. Marvin K. Kaiser* stated: "The crime [of incest] is also punished to promote and protect family harmony, to protect children from the abuse of parental authority, and because society cannot function in an orderly manner when age distinctions, generations, sentiments and roles in families are in conflict." The more biologically based explanations find favor with those who read the anthropological studies much more restrictively than do most anthropologists. Thus, E. O. Wilson (1998: 190–91) cites the study by Arthur Wolf of Taiwanese girls who resisted marriage to the boy they were contracted to marry if they were under thirty months of age when they were first brought into the household of their future spouse, and the studies of Israeli kibbutzim in which boys and girls raised in the communal "children's house" regarded one another as being like siblings and very rarely married someone with whom they were so raised. Wilson takes this as proof of the hypothesis of Edward Westermarck that individuals spurn as mates those with whom they were raised in early life. But there is no proof that this revulsion is not caused by cultural constraints rather than any natural repugnancy (see Spiro 1958 and Wolf 1995). That thirty-eight states prohibit marriage to first cousins whereas the rest do not, that recent studies demonstrate that occasional first-cousin marriage is no more likely to yield deleterious results than other alliances, and that until the nineteenth century, marriage to a wife's sister (even if the wife herself was dead) was regarded as incestuous, should suggest the contingent and malleable nature of the incest taboo even within our own culture.[6] Although some incest boundary does apply in almost every culture, no one theory seems to account for all instances. Thus, one of the most intriguing variants on the role distinctiveness explanation is that of Margaret Mead, who suggested that there must be some domestic zone within which actions that might otherwise carry sexual overtones—various states of undress, caressing, and so forth—would carry only implications of nonsexual intimacy. But even this theory can hardly yield answers as to whether that bounded zone must necessarily be correlated with residence, affinity, or age (Mead 1970).

In recent years, social scientists have also demonstrated that many ostensibly objective theories of universal human nature are, in fact, projections of (or at least deeply suffused by) their proponents' own cultural assumptions. An example that is particularly pertinent to the present discussion is that of mother-infant 'bonding.' This theory claims that an infant needs to 'bond' immediately with its mother—basically by putting the newborn on the mother's tummy and having her nurse it—and that if the process is successful, much subsequent psychological harm to the child may be avoided. But as Diane Eyer has demonstrated, this 'theory' grew out of a single highly suspect article published in 1972, that coincided with women who were moving out into careers feeling guilty about not being constant caregivers to their children, and it thus constituted an explanation and course of action that had great credibility, given the psychological and economic factors of the time. The theory turns out to be scientific nonsense, but to have made eminently good sense in the cultural moment in which it was placed. Once again, as in so many other domains, what was claimed in the name of social science turns out to be a feature whose own circumstances explain its attractiveness.[7]

Indeed, anthropological information, among other sources, has long confounded ideas of sexuality itself. Instances of cultures that construe male sexual identity as being granted first through a homosexual rite, and only later through heterosexual ties, or that conceptualize multiple genders each with its attendant social role, are brought home to us when, as a result of our own medical knowledge or procedures, the very gender of an individual becomes open to question.[8] American law must now decide whether a transgender individual may use the bathroom of his/her choice, is validly married (depending, perhaps, on whether there was a transgender operation before or after the wedding), or whether a prisoner has a valid claim against officials who do not assign him/her to a prison environment consonant with his/her claimed gender.[9] Once again, scholars and courts may cite anthropological instances, but they usually do so as idiosyncratic instances that are meant to signal human universals.

Anthropologists were themselves quite exercised for a time over issues of universality, and such subjects as marriage and the family could hardly escape such concern. As a result, assertions continue to be made about the family, citing various anthropological examples. To the question 'is marriage universal?' examples would be cited such as the Nayar of coastal India. There, a woman is ritually 'tied' to a man of equal or higher caste, but her only duty is to mourn him on his death. She is free to have sexual liaisons with any appropriate caste male, though some individual must step forward to assert himself as a legitimizing progenitor. Kathleen Gough, who studied the Nayar firsthand, argued that this *is* marriage inasmuch as the ritual tie and acknowledgment constitute validations of permissible sexuality, legitimacy of birth, and even rights of exclusive sexual access, since only men of certain castes are allowable lovers.[10] But if 'marriage' may involve no intimate contact between spouses, why, a number of anthropologists have argued, should we not abandon attempts at defining marriage altogether? Pierre Riviere (1971) thus wrote: "I am left in the position of claiming that if we are not to condemn ourselves forever to the tautologies of functionalist explanations we must come to realize that marriage as an isolable phenomenon of study is a misleading illusion." Similarly, Rodney Needham (1971: 7–8) argued: "So 'marriage,' too, is an odd-job word: very handy in all sorts of descriptive sentences, but worse than misleading in comparison and of no real use at all in analysis." However, as even these two scholars note, while no strict definition of marriage may be possible, the anthropological record and changing family patterns continue to raise questions that, while failing to produce universals, nevertheless call for comparative analysis. Thus while the Nayar may have seemed to press the limits of what Westerners understand by marriage, the recently described Na of China would appear to press them to the null point.

The Na, a tribal people of Tibetan-like Buddhists living in southern China, recognize no paternity, allow women to receive sexual visits from any man not part of their household (sex within that domain being unthinkable incest), do not form solidary groups based on descent or alliance, and demonstrate no jealousy in relation to 'visits' by a woman's other lovers. No words exist in their language for 'promiscuity,' 'bastard,' or 'infidelity'; brothers and sisters live together all their lives with some of their maternal kin; and since paternity is not socially recognized, a man may on occasion even wind up sleeping with his own daughter. The account of the Na by the French-trained anthropologist Cai Hua comes with endorsements from Claude Lévi-Strauss and others, and has been very favorably reviewed by leading anthropologists.[11] The example of the Na, therefore, suggests that it is sexuality rather than genealogical ordering on which this society is constructed, and that the 'naturalness,' to say nothing of the universality, of family and descent are once again in play. Indeed, as we shall see later, the question arises whether the Na are truly unusual or whether Western societies are themselves becoming like the Na in certain crucial ways. The Na thus pose a new test for anthropological comparison—and a challenge to generalizations about kinship generally. They do so, among other ways, by challenging some of the working notions that relate to the functions of families in general.

Family functions

In 1950, a group of social scientists associated with Harvard's short-lived Social Relations Department published an article entitled "The Functional Prerequisites of a Society."[12] In it they listed, among other prerequisites, the need for "shared cognitive orientations," "a "shared articulated set of goals," the regulation of both means and affective expression, and the effective recruitment of members who would then be properly socialized to the standards of the group. One problem, however, was that the authors were unable to show any relationship between form and function. Thus while it seems reasonable to suggest that some human endeavors must benefit from cooperation, or that children need to be fed, there is no demonstrable correlation between these endeavors and the ways in which they may be accomplished. Form not only does not follow function, but multifarious forms challenge the concept of function itself. If children can be raised in a separate children's house (as in the classic Israeli kibbutz), or if paternity is irrelevant in a given society (as among the Trobrianders), it is difficult to maintain a strict list of societal requirements. The Harvard enterprise thus fell into disfavor for much the same reason that family law has become so problematic in Western countries—because the multitude of forms has overwhelmed former certainty about function.

The alterations that have occurred in Europe and the United States clearly demonstrate how much form has outstripped function. In the last quarter of the twentieth century, roughly twenty-five percent of all pregnancies in America were aborted, half of the marriages ended in divorce, and three-quarters of African-American children were raised without a resident father.[13] Of late in the United States, 79 percent of children spend some time in day care (39 percent spending more than thirty hours per week).[14] The rate of births to unwed parents in Europe has, in recent years, ranged from 49 percent in Norway, 38 percent in Britain, and 41 percent in France, to 62 percent in Iceland, and even 31 percent in Catholic Ireland (Lyall 2002). Many parents still marry at some point in time, but since cohabiting and married couples may differ in their economic attitudes and knowledge of public policy, it may be, as one commenter on the Swedish example suggests, that "[t]he formal similarity between consensual unions and marriage does not necessarily imply that the 'social contract' between the partners is the same" (Björnberg 2001: 359). Governmental programs have changed along with these familial alterations: Britain has abandoned most policies that favor the traditional family form, Swedish income taxes are neutral on all matters of civil status, and even rights of succession are beginning effectively to alter as the distinction between children born in or out of wedlock has evaporated. Such profound alterations are hardly unique in the West. Studies of family history suggest that children in early modern Europe were often raised outside of their natal homes, that marriage became a concern of the state only in the sixteenth century (and indeed a sacrament only in the early Middle Ages), and that nineteenth-century Americans found many ways around the difficulty of obtaining a divorce, thus reinforcing H. L. Mencken's famous quip that in America "adultery is democratized marriage."[15]

Notwithstanding increased awareness of these contemporary and historic alterations in family forms, many judges, scholars, and policymakers remain attached to a functionalist conception of marriage and the family, whatever their views on the proper role of the state in such matters. Many law scholars, too, cannot shake loose from their functionalist orientations. Martha Fineman, for example, calls for the abolition of marriage as a legal category, but demonstrates her functionalist leanings when she also rhetorically asks: "If the terms of the marital contract are altered, should we not reflect on whether the functional role that the family plays within society must, of necessity, also be altered?"[16] Others are more explicit in the functions they expect marriage and the family to perform, as are many legislators and courts. In supporting no-fault divorce legislation that was finally enacted in 1970, the California Supreme Court in the 1952 case of *DeBurgh v. DeBurgh* first outlined the functions of the family, and then held that when those functions were no longer being performed, the parties should be able to terminate the relationship:

> The family is the basic unit of our society, the center of the personal affections that ennoble and enrich human life. It channels biological drives that might otherwise become socially destructive; it ensures the care and education of children in a stable environment; it establishes continuity from one generation to another; it nurtures and develops the individual initiative that distinguishes a free people. Since the family is the core of our society, the law seeks to foster and preserve marriages. But when a marriage has failed and the family has ceased to be a unit, the purposes of family life are no longer served and divorce will be permitted.

On the opposite end of the sociopolitical spectrum, the 16 million-strong Southern Baptist Convention in 1998 specified the functions each spouse must play in a marriage when it changed its statement of beliefs to read:

> [A husband] has the God-given responsibility to provide for, to protect and to lead his family. A wife is to submit graciously to the servant leadership of her husband even as the church willingly submits to the headship of Christ.[17]

But if many of the purported functions of marriage and the family can be performed without publicly institutionalized regularization, it is difficult to know what 'functions' are being assumed.[18] This is true even in the domain of child welfare, since it is by no means clear that one or another family form best serves a child's needs. In their consideration of same-sex marriage, the Hawaiian courts, for example, held that the optimal development of children had not been proved to be adversely affected by rearing in a same-sex household, a position not unlike that taken by the majority in the U.S. Supreme Court's decision on same-sex marriage, though strenuously objected to by the dissenters.[19] Similarly, studies can be cited on either side—quite often as a matter of what I would call 'the higher personal politics'—to support or attack the proposition that divorce has adverse consequences for children.[20] And if there is support for the recent, though quite controversial, studies by Judith Rich Harris, who argues that peers are far more important than parents to a child's psychological development, the examples of other societies—from the children's houses of the kibbutz to the intense day care situations found in some parts of Italy—may yet affect the entire discourse of functioning families and child welfare (Gladwell 1998).

Polygamy may constitute a similar example. The U.S. Supreme Court in the 1890s, as part of the national attack on Mormonism, characterized polygamy as barbarous and dysfunctional. And the decisions by recent courts supporting same-sex marriage profess to distinguish polygamy. Yet the functionalist arguments for and against the practice based on anthropological findings probably support neither position. That a number of individuals live in de facto polygamous unions—as many as 30,000 in the state of Utah alone—may ultimately lead to cases that challenge the legal opposition to these arrangements, much as was the case with same-sex marriages. Indeed, the Tenth Circuit Court of Appeals, in *Brown v. Buhman*, overruling a lower court that had thrown out a Utah state anti-polygamy statute, reinstated that law, even though state officials have indicated they would only enforce it if there was some fraud or abuse involved (see Wang 2016). But it will be the systemic connections to other issues—property, custody, parental rights, etc.—that will once again underscore how connected marriage is to more than the realm of personal relationships alone (Figure 4.1).[21]

FIGURE 4.1 Polygamous family of Jos. F. Smith, president of Mormon Church (1904).
Source: Unknown photographer; public domain.

To some extent, of course, all social scientists and legal scholars are functionalists: We see usefulness and connection even when we may append other theories (Marxist, behavioral, structuralist, evolutionary, economistic) to the functional foundation. The irony is that much of the debate about the abolition of marriage is being carried on in terms of functionalism, even though functionalism is rife with limitations. In particular, functionalism has always had great difficulty conceptualizing change or, since everything is said to contribute to the working of the whole, establishing criteria for the 'dysfunctional.'[22] Indeed, as the variety of 'familial' forms expands, in both our anthropological awareness and our everyday experiences, it becomes ever more difficult to assume universal propositions about social functioning at all. So it is striking to see the terminology of functionalism remaining so central to the abolition of marriage debates. Thus when courts, like those in Canada and Massachusetts, held that it is unconstitutional to impose differences on same-sexed, as opposed to opposite-sexed, couples, it was noteworthy that they relied on ideas of the ways in which non-marital relations are functionally like those receiving state sanction, even though nowadays courts commonly renounce any single functional model.[23] The result is a kind of approach to vagueness: Neither courts nor commenters can quite give up regarding marriage as 'doing something' for people and society at large, yet as they expand the range of 'equivalent' forms, they can no longer specify with clarity what those functions are.

One way to finesse the issue is to try to remove sexuality from the question altogether. For example, it has been argued that it is inappropriate to consider sexuality when deciding the role of the state in relationships, since the only legitimate interests of the state should go to the well-being of individual children or partners. The comparison to the Na is intriguing, for it could be said that we are becoming more like the Na than like our earlier selves—rendering sexuality central, but without specifically distinctive spousal implications. Indeed, the anthropological literature could be used to suggest that functionalism is either in the eye of the beholder or distinctive to a given culture, and that claims to naturalness, necessity, or universality are claims for legitimacy of one's position, not claims to scientific validation.[24] However, we need to consider one other matter, that of legitimacy itself, before we can explore the ways in which the anthropological approach to culture may be able to address the relation of structure and function in marriage and the family.

Creating legitimacy

What is it one seeks in asking outside persons or institutions to ratify one's conjugal or familial relationship? Obviously, that answer varies with each culture, and any universal response falls into the same trap of functionalism or generalization that always beckons. But if in the American context, one poses the question in this way, both the contributions and the limitations of anthropology to the discussion can be explored. The central question in legitimacy is: Why should

I do what someone else says, or at least seek their approval for my own actions? But what we seek to legitimize is complex. It may be recognition that we are members of the group, or that we have done things the 'right' way. It may be that we have reached a given stage in life and are allowed to possess and feel the things that society has assigned to such a position or role. It may be that we are now licensed to engage in acts previously denied us. Legitimization may be a bald-faced statement that, whatever others may do, this is who *we* are. Indeed, legitimacy may be the assignment of a dangerous capability that must nevertheless be contained if society itself is to be replicated. Or it may simply be a grant of power that we seek, as Paul Valéry said, with no particular goal in mind, never knowing to what uses we may have to put it.

Specific examples of each of these factors can be found in our own, as in any society's, history. Thus, as we have noted, in the West, marriage moved only in recent centuries from the concern of religion to that of the state, as the state itself sought to have its citizens depend on and identify their well-being with the burgeoning central government. Marriage may even have legitimized extramarital relations, as long as they were discreet and the needs of social replication—by class, race, or symbolic appropriation—were fulfilled. For others, marriage may have come to mean the relief that accompanies no longer having to compete for a mate in a marketplace of relations. Indeed, marriage may be less about the relationships of individuals or groups than about legitimization itself—about the capacity of government or religion to tell us what we may do. As a consequence, for revolutionaries—in Britain in the seventeenth century, in Russia at the time of the Bolshevik revolution, in the United States in the 1960s—sex, marriage, and family form could serve as vehicles for protest against the claims of the state.[25] To alter the terms of the relationships may, therefore, be to call into question legitimacy itself.

If, as we shall see, anthropology suggests that every domain of a socio-cultural system has some bearing on every other, then changes, or proposed changes, in the legal status of marriage and the family would be expected to have systemic effects. Some of these effects are more easily missed than others if one did not assume from the outset—based on a wide range of comparative ethnographic instances—that such connections invariably do exist. If, then, we were, for example, to take up the suggestion that marriage should be returned to the domain of religion, or be rendered an entirely contractual matter, with the state playing only the role of enforcing private agreements, and deferring all of its own objectives to the realm of individual support (rather than trying to get the family to do its work for it),[26] one might ask the relevant anthropological question in either of two ways: What supportive changes elsewhere in the sociocultural system will affect the course and success of the outcome? Or: What systemic alterations can one look for that might not at first seem to be connected to these changes, but given comparative studies, do indeed appear likely to be implicated?[27]

Some of these connections are predominantly legal in origin, others more broadly cultural. Martha Fineman (2006: 58), for example, suggests that "ameliorating doctrines would fill the void left by the abolition of family law. In fact, it seems apparent to me that a lot more regulation (protection) would occur once the large category of interactions in families removed from behind the veil of privacy that now shields them." But the very idea of privacy may be affected in the process, and with it notions of responsibility, the religious images that support ideas of the family, and even concepts of time as the stages of life or indicators of personal development are reconceptualized. Similarly, if one moves to a wholly contractual system, numerous questions arise: Will the 'covenant marriage' contracts now permitted in several states (and under consideration by a number of others)—contracts that allow parties to agree to more limitations on exiting their marriages than exist under current state laws—affect personal identity and ideas of democracy, as individuals have different relationships to the state and children identify their parents' relationships differently?[28] Will use of the Uniform Premarital Agreement Act, particularly its provision allowing agreements about the behavior of each party, affect ideas of free will, choice, the American romance of romance, and the image we have of our inalienable right to the pursuit of happiness?[29] If marriages are fraught with explicit contractual elements, will they really be seen as binding contracts for which few changes in circumstance would constitute grounds for revision, or will they be seen as moral agreements, metaphors of intent, or similar to international treaties from which parties may exit when it is in their 'interest' to do so (Scott and Scott 1998)? And if the effects are moral rather than legally enforceable, what impact will this have on images of the self and the arrangements to which marriage has become analogized? Indeed, the use of such contracts highlights the problematic nature of the state itself. For as Judith Butler argues, if the state uses the family as a domain for replicating the composition and structure of national distinctiveness, does shifting away, say, from the image of the family as grounded on heterosexual kinship affect such other factors as the place of immigration in the symbolic image of the nation, or the claim that state policy is not based on nationalism, but on some ineffable natural principles (Butler 2002)?

Even if one does not agree with the proposition that society may, through the institutions of the state, withhold its imprimatur from certain relationships, there is little doubt that 'informal' mechanisms—from metaphoric shifts to revised views of the person—will be affected by the contest over state validation. As legitimacy and privacy are altered, so, too, will be all those other cultural elements connected with them. And like other such instances of significant social and cultural change, the uses to which anthropological information is put, and the repercussions for theoretical development within the discipline itself, will also be profound. How, if at all, one should approach these impending alterations is also worthy of brief consideration.

What is to be done—anthropologically?

> Marital Status (circle one):
> Married. Single. Not sure.
>
> *—magazine questionnaire*

'Not sure' may seem the safe answer all around. Far from being a predictive science, anthropology has enough difficulty stating what's what at any given moment. Of course, prediction and certainty are not the criteria for judging every disciplinary insight, nor is science the singular, invariant entity our mythologies often make it out to be.[30] Courts and legislatures may draw cultural assumptions from the human sciences as much as they may influence those disciplines. Nevertheless, it may be well to match up the occasional uses to which anthropology is put by those who debate the issues surrounding the abolition of marriage with the more realistic claims with which anthropologists (at least those with whom the present author identifies) may be tagged. Here, it may be worth repeating how it is that anthropologists such as I myself conceive of culture and how, working from such an approach, we may be able to cast more useful light on the subject of marriage, family, and the state.

Put very simply (if somewhat repetitively): Human beings are unique for their capacity to create the categories of their own experience. Indeed, we achieved this capability before we acquired our present speciation. The existence of this capacity for culture, while hardly rendering us nonbiological entities, means that instinct has very largely been replaced by culture, and that, as we have gone about creating and re-creating our own experience, we have had to adapt to our own constructs. The universe of meanings, no less than of relationships, and the conceptualizations of our surroundings, no less than the ways we organize our social relations in terms of our cosmological understandings, are factors of our own design, and as those designs have changed, so have the ways we envision and organize ourselves. The range of variation seen in human social and cultural forms is not a simple function of biological or environmental necessity, or the permissible leeway of either; it is the direct expression of that very ability evolution has yielded by which we fashion our own fabric of meaning. Therefore, one cannot take instances out of their contexts without doing them great violence, for what is central to our human identity is an inherent capacity to create an 'artificial obvious' rather than to be dependent on specific solutions required by nature.[31]

There is a Yiddish saying: "For example is no proof." Nowhere is this truer than in the uses of anthropological findings. To take, say, an individual example of marital arrangements or familial forms and use it, in law or in policy, to prove (or disprove) an asserted universal proposition about all marriages or all families, misses the category of which these practices are an instance. For it is not some particular view of marriage or family that these instances can establish, but that what is being demonstrated is a capability, indeed a mode of that capability's expression. To say that the Na prove marriage can be dispensed with or that the kibbutz proves that children do not need parents, misses the anthropological point: What each instance demonstrates is that the nested webs of relationship, organization, concepts, and histories must be unpacked, so that the sense they make becomes a demonstration of the sense-making of culture as the quintessentially human capacity.

Toward this end, as we have seen, anthropologists look for the reverberations across and among diverse domains of a culture, precisely because it is this replication that gives a set of cultural notions its greatest power—the power to appear, to those who conceive of their lives in its terms, as natural. Whether this is because one cannot, so to speak, constantly reinvent each experience, or because this capacity serves to replicate society with enormous success, the evidence all suggests that, however contested and inexact, however open-textured or ambivalent, cultures achieve their integrity through reinforcement across domains. And that means that what anthropology can contribute most is sensitivity, through diversified examples, of how the processes of replication and integration, in all their variations of mode and result, may work for this most distinctive of species.

To follow such an approach is certainly not to pursue mindless relativism. Critics consistently misunderstand anthropologists in this regard. Thus, in a document drafted by his successor Benedict XVI, Pope John Paul II, in the longest encyclical of his papacy, castigated anthropological findings in particular for contributing to moral decline. He noted the "doubts and objections of a human and psychological, social and cultural... nature" that question the Church's teachings "on the basis of certain anthropological and ethical presuppositions end by detaching human freedom from its essential and constitutive relationship to truth." The dangerous result, he argued, will be that in matters of morality, the Church will only be able to propose values, while "each individual will independently make his or her decisions and life choices" (John Paul II 1993). But anthropologists do not equate all cultures on some moral scale. To the contrary, we suspend disbelief about all specific practices in order to investigate the ways in which, to the people themselves, their ideas and relationships form some ordered sense by being suffused through multiple domains of their lives.

Nor does anthropology deny that there may indeed be some singular truths out there that comparison can highlight. But what such a theoretical and investigative stance does imply, is that if human beings are the producers of their own comprehension, then we cannot prejudge the results by limiting truth claims to our own values, or lose sight of the crucial human propulsion to generate categories and link them across seemingly separate realms. Claims for sociobiological determinism thus miss the distinctively biological nature of culture—that the capacity for culture arose through biological forces and may well remain subject to biological aspects, but that at every point it is the ability to conceptualize our own situations that is dominant. Similar criticisms, as we will see in greater detail in a later chapter, can be raised about the approach from natural law. Justice Antonin Scalia, for example, went so far as to assert that democracy obscures

God's law and the natural law presuppositions it embraces: "The reaction of people of faith to this tendency of democracy to obscure the divine authority behind government should not be resignation to it, but the resolution to combat it as effectively as possible" (quoted in Wilentz 2002). Alan Dershowitz (2002), on the other hand, says: "'Natural law' is little more than a matter of personal opinion or belief dressed up as the objective law of nature or God. One judge's notion of what is natural is another's sense of what is unnatural." In sum, it can be argued that claims of natural law are like any other cultural product: They are concepts that, by proliferating through, and linking, diverse aspect of one's culture, take on the air of being beyond human construct. We are not, therefore, ever dealing with natural law, but with the naturalization of law—a process that is no less true for a legal concept than for any other cultural artifact.

To move from the domain of human culture to the specifics of marriage and family is not, then, so great a leap. If one abolishes marriage (in the sense of removing the state, or making marriage more fully contractual, or returning it to religion), it will be the reverberations across diverse realms of cultural life that will be called into play. Metaphors—the most critical means by which we make connections among domains—will play out in ways whose implications will be vast, yet unpredictable. Justifications, whether through the capturing of the institutions of legitimacy or resource allocation, will affect such seemingly tangential aspects of life as concepts of time and space. Reformulations of the state's role in family support will be tied up with changes that occur in the concept of the person and the sense of self-worth. It is not that 'nature' will always reassert itself: It is that culture works by appearing to its adherents as the proof and product of naturalization. It is not, as the French seem to believe, that the national assembly must be half female because nature has divided us in twain. It is that naturalizing the state in these terms constitutes a reaction to fears of multiculturalism, a sense of national purpose slipping away. New marital covenants or contracts will most likely yield a new functionalism, as people assume that the purposes of these arrangements fulfill ends beyond themselves. And as much as comparison will once again demonstrate the indubitable fact that each solution is a product of human endeavor, the power of culture to make each approach appear imminent will almost certainly lead even those who should know better to use anthropology selectively to 'prove' that they are merely describing a human necessity rather than a momentary human solution.

Universal donor, perhaps; universal source for poaching, almost certainly. The vital lesson of anthropology—connections—carries implications that are easily dismissed as standardless relativism, inapposite practices from distant climes and peoples, or alternative ways of being that we should adopt piecemeal as more fulfilling, or reject wholesale as less than truly human. But if we use comparative examples to think through the variable nature of family organization, we may find that the 'answer' to the debate over the abolition of marriage—like many other issues in law and social policy—does not lie in some arcane example proving or disproving a universal proposition, but in the comprehension of how, in each society, linkages are configured. Variation being as central to culture as it is to biology, only the most responsible use of comparative examples, whether in law or other institutions, will help us to understand the potential implications of our own actions.

Notes

1 *Compare* Nussbaum (2010): 672 ("it would be a lot better... if the state withdrew from the marrying business, leaving the expressive domain to religions and to other private groups"), *and* Coontz (2007) ("Perhaps it's time to revert to a much older marital tradition. Let churches decide which marriages they deem 'licit.' But let couples—gay or straight—decide if they want the legal protections and obligations of a committed relationship."), *with* Karlan (2010) (states may not have the constitutional right to abolish marriage). See also, Pender (2015) (reaction to Supreme Court same-sex marriage decision).

2 See, Brinig (2010).

3 On the application of social science claims in family law, see the discussion by Canadian judge Williams (1996). See generally the discussion of such matters in Monahan and Walker (2014).

4 For a similar denial of the role of culture as other than secondary, taken from the vantage of environmental determinism (and citing only those writers in cultural evolutionism who have, in fact, long since rejected their earlier theories), see Diamond (1997).

5 Epstein (1995: 336). The bracketed addition is from Eskridge and Hunter (1998: 40).

6 Eleven states and the District of Columbia prohibit stepsibling marriage; Alaska and Louisiana prohibit marriage within four degrees of relatedness; and Utah prohibits marriage within five degrees of affinity. See Eskridge and Hunter (1998). On recent discoveries about the genetics of first-cousin marriage, see Grady (2002). On sister-in-law marriage, see Twitchell (1987); and Héritier (1999).

7 Eyer (1992). Fathers, too, could bond by donning a 'male nursing bra' in which two baby bottles were placed for nursing the child. Goldstein, et al. (1973) argued for custody to be given exclusively to a child's "psychological parent," a proposal adopted by many courts in the U.S. in the 1970s–80s (e.g., *J.A.L. v. E.P.H.*).

8 See the anthropological sources and arguments as discussed for law students in Eskridge and Hunter (1998): 209–11.

9 *Compare, M. T. v. J. T.* (individual who has made his body conform to his psychological self has changed gender for purposes of marriage), *with, In re Elaine Frances Ladrach*, (postoperative transsexual not granted marriage license). On transsexual as an adopting parent, see Canedy 2002; on placement of transsexual in prison population, see *Murray v. United States Bureau of Prisons, et al.*

10 Gough (1959); and Fuller (1976). *Compare* the definition of marriage given in Royal Anthropological Institute (1951: 110) ("a union between a man and a woman such that children born to the woman are the recognized legitimate offspring of both partners"), *with* the critique of that definition in Leach (1955: 182–86). For additional comparisons, see Marshall (1968) and Barnard (1994).

11 Hua (2001). See also the review of Hua's book by Geertz (2001). Geertz expresses concern, however, that Hua does not give a fuller description of how these sexual and procreative customs relate to a broader range of Na cultural features. One might also ask why the Na are so secretive about these sexual visits if they see no reason to be concerned about their legitimacy or effects on other social relationships.

12 Aberle (1950). For a more recent—and, despite its lengthy enumeration, far more vague—set of universals, see Pinker (2002).

13 Cited in Witte (2000): 92. The divorce rate has actually been declining, from 5 per thousand in 1985, to 4.7 in 1990, to 4.1 in 1995. DiFonzo (2000: 877–78). The numbers have declined still further in the first part of the twenty-first century.

14 McCartney (2002). McCartney's study (1990) of more than 1,350 children shows no adverse consequences to such care when the child also has good parental attention.

15 On the early modern period, see Stone (1977) and Wrigley (1997). On America, see Hartog (2000). See also, Cott (2000) and De Rougement (1956).

16 Fineman (1998). See also, Fineman (1995).

17 Niebuhr (1998). It was this change in position that led former President Jimmy Carter and his wife Rosalind Carter to leave the Convention. Indeed, for whatever reasons, the Convention lost 236,000 members in one recent year, membership having dropped to 15.5 million from its peak of 16.3 (Smietana 2015).

18 See generally, Clive (1980).

19 *Baehr, et al. v. Milke.* See also the Supreme Court's same-sex decision in *Obergefell v. Hodges.* One particularly specious study, often still cited by opponents of same-sex marriage, claimed to show that same-sex parents had deleterious effects on the children they raised. See Sprigg (2012). These purported findings by University of Texas sociologist Mark Regnerus, were, however, shown to concern only two such couples and that the children showing greatest problems had been adopted from abusive homes. Regnerus' flawed study was condemned by his professional association, his own academic department, and by the Court of Appeals for the Sixth Circuit which upheld Michigan's anti-gay marriage law as constitutional, but nevertheless characterized Regnerus' testimony at trial as "entirely unbelievable and not worthy of serious consideration" (*Deboer v. Snyder*, decision of November 6, 2014; combined with other cases as the *Obergefell* case decided by the Supreme Court). Regnerus later recanted his claims and still later partially recanted his recantation, still claiming homosexual couples are "inherently" unstable. See Ford (2012), Blue (2015), and Parke (2015).

20 *Compare* the citations and discussions of the work of Judith Wallerstein and others, who claim to have demonstrated the ill effects on children of divorce (cited in DiFonzo 2000: 925–26), *with* Hetherington 2002, who argues that any ill effects are not long-lasting. The politics of the former position are evident in the work of James Q. Wilson (2002). After criticizing him for his failure to cite Hetherington's work, a reviewer of Wilson's book notes:

> Why does he dabble in tinhorn biology to claim that men are better at climbing the corporate ladder and more likely to work longer hours because he-man aggressiveness was once an evolutionary advantage? Or declare that a mother wonders whom the baby resembles, while a father suspects that 'the infant looks like—well, a baby'?
>
> *(Cohen 2002)*

21 See, *Obergefell v. Hodges.* See generally, Symposium (2015).

22 On the question of functionalism in social theory and comparative law, see Rosen (2002).

23 See generally, Cossman and Ryder (2001: 288) who quip, apropos the use of a baseline of the idealized marital relationship: "Indeed, it is tempting to speculate how many marriages would fail to qualify as 'marriage-like' if they were subjected to similar scrutiny."

24 As Clifford Geertz (2000: 135) has put it: "If you want a good rule of thumb generalization from anthropology, I would suggest the following: Any sentence that begins, 'All societies have ...' is either baseless or banal."

25 See Hill (1972); and Massell (1974).

26 See Fineman (2006); and Bernstein (2006).

27 For the argument in favor of returning marriage to religion, see Cossman and Ryder (2001). On converting marriage to a largely contractual matter, see DiFonzo (2000): 934–45.

28 See generally, Difonzo (2000): 934–37. See also the Web site of the Institute for American Values (www.americanvalues.org), a conservative action group, for information on faith-based support for marriage and agreements to stay married.

29 See generally, Difonzo (2000): 954–59. The Pennsylvania Supreme Court has even refused to engage any longer in the "business of policing the reasonableness of premarital bargains" (Note 1991: 1400).
30 See, e.g., the discussion in Geertz (2000): 155.
31 The phrase 'artificial obvious' is borrowed from Bates (1960).

References

Aberle, David Friend, Albert K. Cohen, Arthur K. Davis, Marion J. Levy Jr., and Francis X. Sutton 1950, "The Functional Prerequisites of a Society," *Ethics*, vol. 60, pp. 100–11.

Barnard, Alan 1994, "Rules and Prohibitions: The Form and Content of Human Kinship," in Tim Ingold, ed., *Companion Encyclopedia of Anthropology*, London: Routledge, pp. 783–812.

Bates, Marston 1960, *The Forest and the Sea*, New York, Signet.

Bernstein, Anita 2006, "Afterword: Narrowing the Status of Marriage," in Anita Bernstein, ed., *Marriage Proposals: Questioning a Legal Status*, New York: New York University Press, pp. 217–36.

Björnberg, Ulla 2001, "Cohabitation and Marriage in Sweden: Does Family Form Matter?" *International Journal of Law, Policy and the Family*, vol. 15, pp. 350–62.

Blue, Miranda 2015, "Mark Regnerus Defends Flawed Research on Same-Sex Parenting," *Right Wing Watch*. www.rightwingwatch.org/content/mark-regnerus-defends-flawed-research-same-sex-parenting (accessed January 5, 2017).

Brinig, Margaret F. 2010, *Family, Law, and Community: Supporting the Covenant*, Chicago, IL: University of Chicago Press.

Butler, Judith 2002, "Is Kinship Always Already Heterosexual?" *Differences: A Journal of Feminist Cultural Studies*, vol. 13, no. 1, pp. 14–44.

Canedy, Dana 2002, "Sex Change Complicates Battle over Child Custody," *New York Times*, February 18.

Clive, Eric 1980, "Marriage: An Unnecessary Legal Concept?" in John Eekelaar and Sanford Katz, eds., *Marriage and Cohabitation in Contemporary Societies*, London: Butterworths, pp. 71–81. (Excerpted in J. Eekelaar and M. Maclean, eds., 1994, *A Reader on Family Law*, Oxford: Oxford University Press, pp. 175–91).

Cohen, Patricia 2002, "From 'I Do' to 'I Don't': Review of James Q. Wilson, The Marriage Problem," *New York Times Book Review*, March 24, p. 16.

Coontz, Stephanie 2007, "Taking Marriage Private," *New York Times*, November 26.

Cossman, Brenda and Brian Ryder 2001, "What Is Marriage-Like Like? The Irrelevance of Conjugality," *Revue Canadienne de Droit Familial*, vol. 18, pp. 269–326.

Cott, Nancy F. 2000, *Public Vows: A History of Marriage and the Nation*, Cambridge, MA: Harvard University Press.

Dershowitz, Alan M. 2002, *Shouting Fire: Civil Liberties in a Turbulent Age*, Boston, MA: Little, Brown.

Diamond, Jared 1997, *Guns, Germs, and Steel: The Fates of Human Societies*, New York: Norton.

De Rougement, Denis 1956, *Love in the Western World*, New York: Pantheon.

DiFonzo, J. Herbie 2000, "Customized Marriage," *Indiana Law Journal*, vol. 75, pp. 875–962.

Epstein, Richard 1995, "Two Challenges for Feminist Thought," *Harvard Journal of Law and Public Policy*, vol. 18, no. 2 (1995), pp. 331–47.

Eskridge, William N. Jr. and Nan D. Hunter 1998, *Sexuality, Gender, and the Law: 1998 Supplement*, Westbury, NY: Foundation Press.

Eyer, Dorothy 1992, *Mother-Infant Bonding: A Scientific Fiction*, New Haven, CT: Yale University Press.

Fineman, Martha Albertson 1995, *The Neutered Mother, the Sexual Family, and Other Twentieth Century Tragedies*, New York: Routledge.

——1998, "Contract, Marriage and Background Rules" in Brian Bix, ed., *Analyzing Law: New Essays in Legal Theory*, Oxford: Clarendon Press, pp. 183–95.

—— 2006, "The Meaning of Marriage," in Anita Bernstein, ed., *Marriage Proposals: Questioning a Legal Status*, New York: New York University Press, 2006, pp. 29–69.

Ford, Zack 2012, "Mark Regnerus Admits His 'Family Structures' Study Wasn't about Gay Parenting," *Think Progress*, October 30. http://thinkprogress.org/lgbt/2012/10/30/1110591/regnerus-admits-gay-parenting/ (accessed January 5, 2017).

Fuller, Christopher John 1976. *The Nayars Today*, London: Routledge and Kegan Paul.

Geertz, Clifford 2000, *Available Light: Anthropological Reflections on Philosophical Topics*, Princeton, NJ: Princeton University Press.

—— 2001, "The Visit," *New York Review of Books*, October 18, pp. 27–30.

Gladwell, Malcolm 1998, "Do Parents Matter?" *The New Yorker*, August 17, pp. 54–64.

Glendon, Mary A. 1989, *The Transformation of Family Law: State, Law, and Family in the United States and Western Europe*, Chicago, IL: University of Chicago Press.

Goldstein, Joseph, Anna Freud, and Albert J. Solnit 1973, *Beyond the Best Interests of the Child*, New York: Free Press.

Gough, E. Kathleen 1959, "The Nayars and the Definition of Marriage," *Journal of the Royal Anthropological Institute*, vol. 89, pp. 23–34.

Grady, Denise 2002, "Few Risks Seen to the Children of First Cousins," *New York Times*, April 4.

Hartog, Hendrik 2000, *Man and Wife in America*, Cambridge, MA: Harvard University Press.

Héritier, Françoise 1999, *Two Sisters and Their Mother: The Anthropology of Incest*, New York: Zone Books.

Hetherington, Eileen Mavis 2002, *For Better, for Worse: Divorce Reconsidered*, New York: Norton.

Hill, Christopher 1972, *The World Turned Upside Down: Radical Ideas during the English Revolution*, London: Temple Smith.

Hua, Cai 2001, *A Society without Fathers or Husbands: The Na of China*, New York: Zone Books.

John Paul II 1993, *Veritatis Splendor* ("The Splendor of Truth"), August 6. http://w2.vatican.va/content/john-paul-ii/en/encyclicals/documents/hf_jp-ii_enc_06081993_veritatis-splendor.html (accessed January 5, 2017).

Karlan, Pamela S. 2010, "Let's Call the Whole Thing Off: Can States Abolish the Institution of Marriage?" *California Law Review*, vol. 98, pp. 697–707.

Leach, Edmund 1955, "Polyandry, Inheritance and the Definition of Marriage," *Man*, vol. 55, pp. 182–86.

Lyall, Sarah 2002, "For Europeans, Love, Yes; Marriage, Maybe," *New York Times*, March 24.

McCartney, Kathleen, ed., 1990, *Child Care and Maternal Employment: A Social Ecology Approach*, San Francisco: Jossey-Bass.

—— 2002, Cambridge Forum, National Public Radio broadcast, July 1.

Marshall, Gloria A. 1968, "Marriage: Comparative Analysis," in David L. Sills, ed., *International Encyclopedia of the Social Sciences*, New York: Macmillan and Free Press, vol. 10, pp. 8–19.

Massell, Gregory 1974, *The Surrogate Proletariat: Moslem Women and Revolutionary Strategies in Soviet Central Asia*, Princeton, NJ: Princeton University Press.

Mead, Margaret 1970, "Anomalies in American Post-divorce Relationships," in Paul Bohannan, ed., *Divorce and After*, Garden City, NY: Doubleday, pp. 97–112.

Monahan, John and W. Laurens Walker 2014, *Social Science in Law*, 8th edn., St. Paul, MN: Foundation Press.

Needham, Rodney 1971, "Remarks on the Analysis of Kinship and Marriage," in Rodney Needham, ed., *Rethinking Kinship and Marriage*, London: Tavistock, pp. 1–34.

Niebuhr, Gustave 1998, "Southern Baptists Declare Wife Should 'Submit' to Her Husband," *New York Times*, June 10.

Note 1991, "Recent Developments, Family Law. Prenuptial Agreements. Pennsylvania Supreme Court Rejects Substantive Review of Prenuptial Agreements. Simeone v. Simeone, 581 A.2d 162 (Pa. 1990)," *Harvard Law Review*, vol. 104, pp. 1399–1406.

Nussbaum, Martha C. 2010, "A Right to Marry?" *California Law Review*, vol. 98, pp. 667–96.

Parke, Cole 2015, "World Congress of Families to Feature Anti-LGBTQ Family Scholars," August 14. www.politicalresearch.org/tag/mark-regnerus/ (accessed January 5, 2017).

Pender, Geoff 2015, "Lawmaker: State Could Stop Marriage Licenses Altogether," *The Clarion-Ledger* [Jackson, Mississippi], June 26.

Pinker, Steven 2002, *The Blank Slate: The Modern Denial of Human Nature*, London: Penguin/Allen Lane.

Posner, Richard 1992, *Sex and Reason*, Cambridge, MA: Harvard University Press.

Riviere, Pierre 1971, "Marriage: A Reassessment," in Rodney Needham, ed., *Rethinking Kinship and Marriage*, London: Tavistock, pp. 57–74.

Rose, Carol M. 1994, *Property and Persuasion: Essays on the History, Theory, and Rhetoric of Ownership*, Boulder: Westview Press.

Rosen, Lawrence 2002, "Beyond Compare," in Pierre Legrand and Roderick Mundy, eds., *Comparative Legal Studies: Traditions and Transitions*, Cambridge: Cambridge University Press, pp. 493–510.

Royal Anthropological Institute 1951, *Notes and Queries on Anthropology*, London: Routledge and Kegan Paul.

Scott, Elizabeth S. and Robert E. Scott 1998, "Marriage as Relational Contract," *Virginia Law Review*, vol. 84, pp. 1225–1334.

Smietana, Bob 2015, "As Church Plants Grow, Southern Baptists Disappear," *Christianity Today*, June 12. www.christianitytoday.com/gleanings/2015/june/southern-baptist-decline-baptism-church-plant-sbc.html (accessed January 5, 2017).

Spiro, Melford E. 1958, *Childhood in the Kibbutz*, Cambridge, MA: Harvard University Press.

Sprigg, Peter 2012, "New Study of Homosexual Parents Tops All Previous Research." www.frc.org/issuebrief/new-study-on-homosexual-parents-tops-all-previous-research (accessed January 5, 2017).

Stone, Lawrence 1977, *Family, Sex and Marriage in England, 1500–1800*, New York: Harper and Row.

Symposium 2015, "Polygamous Unions? Charting the Contours of Marriage Law's Frontier," 64 *Emory Law Journal*, vol. 64, pp. 1669–2139.

Twitchell, James B. 1987, *Forbidden Partners: The Incest Taboo in Modern Culture*, New York: Columbia University Press.

Wang, Yanan 2016, "Utah's Polygamy Ban Restored in Big Defeat for 'Sister Wives'," *Washington Post*, April 12.

Wilentz, Sean 2002, "From Justice Scalia, a Chilling Vision of Religious Authority in America," *New York Times*, July 8.

Williams, R. James (Jim) 1996, "Grasping a Thorny Baton... A Trial Judge Looks at Judicial Notice and Courts' Acquisition of Social Science," *Canadian Family Law Quarterly*, vol. 14, pp. 179–232.

Wilson, Edward O. 1998, *Consilience: the Unity of Knowledge*, New York: Vintage Books.

Wilson, James Q. 2002, *The Marriage Problem: How Our Culture Weakens Families*, New York: HarperCollins.

Witte, John Jr., 2000, "An Apt and Cheerful Conversation on Marriage," in R. Bruce Douglass and Josh Mitchell, eds., *A Nation Under God? Essays on the Fate of Religion in American Public Life*, Lanham, MD: Rowman & Littlefield Publishing Co., pp. 91–110.

Wolf, Arthur P. 1995, *Sexual Attraction and Childhood Association: A Chinese Brief for Edward Westermarck*, Stanford: Stanford University Press.

Wrigley, Edward Anthony 1997, *English Population History from Family Reconstitution, 1580–1837*, Cambridge: Cambridge University Press.

Cases cited

Baehr et al. v. Milke, 1996 WL 694235 (No. 91-1394, Hawaii Cir. Ct., 1st Cir. 1996).

Brown v. Buhman, Appellate case no. 14-4117 (10th Circuit April 11, 2016).

DeBurgh v. DeBurgh, 39 Cal.2d 858, 250 P.2d 598 (Cal. 1952).

In re Elaine Frances Ladrach, 32 Ohio Misc. 2d 6, 513 N.E. 2d 828 (Probate Ct. for Stark Cty., Ohio 1987).

J.A.L. v. E.P.H., 453 Pa. Superior Ct. 78, 682 A.2d 1314 (Pa. Super. 1996).

M.T. v. J.T., 140 N.J. Super. 77, 355 A.2d 204, *cert. denied*, 71 N.J. 345, 364 A.2d 1076 (N.J. App. Div. 1976).

Murray v. United States Bureau of Prisons, et al., 106 F.3d 401, 1997 WL 34677 (6th Cir. 1997).

Obergefell v. Hodges, 576 US___ (2015).

State v. Marvin K. Kaiser, 34 Wash. App. 559, 663 P.2d 839 (Wash. Ct. of App. 1983).

5

WHAT'S WRONG WITH INCEST?

Perception and theory in a shifting legal environment

Picture the following situation: A brother and sister are separated at birth, meet for the first time as adults, fall in love, and arrive at the marriage license bureau only for the official to notice from the records that they are siblings. Told by the clerk that incest could create malformed offspring the young man offers to have a vasectomy; told that it is against God's law the couple insist that the state has no right to tell them what religious beliefs they may hold.[1]

Why exactly should they not be able to wed? What if they just live together or do have children together—what business is it of the state? And if the rationales for the incest prohibition have changed over time—and if all of them have flaws—what reason, if any, would presently pass inspection to bar such relationships? Where, too, should the boundary be set in incest as an issue of marriage and as an issue of sexual contact? On a personal note, my great uncle and great aunt were first cousins. When, in the early twentieth century, they wanted to marry they were up against a state statute that forbade unions between first cousins. So they crossed the Ohio River from their homes in Louisville to the state of Indiana to be wed. They then lived their entire lives in the state of Kentucky. Presumably, had anyone challenged the validity of their marriage—during their lives or in the administration of their estates—their marriage could have been declared invalid. But what rationale, other than states' rights, would support such a union being incestuous on one side of a country's river and not on the other? Incest laws and customs thus afford us an excellent opportunity to test some of the situations in which cultural concepts make their way into the law. Because the reasons given for the prohibition have changed markedly over the past century, it also affords an example of how courts contend with uncertainty, science, custom, and so-called common sense as they seek approaches that will not simply possess the air of consistency and predictability but will sound such a note of familiarity that the law's own legitimacy will not be jeopardized. And as same-sex marriage has become legal, what reasons shall pass muster for forbidding relations between, say, step-siblings? Indeed, now that a sperm donor may foster any number of children, what reason will be offered for withholding from individuals knowledge that they may, in fact, be siblings? As practices and rationales shift, incest thus offers itself as an intriguing test case for the relation of culture to biology, social roles, and the law.

★ ★ ★

In 1997, a Wisconsin appellate court upheld the conviction of a brother and sister who had been sentenced to 8 and 5 years' imprisonment respectively on charges of felony incest. Allen and Patricia Muth had been separated as infants, Patricia having been reunited with her biological parents at the age of 18. The siblings, aged 45 and 30 when tried, had at least three children together (the father of a fourth child possibly being that of another man). The case went forward notwithstanding that felony incest is "a crime rarely prosecuted in Wisconsin against consenting adults" (Murphy 1998). Moreover, under a law unique to the state the couple was also deprived of their parental rights solely for having had children through an incestuous relationship. In sentencing them, the trial judge said the punishment was the only way to keep them apart and prevent them from having sex, notwithstanding the fact that "[t]he woman, her voice breaking, pleaded: 'I just want to have a chance to be out there. I'd separate from my brother'."[2]

In 2012 the European Court of Human Rights (ECHR) upheld the conviction by a German court in a similar case. Patrick Stuebing, who was born in 1976 and placed in a children's home at age three before being adopted, did not meet his sister, Sarah Karoleski, until 2000, after their biological mother had died. They began a relationship that resulted in four children, two of whom are mentally and physically disabled, while a third required a heart transplant. The couple insisted that their relationship was no different from any other bond of love, that they had a right to their own family form, and that the state's claim that resultant children would be disabled was discriminatory since others who might produce such offspring are not barred from marriage. Noting that most member states of the European Union ban such marriages, the European Court of Human Rights (ECHR) upheld Stuebing's prison sentence as well as the lower court's decision not to punish the sister who, it said, has a personality disorder that rendered her "only partially liable" for her actions. "The main basis for punishment for the incest, the ECHR said, was 'the protection of marriage and the family' because it blurs family roles. It also noted 'the risk of significant damage' to children born of such a relationship" (Agence France-Presse 2012). Two years after the Steubing decision the highest court in New York State, in *Nguyen v. Holder*, held that the marriage between a 24-year-old Vietnamese-born naturalized American and his 19-year-old immigrant bride did not violate the state's incest statute even though the man's wife is the daughter of his own half-sister. While marriage between a full uncle and niece is prohibited in New York, the court ruled that the risk of any genetic defects for this couple was no greater than those involving first cousins, who are permitted to marry. Indeed, as one of the judges noted, until 1893 a marriage between a full uncle and niece was allowed in the state. He continued: "We are not geneticists, and the record and the briefs in this case do not contain any scientific analysis; but neither party disputes the intuitively correct-seeming conclusion that the genetic risk in a half-uncle, half-niece relationship is half what it would be if the parties were related by the full blood." While concurring in the decision a second judge suggested that the state legislature might wish to revisit the statute:

> From a public policy perspective, there may be other important concerns. Such relationships could implicate one of the purposes underlying incest laws, i.e., 'maintaining the stability of the family hierarchy by protecting young family members from exploitation by older family members in positions of authority, and by reducing competition and jealous friction among family members' (Benton v State, 265 Ga 648, 650, 461 SE2d 202, 205 [1995, Sears, J., concurring]). Similar intra familial concerns may arise regardless of whether the uncle or aunt in the marriage is of whole or half blood in relation to the niece or nephew. The issue of unequal stature in a family or cultural structure may not be implicated in this case but certainly could exist in other contexts, and a number of states have retained statutory prohibitions involving such marriages.

Courts faced with incest cases must confront not only their own legal histories but a tangled course of cultural and scientific assumptions. However, states may choose to legislate on the matter, the sheer variation in incest prohibitions over the course of time, as well as within and across cultures, is enormous. For example, in the Arab world it is incest to marry or have sex with someone who was nursed by the same wet-nurse, the usual term employed being 'milk-siblings.' (Interestingly, Saddam Hussein, in addition to his other illegal acts, was married to just such a milk-sibling.) A number of courts review the religious and historical foundations of their laws when addressing such cases.[3] Thus, the change in the New York law mentioned by the judge in the preceding case may, as he went on to speculate, have been influenced by early developments in eugenics, or it may also have been influenced by the late nineteenth century emphasis on the nuclear family as the focus of procreation and the desire to assimilate immigrants whose patterns of marriage were frowned upon by the majority legislators and their constituents.[4] Throughout the century, familial patterns were changing. Until the early twentieth century, for example, marriage to the sister of one's wife was regarded as incest. The allure of the sister-in-law, particularly if the elder daughter had to be married off first, was regarded as so menacing to society that categorizing the relationship as incest applied even if the sister-wife was deceased.[5] Indeed, the threat of chaos posed by the temptation of the younger sister-in-law was so pervasive that one version of the last stanza of the famous ballad "My Darling Clementine" ended: "So I kissed her little sister/ and forgot my Clementine!" Other historical examples have long been claimed as indicative of the dangers of incest. Thus, brother-sister marriage in ancient Egypt was taken as the archetype of royal decadence even though the practice turns out to have involved a wider range of that society.[6] Similarly, the first cousin marriages of such figures as Charles Darwin, Edgar Allan Poe, H. G. Wells, Frances Galton, and Jesse James were the subject of differential acceptance as incest boundaries altered in the light of changing social and scientific trends.[7]

At present, too, the range of variation in approaches to incest is seldom fully appreciated. In the United States, neighboring states may have very different rules. For example, states are almost equally divided between those allowing first cousin marriage and those barring it, though only a small handful of states punishes such cousins for having sexual relations with one another or co-habiting. Some commenters suggest that many state statutes obscure the difference between the presence and absence of consent when incest is involved (Note 2006). In terms of penalties, Rhode Island has repealed its criminal incest statute and only criminalizes incestuous marriage, Ohio "targets only parental figures" in its criminal incest statute, and New Jersey does not apply any penalties when both parties are 18 years of age or older.[8] China, Israel, the Ivory Coast, the Netherlands, Russia, Spain, France, Turkey, Japan, and Brazil are among the countries that allow consensual sex between related adults, while others (Slovenia, Sweden) have eliminated criminal penalties for incest in part to remove the stigma of that term from innocent victims while retaining other laws for the protection of minors. A government-appointed ethics committee in Germany has also recommended dropping criminal charges for incest, except those relationships involving a parent and child, arguing that such laws are an unacceptable intrusion on the right of sexual self-determination. "Criminal law is not the appropriate means to preserve a social taboo," the German Ethics Council said: "The fundamental right of adult siblings to sexual self-determination is to be weighed more heavily than the abstract idea of protection of the family."[9] On the other hand, an Australian judge who suggested abolition of incest penalties was roundly excoriated by the crown prosecutor who labeled the judge's remarks "completely disgraceful" (Pearlman 2014).

New technologies have raised additional problems. A single sperm donor may sire literally hundreds of children who may not know they are related (Mroz 2011; see also the 2013 film "Delivery Man"). Some countries (e.g., Britain, France, Sweden) limit the number of children a sperm donor can father, while private donor sibling registries can show if one shares a donor with other half-siblings or indicate to a donor how many children he has fathered. Given rates of divorce and remarriage (to say nothing of co-habitation), the issues surrounding step-siblings' sexual relations and marriage have exercised the attention of commenters and courts in various countries. For example, in 1984 a Church of England panel recommended that step-parents and their step-children, as well as step-siblings, be allowed to marry as a way of discouraging secret sexual relationships. The majority report stated, "[T]he prohibition is based simply on tradition and cannot now be justified on any logical, rational or practical ground" (Anonymous 1984). In fact, current UK law permits marriage between adopted siblings, between a step-child and an unrelated adopted brother or sister, but not with an adopted son or daughter. At the same time a 2004 revision of the United Kingdom's Sexual Offenses Act toughened penalties and revised incest offences to cover not just blood relatives but also foster and adoptive parents and live-in partners. By comparison, in the Netherlands special permission must be obtained to marry one's adoptive sibling, while in Sweden half-siblings may marry only with government approval. Since same-sex marriage was recognized in 2015 by the U.S. Supreme Court in *Obergefell v. Hodges* the question arises whether the same grounds for its constitutional support should not bar government interference in any form of adult marriage. Similarly, decisions striking down sodomy laws have been cited as a basis for permitting sexual relations regardless of any relatedness between the consenting adults. Indeed, the support of a very broad political spectrum in favor of same-sex marriage in the United States may be based in large part on the claim that one's private life is simply not the business of the government, while opponents see a slippery slope ending in polygamy and the legalization of incest. While the U.S. Supreme Court's opinion recognizing same-sex marriage, like the explicit statements of lower appellate courts, indicates that polygamy is a distinguishable issue, it remains arguable whether the logic of the same-sex cases really does constitute an adequate basis for disallowing either polygamy or sexual relations between consenting adult relatives.[10]

As practices and rationales have changed over time, the question then arises as to what theories may account for the incest prohibition. It will be useful to take each of these theories in turn to see how courts have addressed them and what, if any, validity they still possess. It in no way diminishes the seriousness of the issue if each is considered under a somewhat droll heading.

"The kids will look weird"

Biological theories that profess to account for the incest taboo come in a variety of forms, but they share the claim that the offspring of close relatives have a significant chance of suffering physical or mental problems. Prior to the science of genetics approaches to the incest taboo were based on little more than a metaphorical image of 'bad blood' or observations from barnyard experiments gone amiss. In fact, a great many scientists and anthropologists argued well into the twentieth century that incest lacked any biological rationale.[11] Although people had long bred animals closely in order to produce desired qualities, it was commonly thought that where humans were concerned such close matching almost always involved a barrier—especially parent/child and brother/sister—beyond which one could not go without risk of disaster. Far from resolving the matter, modern genetics has, in some respects, actually muddied these waters as science and cultural assumptions may pull in different directions.

Geneticists have indeed established that deleterious effects tend to be carried on recessive genes and that the likelihood of their being expressed increases with close inbreeding.[12] But the science does not point in only one direction. If the effects are indeed maladaptive then inbreeding should lead to their elimination. Some studies show that frequent first cousin unions do significantly increase the expression of adverse genetic results, but even here, the studies are widely variant in their statistics and conclusions.[13] It is also true that some cultures practice preferential marriage to a close cousin believing that such unions reduce domestic conflict and maintain property within the kin group. But for sustained biological harm to affect a significant proportion of the population, it is all but indispensable that such unions take place over the course of a number of generations: The occasional combination only raises the percentage of deleterious outcomes a few points. In addition, people would have to regard such outcomes as undesirable and they would have to trace causality to biological relatedness. Most animal studies that suggest a natural aversion to close inbreeding either assume that one can extrapolate to humans from non-human populations or that evolution has eliminated those who bred too closely.[14] Neither of these propositions has been established to the level of scientific acceptability. The result is that a singularly biological basis for the incest taboo is at best unproven. And when it comes to claims about the sources, whether social or biological, of the incest taboo William Durham (2005: 135) is almost certainly correct when he says, "I question whether we'll ever, in the foreseeable future, know enough to fairly test alternative hypotheses about [the taboo's] origin."

"Familiarity breeds contempt"

An alternative set of theories suggests that some combination of biology and culture is working to produce a universal, if somewhat variably structured, avoidance taboo. The version associated with Sigmund Freud holds that males want to have sexual access to their mothers and sisters, jealousy of the father resulting in the combination of guilt and anger that is the price society and the individual pay for collective avoidance and personal repression of such desires. In his variation on Freud's theme, Robin Fox suggests that adult males in the primal horde, seeking to control the sexual choices of the younger males, actually wind up in league with the youngsters by accepting the terms of competition, a competition that was further encouraged by the females. The evolutionary result was not only an increase in the brain's ability to handle such relations but selective pressures that pushed younger males away from sexual access to closely related females and towards greater calculation of the advantages and disadvantages of alternative mates.[15] Each of these theories was, to a considerable extent, built on the ideas of the Finnish anthropologist, Edward Westermarck.

Westermarck's version of this class of explanations is often misconstrued as simply holding that there is some innate aversion to sex with parents or siblings—what my students, contemplating such a relationship with a parent or sibling, invariably refer to as the 'yuck' factor. But Westermarck was actually arguing that the aversion results primarily from being raised in close proximity to such relatives, not because of some 'hard wired' biological repulsion. After all, siblings raised apart and never knowing that they are related do not experience automatic disgust if they accidentally encounter one another sexually as adults.[16] Here the proponents usually point to studies of the classic Israeli kibbutz and the occasional Taiwanese practice of raising children together who are intended in marriage to one another. In the former study, it has been shown that it is exceedingly rare for two individuals to have sex or get married who were raised separated from their natal parents but with one another in the children's house of a kibbutz.[17] In Taiwan, children pledged to one another in marriage and then raised together in the same household are also said to show distinct signs of aversion when they grow to sexual and marital maturity.[18] While other factors than being raised together may affect these outcomes, the argument is that biology and culture interact such that it is the former that makes sex close to home unattractive while it is the particular culture that makes the adverse results of close inbreeding less likely to occur by, for example, creating the co-residential circumstances within which children learn to think of such alliances as naturally repugnant.[19] Different versions of these theories stress different elements, but they all share the assertion that biology plays an indispensable, if imprecisely determinable, role along with culture in the origin and expression of incest avoidance and taboos.

"Marry out or die out"

A third approach tends to play down the biological and to play up the cultural in a very particular way. It suggests that in the development of our species and the continuing well-being of individual communities it is necessary for alliances to be built with groups beyond a narrow kin-based set of individuals. If, for example, trade across ecological zones is facilitated by marriage then one may be able to vary and hedge one's reliance beyond a single productive area; if your grandchildren are resident among an outsider group into whom your children have married you are presumably less likely to go to war with that group; and if your gene pool is more mixed, the chances of your descendants having fewer physical or mental problems may be more readily perceived. While a corollary of the theory holds that there may, among groups of hunter-gatherers in particular, be an insufficient number of mates of the right age and gender to go around—thus prompting a simple demographic need to seek mates outside of the immediate kin group—the primary emphasis in this set of theories is on the sociological advantages of forming external alliances. The theory has a long history but is, in modern times, most often associated with the French structuralist Claude Lévi-Strauss, who wrote:

> It will never be sufficiently emphasized that, if social organization had a beginning, that could only have consisted in the incest prohibition. ... [T]he ultimate explanation is probably that mankind has understood very early that, in order to free itself from a wild struggle for existence, it was confronted with the very simple choice of 'either marrying-out or being

killed-out.' The alternative was between biological families living in juxtaposition and endeavoring to remain closed, self-perpetuating units, over-ridden by their fears, hatreds, and ignorances, and the systematic establishment, through the incest prohibition, of links of intermarriage between them, thus succeeding to build, out of the artificial bonds of affinity, a true human society, despite, and even in contradiction with, the isolating influence of consanguinity.[20]

Marriage as alliance has its advantages, but it is not the only—and not necessarily the best—vehicle for creating a wide range of affiliations. Moreover, it is unclear why the push of an incest taboo is more powerful than the pull of intergroup trade, political attachment, or ecological hedging. Combining alliance theory with a Freudian or Westermarckian theory can offer a rationale for the push but retains the same caveats that accompany each of those theories. And it is difficult to see alliance theory as a rationale for modern incest prohibitions in complex and open-ended societies.

"I'm my own grandpa"[21]

Role confusion is another possible basis for the incest taboo. If a man marries his father's brother's daughter in a patrilineal system, it may be possible to keep property within the lineage if the husband dies or divorces his wife. However, some solution must be available when, during the course of the marriage, husband and wife disagree, for the wife's father is simultaneously the husband's paternal uncle to whom he should probably defer and his father-in-law whose interference he might well regard as undermining his authority as the head of his own household. Role confusion may, therefore, be an inherent problem when close kin interbreed and intermarry. But that does not mean that it is an insoluble problem. Many societies have institutionalized mechanisms that address the issue, such as physical avoidance or joking patterns whereby the potentially disruptive conflict of roles is finessed by spatial separation, compartmentalized roles, social opprobrium, or licensed outlets for antipathy. Nevertheless, it is not unreasonable to wish to avoid the risk of such confusion, particularly where mechanisms are not in place to offer a set solution.

A corollary to the role confusion theory of incest avoidance is often stated rather vaguely as preserving 'family integrity.' An interesting test of this concept is posed by the practice of adopting an adult lover as a way of immunizing some of one's assets from taxation or safeguarding the lover from a contest over the benefactor's estate. The question that can then arise is whether continued sexual relations with the adopted individual constitute incest. One law professor, noting that it cannot be about eugenics or instinctual repulsion, concludes: "Generally, society has been confused on these issues throughout history and into the present day. Or are we asking the wrong question altogether? Should the inquiry instead be case-by-case whether a true parent-child relationship exists rather than distinguishing between blood or adoption?" (Turnipseed 2012). The result of litigation in this domain may affect whether it is the legal tie or the actual social relationship that should be key to the definition of incest.

"All in the family"

Anthropologist Margaret Mead offered an intriguing alternative reason for the maintenance of the incest taboo. She argued that there should be a zone within which actions that might otherwise carry overtones of sexuality should be free from such implications. Thus, wandering around the house partially clothed or cuddling in a housemate's lap should be treated as actions of intimacy devoid of sexual implication. To maintain the incest bar while simultaneously retaining these gestures of affection and familiarity is, she argued, vital to psychological development and well-being. Here, the emphasis comes down on the household as the primary unit of consideration, rather than kinship or possibly even gender. The rationale could, of course, be extended to other relationships. In ancient China teacher-student sex or marriage was regarded as incest, and many people in our own culture feel uncomfortable at the thought of a sexual relation between a teacher and student who are both consenting adults, notwithstanding the fact that we do not bar the relationship altogether. Mary Case (2009) even wonders whether an incest taboo in the workplace might not be a partial approach to issues of sexual harassment, and one could imagine other spaces where joking or gestures might undergo reinterpretation if actual sex carried the stigma of incest.

The idea that one could create such additional incest boundaries may seem unlikely: If they come into existence shouldn't they somehow appear 'naturally'? But this, of course, is only one example of a tendency to imagine that incest must derive from nature rather than from interaction with, if not origination in, cultural orientations. Take the example of the incest taboo in colleges. The terminology and boundaries vary. It may be referred to as *dormcest* or *hallcest*, but in each instance students maintain that sexual relations between those within the bounded domain are to be avoided—indeed that others living within this zone should use the pressures of gossip, scandal, and avoidance to insure its prohibition. The reason offered is almost always the same: If the couple later has difficulties, the neighbor/friend does not want to have to take sides and thus risk ongoing disruption or losing the friendship of one or both of the parties.[22] Pressures to have sex outside of other boundaries may partake of a similar rationale. At my own university, students refer to *debatecest*, by which they indicate that members of the debate team should not be sexually involved since an opponent on one occasion may be a partner on another and the breakup of a couple sexually involved may be disruptive of the entire team's prospects. By contrast, members of the rowing teams say there are pressured to 'date' exclusively other rowers because the shells are separated by gender, that pressures from fellow rowers can actually benefit the relationship through any rocky moments, and that since the members of the couple operate in separate boats there will be no risk to team cooperation should they break up. Clearly, in each of these instances no biological aversion is at work, and any reason for taboos would be purely sociological.

★ ★ ★

Given the alternative theories about incest—some of which claim exclusive explanatory power, others that easily combine with alternatives—how have courts approached the issue in recent times? Biology continues to figure in some, though a diminishing, number of instances. This may, of course, be a function of the cases presented. Parent-child cases are more likely to raise questions of abuse than sexual freedom while often-outdated statutes may not speak to current reproductive technologies or residential arrangements. But even here, some relationships many thought beyond alteration are being challenged. When Columbia University Professor David Epstein began a consensual sexual relationship with his 24-year-old daughter, he was charged with third degree criminal incest. Although he later pleaded guilty to a misdemeanor, the incident precipitated widely divergent viewpoints.[23] Many commenters argued that consenting adult sex is none of the state's business: If recent legal decisions have eliminated criminal statutes for sodomy and same-sex marriage has now gained legal recognition, then relatedness should be irrelevant to consensual adult sex.[24] Cases were cited where a vasectomy precluded any biological implications yet the relationship was still penalized, a result that would appear to vitiate the biological argument altogether.[25] Some opponents abandoned biology as an explanation, standing their ground instead on a claim of 'family integrity.' Already in 1954, in the case of *In Re Enderle* (1954: 120), a Pennsylvania court, overruling the county clerk's refusal to issue a marriage license to first cousins by adoption, articulated the reasons characteristic of that period, holding that:

> The purpose of the legislature in prohibiting marriages within certain degrees of consanguinity and affinity is at least threefold: (1) To maintain the Divine Law forbidding the marriage of close relatives; (2) for eugenic reasons, to preserve and strengthen the general racial and physical qualities of its citizens by preventing inbreeding, and (3) to maintain the sanctity of the home and prevent the disastrous consequences of competition for sexual companionship between members of the same household or family.

Thus the court, while refusing to create a fictive biological tie through the adoption of cousins, was still using the language of race, biology, and jealousy in its opinion. The court in *Enderle* had said it was not deciding an instance in which the parties might be more closely related than cousins. But when, in 1977, another Pennsylvania court was in fact confronted with a case involving unrelated individuals who became siblings through the adoption by his step-mother of the 16-year-old boy, the emphasis on family ties was given prominence: "An important consideration in this case is the integrity of the family which the law has a duty to protect. To authorize and encourage marriages of brothers and sisters by adoption would undermine the fabric of family life" (*Marriage of MEW and MLB* 1977: 59). The majority stressed that, "While the applicants did not live and grow up together in the same household from early childhood, they have for at least part of their lives, lived together as brother and sister in the family residence of their respective parents" (*Id.*). However, the dissenting judge pointed out that, "This is not a case where a male infant and a female infant were adopted and raised to maturity by the adopting parents in the same household" (*Id.*: 62). In fact they lived together only a couple of months, and both sides had stipulated that "as children, the applicants grew up separately and apart from one another."[26]

What is curious in this last case is that, absent any biological basis for refusing the marriage license, the majority extended the sociological basis for including the union within the terms of the state incest statute by finding that any co-residence—or is it any use of words like 'brother' and 'sister'?—should trigger a bar to the union. Even the separate concurring opinion in the case argued that adoption creates the legal equivalent of a blood bond and that one should not be able to pick and choose among the benefits and obligations of the adoption tie. In short, it is clear that, absent a decisive theory on the subject, the Pennsylvania court at this moment in time was shifting conceptual categories while still holding on to the cultural notion that somehow being a brother and sister does not feel like it belongs in the same category as marriage. Conceptual boundaries are also tested in those instances in which one partner in an adult gay couple has adopted the other prior to the legalization of same-sex marriage and now the couple wishes to dissolve the adoption and be wed (see, Green 2015; Wang 2015).

The ground was also being cut out from under those who sought justification for an incest prohibition based on its claimed universality. Courts may not have been influenced by those anthropologists who asserted that there is no universal taboo, but it is true that throughout the latter half of the twentieth century many scholars were moving away from universals and towards more emphasis on the practices of particular cultures.[27] Courts had long emphasized the history and traditions of various practices, and incest prohibitions were often viewed in this light. But as arguments of biology and state power began to be worn down in the sodomy and same-sex cases, the courts turned increasingly to arguments about family integrity.

Consider, for example, a 1999 case dealing with sex between an uncle and niece: "The indictment charged and it is not disputed that the appellant was involved in an incestuous relationship with her paternal uncle. The appellant does not deny this relationship. We are able to glean from the sparse record before us that the incestuous relationship began while the appellant was still a minor and continued into her majority. Her uncle was in his mid-thirties when the relationship began. No children were born as a result of this relationship. The appellant's brief indicates that she suffers from various psychological disorders and was

18 years old when charged with the offense" (*Smith v. State of Tennessee*, note 1). The court then framed the issue in the following way:

> The taboo against incest has been a consistent and almost universal tradition with recorded proscriptions against incest existing as early as 1750 B.C.[10] The incest taboo has been characterized as one of the most important human cultural developments and is found in some form in all societies. Being primarily cultural in origin, the taboo is neither instinctual nor biological and has little to do with actual blood ties.[11] See Benton v. State, 265 Ga. 648, 461 S.E.2d 202, 205 (1995) (Sears, J., concurring). Anthropologists and sociologists claim the significance of the incest taboo is twofold: (1) the restriction forces family members to go outside their families to find sexual partners, requiring people to pursue relationships outside family boundaries that help form important economic and political alliances, and (2) to maintain the stability of the family hierarchy by protecting young family members from exploitation by older family members in positions of authority and by reducing competition and jealous friction among family members.

The court went on to trace the adoption by the state of the historic approach of the common law from its development in England to its current incarnation in the courts of Tennessee. Building on earlier U.S. Supreme Court precedent, the judges argued that there is no fundamental right to any sexual relationship, the criteria for discerning a fundamental right being based in no small part on whether such a practice does indeed derive from the 'traditions of our people.' The court then concluded:

> Specific to our concern, Tennessee has traditionally recognized the proscription against incest as a punishable offense.... There is nothing to suggest a movement away from the historical treatment of incest; Tennessee, as other states, continues to condemn it as a grave public wrong.
>
> To conclude that there exists a "fundamental right" to engage in an incestuous relationship, this court would be called upon to contradict centuries of legal doctrine and practice; which this court declines to do. See, e.g., Glucksberg, 521 U.S. at 723–24, 117 S.Ct. at 2269; Jackman v. Rosenbaum, 260 U.S. 22, 31, 43 S.Ct. 9, 9–10, 67 L.Ed. 107 (1922) ("If a thing has been practiced for two hundred years by common consent, it will need a strong case for the Fourteenth Amendment to affect it."). The evidence is plain; the incest taboo is deeply rooted in Anglo-American history and traditions.
>
> Although the individual has a right to govern the course of his life, society, also, has its interests....The balance to be achieved is the toleration of the maximum individual freedom that is consistent with the integrity of society. The law must protect the institutions and the community of ideas, political and moral, without which people cannot live together....

The prohibition against incest is aimed at the protection of children and of the family unit....Society is concerned with the integrity of the family... because society cannot function in an orderly manner when age distinctions, generations, sentiments, and roles in families are in conflict.... The state has a legitimate and rationally based objective in prohibiting sexual relations between those related within the proscribed degrees of kinship to promote domestic peace and purity. We conclude that the state, in the exercise of its legislative function, may legitimately proscribe against acts which threaten public order and decency, including prohibitions against interfamilial sexual relations.... Our pronouncements of these principles are consistent with and not contrary to deeply rooted traditions. (Smith v. State of Tennessee, at 514)

Leaving aside the curious reference to "purity"—which is commonly replaced with the word "sanctity" or "integrity" in other opinions—the Tennessee court clearly moved towards a sociological theory of incest. This means that as society changes, the theory may have to permit formerly proscribed practices or the choice of theories will have to change. As we shall see in the U.S. Supreme Court's uses of natural law in the next chapter, it is unclear when a tradition applies and when it changes. Yet courts can render their decisions connected to their culture by such a concept and appear to be drawing from society's own legitimization force in doing so. As in many other areas we have been considering, cultural assumptions operate to fill the interstices as courts, constantly addressing issues the legislature has not considered, seek to make their decisions appear at once timeless and consistent with the age. Call it tradition or integrity or even purity, the law relies on cultural propositions even when it is trying to build an internal consistency to the law that seems to rely predominantly on the rules of logic and precedent. In that two-pronged process lies much of the willingness of the populace to follow its decisions. Throw culture out the door and it will indeed come flying back in through the window—whether in the approach to issues of incest or, as we shall continue to see, many other domains of the law.[28]

Notes

1 For the actual case of twins separated at birth who only discovered their relationship after marriage, see Baron (2008).
2 Anonymous (1997). In a case brought in the interests of Muth's daughter, the Wisconsin appellate court held the statute terminating parental rights of an incestuous couple constitutional (*In re Tiffany Nicole M.*). Allen Muth, from his prison cell, then appealed for a writ of habeas corpus in federal court claiming the incest statute was inconsistent with the U.S. Supreme Court's decision in *Lawrence v. Texas* barring a state from criminalizing homosexual relations. The federal court of appeals denied his claim and upheld the state incest statute as constitutional (*Muth v. Frank*). See also Hammer (2007) (court in *Muth* was wrong to disallow consensual adult sex between close relatives).

3 See, e.g., *State v. Lowe.*

4 On changing family structures, procreation, and history of first cousin marriage, see Ottenheimer (1996: 7).

5 See, Twitchell (1987); Frew (2012).

6 See Frandsen (2009).

7 See Kuper (2009) and Corbett (2008). More extreme was the notorious affair of George Gordon, Lord Byron with his half-sister: see Twitchell: 4–6.

8 Ohio and New Jersey are the only states that include in their "Sexual Battery" and "Sexual Assault" laws (their respective statutes that concern incest) those *in loco parentis* to a forbidden partner. Whether this would include a teacher is unclear, no cases on point having been found. Ohio Rev. Code Ann. § 2907.03(5); N.J. Stat. Ann. 2C: 14-2 (2013).

9 A press release summarizing the ethics committee report can be found at www. ethikrat.org/press/press-releases/2014/press-release-08-2014 (accessed January 5, 2017). The full report in German can be accessed at http://www.ethikrat.org/dateien/pdf/stellungnahme-inzestverbot.pdf (accessed January 5, 2017). Opposition to the proposal, including that of Chancellor Angela Merkel, has thus far blocked acceptance of the recommendation.

10 Among the more interesting recent legal decisions bearing on polygamy are: *Baskin v. Bogan, Bostic v. Rainey,* and *Brown v. Buhman.* An earlier statement worth noting is *In re State of Utah* (Henriod, J. concurring).

11 See, e.g., Malinowski (1927: 243) ("[B]iologists are in agreement that there is no detrimental effect produced upon the species by incestuous unions."); White (1948: 417) ("Inbreeding as such does not cause degeneration; the testimony of biologists is conclusive on this point.").

12 For studies of a number of countries, mainly Arab, where the rates of close-kin inbreeding are comparatively high, see Teebi (1994), Modell and Darr (2002), and Cherkaoui (2009).

13 A 2002 study by a National Society of Genetic Counselors task force found that cousin couples were only 1.7–2.8 percent more likely than non-related couples to have a child with a significant genetic or birth defect. Bennett (2002: 115). See also the studies discussed at Twitchell (1987: 15). Other studies indicate that excess morbidity due to first cousin unions may range anywhere from 4 to 20 percent (Bittles 2005: 53). Rates of first cousin marriage vary enormously among cultures that permit or encourage such unions: Rates as high as 33 percent of all marriages have been reported in a Mennonite community of Kansas and 75% among Pakistanis living in Bradford, UK (Anonymous 2005).

14 *Compare* Bateson (2005), and Bittles (2005: 38–60), *with* Fessler (2004) and Lieberman (2007: 730) ("The tight mesh between theoretical expectations and empirical tests provides strong support for the hypothesis that humans have a system designed by selection to detect genetic relatedness.") This latter study claims that watching one's mother care for a younger sibling or the amount of time spent in co-residence triggers an instinct of aversion. On extrapolating to humans from animal studies, see the discussion of animal experiments that actually show preference for first cousin mates in Gould (1993: 378–80).

15 Fox (1980). See also, David Aberle, et al. (1963).

16 There are, however, those who claim that if related persons meet after long separation there is indeed a "genetic sexual attraction (GSA)" that draws them to one another. This alleged biological attraction has even been asserted as a defense in some criminal incest cases and as a basis for needed legislative changes. The 'theory,' first promulgated by a non-scientist advocate in the 1980s, has received little scholarly support, though some behavioral psychologists (e.g., Fessler 2004) claim to have found it in posing hypotheticals to test subjects.

17 See, Sepher (1971); Talmon (1965); Spiro (1969: 326–35, 347–50).
18 See, Wolf (1995). Instances in which the young girl is brought into the home of the boy are, however, very rare: see Wolf (1980).
19 Examples of work in this vein, besides the various studies by Arthur P. Wolf, include Turner (2005).
20 Lévi-Strauss (1960: 278). For an argument in this same mode, see Héritier (1999).
21 The song written by Dwight B. Latham and Moe Jaffe's called 'I Am My Own Grandpa' was based on a true story: "There was a widow and her daughter-in-law, and a man and his son. The widow married the son, and the daughter the old man; the widow was, therefore, mother to her husband's father, consequently grandmother to her own husband. They had a son, to whom she was great-grandmother; now, as the son of a great-grandmother must be either a grandfather or great-uncle, this boy was therefore his own grandfather" (*The Genealogue*, September 22, 2006, relying on a source from 1822). www.genealogue.com/2006/09/someone-really-was-his-own-grandpa.html (accessed January 5, 2017).
22 See, e.g., Peitzman (2015).
23 See, Jacoby (1998). See also, Anonymous (1980); Tsouli-Reay (2015).
24 But see, Turnipseed (2009).
25 See, Twitchell (1987: 1–3) for the case of siblings separated as children who only learned they were siblings later on and were punished even though the male had a vasectomy.
26 *Marriage of MEW and MLB* (1977: 52). A close case concerns the Na, a Tibetan Buddhist people, discussed in greater detail above in chapter four. While possessing a definite concept of incest they have no marriage, no nuclear families, and no recognition of paternity, such that a man might accidentally sleep with his daughter. Hua (2008). See also the review of Hua's book by Geertz (2001).
27 See, e.g., Needham (1971: 25) ("I conclude that 'incest' is a mistaken sociological concept and not a universal."); Schneider (1976: 168) (the incest taboo is "a mistaken sociological concept").
28 For further discussion of the inadequacy of prevailing theories, see Twitchell (1987: 243–59).

References

Aberle, David et al. 1963, "The Incest Taboo and the Mating Patterns of Animals," *American Anthropologist*, vol. 65, no. 2, pp. 253–65.
Agence France-Presse 2012, "German Loses Human Rights Appeal over Incestuous Relationship with Sister," *Telegraph* [London], April 12. www.telegraph.co.uk/news/worldnews/europe/germany/9200876/German-loses-Human-Rights-appeal-over-incestuous-relationship-with-sister.html (accessed January 5, 2017).
Anonymous 1980, "Attacking the Last Taboo: Researchers are Lobbying against the Ban on Incest," *Time*, April 14, p. 72.
Anonymous 1984, "Allow Step-parents, Children to Marry, Church Panel Says," *Chicago Tribune*, May 31, p. 12.
Anonymous 1997, "Incestuous Wisconsin Pair Sent to Prison," *The Atlanta Journal and Constitution*, November 12, p. 3.
Anonymous 2005, "Labour MOP Calls for End to Cousin Marriage following Newsnight Investigation," bbc.co.uk, November 16.
Barton, Fiona 2008, "Shock for the Married Couple Who Discovered They are Twins Separated at Birth," *Daily Mail*, January 11.

Bateson, Patrick 2005, "Inbreeding Avoidance and Incest Taboos,' in Arthur P. Wolf and William H. Durham, eds., *Inbreeding, Incest, and the Incest Taboo: The State of Knowledge at the Turn of the Century*, Stanford: Stanford University Press, pp. 24–37.

Bennett, Robin, et al. 2002, "Genetic Counseling and Screening of Consanguineous Couples and Their Offspring: Recommendations of the National Society of Genetic Counselors," *Journal of Genetic Counseling*, vol. 11, no. 2 (April), pp. 97–119.

Bittles, Alan H. 2005, "Genetic Aspects of Inbreeding and Incest," in Arthur P. Wolf and William H. Durham, eds., *Inbreeding, Incest, and the Incest Taboo: The State of Knowledge at the Turn of the Century*, Stanford: Stanford University Press, pp. 38–60.

Case, Mary Anne 2009, "A Few Words in Favor of Cultivating an Incest Taboo in the Workplace," *Vermont Law Review*, vol. 33, pp. 551–58.

Cherkaoui, I., et al., 2009, "Consanguineous Marriages in Morocco and the Consequence for the Incidence of Autosomal Recessive Disorders," *Journal of Biosocial Science*, vol. 41, pp. 575–81.

Corbett, Mary Jean 2008, *Family Likeness: Sex, Marriage, and Incest from Jane Austen to Virginia Woolf*, Ithaca, NY: Cornell University Press.

Durham, William H. 2005, "Assessing the Gaps in Westermarck's Theory," in Arthur P. Wolf and William H. Durham, eds., *Inbreeding, Incest, and the Incest Taboo: The State of Knowledge at the Turn of the Century*, Stanford, CA: Stanford University Press, pp. 121–38.

Fessler, Daniel M. T. 2004, "Third-Party Attitudes toward Sibling Incest: Evidence for Westermarck's Hypotheses," *Evolution and Human Behavior*, vol. 25, no. 5 (September), pp. 277–94.

Fox, Robin 1980, *The Red Lamp of Incest*, New York: E. P. Dutton.

Frandsen, John Paul 2009, *Incestuous and Close-Kin Marriage in Ancient Egypt and Persia; An Examination of the Evidence*, Chicago, IL: University of Chicago Press (as distributor for Copenhagen: Museum Tusculanum Press).

Frew, Charlotte 2012, "Marriage to a Deceased Wife's Sister Narrative: A Comparison of Novels," *Law & Literature*, vol. 24, pp. 265–91.

Geertz, Clifford 2001, "The Visit," *New York Review of Books*, October 18.

Gould, Steven Jay 1993, *Eight Little Piggies*, New York: Norton.

Green, Elon 2015, "The Lost History of Gay Adult Adoption," *New York Times*, October 19.

Hammer, Brendan J. 2007, "Tainted Love: What the Seventh Circuit Got Wrong in *Muth v. Frank*," *DePaul Law Review*, vol. 56, pp. 1065.

Héritier, Françoise 1999. *Two Sisters and Their Mother: The Anthropology of Incest*, New York: Zone Books.

Hua, Cai 2008, *A Society without Fathers and Husbands: The Na of China*, New York: Zone Books.

Jacoby, Jeff 1998, "Query for Liberals: Should Incest be a Crime?" *The Boston Globe* (January 27), p. A17.

Kuper, Adam 2009, *Incest and Influence: The Private Life of Bourgeois England*, Cambridge, MA: Harvard University Press.

Lévi-Strauss, Claude 1960, "The Family," in Harry L. Shapiro, ed., *Man, Culture, and Society*, New York: Oxford University Press, pp. 261–85.

Lieberman, Debra, John Tooby, and Leda Cosmides 2007, "The Architecture of Human Kin Detection," *Nature*, vol. 445 (February 15), pp. 727–31.

Malinowski, Bronislaw 1927, *Sex and Repression in Savage Society*, London: Kegan Paul.

Modell, Bernadette and Aamra Darr 2002, "Genetic Counselling and Customary Consanguineous Marriage," *Science and Society, Nature Reviews Genetics,* vol. 3 (March), pp. 225–29.

Mroz, Jacqueline 2011, "One Sperm Donor, 150 Offspring," *New York Times,* September 5.

Murphy, Mary Beth 1998, "Court Upholds Incest Law Terminating Parental Rights," *Milwaukee Journal Sentinel* (January 28), p. 3.

Needham, Rodney 1971, "Remarks on the Analysis of Kinship and Marriage," in his *Rethinking Kinship and Marriage,* London: Tavistock.

Note 2006, "Inbred Obscurity: Improving Incest Laws in the Shadow of the 'Sexual Family'," *Harvard Law Review,* vol. 119, pp. 2464–85.

Ottenheimer, Martin 1996, *Forbidden Relatives: The American Myth of Cousin Marriage,* Champaign, IL: University of Illinois Press.

Pearlman, Jonathan 2014, "Australian Judge Says Incest May No Longer Be a Taboo," *The Telegraph* [London], July 10.

Peitzman, Louis 2015, "Dormcest: The Other Taboo," *The Daily Californian,* August 9. http://archive.dailycal.org/article.php?id=102288 (accessed April 30, 2016).

Schneider, David 1976, "The Meaning of Incest," *Journal of the Polynesian Society,* vol. 85, pp. 149–69.

Sepher, Joseph 1971, "Mate-Selection among Second-Generation Kibbutz Adolescents and Adults: Incest Avoidance and Negative Imprinting," *Archives of Sexual Behavior,* vol. 1, pp. 293–307.

Spiro, Melford E. 1969, *Children of the Kibbutz,* New York: Schocken Books, 1969.

Talmon, Yonina 1965, "The Family in a Revolutionary Movement: The Case of the Kibbutz in Israel," in M. F. Nimkoff, ed., *Contemporary Family Systems,* Boston: Houghton Mifflin, pp. 259–56.

Teebi, Ahmad S. 1994, "Autosomal Recessive Disorders among Arabs: An Overview from Kuwait," *Journal of Medical Genetics,* vol. 31, pp. 224–33.

Tsoulis-Reay, Alexis 2015, "What's It Like to Date Your Dad?' *New York Magazine,* January 15. http://nymag.com/scienceofus/2015/01/what-its-like-to-date-your-dad. html (accessed January 5, 2017).

Turner, Jonathan H. 2005, *Incest: Origins of the Taboo,* London: Routledge.

Turnipseed, Terry L. 2009, "Scalia's Ship of Revulsion has Sailed: Will *Lawrence* Protect Adults who Adopt Lover to Help Ensure Inheritance from Incest Prosecution?" *Hamline Law Review,* vol. 32, pp. 95–132.

——— 2012, "A Florida Millionaire Adopted His 42-Year-Old Girlfriend. Isn't that Incest? Maybe. But It Is Also a Good Way to Shield His Fortune from the Law," *Slate,* February 7. www.slate.com/articles/news_and_politics/jurisprudence/2012/02/should_a_florida_millionaire_be_prosecuted_for_incest_because_he_adopted_his_girlfriend_.html (accessed January 5, 2017).

Twitchell, James B. 1987, *Forbidden Partners: The Incest Taboo in Modern Culture,* New York: Columbia University Press.

Wang, Yanan 2015, "Men Become 'Father and Son'. Now They Want to Get Married but Can't," *New York Times,* November 5.

White, Leslie 1948, "The Definition and Prohibition of Incest," *American Anthropologist,* vol. 50, no. 3, part 1, pp. 416–35.

Wolf, Arthur P. 1980, *Marriage and Adoption in China, 1854–1945,* Stanford, CA: Stanford University Press.

——— 1995, *Sexual Attraction and Childhood Association: A Chinese Brief for Edward Westermarck,* Stanford, CA: Stanford University Press.

Cases cited

Baskin v. Bogan, 12 F. Supp.3d 1144 (S. D. Ind. 2014), *aff'd*. 766 F.3d 648 (7th Cir. 2014).

Bostic v. Rainey, 970 F. Supp.2d 456 (E.D. Va. 2014), *aff'd*. 760 F.3d 352 (4th Cir 2014).

Brown v. Buhman, 947 F. Supp.2d 1170 (D. Utah 2013).

In re Enderle Marriage License, 1 Pa. D. & C.2d 114 (Common Pleas Court, Philadelphia County, PA, Orphans Division 1954).

In re State of Utah, 3 Utah2d 315 (Utah 1955).

In re Tiffany Nicole M., 571 N.W.2d 872 (Wis. Ct. App. 1997).

Lawrence v. Texas, 539 U.S. 558 (2003).

Marriage of MEW and MLB, 4 Pa. D. & C.3d, 51 (Common Pleas Court, Allegheny County, PA, Orphans Division 1977).

Muth v. Frank, 412 F.3d 808 (7th Cir. 2005), *cert. denied* 126 S. Ct. 575 (2005).

Nguyen v. Holder, 2014 NY Slip Opinion 07290, October 28, 2014, Court of Appeals.

Obergefell v. Hodges, 576 U.S. ___ (2015).

Smith v. State of Tennessee, 6 S.W.3d 512 (Tenn. Crim. App. 1999).

State v. Lowe, 112 Ohio St.3d 507, 861 N.E.2d 512 (2007).

6

NATURAL LAW OR LAW NATURALIZED?

Nature v. culture in the U.S. Supreme Court

"Throw nature out the door and it will rush back in through the window."
—*Lucretius*

For as long as people have worried over the ultimate sources upon which a just law may be applied by fallible humankind there has been a belief that the sources of that certainty, however well grasped by reason, must lie outside of us. Whether that belief stems from a deep suspicion about human motives and dispositions, or appears to result in ends we wish for ourselves, the belief in a set of propositions that are not dependent on our own mortal failings has been hard to resist. Sceptics of the propositions on offer, however, have been as numerous as the purveyors of one scheme or another. Told that it is in the law of nature that we render help to our offspring, they counter that teaching independence is the only guarantee of individual or collective success; told that nature says we must do to others as we would to ourselves, they reply that evolution demands nothing more or less than that our selfish genes find a home in a very narrowly bounded group of persons. In the name of natural law and natural rights, we incorporate our own cultural norms, however much they may be couched as universal good.

Natural law has always had a way, then, of creeping into Western legal action. It may do so under other names, only to be challenged at every turn, and evade easy generalization. In this chapter our subject will, however, be rather circumscribed, as we will look at the particular ways in which natural law thinking appears to be present in the judgments of members of the contemporary U.S. Supreme Court. As in all other instances, we cannot enter the minds of judges—who may not know their own—but we can study the terms of their discourse, the passing traces of that which appears to influence them, and in the process, hone in to a degree on yet another way in which cultural concepts, here portrayed as transcending any particular culture, nevertheless inform decisions made by a nation's highest court.

★ ★ ★

In a sense, this chapter might seem to have no raison d'être. After all, 'natural law' has never had a formally legislated place as one of the 'sources' of American law.[1] Scholars and judges may, at times, have argued that their approaches are based on conformity to universal rights, to a supposed state of the cosmos, or to something that could be denominated as 'human nature.' John Adams, for example, could speak of laws as founded "in the frame of human nature, rooted in the constitution of the intellectual and moral world." Indeed, Adams succeeded in convincing the Second Continental Congress to include reference to the laws of nature, though apparently in the same spirit in which Sir Edward Coke and others sought in such laws a check on the powers of King and Parliament. As Corwin notes (1955: 46, 75, and 89; original italics), that this natural law was seen (in Coke's words) as "written with the finger of God in the heart of man," actually resulted in its separation from the divine:

> The receptive and candid attitude evinced toward natural law ideas... made allies of sixteenth-century legalism and seventeenth-century rationalism, and the alliance then struck has always remained, now more, now less vital, in American constitutional law and theory.... The point of view is thoroughly deistic; reason has usurped the place of revelation, and without affront to piety.... [I]n the American *written Constitution*, higher law at last attained a form which made possible the attribution to it of an entirely new sort of validity, the validity of a *statute emanating from the sovereign people.*[2]

In the late nineteenth century the Supreme Court of Massachusetts, in *Commonwealth v. Perry*, could be more direct when it noted that: "A right of privacy in matters purely private is therefore derived from natural law....It may be said to arise out of those laws sometimes characterized as immutable, 'because they are natural, and so just at all times, and in all places, that no authority can either change or abolish them'." Some scholars, like Lon Fuller (1946: 378), could argue that the antidote to personal predilection is for the judge to "discover the natural principles underlying group life," while others have argued that in the consent of the governed, the operation of natural law's most vital aspect is revealed (Wright 1994–95: 466). A number of jurists have avoided direct reference to natural law, while nevertheless expressing their distrust of legislative power, by recourse (in Chancellor Kent's terms) to "a deep and universal sense of justice."[3] There have also been times when judges and scholars have criticized one another for hiding, sometimes in plain sight, their basis for legal decision-making under the guise of natural law. Thus Justice Hugo L. Black rejected Justice Felix Frankfurter's reliance on the 'traditions' of the American people for assessing the constitutionality of legislation as a form of inappropriate dependence on what he called 'natural law' and the overabundance of discretion embraced in that approach (Wiecek 2001). Even if natural law is not mentioned specifically, it may, therefore, be discernible in various forms and through other terms in American legal thought. One would not expect a present-day court to express its moral claims as baldly as did earlier justices. Thus Justice Fields said: "Bigamy and polygamy are crimes by the laws of all civilized and Christian countries....To extend exemption from punishment for such crimes would be to shock the moral judgment of the community" (*Davis v. Beason* 1890: 341). Nor would we expect even the present-day Catholic conservative justices who dissented in the 2010 case of *Christian Legal Society v. Martinez* to adopt the language of one of the briefs that spoke of adultery as "sins against nature." Instead, the terms and bases for natural-law thinking are nowadays both subtle and diverse.

Generally speaking, there are three main types of natural law: (1) one based on the natural sciences or the perceived laws of the human psyche or marketplace, (2) one derived from divine injunction, commonly inscribed in sacred text, and (3) one grounded in a set of discernible moral propositions that are not necessarily linked to a specific religious or scientific doctrine. Variants and admixtures exist for each of these three types. Those based on science may be regarded as 'facts,' to which courts should grant judicial notice or strong evidential weight, facts that are said to be provable by impartial and stringent criteria. For example, the district court judge who heard the challenge to a state statute requiring the teaching of creationism alongside evolution stated that

> the essential characteristics of science are: 1. It is guided by natural law; 2. It has to be explanatory by reference to natural law; 3. It is testable against the empirical world; 4. Its conclusions are tentative, i.e., are not necessarily the final word; and 5. It is falsifiable.
>
> (*McLean v. Arkansas Board of Education 1982: 1267*)[4]

Alternatively, natural-law theorizing may derive from a single religious tradition, thereby its exclusive access to the truth, or from features that are said to inform all faiths, thus avoiding the appearance of favoring any particular religion. Those natural-law orientations based on the concept that morality has become so entrenched and pervasive within a society, commonly regard the natural as readily available through ordinary common sense, sometimes taking as their starting point, Kant's wonder at "the starry sky above and the moral law within."

To some extent, the appeal to each basis of natural law is the same, notwithstanding sharply divergent implications, for, as Stephen Jay Gould put it (1987: 119): "Natural laws are constant in space and time. Philosophers have long recognized that assumptions about the invariance of natural law serve as a necessary warrant for extending inductive inference into an unobservable past," thus allowing proponents of whatever stripe to claim a legitimizing constancy for present-day events. The foundational view in the western world of a universal natural law, drawn from Greek and Roman sources and elaborated in early Christian thought, holds that it represents the mind of God, which is by definition reasonable, and that the gift of reason allows man in turn to grasp these universal principles. Cicero (*On the Republic,* 3.22.33) could thus be cited by the American Founders for the proposition that "true law is right reason in agreement with Nature, it is of universal application, unchanging and everlasting.... There is now and will be forever one law, valid for all peoples and all times."[5] Each form of natural-law thinking, of course, requires some degree of interpretation, although the first type claims its legitimacy on the basis of imagined universality and neutral methods, the second on the basis of divine revelation, and the third on being sufficiently widespread and vital to social stability as to appear self-evident. Garet (1988: 255) offers an example of a view that spans several of these categories:

> The aspiration toward natural law, as I conceive it, has always regarded nature as an educator as well as a promulgator. Natural right has served as a means not of concealing but of exposing the lines of justification; natural command has tried not to suppress but to evoke and express fundamental moral experience. In these respects, natural law represents an attitude toward nature that is as opposed as the scientific attitude, although in different ways and for different reasons, to a view of nature that enlists it in the service of arbitrary and unquestionable commands.

An example of the claim of universality as the basis for substantive propositions of natural law, at least as it relates to one style of conservative American legal thinking, can be found in the writings of Richard A. Epstein (1989, 2005, 2012). His work, however, demonstrates quite vividly what Clifford Geertz once asserted—that claims to universality, when applied to human communities, "are so general as to be without intellectual force or interest, are large banalities lacking either circumstantiality or surprise, precision or revelation, and thus of precious little use....Any sentence that begins, 'All societies have...' is either baseless or banal" (Geertz 2001: 134–35). So, for example, Epstein fails to understand that nuclear families, for example, are not universal, that the variant forms of human social arrangements contradict the level of generalization he employs, and that discerning what is a "low value transaction" is itself a value judgment that is not objectively determinable. (For an example of a kinship pattern that would not fit most universal claims, see the discussion of Hua 2001 in the preceding chapter.) Other professed universals drawn from nature are similarly insupportable: that humans are rational (but see the work of experimental social psychology), that nature favors the preservation of life (but what of the death penalty, heroic acts, etc.), that whatever pertains to the inclination to live in society is good (but what of religious ascetics), or (to cite Aquinas' prime example of natural law) that nature favors parental education of offspring (but what about the Israeli kibbutz, the Spartans, or the Victorian public school). It was examples such as these that led philosopher Richard Wollheim (1967: 451) to conclude: "it is idle to pretend that we can extract a uniform message from nature."[6]

In addition, natural law, in its diverse renderings, often serves as the justification for a particular form of political order, including (but not limited to) the authoritarian and the revolutionary. As Max Weber (1968: 96) noted: "The invocation of natural law has repeatedly been the method by which classes in revolt against the existing order have legitimated their aspirations, in so far as they did not, or could not, base their claims upon positive religious norms or revelation.... [N]atural law has also served to legitimate authoritarian powers of the most diverse types." So, too, natural law has been thought by many post-war Germans to have shown its failure during the Nazi regime just as others argue that the cult of natural rights played a major role in the thinking of the French revolutionaries (Edelstein 2010).

Moreover, each form of natural law may be made explicit by judges or may be cast in terms that, whether intended or not, mask the underlying basis of claimed authority. Thus to some, 'natural' law is either vacuous or nothing more than a veil cast over personal beliefs. Thomas Huxley, for example, argued that the idea that God created life through some form of natural law lacked any "intelligible meaning at all," such an *"explanation* of creation" being no more than a claim that it was an "orderly miracle" (quoted in Desmond and Moore 1991: 414, original italics). Alan Dershowitz (2005) writes: "Nobody today believes in an objective natural law inscribed in the nature of things which, if it were transcribed, would suffice to yield a positive law"(see also, Foriers and Perelman 1968: 26). Others come to similar conclusions from more radical positions. Thus Jean-Paul Sartre argued that "there is no human nature, because there is no God to have a conception of it," while José Ortega y Gasset maintained that *"Man, in a word, has no nature; what he has is—history.* Expressed differently: what nature is to things, history, *res gestae*, is to man" (quoted in Garet 1988: 250–51, original italics).[7] For other commenters, the accepted sources of the law—statutes, constitutions, and case law—are themselves (at least when 'correctly' applied) but the overt expressions of natural law's deeper structure. That the entire matter may, therefore, seem to exist only in the eye of the beholder, or as a way of rationalizing and legitimizing what may not be acknowledged, overtly gives to this subject both its sought-for reason-for-being and its distinctive flavor in particular jurisprudential contexts.

In what follows, I will trace briefly some of the ways in which natural law—whether called that or not—has found its voice at certain moments in American law. Then I want to turn to the present U.S. Supreme Court, and consider in what ways natural law, in its various guises and denominations, might be playing a role in the thinking of the conservative members of the Court and the wider jurisprudential setting within which their thinking appears to be grounded. We will see, too, that myriad cultural assumptions become entangled in different presentations of natural law, and that, as a consequence, an opportunity is presented to excavate down through the terminologies employed, to some of the social propositions upon which contemporary claims for natural law are employed by the Court.

It should be noted at the outset that, until the death of Justice Scalia in February 2016, there were for many years, six Catholics on the Court, four of whom—Scalia, Roberts, Alito, and Thomas—were very conservative (whereas Kennedy and Sotomayor are respectively more moderate and liberal). The relevance of a judge's religion to his or her decisions is obviously a contentious issue. Judge Richard Posner (2016) has indicated that the Catholicism of many of the justices of the present U.S. Supreme Court bears directly on their decisions. Justice Scalia took umbrage when Prof. Geoffrey Stone suggested that their Catholic faith was crucial to the decision by the conservative Catholic justices in an abortion case (Stone 2009, 2016). However, in the Court's same-sex marriage decision, Scalia castigated the Court for being insufficiently diverse in its members' religious af-filiations, a position quite at odds with claiming that religion plays no part in such decision-making. In his dissent, speaking of the Court's composition, he wrote:

> Not a single evangelical Christian (a group that comprises about one quarter of Americans), or even a Protestant of any denomination. The strikingly unrepresentative character of the body voting on today's social upheaval would be irrelevant if they were functioning as judges, answer-ing the legal question whether the American people had ever ratified a constitutional provision that was understood to proscribe the traditional definition of marriage. But of course the Justices in today's majority are not voting on that basis; *they say they are not*. And to allow the policy question of same-sex marriage to be considered and resolved by a select, patrician, highly unrepresentative panel of nine is to violate a principle even more fundamental than no taxation without representation: no social transfor-mation without representation" (*Obergefell v. Hodges*, original italics; inter-nal citation eliminated).

Given the revitalization of Catholic natural-law thinking, the allusions by some of the justices to such principles may be relevant to understanding their decision-making.[8] Following the language they use to import natural-law think-ing is thus vital, because even when one cannot penetrate the true motivation of a judge, the fact that he or she must articulate reasons for a decision reveals a good deal about the concepts that are actually in play. Finally, I will suggest that the apparent attachment of some members of the court to natural law is one that American politicians and commenters have not always adequately addressed, particularly in the questioning by members of the Senate Judiciary Committee of recent nominees to the Supreme Court. In this regard we also have a chance to see how competing cultural paradigms may be influenced by the politics of natural law.

★ ★ ★

Natural law in the Western theological context generally refers to those princi-ples God is said to have fixed in the natural world, and which can be discerned by human reason. It may incorporate revealed law 'written in the hearts of man' (as Paul says in Romans 2:14ff) but may be so contested or vague as to mean that

"Natural Law underwrites morality as such, rather than any particular moral code."[9] Europeans, especially Germans, had been moving away from natural law throughout the Enlightenment: Friedrich Schlegel could ridicule the philosophical jurists who "in addition to the other laws, which are often so unjust, also have a Natural Law, which not rarely is even more unjust," while Joseph von Eichendorff said of his legal education that "the jurists were teaching a so-called Natural Law, which was valid nowhere and never could be valid" (quoted in Ziolkowski 1997: 193). The natural law view of the Renaissance humanists, who found in it one of the bases for the very idea of a humanly created state, is neatly captured in the following summation by Quentin Skinner (1978: 149): "[T]he law of nature provides a moral framework within which all human laws must operate; conversely, the aim of these human laws is simply to give force in the world to a higher law which every man already knows in his conscience" (see also Brett 2011).

The founders of the American republic were not unaware of the issues. There were those who envisioned the new nation as freed from the history of Europe, so that man's nature could fully express itself, a place where, contrary to the fabrications of British common law, it would be possible to forget "models of Saxon barbarity," and instead, "to resolve every argument into principles of natural reason, universal justice, and present convenience."[10] Notwithstanding the views of those like John Adams, who, in the post-revolutionary decades, imagined that the law might develop with as great a degree of conformity to the laws of nature as does Newtonian physics, it proved impossible to separate the romance of the common law as an expression of Christian and natural ideals from the workaday needs of an independent people. The particular laws of individual nations, many hoped, would accord with 'the immutable law of moral obligations' protected by public opinion. But for all their claims that (as Professor D. T. Blake exhorted young lawyers in 1810) "the science of the Law is, of all others, the most sublime and comprehensive," and for all their flirtation with European civil law in this period, as Perry Miller (1965: 165–66; original italics) notes: "Despite their noble endeavors to make the Common Law appear a systematic wisdom, to invest it with the halo of Blackstone, they could never quite fumigate it of the smell of the grubby. It *had* grown up by accident, out of low contention." That is not to say that forms of natural-law thinking did not, at important moments, play a central role in some of the nation's most trying disputes. William Seward's maiden speech before the Senate in the 1850 debate over the extension of slavery to the new territory in the West, became famous for its claim that:

> there is a higher law than the Constitution, which regulates our authority over the domain [of slavery], and devotes it to the same noble purpose. The territory is a part, no inconsiderable part, of the common heritage of mankind, bestowed upon them by the Creator of the universe. We are his stewards, and must so discharge our trust as to secure in the highest attainable degree their happiness.[11]

But such claims to "a higher law" did not become integral to American judicial decision-making. At various times, the due process clause of the Constitution, whether viewed restrictively (as was the case from the 1870s until the 1930s), served as the vehicle for debating whether powers and rights other than those made explicit in the Constitution could receive judicial recognition. But those who couched such rights in naturalistic terms, were never able to dominate the discourse.[12] Indeed, in the context of American jurisprudence, we can trace a definitive move against any form of natural law to the period after the Civil War when Justice Holmes and others—following on Bentham's famous assertion that both natural law and natural rights are "a mere work of the fancy...nonsense on stilts"—revolted against the idea that there are objective concepts of right and wrong to which judges may appeal.[13] Moreover, by the late nineteenth century, even the reference to 'natural law' had been largely replaced by 'natural rights,' a phrasing that not only called up the Founders' terminology but, perhaps more significantly, implied a shift from a vision based on communitarian values to one based more in the private property rights of individuals.[14] This is the kind of shift that was to be replicated, in one of those categorizing moves to which we will have further reference, by a number of present-day conservative legal scholars and judges as well.

Among the current scholars who have sought to revive natural law in the American setting, we see several distinct concepts—and political alliances—at work. For while multiple streams have merged in the present revival, what has occurred most dramatically is a political confluence of Catholics and Evangelicals, two groups that have more often been opposed than united in the nation's past. Brought together in large part by shared social issues—anti-abortion, increased government 'accommodation' of (if not direct involvement with) religion, limitation of sexual expression, maintenance of traditional family forms, and a vision of more restricted federal power—the two have engaged in a kind of division of labor, with the Catholic intellectuals doing the heavy lifting on the theological and philosophical side, and the Evangelicals adding local political clout in regions previously ill-disposed to the Church of Rome.[15] Economically, both religious groups have prospered and moved into higher status positions in recent decades, a factor that may also have prompted each to move away from a communal emphasis to one based on private property. Politically, the combination of the two—in what they, adopting a term redolent of allies facing a common enemy, have themselves sometimes denominated a posture of 'co-belligerency'[16]—was particularly compatible with the presidency of George W. Bush who, it may be argued, found in natural-law thinking, a way to imagine that if the obstacles to freedom and the American Way were simply eliminated—as, say, in Iraq—democracy and right action would take their natural, democratic course.[17] As we will see, this Catholic-Evangelical alliance also undoubtedly influenced President Bush's choice of Supreme Court nominees.

On the intellectual side, the Catholic natural law movement has found in such scholars as John Finnis, Robert George, Germain Gabriel Grisez, and others, the advocates for drawing natural law back into American jurisprudence.[18] Robert George (2008), characteristically, argues that certain communitarians and individualists share a mistaken view of human nature and the human good. For him, humans incorporate reason and freedom, and he thus regards it as a matter of practical reasoning to apply natural law principles to everyday adjudication.[19] Judges may deduce precepts from the natural law, then, just as mathematicians or natural scientists do in their realms. Key words like 'flourishing,' 'fulfillment,' and 'dignity' that are associated with natural law, form a central part of this discourse and, as we shall see, find their way into some judicial opinions.

Note that in this view, several conceptual shifts occur. Natural law is elided with practical reasoning (in line with Thomistic thinking), history and tradition are invoked as demonstrations of the depth and truth of the substantive propositions raised, and even Holmes' 'descriptive sociology' is folded within this new natural law to further support its universal claims. Deeper sources are cited more specifically by other proponents of the new natural law. Nicholas Wolterstorff (2008) says there can be no independent base for the morality of law, since even for those who are secularists or unbelievers, it is from the biblical sources that the precepts of the law stem. Anthony D'Amato (2007–8) argues that natural law is an expression of that universal inference from the nature of human society which holds that no party may take advantage of another. Like many of the natural-law thinkers, however, D'Amato's argument is both vague and circular: He speaks of the inherent limitation and boundaries of natural law, but does not specify what they are, incorrectly asserts that the diminished importance of natural law led (as only a libertarian, and one tone deaf to the civil rights movement, might claim) to the shrinking of freedom, and demonstrates (by focusing solely on the free-rider issue) that that issue is a libertarian obsession, not a social constant. In each instance, the connection to America is made through a particular reading of the U.S. Constitution and its predecessor documents.

To the current group of natural law proponents, the Constitution needs to be seen against the backdrop of such documents as the Declaration of Independence, which is itself read as grounded in Christian doctrine.[20] Seeing the U.S. as a Christian nation they cite the Declaration, for example, for its reference to the "Laws of Nature and of Nature's God," and take this to mean the Christian view thereof.[21] In support, they cite not the Founders' deism but their frequent references to the Creator—even though almost none of these references is specifically to Christ or to Christianity proper, and none appears in the final Constitution.[22] The stakes are obvious: As Martin Marty has said, "The more you can associate Christianity with the founding, the more you can sway the future Supreme Court....Establish the founders as Christians, and you have it made."[23]

Nor are the present natural-law thinkers the first to cite the Declaration in this fashion. They note that Abraham Lincoln, like Daniel Webster and Justice Joseph Story, believed that the concept of equality in the Declaration informed the provisions of the Constitution, and was, indeed, a vehicle through which flaws in that document could be corrected (see, e.g., Lowry 2011). However, Lincoln did not see the Declaration as law: Instead, as in his speech in Philadelphia on February 22, 1861, he said: "I have never had a feeling politically that did not spring from the sentiments embodied in the Declaration of Independence," which is hardly the same as seeing it as a formal source of law. It is true that over the years, a number of cases have cited the Declaration, even though it forms no part of American law.[24] Robert George has referred to the Constitution itself as a kind of transparency or overlay, beneath which one can read the Declaration, and beneath both, Sacred Text (as most authoritatively interpreted, for these believers, by the Roman Catholic Church) to understand the original meaning and intent that informs the provisions of the later documents.[25] Indeed, it is often assumed by the proponents of Catholic natural law—as, in a sense, they must—that such law, being natural and universal, must exist irrespective of a particular faith's recognition of it. Father John Courtenay Murray (2005 [1960]: 55 and 51) is among those often quoted, then, for the assertion that:

> Catholic participation in the American consensus has been full and free, unreserved and unembarrassed, because the contents of this consensus— the ethical and political principles drawn from the tradition of natural law—approve themselves to the Catholic Intelligence and conscience.... It is not an American belief that free government is inevitable, only that it is possible, and that its possibility can be realized only when the people as a whole are inwardly governed by the recognized imperatives of the universal moral law.

The clearest proponent in recent years of the use of non-Constitutional sources for legal decision-making—and the clearest proponent on the bench of natural-law thinking generally—was, of course, Justice Antonin Scalia.[26] It is true that he never overtly said that natural law is a proper source for judicial decision-making. Thus, in his Vaughan Lecture at Princeton University on December 10, 2012, Scalia, in response to a student question about the proper bases for constitutional interpretation, responded rhetorically by asking: "If we don't use originalism and textualism what do we use? Natural law? We don't agree on what that is." It is noteworthy that the questioner had not raised natural law as a possibility but that Scalia went to that as his example, and rather than saying that natural law would not be an appropriate basis for adjudication, he instead said that he could not garner agreement as to its content.[27] However, in a statement that received a great deal of attention, Scalia referred to St. Paul for the idea that "government …derives its moral authority from God," and that "[t]hese passages from Romans represent the consensus of thought until very recent times. Not just of Christian or religious thought, but of secular thought regarding the powers of the state." And, in a statement that provoked special controversy, Scalia (2002) went on to say that one can detect "the tendency of democracy to obscure the divine authority behind government." Scalia further stated that "in the words of a Supreme Court opinion from the 1940s 'we are a religious people, whose institutions presuppose a Supreme Being'," and that "[Saint] Paul was correct to assert that government carries the sword as 'the minister of God,' to 'execute wrath upon the evildoer'" (citing *Romans* 13:1–5). This latter article prompted a strong editorial against Scalia's position by *The Washington Post,* and a heated exchange between Professors Sean Wilentz and Laurence H. Tribe (2002). Scalia's position tracks that of the standard conservative view as expressed by one of its main spokesmen: "There are six canons of conservative thought [the first being]: 1) Belief in a transcendent order, or body, of natural law, which rules society as well as conscience. Political problems, at bottom, are religious and moral problems" (Kirk 2001).[28] But rather than invoke natural law directly, Scalia and other conservative judges have brought such matters in under various other conceptual categories.

All legal systems engage in pigeonholing, although perhaps the kinder term would be category displacement or rearrangement. In Continental systems, this may take the form of picking one or another statutory provision under which to place new or changing circumstances. Alternatively, the process may approximate the common law style in its use of what Edward Levi (1949) called "a moving system of categorizing concepts." Indeed, in the common law, what often happens is not so much that a category is chosen that gets the desired result, but rather that a category starts to fill up in a particular fashion through case application, and then comes to have implications that are less favored in a judge's or scholar's view, which in turn prompts a shift to another category, where the overtones are thought to be more favorable. It is interesting to note, too, that Thomas S. Kuhn (1962: 23) analogized paradigm shifts in science to the reasoning process that takes place in the common law. Thus, to take just one example, the federal Constitution's Commerce Clause may have been extended over time to include many civil rights matters, only for it later to become too problematic a category, within which some judges feel comfortable including, say, affirmative action legislation. Similarly, the approach to same-sex unions was affected by a shift from categorizing it as a question of marriage, to one of civil rights. All of this bears on the question of natural law in American jurisprudence, because what may have fit for certain judges under one category or term, may later shift to an alternative.[29]

Two of the primary categories through which natural law may be rendered in other terms are those of history and 'tradition.' Under these rubrics, a number of conservative scholars and judges have argued that one is not merely upholding the cultural identity of a nation, but those deeper precepts of nature that have given rise to our institutions. This may, as Cass Sunstein (2007–8) has argued, be preferable to interpreting such concepts as 'liberty' in whatever fashion is appealing, but may, for example, mean that the concept of 'goodness' with which its proponents work is at best imprecise. Nevertheless, history and tradition are themes that crop up repeatedly in the opinions of various courts. Thus, U.S. District Court Judge Jeffrey White, in striking down the Defense of Marriage Act, wrote: "The imposition of subjective moral beliefs of a majority upon a minority cannot provide a justification for the legislation. The obligation of the Court is 'to define the liberty of all, not to mandate our own moral code'." He also stated: "Tradition alone, however, cannot form an adequate justification for a law....The 'ancient lineage' of a classification does not render it legitimate.... Instead, the government must have an interest separate and apart from the fact of tradition itself" (*Golinski v. Office of Personnel Management* 2012: 994 and 993). At the level of the Supreme Court, Chief Justice Rehnquist cited history in support of restricting the ability of Native Americans to engage in certain religious practices, Justice White cited tradition in the rejection of challenges to state sodomy laws, and Justices Scalia and Thomas referred to the 'traditions of our people' in support of the display of religious symbols on government lands. By comparison, Justice Kennedy prefers the term 'dignity,' as in his opinion in *United States v. Windsor*, a usage that may owe less to his Catholicism than to Thomas Aquinas and Immanuel Kant ("In the kingdom of ends everything has either a *price* or a *dignity*"; see Baertsch 2012; Rosen 2012). However, Judge Richard Posner (2008: 311) says that "Kennedy is a natural lawyer—a believer in the existence of universal moral principles (the sources of his 'own sense of ethics and morality') that inform—and constrains—positive law" (Posner 2008: 257, quoting an interview the Justice gave in 2006; see generally, Colucci 2009; Jelliff 2013; Knowles 2009). The use by Kennedy and more moderate Catholics of the term 'dignity' may, then, be an attempt to wrest that concept from the conservatives and to imbue it with less authoritarian implications, as when Justice Clarence Thomas placed emphasis on 'human dignity' in his own early statements.[30]

That 'traditions' change, yet seem to bespeak a sense of collective identity, poses the dual questions: whether a people are entitled to some sense of cultural integrity ('we are the people who do not eat dogs and horses even though we understand that others might'), and whether something old enough (or sufficiently shared?) can qualify as a 'tradition.'[31] Clearly one cannot say with certainty that these rationales have no other source than the religious beliefs of these judges, but some of their other utterances do suggest strong correlations, both in their own searching comments about the relation of their faith to their judicial decision-making, and in their choice of terms in the opinions they have rendered. Unlike many conservatives, Scalia did not appear to regard the Constitution itself as a sacred document: He professed willingness to enforce it if changed by proper legislative means, which would hardly be appropriate for sacred text. Accordingly, it might be argued that he saw natural law as 'denatured,' shorn of its invariant view of human nature, as well as displaced, in the sense of being rooted in divine inspiration, but not constituting a direct readout for judicial judgment. In place of these elements, Scalia's cleaving to the original text becomes the methodological equivalent of the classical transition from natural law to positive law, a process that shares its intellectual-procedural features with the style of natural-law thinking practiced within the Catholic tradition (see generally, Garet 1988; see also Fallon 1997: 40; Note 1990: 175–80). How personal faith and judicial decision-making should bear on one another is, however, a vexed and controversial issue.

Catholic judges and scholars have been as concerned as any about the appropriate relation of their religious beliefs to judicial decisions.[32] Scalia himself should be taken at his word when he said that his religion had no bearing on his work as a justice, although perhaps no case—certainly not the death penalty cases—had, to my knowledge, arisen in which he stated that he had to rule one way as a judge while feeling compelled to decide differently as a believer. Scalia (2002) had said that if that were the case, a judge would have to go along with the statute or resign his post: "If a state were to permit abortion on demand, I would—and could in good conscience—vote against an attempt to invalidate that law…because the Constitution gives the federal government (and hence me) no power over the matter." He acknowledged, particularly in the death penalty situation, that so far, Church doctrine fortunately did not require him to change his opposition to the abolition of the death penalty. In a speech at Duquesne University, he said: "If I thought that Catholic doctrine held the death penalty to be immoral, I would resign. I could not be a part of a system that imposes it" (Majors 2011).[33] Expectedly, commenters have been on all sides of the issue. Arguing that one's beliefs *should* be relevant to a judge's confirmation, Tennessee Judge D'Army Bailey argues that they would be especially relevant to matters from which the judge might have to recuse himself. Failure to ask about the beliefs of Supreme Court nominees, he says, may be "polite," but he adds: "In reality, however, the judges have beliefs, their beliefs are relevant to their decision-making, and sharing those beliefs will not threaten impartial justice. Those beliefs should be open to inquiry."[34] Some regard any such inquiry as starting down the path of asking what *kind* of Catholic, etc. one is.[35] Others seem either disingenuous or to be ducking the issue altogether when, like Judge William H. Pryor (2006: 358), they say that "Catholics should welcome a conversation about the religious faith of federal judges," but then go on to say that "a federal judge has no authority to use natural law as a way to subvert the *clear commands* of the positive law," without indicating what should be done when matters are *not* clear (as is commonly true for a case that makes it to appeal, much less to the nation's highest court). Regrettably, much of this discussion never quite addresses whether natural law, based in one's faith, may be drawn upon in such adjudication. The result is either to leave the question aside for fear that it will spark inappropriate questioning of one's religion, or to drive the discussion into other categories that obscure the sources to which a believing judge may in fact turn when matters are unclear.

For example, in the creationism case, Justice Scalia referred to 'evidences,' a concept drawn from Catholic thinking that implies indications in this world of the underlying natural-law precepts of revealed religion.[36] It is true that in a case concerning the display of the Ten Commandments, *McCreary County, KY v. American Civil Liberties Union*, Scalia relied on their historical significance to claim that the Mosaic Law possessed only a secular purpose, while in another case, he denied any right of visitation to the father of a child whose mother was married to another man, because such a family form was not "rooted in the traditions and conscience of our people."[37] Scalia especially emphasized traditional practices in his decisions concerning homosexuality, as for example in *Romer v. Evans*, where he characterized Justice Kennedy's reference to state "animosity" to homosexuals as being "animosity to evil," when Kennedy never made use of the word 'evil.' And his decision in *United States v. Virginia*, a case requiring a state to admit women to an all-male military academy, clearly relied on the idea that a state may reasonably conclude that the particular style of that academy's programs is unsuited for females, because of the women's very nature. There, as in other writings (Scalia 2011), the Justice repeated his belief that protection for women against discrimination is not mandated by the Constitution: "Certainly the Constitution does not require discrimination on the basis of sex. The only issue is whether it prohibits it. It doesn't." It is, of course, perfectly valid to claim that the Constitution leaves many matters of morality to the states, but it is difficult, if not impossible, to find a case in which Scalia or the other conservatives on the court have, notwithstanding assurances to the contrary, actually ruled for a state practice about which they had moral reservations. One possible exception was Scalia's willingness to join the Brennan majority in the flag-burning case, *Texas v. Johnson*, a position made all the more curious because Scalia later argued in *Employment Division v. Smith* in favor of a lower standard of scrutiny for state action than the Brennan majority accepted in *Lawrence v. Texas*, a case involving anti-sodomy laws. Thus while we cannot say that natural law underlies many of these justices' decisions, we can point to instances in which attachment to natural law appears very close to the surface, and in which the language of the natural law movement has shifted to embrace a widening range of discourses and legal results.

One of those streams to which the contemporary natural law movement has attached itself is that of 'natural rights'. This has, of course, been a key part of natural-law thinking for ages, but its current manifestation carries with it several distinctively American implications.[38] First, it associates natural law with the rights expressed in the pre-Constitutional documents of the Republic. Second, it forges a link to the arguments of one of the key intellectuals the conservative movement as a whole has taken to heart, namely Leo Strauss, particularly as set forth in his *Natural Right and History* (1999 [1953]). Although his own politics were ambiguous, and his view of nature one of possibilities and questions rather than positivistic certainties, the Straussians have taken a simpler and more absolute stand, indicating, for example, that men may naturally have precedence over women, or—as Hadley Arkes, an enthusiastic Straussian and recent convert to Catholicism, argues—that marriage manages nature.[39] Thirdly, switching to a discourse of natural rights also marks a move from the more communitarian view associated with natural law, to a greater emphasis on individually held private property, a move that further links the natural-law proponents to the conservative movement more generally.[40] The concept of natural law may even be extended, fourthly, to take over the civil rights discourse, usually associated with the liberal wing of the American political spectrum, as when Associate

Justice Clarence Thomas, in his confirmation hearing, stated that in his prior work as a "part-time political theorist for [the] Equal Employment Opportunity Commission… my interest in this area of natural rights was…looking for a way to unify and strengthen the whole effort to enforce our civil rights laws."[41] In these multiple synergies, then, the natural-law thinkers, employing a wide range of terminologies, have successfully imported natural law into the contemporary political and juridical environment.[42]

Perhaps nowhere has the issue of natural law been raised—and ducked—more openly than in the confirmation hearings of recent conservative Catholic nominees to the Supreme Court. The process really began at the hearings for Clarence Thomas.[43] It was Senator (later, Vice President) Joseph Biden, then chair of the Judiciary Committee that reports out a nominee for the full Senate to vote on, who focused on natural law. He may have been provoked by a number of comments Clarence Thomas had made in earlier speeches, such as his statement that: "Without recourse to higher law, we abandon our best defense of a court that is active in defending the Constitution but judicious in its restraint and moderation. Higher law is the only alternative to the willfulness of both runamok majorities and runamok judges."[44] Or the committee may have been concerned about Thomas' assertion (1987) that constitutionalism would be meaningless without recourse to a higher law: "Men cannot rule others by their consent unless their common humanity is understood in light of transcendent standards provided by the Declaration's 'Laws of Nature and of Nature's God.'" Thomas went on to say that natural law, by its provision of a baseline for human dignity, makes it possible to decide whether people are just or unjust.[45]

Introducing the hearings on Thomas' nomination, Senator Biden referred to the "radical" types of natural law then being debated among scholars, and to the "radical change in direction that some are urging on the Court under the banner of natural law." A Catholic himself, Biden made clear that he thought natural law was at the heart of the entire confirmation inquiry.[46] Yet in his questioning, Biden made two mistakes: He focused on natural-law debates, rather than on where the candidate himself would go for guidance when the law is unclear, and he failed to pin the candidate down to some hypotheticals or well-established precedents, through which to explore the actual content of his natural-law thinking. Perhaps in the grip of sounding like one who can also play the game of natural-law philosophizing, Biden (a self-admitted poor student in law school) was so embroiled in his own demonstration of intellectuality that he left the door open for Senator Alan Simpson, a Republican conservative not particularly noted for his command of abstruse philosophy, to undercut Biden's line of inquiry by showing that there were numerous debates within the ranks of Straussians, natural-law thinkers, and theologians, so that, in his response, Judge Thomas was able to render the entire matter one of mere mental exercise rather than a source for adjudicating in an environment of uncertainty.

The result of the misguided discussion in the Thomas hearing was that further consideration of natural law largely fell to the wayside when subsequent nominees appeared before the Committee. Thus, by the time John Roberts was being considered as the Chief Justice in 2005, Biden had shifted from asking about natural law to asking about following precedent under the rule of *stare decisis*, and the hearings the following year for Samuel Alito barely touched on the topic. The nomination by President George W. Bush of Harriet Miers in 2005, showed that without some clear indication, whether through natural law/natural-rights thinking, or a deep record of decisions consonant with it, even a conservative nominee might not garner conservative support. A Catholic convert to Evangelical Christianity, Miers would seem to have neatly straddled the two parts of the co-belligerency alliance. Indeed, Bush made her faith an indicator of her reliable conservative credentials when he said (in the proper code words for the faithful): "Well, we know her religious beliefs."[47] But conservatives—perhaps recalling how they felt betrayed by the assurances of Bush's father about the proclivities of Justice David Souter—reacted sharply to the nomination. They felt her record was too thin to be sure she really would support their agenda. Though Bush told his allies to "trust me" on this appointment, and emissaries were sent to mollify all sides, it was not enough: The conservatives would not support the nomination, and Miers found it more convenient to withdraw.[48] The whole issue of natural law and natural rights in confirmation hearings came to a ludicrous halt when, in 2009, one senator, perhaps thinking he could trap even a liberal Catholic into supporting his view, asked Judge Sonia Sotomayor whether she agreed that gun ownership was a God-given natural right, a question which (like so many others) the nominee easily ducked.[49]

★ ★ ★

Like nature, in the formulation of Lucretius, natural law may always be with us, whether as supplement, control, or motivating factor.[50] When used to fill in the perceived deficiencies of the positive law, to address changing social practices, or to justify political or moral views, natural law—by whatever name—may be vital to the capacity of a legal or political directorate to muster support. Whether one distinguishes natural law from natural rights, or seeks to reconfigure one set of approaches in the terminology of another, the process of looking beyond the humanly fabricated will always have great appeal. This is particularly true for conservatives at the present time in the United States, since they clearly seek a foundation for their beliefs—whether economic, familial, or governmental—that can lay claim to legitimacy based on the 'nature' of the marketplace, the biology of the species, or the guided genius that set forth the structure of the Constitution. Others, like Ronald Dworkin (2013), arguing from the non-religious side, see in the awe with which one needs to confront the universe, a set of moral propositions which, for purposes of constitutional interpretation, serve many of the same functions as a religious-based view of natural law. Judge Richard Posner, by contrast, notes that judges must always fill in the gaps, whether they call it natural law, or whatever they please. Although he speaks of "the discredited idea

of a universal natural law," Posner nevertheless writes (2004): "I have a qualified sympathy for the idea of natural law. If a novel case arises—one that cannot
be decided by subsumption under clear statutory or constitutional language or
precedent—the judge will have to look elsewhere, and if one wants to call the
elsewhere 'natural law' I have no strong objection, as long as it is understood not
to be Thomas Aquinas's concept of natural law."

Pinning down the attachment to natural law is easier when viewing the utterances and writings of politicians, academics, and pundits: It is far more slippery
when it comes to finding its presence in judicial opinion-making. But it may well be
that the conservatives' attachment to 'strict construction' or 'originalism' is actually
a secondary manifestation of a deeper need for certainty, a place where ambiguity
and human judgment come up against something that can indeed be regarded as
foundational.[51] Such a propensity is not necessarily consonant with being authoritarian or inflexible, but it may fulfill a personal need to ground decisions in a source
that transcends the personal, the momentary, and the untrustworthy.[52] Then a given
document can be approached, not simply for its content, but for its felt solidity, just as
one might find similar certainty through religious or scientific attachments.

It is impossible to state that natural-law thinking—grounded, say, in Catholic
legal thinking—is undoubtedly at the base of any American judge's decisions.
The direct use of natural law in such decisions would be wholly inappropriate, as
well as unwise, since Americans profess to import religion into the law only in
the most generalized of ways, if at all. Nor is the argument that there is an unmis-
takably Catholic-Evangelical alliance in any way an assertion that this constitutes
some sort of illegitimate cabal. To the contrary, it is a perfectly legitimate quest
for understanding and influence within the American political system. It is also
clear that one of the intellectual and political tactics of the movement has been
to appropriate concepts that are not linked exclusively to the form of natural law
the proponents profess, as they have set out to gain wider acceptance of their
natural-law style of legal thinking.

It is also quite clear that the conservative Catholics on the court, regardless of
how central their attachment to natural law may be, almost always vote in a bloc.
In the opinion of court-watcher Jeffrey Toobin (2009):

> After four years on the Court, however, Roberts's record is not that of
> a humble moderate but, rather, that of a doctrinaire conservative. The
> kind of humility that Roberts favors reflects a view that the Court should
> almost always defer to the existing power relationships in society. In
> every major case since he became the nation's seventeenth Chief Justice,
> Roberts has sided with the prosecution over the defendant, the state over
> the condemned, the executive branch over the legislative, and the corpo-
> rate defendant over the individual plaintiff. Even more than Scalia, who
> has embodied judicial conservatism during a generation of service on the
> Supreme Court, Roberts has served the interests, and reflected the values,
> of the contemporary Republican Party.

Thus:

> In a case about the free-speech rights of students, Roberts wrote the opin-
> ion approving the suspension of a high-school student in Alaska for holding
> a sign that said 'BONG HiTS 4 JESUS' on a street off school grounds. The
> Chief Justice said the school had the right to 'restrict student speech at a
> school event, when that speech is reasonably viewed as promoting illegal
> drug use.' Thomas, characteristically, wrote a concurring opinion urging
> the Court to go farther and hold that students have no First amendment
> rights at all. But the larger point remained that Roberts, Scalia, and Thomas
> voted together in that case, as they do virtually all the time. 'These kinds of
> distinctions among the conservatives are just angels-on-the-head-of-a-pin
> stuff,' says Theodore B. Olson, the former Solicitor General.

As we have seen, the particular use of such concepts as 'natural rights,' 'tradition,' 'conscience,' and the like has facilitated the merging of various political
and religious streams into a shared confluence that possesses greater appeal and
acceptability by being cast in these terms, rather than under the rubric of natural
law. The political movement that draws on this orientation has proven very successful as a vehicle for supporting judicial nominees (as well as choosing Justice
Department officials and Supreme Court clerks), and has formed a crucial basis
for allying several Christian denominations that have previously been reluctant
to form a coalition.[53] Indeed, we can see this movement as part of a larger pattern
of the divisions and decisions of the current Supreme Court.

The Court has properly been characterized as one whose members are, on
each side of the liberal-conservative divide, in lock-step with one another on a
wide range of issues—and with the political party of the president who appointed
them.[54] But while some would argue that each side lacks an overarching theme
that draws together decisions on such diverse matters as abortion, states' rights,
affirmative action, environmental concerns, same-sex marriage, gays in the military, etc., it might be suggested that, for the conservatives, that theme can be
described as an attachment to the proposition that the more decentralized the
government the more influence ethical leaders may be able to exercise on both
the laws and the extra-legal moral pressures that should govern the central concerns of our lives. So one might interpret the Supreme Court's decision in *Bush
v. Gore* as incorporating the notion that voters, not the state of Florida, are the
ones who must be responsible for making their choices clear, or that cities like
Washington and Chicago ought not to severely limit gun use, since it is the individual whose ethical conduct is the appropriate governing point.[55] The quest for
rock-hard certainty (and hence the antipathy to any form of relativism[56]) leads
many conservatives to focus on such foundational American values as individualism and extra-governmental ethical leadership.

Finding certainty in natural-law thinking also has a very American cultural
aspect when it is thought to be as determinable as the laws of science. Thus,

in the case of abortion, one can claim that an ultrasound 'proves' the fetus is a person, or that medicine and psychiatry show that homosexuality is 'curable.'[57] Similarly, the dissenting opinions in the Court's decision on same-sex marriage, particularly that of Justice Thomas, once again reiterate the 'natural' basis for denying protection under the Constitution.[58] Human rights are frowned upon as human creations, because that might, for example, militate against the use of capital punishment, a penalty the American conservatives' version of natural law commonly permits. And all of this may be wrapped within a blanket of national exceptionalism, itself imagined as a gift of God.

Such themes, of course, need not be made explicit to be dispositive; indeed, such a connective idea may be left unarticulated for various reasons. We can see, for instance, that in the period surrounding the presidential campaign of 2012, the Republican party had no dominant ideology, a factor that may have made it all the more possible for such diverse groups as the Evangelicals and the Catholics to find a common space that clearer expressions of ideology might otherwise preclude.[59] Similarly, the conservative wing of the Court, as we have seen, has not been unified on all issues and may, for a time, have benefited from not pushing a singular ideology too explicitly. What links the decisions of this wing, then, is not a logic of case decisions of the sort a law professor may wish to reconcile in order to show what 'the law' really is at a given moment. It is rather the logic one finds in any culture, in which the themes that are operative, partake of a central aspect of indirection, ambivalence, and indeterminacy, even as alternative categories compete for the definition of any given situation. In American culture, no less than in American law, Max Gluckman's (1965: 326) general formulation continues to apply: "The 'certainty' of law resides in the 'uncertainty' of its basic concepts."

We cannot, therefore, know with any certainty when beliefs in religion or natural law are substantively influencing a judge's decision. Justice Thomas, for example has said: "'I quite frankly don't know how you do these hard jobs without some faith. I don't know. Other people can come to you and explain it to you. I have no idea," he said. "I don't know how an oath becomes meaningful unless you have faith. Because at the end you say, 'So help me God.' And a promise to God is different from a promise to anyone else."[60] While no one can enter the mind of any judge to determine whether he or she has actually made a decision on the basis of religious, political, or psychological motivations, there is, however, certainly enough evidence from earlier decisions to indicate that personal orientations have been central to particular decisions. A justice who, in the late nineteenth century, can say that 'divine law' and 'the nature of things' precludes a woman from becoming a member of the bar,[61] the fact that as many as twenty-seven justices who owned slaves may have been influenced by their belief that slavery was not inconsistent with God's law, or the claim that the American flag is rendered sacred, not simply by emotional attachment, but by its symbolizing the state's legitimacy as 'God's minister,' are all propositions that have had persuasive force in their day.

American courts may have appealed to higher law under such varied rubrics as due process, fundamental rights, equal protection, and the like, and in that sense have indeed employed some form of superordinate law, even if it was cast in terms of the Constitution, common sense, or shared history and values. Yet when one sees conservative justices who find a concept like 'substantive due process' to be vague and only a function of personal interpretation, yet readily employ notions of 'tradition' and 'the conscience of our people,' it is clear that they are driving a wedge between generalized notions of universality and the particular form of higher law to which they believe judges may turn. Opponents may be forced into much the same language at certain moments. They, too, may speak of 'unfair' competition, practices that 'shock the conscience,' or the emerging standards of 'universal human rights,' and in doing so, may seem to be little different from their natural-law-oriented brethren. But still the differences stand out. For one does not have to say that beliefs grounded in natural law are necessarily right or wrong, or claim that natural law has some positivistic existence, or (to recycle my own view) that 'there is no such thing as natural law, only law naturalized,'[62] to appreciate that the terms one chooses, the line of thinking to which one attaches oneself, have very different consequences, however much they share in the common problem of seeking guidance—whether absolute or relative to the moment—when available sources appear inadequate to the task.

Cultural concepts may enter the law through a wide array of doors, whether through the terms of biology, market forces, behavioral psychology, claims of divine inspiration, or what 'our people' have 'always' done. Natural-law thinking is yet another avenue for such inclusion. Whatever else may be true, a review of the cases and commentary suggests that, in the American context, to fail to consider the role of natural law in the current thinking of those justices (and other judges, legal scholars, and politicians) who profess a sincere attachment to it, because we are afraid of appearing critical of another's religious beliefs,[63] is not only to fail to take seriously those who honestly seek to persuade us of their arguments, but to hide from the factors that may be influencing, directly or indirectly, the course of American jurisprudence.

Notes

1 Thomas Jefferson and Joseph Story famously differed on the related issue of whether Christianity formed part of the common law. Jefferson insisted it did not (he called such an assertion by courts a "forgery," said that the judges "stole this law upon us," and described the doctrine as "the most remarkable instance of Judicial legislation, that has ever occurred in English jurisprudence, or perhaps in any other"). Justice Story insisted that Christianity was part of the common law in the sense that it formed an historic base for the common law, that English law recognized Christianity as true, that Christianity served as a broad support for society, and that its incorporation in the common law could serve as a basis for prosecuting blasphemy even though all persons were certainly not required to be Christians. See generally, Allison (2012). As concerns natural law, Helmholz (2015) does argue it formed the

basis for a number of procedural and substantive propositions in American, as well as British and European, law.

2 On the debates in the Continental Congress, see Corwin (1955: 79–82). For other Americans, natural law continues to be seen as entirely separable and superior to state law, precisely because it is grounded in religious doctrine. See, e.g., DeMar (2012). For an example of those Southern Baptists who see natural law as unifying and state law as divisive, and who therefore avoid the state legal system, see Greenhouse (1989). On the historic avoidance of natural law in common law legal development, see Singer (1983). For a good discussion of deism and the Founders, see Nelson (2007).

3 For an analysis of these and other assertions, see Haines (1930: 52–59), 77–103. Writing mainly about cases through the late nineteenth century, Haines (1916: 625) says:

> It is the practice to insist that while references to these phrases [referring to natural law] are somewhat frequent the utterances are almost invariably in the form of dicta.... [However,] by a citation of cases, federal and state, attention will be called to the tendency to use natural law principles as a direct basis to invalidate legislation and also as an implied ground to broaden and render more effective the specific language of written constitutions in the development of judicial review of legislation.

It should also be noted that, following the Treaty of Westphalia in 1648, when the distinction between the natural law of states (based on the compact of its citizens) and the natural law applicable to individuals became prominent, scholars and judges found in this conception an often unspoken basis for limiting state action against individuals. In this particular sense it may be said that there remains a tacit natural-law assumption in the mentality of American law to this day.

4 See generally, Rosen (1988). For an assessment of law as derived from the nature of society, see Barden and Murphy (2010), especially pp. 189–204 on natural law.

5 But even commonly perceived natural laws may be infused with very different content and meanings. This more relativistic view may inform approaches to 'the natural' based on an anthropological demonstration that a given practice (e.g., the parent-child, sibling incest taboo) is not, in fact, universal. Thus a Connecticut Supreme Court opinion denying the validity of a marriage between an uncle and a niece of the half-blood undertaken in India, quoting sources from the time of Henry VIII presented by the defendant, held that since the prohibition of '"uncle-niece marriages, especially those between relatives of half blood, are not the object of universal condemnation, the Court will not be at odds with "natural law" if it adopts the construction [advocated] by [the parties].' We are not persuaded by any of these claims" (*Singh v. Singh*). However, it is not clear whether the court in *Singh* was rejecting the claim of relativism or accepting the relevance of natural law, since its decision was based mainly on statutory interpretation. For more relativistic views, see the cultural defense cases discussed in Renteln (2004); and Chapter 1.

6 For an example of a kinship pattern that would not fit most universal claims, see the discussion of Hua (2001) in the preceding chapter.

7 For some of the current debates on the applicability of natural law, see the selections in Laing and Wilcox (2013: 297–341).

8 Although the four commonly voted the same way, they were not always in total accord. Referring specifically to the difference between himself and Clarence Thomas, Justice Scalia, for example, told one reporter: "I'm a conservative, I'm a textualist, I'm an originalist, but I'm not a nut" (quoted by Jeffrey Toobin in an interview with Terry Gross on National Public Radio's *Fresh Air* program, September 19, 2007). The overall rift between liberals and conservatives on the Court is reflected in the fact that even their clerks are now largely chosen for their political compatibility. Scalia's claim that he always picked at least one liberal clerk to challenge him is misleading. As L. Greenhouse (2016) notes: "And while earlier in his Supreme Court tenure,

he [Scalia] prided himself on hiring one politically liberal law clerk among his four clerks every year, he abandoned that practice at least a decade ago." On the tendency towards ideological matching of clerks to the justices they work for, see Baum (2014) and Devins and Baum (2016). Indeed, the justices themselves rarely visit each other's offices, and communicate mostly in writing with one another. Liptak (2010). As Justice Thomas (1998: 1–2) remarked: "[W]e simply do not see each other on a frequent basis....For the most part, we will only see each other when we have conferences [where decisions are voted upon], a formal event, or when we sit [to hear oral argument in a case]. There is rarely contact beyond that." See also, Toobin (2007: 117–8)."

9 "Natural Law," in Cross and Livingstone (2005: 1139). Aquinas refers to natural law as "rational creatures' participation in the eternal law." See generally, d'Entreves 1970. The fuller quote from Romans (2:14–15, Revised Standard Version) reads: "When Gentiles who have not the law do by nature what the law requires...[t]hey show that what the law requires is written on their hearts, while their conscience also bears witness and their conflicting thoughts accuse or perhaps excuse them...."

10 Quoting a statement made in 1823 by William Sampson, an Irish Protestant lawyer known for his defense of religious liberty in Ireland and America, in Miller (1965: 107). See also Zuckert (1997).

11 On the broader background to the concept of the U.S. Constitution as the declaration and enactment of a higher law emanating from a sovereign people, see the famous essay by Edwin S. Corwin (1955), first published in the *Harvard Law Review* in 1928–29. On the relation of the Constitution to current American attachments to the higher law of religion, see Levinson 2011.

12 But see Wolfe (1994). Justice Benjamin Cardozo (1924: 49), for example, wrote: "If there is any law which is back of the sovereignty of the state, and superior thereto, it is not law in such a sense as to concern the judge or lawyer, however much it concerns the statesman or moralist."

13 Alschuler (2002: 9–10). See generally, Hoffheimer (1992) and Biddle (1961). Justice Holmes (1920: 312) wrote: "The jurists who believe in natural law seem to me to be in that naïve state of mind that accepts what has been familiar and accepted by them and their neighbors as something that must be accepted by all men everywhere."

14 See, Seagrave (2014) and Tierney (2014).

15 One of the events that may have helped to initiate this alliance was, ironically, the decision (written for the majority by Justice Scalia) in *Employment Division v. Smith* supporting a state statute restricting Native Americans' religious use of peyote and setting the standard of Constitutional review only at the level of a 'rational relationship' rather than 'strict scrutiny,' thus potentially allowing states to limit various religious practices. As a result, numerous religious groups coalesced to get Congress to set the standard as one of 'compelling state interest' under the Religious Freedom Restoration Act, 42 U.S.C. §§ 2000bb-4, a law that was in turn deemed by the Court, in *City of Boerne v. Flores*, an unconstitutional infringement of the Court's power to set the standards of review.

16 The foundational document for this alliance that is commonly cited, and in which the signatories "confess that we have sinned against one another and against God," resulted from consultation with and approval by a large number of leaders of both faiths, the primary authors apparently being Father Richard John Neuhaus and Charles W. Colson (1994: 21). On the concept of co-belligerency and its organizational implications, see Mohler 2003, as well as articles in that same issue by Robert George and Father Neuhaus. See also Wills (2005), Boyer (2010), and Linker (2007). It is also perhaps noteworthy that the line between Catholic and Evangelical has been further blurred by many believers, including many Hispanics, who have no qualms about attending services of both denominations. See, e.g., Oppenheimer (2010).

17 On the Bush administration's connection of the 'natural' to policies promoting wars of democratization, see Sahlins (2008: 42). During the 2012 Republican primary

race, several candidates were explicit in their support of natural law. Former Senator and presidential candidate Rick Santorum (2006) wrote that: "The promise of natural law is that we will be the happiest, and freest, when we follow the law built into our nature as men and women." On these grounds, Santorum subsequently came out against contraception and the recognition of a Constitutional right of privacy (Worthen 2012).

18 See generally, Bamforth (2011).

19 See generally, Finnis (2011), Biggar and Black (2000), and Forte (1998). For an analysis of these and other contemporary approaches to natural law, see Weinreb (1990). For the argument that many scholars misunderstand Aquinas' arguments, see Rogers (2013). See also, Soper (1992). In a case concerning the constitutionality of a state referendum banning legal protection for homosexuals, Robert George and John Finnis appeared as expert witnesses opposite Martha Nussbaum, each of whom offered testimony in which the history and applicability of natural law figured significantly. See Mendelsohn (1996).

20 On the relation of natural law to the Declaration, particularly as the founders referred to classical political philosophy, see Fears (2000).

21 Over one hundred U.S. Supreme Court opinions have mentioned the Declaration of Independence—commonly to distinguish it from the final Constitution—though none has used it as the basis for a decision. See, http://candst.tripod.com/doisussc. htm (accessed January 5, 2017). Compare Justice Stevens' dissent in *Meachum v. Fano* (1976: 230) with Justice Scalia's dissent in *Troxel v. Granville* (2000: 91–92). It is also noteworthy that a working draft of the Bill of Rights, drawn up by Representative Roger Sherman in July 1789, used the phrase "The people have certain natural rights," wording that was not, however, incorporated in the final document (Mitgang 1987).

22 See, e.g., Shorto (2010). Conservatives also claim that by citing the Declaration as the first entry in the U.S. Statutes at Large (under the heading "The Organic Laws of the United States of America") the Declaration is part of the basic laws of the nation (but see footnote 24 below). See Sandefur (2013). For a very different reading of the Declaration, see Allen (2014), and the review of her book by Wood (2014).

23 Quoted in Shorto (2010).

24 In an 1892 decision, *Church of the Holy Trinity v. U.S.*, the Supreme Court cited the Declaration in holding that an anti-sweatshop law cannot bar a congregation from bringing into the country a minister of its choice. But see generally, Fletcher (2001). Columnist George Will (2014) notes that since 1864 admission to statehood has been conditioned on acceptance of both the U.S. Constitution and the Declaration. He too points out that the Declaration appears on the first page of the first volume of the United States Statutes at Large under the caption "The Organic Laws of the United States of America." What he fails to note, is that the reprinted Declaration is immediately followed (pp. 4–9) by a copy of The Articles of Confederation, which is hardly the law, any more than is the Declaration. See generally the articles at Declaration of Independence Symposium 2016.

25 Introduction to the first Walter Murphy Lecture at Princeton University, April 2000. See also George (2012, 2013: 71–90, especially 71–73), Sandefur (2013), Arkes (2013), and Kozinski (2013). The Constitution is regarded by many American religious conservatives as divinely inspired, if not actually divinely revealed: see, e.g., Freedman (2010) and Rosen (2010).

26 See generally, Biskupic (2010). Many of Scalia's opinions are collected in Ring (2004).

27 For a discussion of the December 10, 2012, Princeton remarks, see http://usnews. nbcnews.com/_news/2012/12/11/15841049-gay-student-asks-justice-scalia-to-defend-his-bestiality-comments?lite (accessed January 5, 2017).

28 For an argument that Scalia's jurisprudence can only be understood against his background as a conservative Catholic, see Murphy (2015).

29 For what he calls "a collection of catchwords and catch phrases invoked by judges who would strike down under the Fourteenth Amendment laws which offend their notions of natural justice" see Justice Hugo Black's dissent in *Griswold v. Connecticut* (1965: 527, note 2/4). See also the opinion of Justice Cardozo in *Palko v. Connecticut* (1937: 325).

30 Kennedy may have been more directly influenced by the papal Declaration on Religious Freedom, initiated by Pope John XXIII at the Second Vatican Council, and brought to publication by his successor Paul VI under the title *Dignitatis Humanae* (1965). The content of that document certainly coincides with Kennedy's stress on the individual, and with the Declaration's recognition of religious freedom as a social and civil right, grounded in "the dignity of the human person as this dignity is known through the revealed word of God and by reason itself."

31 See, e.g., the opinion of Judge Posner in *Baskin v. Bogan*. By comparison, the trial judge who ruled unconstitutional the California law banning same-sex marriage wrote: "Tradition alone, however, cannot form a rational basis for a law. The 'ancient lineage' of a classification does not make it rational. Rather, the state must have an interest apart from the fact of the tradition itself" (*Perry v. Schwarzenegger*).

32 For a particularly thoughtful approach, see Noonan (2009). Although Judge Noonan's essay is not focused on the situation of believing Catholics, he does insist that: "I do not understand the authority attributed to conscience unless in some way it is responsive to God" (Noonan 2009: 238–39). See generally, Idleman (2005); and the symposium edited by Gross (2015).

33 On the questionable implication of his statement that the Catholic Church does not oppose the death penalty, see Miller (2011). For an analysis of whether American judges and politicians must follow Church teaching, see Kmiec (2009). By contrast, decisions by Justice Frankfurter in *Louisiana ex rel. Francis v. Resweber* and Justice Blackmun in *Furman v. Georgia* included statements that, although their personal beliefs were to the contrary, they were required by their judicial role to apply laws they found morally repugnant. Contrast Blackmun's eventual rejection of the death penalty with Scalia's support for it in *Callins v. Collins*.

34 Bailey (2006: 446). See also Carter (1989: 943) ("the religiously devout judge ought to be free to rest her moral knowledge on her religious faith" in the performance of her judicial duty). See generally, Greenawalt (1994). On the concealment of a judge's religious beliefs, see Idleman (2005).

35 Franck (2006: 452). Prof. Franck, however, never addresses a nominee's possible attachment to natural law, rather than religious beliefs generally.

36 *Edwards v. Aguillard.* See also, Rosen (1988). In *Barnes v. Glen Theatre, Inc.* (1991: 575) Scalia, concurring, wrote: "Our society prohibits, and all human societies have prohibited, certain activities not because they harm others but because they are considered in the traditional phrase, '*contra bonos mores*,' i.e. immoral," a phrase, however, used in a number of earlier cases, e.g., *Harris v. Runnels* (1851: 83) ("The common law...prohibits everything that is unjust or *contra bonos mores*"), *Jones v. Randall* ("Whatever is contrary, bonos mores est decorum, the principles of our law prohibit"), and *Kardo Co. v. Adams* (1916: 969) ("That term [contra bonos mores] may be difficult of definition applicable to all cases; but there can be no doubt that when conduct is of such character as to offend the average conscience, as involving injustice according to commonly accepted standards, it is contra bonos mores."). With Justice Thomas joining, Scalia, concurring in the judgment, also wrote in *Erie v. Pap's AM* (2000: 310; original italics): "The traditional power of government to foster good morals *(bonos mores),* and the acceptability of the traditional judgment (if Erie wishes to endorse it) that nude public dancing *itself* is immoral, have not been repealed by the First Amendment."

37 *Michael H. v. Gerald D.* (1989: 123), citing Justice Cardozo in *Snyder v. Massachusetts* (1934: 105) and *Palko v. Connecticut* (1937: 328). Scalia refers to "tradition" forty-one

times in his opinion. The dissent by Justice Brennan in *Michael H.* also discusses tradition, but finds it too subjective in most instances: "...the plurality pretends that tradition places a discernible border around the Constitution...Because reasonable people can disagree about the content of particular traditions, and because they can disagree even about which traditions are relevant to the definition of 'liberty,' the plurality has not found the objective boundary that it seeks" (*Id.*: 137). See also Scalia's opinion in *Rutan v. Republican Party* (1990: 95–96) ("traditions are themselves the stuff out of which the Court's principles are to be formed"). Compare, too, the case of *Troxel v. Granville*. For both cases, see Dubler (2008). "Liberal" justices also refer to the *Snyder* phrasing: See the concurrence of Justices Goldberg, Warren, and Brennan in *Griswold v. Connecticut* (1965: 486–91). On Scalia's opportunistic use of 'tradition,' see Strauss (1991).

38 For an argument that seeks to unite natural law and natural rights that Leo Strauss and others have sought to regard as incompatible, see Seagrave (2014).

39 See generally Norton (2004: 75–94). On Strauss as a practitioner of esoteric philosophy, in which the writer purposely obscures his precise meaning and its implications in the manner of many earlier philosophers, see Melzer (2014).

40 See generally, Merrill (2015).

41 Quoted in Flax (1998: 26).

42 See generally, Lane (2008). Justice Scalia, in his Vaughan Lecture at Princeton said: "Not all natural rights are in the Constitution." It is not clear, however, whether he believed that one may seek unenumerated natural rights in other foundational documents, and then read those documents into one's interpretation of the Constitution proper.

43 The issue of natural law arose tangentially in the confirmation hearing of Antonin Scalia when then Senator Biden sought to get the nominee to acknowledge that there exists a right of privacy, even though it is not mentioned in the Constitution and was not a widely shared value at the time of that document's adoption. Committee on the Judiciary, United States Senate 1986: 103. Scalia ducked the issue, at which point Biden phrased the question in terms of whether Scalia would accept the idea that most people now acknowledge some right to privacy, a proposition with which the nominee agreed without stating its foundations or scope in particular cases. Quite aside from Senator Biden's concern, the hearings may have been kept brief and unspecific for various reasons. President Reagan had just had his nomination of Robert Bork turned down in a bitter Senate fight, and his replacement nominee, Douglas Ginsburg, had to withdraw after questions arose about his use of marijuana. Scalia was confirmed by the Senate 98–0. Moreover, the movement of Catholic natural law was just gathering political force when Scalia was nominated in 1986 to replace William Rehnquist, who was being moved up to Chief Justice.

44 Federalist Society for Law and Public Policy Studies, University of Virginia School of Law, March 5, 1988. All of Thomas' comments quoted here were appended to the public record of the confirmation hearings and may be found at www.loc.gov/law/find/nominations/thomas/hearing-pt1.pdf (accessed January 3, 2017). Thomas also said:

> The American conception of the rule of law presupposes appreciation for the political philosophy of natural rights in all departments of government. The conservative failure to appreciate the importance of natural rights and higher law arguments culminated in the spectacle of Senator Biden, following the defeat of the Bork nomination, crowing about his belief that his rights were inalienable and came from God, not from a piece of paper. We cannot expect our views of civil rights to triumph, by conceding the moral high ground to those who confuse rights with willfulness.

45 In his Pacific Research Institute Speech of August 10, 1987, Thomas also said: "...a renewed emphasis on economic rights must play a key role in the revival of the

natural rights philosophy," which he marked as responsible for the last two hundred years of the nation's success. Thomas' opinion in the same-sex decision (*Obergefell*) by the Court confirms this orientation.

46 In his opening statement to the nominee, Biden said: "Judge Thomas, you come before this committee, in this time of change, with a philosophy different from that which we have seen in any Supreme Court nominee during my 19 years in the Senate, for, as has been widely discussed and debated, you are an adherent of the view that 'natural law' philosophy should inform the Constitution. Finding out what you mean when you say you would apply a 'natural law' philosophy to the Constitution is, in my view, the most important task of these hearings."

Biden then went on to describe several types of natural-law thinking before asking his questions of the candidate. He was thus following up on a statement he had made in his opening remarks at the confirmation hearing of Judge Robert Bork, when he said: "As a child of God, I believe my rights are not derived from the Constitution. My rights are not derived from any government. My rights are not derived from any majority. My rights are because I exist. They were given to me and each of my fellow citizens by our creator and they represent the essence of human dignity." In a fuller statement of his views, published during Thomas' confirmation hearings, Biden (1991) wrote:

> If Clarence Thomas believes that the Supreme Court should apply natural law above the Constitution, then in my view he should not serve on the Court....As I argued during the Bork confirmation debate, the American tradition of natural law has been to protect the rights of individuals to make decisions about matters of moral significance—free from both the interference of the will of the majority, as Robert Bork would have permitted, or from judges imposing their particular moral code, as some believe Clarence Thomas would have it....Judge Thomas has said that 'the thesis of natural law is that human nature provides the key to how men ought to live their lives'—suggesting that natural law dictates morality to us, instead of leaving matters to individual choice.

A number of academic lawyers expressed to the Committee their concerns about Thomas' views on natural law: see Margolick (1991).

47 Quoted in Bailey (2006: 445). On the Miers appointment, see Toobin (2007: 329–45). See also, Greenburg (2007).

48 Robert George was reportedly one of these emissaries, as he had been for the nomination of John Roberts as Chief Justice. Kirkpatrick (2005). As on previous occasions, George, a banjo-picking West Virginian and ardent Catholic, could speak to the Evangelicals as well as his co-religionists. In his last days in office, President George W. Bush awarded George the nation's second highest civilian award, the Presidential Citizens Medal; in 2012, he was appointed by House Speaker John Boehner to the U.S. Commission on International Religious Freedom. On George's close ties with Opus Dei, see Eshel (2005).

49 See Dworkin (2010).

50 The distinctions are spelled out in Foriers and Perelman (1968: 23–26).

51 "What the various forms of natural law share, is a longing for unity, for a less complicated and more organic sort of social world. What is wanted is a world in which it would be easier to be certain about 'the public good'.... [N]atural law has always been a philosophy congenial to judges. It guarantees the possibility of an impersonal administration of rules.... In America, the recent successes of natural law are surely part of the general cry for 'national purpose,' for a 'united moral front'" (Shklar 1964: 86, 87, 88–89). Justice Scalia always opposed the notion of a "living constitution": "But you would have to be an idiot to believe that," Scalia said. "The Constitution is not a living organism, it is a legal document. It says something and doesn't say other things" (quoted in Frank 2006).

52 A further example is supplied by the orientation of Supreme Court nominee Robert Bork. Like Thomas, Scalia, and others, Bork apparently needed to ground himself in some solid belief: Like them his originalism may be better understood not as authoritarianism, but as a need for some basis of certainty, including a foundational legal source. Thus it is no surprise that in 2003, at the age of 76 and now married to a woman who had been a nun for fifteen years, Bork converted to Catholicism. His penchant for the absolute was further revealed when he told an interviewer at the time: "I found the evidence of [intelligent] design overwhelming, and also the number of witnesses to the Resurrection compelling. The Resurrection is established as a solid historical fact" (Drake 2012). Indeed, a number of commenters misconstrue the basis on which Bork's nomination was rejected by the Senate. Linda Greenhouse (2013), for example, attributes Bork's failure to win confirmation to his vision of the Constitution, as exemplified by the position of Senator Arlen Spector. But the key swing vote in the Senate Judiciary Committee was not that of Spector but that of Senator Howell Heflin of Alabama. A former chief justice of his state's Supreme Court, Heflin, a democrat, was a conservative who opposed abortion, gun control, NAFTA, GATT, and the Family Medical Leave Act. Initially disposed to support the nomination, Heflin turned against Bork when he began to realize not that Bork was a constitutional originalist, but that he already knew the answers to all questions that might come before the Court, and would not listen to other arguments. To Heflin, this was the antithesis of judicial temperament: At the very least, a justice must consider what counsel, his fellow justices, and the writers of briefs have to say. But Bork clearly indicated he needed to listen to no one else's opinions. Once Heflin grasped this aspect of Bork's persona, he turned against the nominee and was able to bring along several other senators who voted down the nomination. It is, therefore, a mistake to attribute Bork's failure to gain a seat on the Court to his view of the Constitution.

53 On the movement as a whole, and the crucial role of the Federalist Society in particular, see Teles 2010. Like so many commenters, however, Teles does not discuss the natural-law aspect of this movement. See also, Avery and McLaughlin (2013).

54 See, e.g., the remarks by Christopher Eisgruber, "Law at Princeton," October 21, 2010, Princeton University, Law and Public Affairs Reunion.

55 The gun cases are *District of Columbia v. Heller*, and *McDonald v. Chicago*.

56 Pope Benedict XVI, while still a cardinal, was responsible for drafting the document signed by his predecessor, Pope John Paul II, and ratified early in his own papacy, that castigates all those, specifically mentioning anthropologists, who regard morality relativistically. Both popes confuse methodological relativism (trying to understand another culture without initially being judgmental) and asserting that all cultural practices are equally valid (even, by such a view, Nazism). See the encyclical *Splendor Veritatis,* quoted and discussed at Chapter Four above. See also Joseph Cardinal Ratzinger's August 6, 2000 declaration, as the head of the Congregation for the Doctrine of the Faith, *Dominus Jesus.* www.vatican.va/roman_curia/congregations/cfaith/documents/rc_con_cfaith_doc_20000806_dominus-iesus_en.html (accessed January 3, 2017), and, following the cardinal's elevation to the papacy, Pope Benedict XVI's message to youth, www.vatican.va/holy_father/benedict_xvi/messages/peace/documents/hf_ben-xvi_mes_20111208_xlv-world-day-peace_en.html (January 3, 2017).

57 On the recantation by one of the proponents of this 'recuperative therapy,' see Carey (2012).

58 See, *Obergefell v. Hodges*, dissent of Justice Thomas, section A2.

59 In a number of instances, the position of the Catholic Church is closer to that of Evangelicals than to its own parishioners. Thus, a survey in 2004 showed that Pope John Paul II had a more favorable rating among Evangelicals than the most famous of their own preachers, while the Papal position banning the use of contraceptives is closer to the position of many Evangelicals than most Catholics. See Wills (2005).

Donald Trump also played to the "Prosperity Gospel" wing of Evangelical thought, inviting two of its pastors to speak at his inauguration. On this movement generally, see Bowler (2013).

60 Quoted in Moody (2014). As his former clerk, law professor John Yoo (2016: 18) has said: "Thomas rejects social engineering in favor of individual liberty grounded in natural law."

61 *Bradwell v. Illinois* (1872: 141), Justice Bradley concurring ("The natural and proper timidity and delicacy which belongs to the female sex evidently unfits it for many of the occupations of civil life"). But see, Aynes (1999).

62 Rosen (2006: 64–65). Those favoring natural law also commonly portray themselves as apolitical in their judgments. As Judge Richard Posner (2008: 307) says, "Believers in natural law as a source of or limitation on positive law do not think they are politicizing law."

63 Judge Pryor (2006: 347), referring to the hearings in 2003, for his confirmation to the federal circuit court, when several members of the Senate Judiciary Committee asked whether his deeply held religious beliefs were part of an agenda, has written: "When Chairman Hatch responded to these statements by asking me about my religion and then asserting that 'in every case' he could see, I had 'followed the law regardless of [my] personal, deeply felt, strongly felt religious beliefs,' two other Senators [Leahy and Specter] objected to Chairman Hatch's reference to my religion." See generally, Horwitz (2006).

References

Allen, Danielle 2014, *Our Declaration: A Reading of the Declaration of Independence in Defense of Equality*, Liveright.

Allison, Jim 2012, "Is Christianity Part of the Common Law." http://candst.tripod.com/joestor4.htm (accessed January 5, 2017).

Alschuler, Albert W. 2002, *Law without Values: The Life, Work, and Legacy of Justice Holmes*, Chicago, IL: University of Chicago Press.

Arkes, Hadley 2013, "The Natural Law Challenge," *Harvard Journal of Law and Public Policy*, vol. 36, no. 3 (Summer), pp. 961–75.

Avery, Michael and Danielle McLaughlin 2013, *The Federalist Society*, Nashville, TN: Vanderbilt University Press.

Aynes, Richard L. 1999, "Bradwell v. Illinois: Chief Justice Chase's Dissent and the 'Sphere of Women's Work'," *Louisiana Law Review*, vol. 59, pp. 520–41.

Baertsch, Bernard 2012, "Human Dignity as a Component of a Long-Lasting and Widespread Conceptual Construct," *Journal of Bioethical Inquiry*, vol. 11, no. 2, pp. 201–11.

Bailey, D'Army 2006, "The Religious Commitments of Judicial Nominees—Address by Judge Bailey," *Notre Dame Journal of Law, Ethics, and Public Policy*, vol. 20, no. 1, pp. 443–46.

Bamforth, Nicholas 2011, "New Natural Law, Religion, and Same-Sex Marriage: Current Constitutional Issues," *Wake Forest Journal of Law and Policy*, vol. 1, pp. 207–79.

Barden, Garrett and Timothy Murphy 2010, *Law and Justice in Community*, New York: Oxford University Press.

Baum, Lawrence 2014, "Hiring Supreme Court Law Clerks: Probing the Ideological Linkage between Judges and Justices," *Marquette Law Review*, vol. 98, pp. 333–60.

Biden, Joseph R. Jr. 1991, "Law and Natural Law: Questions for Judge Thomas," *The Washington Post*, September 8.

Biddle, Francis 1961, *Justice Holmes, Natural Law and the Supreme Court*, New York: Macmillan.

Biggar, Nigel and Rufus Black, eds. 2000, *The Revival of Natural Law*, Aldershot: Ashgate.

Biskupic, Joan 2010, *American Original: The Life and Constitution of Supreme Court Justice Antonin Scalia*, New York: Farrar, Strauss and Giroux.

Bowler, Kate 2013, *Blessed: A History of the American Prosperity Gospel*, Oxford: Oxford University Press.

Boyer, Peter J. 2010, "Frat House for Jesus: The Entity behind C Street," *The New Yorker*, September 13.

Brett, Annabel S. 2011, *Changes of State: Nature and the Limits of the City in Early Natural Law*, Princeton, NJ: Princeton University Press.

Brooks, David 2016, "How Covenants Make Us," *New York Times*, April 5.

Cardozo, Benjamin 1924, *The Growth of Law*, New Haven, CT: Yale University Press.

Carey, Benedict 2012, "Leading Psychiatrist Apologizes for Study Supporting Gay 'Cure'," *New York Times*, May 18.

Carter, Stephen L. 1989, "The Religiously Devout Judge," *Notre Dame Law Review*, vol. 64, pp. 932–44.

Codevilla, Angelo M. 2010, *The Ruling Class: How They Corrupted America and What We Can Do about It*, New York: American Spectator/Beaufort.

Colucci, Frank J. 2009, *Justice Kennedy's Jurisprudence*, Lawrence: University Press of Kansas.

Committee on the Judiciary, United States Senate 1986, *Nomination of Judge Antonin Scalia*, S. Hrg. pp. 99–1064, August 5–6.

Corwin, Edward S. 1955, *The "Higher Law" Background of American Constitutional Law*, Ithaca, NY: Cornell University Press.

Cross, F. L. and E. A. Livingstone, eds. 2005, *The Oxford Dictionary of the Christian Church*, 3rd rev. edn., Oxford: Oxford University Press.

D'Amato, Anthony 2007–8, "Natural Law—A Libertarian View," *Florida International University Law Review*, vol. 3, pp. 97–111.

Declaration of Independence Symposium 2016, *Southern California Law Review*, vol. 89, pp. 359–671.

DeMar, Gary 2012, "Is a Return to Natural Law a Good Thing?" *The American Vision*, October 16. http://americanvision.org/6505/is-a-return-to-law-a-good-thing/ (accessed January 5, 2017).

d'Entreves, Alessandro Passerin 1970, *Natural Law*, 2nd rev. edn., London: Hutchinson University Library.

Devins, Neal and Lawrence Baum 2016, "Split Definitive: How Party Polarization Turned the Supreme Court into a Partisan Court," William and Mary Law School Research Paper No. 09-276 (March 16). https://papers.ssrn.com/sol3/papers.cfm?abstract_id=2432111 (accessed January 5, 2017).

Dershowitz, Alan 2005, *Rights From Wrongs: The Origins of Human Rights in the Experience of Injustice*, New York: Basic Books.

Desmond, Adrian and James Moore 1991, *Darwin: The Life of a Tormented Evolutionist*, New York: W. W. Norton.

Drake, Tim 2012, "Catholic Convert Judge Robert Bork Dies," *National Catholic Register*, December 19. www.ncregister.com/site/print_article/35784/ (accessed January 5, 2017).

Dubler, Ariela R. 2008, "Constructing the Modern American Family: The Stories of Troxel v. Granville," in Carol Sanger (ed.), *Family Law Stories*, New York: Foundation Press, pp. 95–111.

Dworkin, Ronald 2010, "The Temptation of Elena Kagan," *New York Review of Books*, July.

———— 2013, *Religion without God*, Cambridge, MA: Harvard University Press.

Edelstein, Dan 2010, *The Terror of Natural Right: Republicanism, The Cult of Nature, and the French Revolution*, Chicago, IL: University of Chicago Press.

Epstein, Richard 1989, "The Utilitarian Foundations of Natural Law," *Harvard Journal of Law and Public Policy*, vol. 12, pp. 713–51.

———— 2005, "The Not So Minimum Content of Natural Law," *Oxford Journal of Legal Studies*, vol. 25, no. 2 (Summer), pp. 219–55.

———— 2012, "The Natural Law Influences on the First Generation of American Constitutional Law: Reflections on Philip Hamburger's Law and Judicial Duty," *Journal of Law, Philosophy and Culture*, vol. 6, no. 1, pp. 120–49.

Eshel, Neir 2005, "Spotted History Aside, Opus Dei Forges Close Campus Links," *Daily Princetonian*, March 22.

Fallon, Richard H. 1997, "'The Rule of Law' as a Concept in Constitutional Discourse," *Columbia Law Review*, vol. 97, pp. 1–56.

Fears, J. Rufus 2000, "Natural Law: The Legacy of Greece and Rome," in Edward B. McLean, ed., *Common Truths: New Perspectives on Natural Law*, Wilmington, DE: ISI Books, pp. 19–56.

Finnis, John 2011, *Natural Law and Natural Rights*, revised edition, Oxford: Oxford University Press.

Flax, Jane 1998, *The American Dream in Black and White: The Clarence Thomas Hearings*, Ithaca, NY: Cornell University Press.

Fletcher, George 2001, *The Secret Constitution*, Oxford: Oxford University Press.

Foriers, Paul and Chaim Perelman 1968, "Natural Law and Natural Rights," in Philip Weiner, ed., *Dictionary of the History of Ideas*, vol. 3, New York: Charles Scribner's Sons, pp. 13–27.

Forte, David F. ed. 1998, *Natural Law and Contemporary Public Policy*, Washington, DC: Georgetown University Press.

Franck, Matthew J. 2006, "The Unbearable Unimportance of the Catholic Moment in Supreme Court History," *Notre Dame Journal of Law, Ethics, and Public Policy*, vol. 20, no. 1, pp. 447–53.

Frank, Matthew J. 2006, "That Rascal Scalia!" *National Review*, February 14.

Freedman, Samuel G. 2010, "Tea Party Rooted in Religious Fervor for Constitution," *New York Times*, November 5.

Fuller, Lon L. 1946, "Reason and Fiat in Case Law," *Harvard Law Review*, vol. 59, pp. 376–95.

Garet, Ronald R. 1988, "Natural Law and Creation Stories," in J. Roland Pennock and John W. Chapman, eds., *Religion, Morality, and the Law*, Nomos XXX, New York: New York University Press, 1988, pp. 218–62.

Geertz, Clifford 2001, *Available Light: Anthropological Reflections on Philosophical Topics*, Princeton, NJ: Princeton University Press.

George, Robert P. 2008, "Natural Law," *Harvard Journal of Law and Public Policy*, vol. 31, pp. 171–96.

———— 2012, "Interpreting Freedom: America's Unwritten Constitution by Akhil Reed Amar," *New York Times*, December 21.

———— 2013, *Conscience and its Enemies: Confronting the Dogmas of Liberal Secularism*, Wilmington, DE: ISI Books.

Gingrich, Newt 2011, *A Nation Like No Other*, Washington, DC: Regnery.

Gluckman, Max 1965, *The Judicial Process among the Barotse*, Manchester: Manchester University Press.

Gould, Stephen Jay 1987, *Time's Arrow, Time's Cycle*, Cambridge, MA: Harvard University Press.

Greenawalt, Kent 1994, "The Use of Religious Convictions by Legislators and Judges," *Journal of Church and State*, vol. 36, no. 3, pp. 541–55.

Greenburg, Jan Crawford 2007, *Supreme Conflict: The Inside Story of the Struggle for Control of the United States Supreme Court*, New York: Penguin Books.

Greenhouse, Carol 1989, *Praying For Justice: Faith, Order, and Community in an American Town*, Ithaca, NY: Cornell University Press.

Greenhouse, Linda 2013, "Robert Bork's Tragedy," *New York Times*, online Opinionator, January 9.

—— 2016, "Resetting the Post-Scalia Supreme Court," *New York Times*, February 18.

Gross, Rachel E., ed. 2015, "Do Religious Beliefs of Supreme Court Justices Influence their Decisions?" *Moment*, January/February, pp. 41–45 (also broadcast on CSPAN.com, October 27, 2014).

Haines, Charles Grove 1916, "The Law of Nature in State and Federal Judicial Decisions," *Yale Law Journal*, vol. 25, pp. 617–57.

—— 1930, *The Revival of Natural Law Concepts*, Cambridge, MA: Harvard University Press.

Helmholz, Richard H. 2015, *Natural Law in Court: A History of Legal Theory in Practice*, Cambridge, MA: Harvard University Press.

Hoffheimer, Michael H. 1992, *Justice Holmes and the Natural Law*, New York: Garland Publishing.

Holmes, Oliver Wendell Jr. 1920, *Collected Legal Papers*, New York: Harcourt, Brace and Co.

Horwitz, Paul 2006, "Religious Tests in the Mirror: The Constitutional Law and Constitutional Etiquette of Religion in Judicial Nominations," Social Science Research Network, April 19. http://papers.ssrn.com/sol3/papers.cfm?abstract_id=897816&high=%20paul%20horwitz (accessed January 5, 2017).

Hua, Cai 2001, *A Society without Fathers or Husbands: The Na of China*, trans. by Asti Hustvedt, New York: Zone Books.

Idleman, Scott C. 2005, "The Concealment of Religious Values in Judicial Decision-making," *Virginia Law Review*, vol. 91, pp. 515–34.

Jelliff, Anne 2013, "Catholic Values, Human Dignity, and the Moral Law in the United States Supreme Court: Justice Anthony Kennedy's Approach to the Constitution," *Albany Law Review*, vol. 76, pp. 335–65.

Kirk, Russell 2001, *The Conservative Mind*, 7th rev. edn. Washington, DC: Regnery Publishing.

Kirkpatrick, David D. 2005, "A Year of Work to Sell Roberts to Conservatives," *New York Times*, July 22.

Kmiec, Douglas M. 2009, "Catholic Judges and Abortion: Did the Pope Set New Rules?" *Time*, February 20.

Knowles, Helen 2009, *The Tie Goes to Freedom: Anthony M. Kennedy on Liberty*, New York: Rowman & Littlefield Publishers.

Kozinski, Alex 2013, "Natural Law Jurisprudence: A Skeptical Perspective," *Harvard Journal of Law and Public Policy*, vol. 36, no. 3 (Summer), pp. 977–82.

Kuhn, Thomas S. 1962, *The Structure of Scientific Revolutions*, Chicago, IL: University of Chicago Press.

Laing, Jacqueline A. and Russell Wilcox, eds. 2013, *The Natural Law Reader*, London: Wiley-Blackwell.

Lane, Frederic S. 2008, *The Court and the Cross: The Religious Right's Crusade to Reshape the Supreme Court*, Boston, MA: Beacon Press.

Levinson, Sanford 2011, *Constitutional Faith*, Princeton, NJ: Princeton University Press, rev. edn.

Levi, Edward J. 1949, *An Introduction to Legal Reasoning*, Chicago, IL: University of Chicago Press.

Linker, Damon 2007, *The Theocons: Secular America under Siege*, New York: Doubleday.

Liptak, Adam 2010, "A Sign of the Court's Polarization: Choice of Clerks," *New York Times*, September 6.

Lowry, Rich 2011, "Lincoln's Declaration," *National Review Online*, July 1.

Majors, Dan 2011, "Scalia States His Case for Morals," *Pittsburgh Post-Gazette*, September 25.

Margolick, David 1991, "The Thomas Hearings; Sizing Up the Talk of 'Natural Law': Many Ideologies Discover a Precept," *New York Times*, September 12.

Melzer, Arthur M. 2014, *Philosophy between the Lines: The Lost History of Esoteric Writing*, Chicago, IL: University of Chicago Press.

Mendelsohn, Daniel 1996, "The Stand: Expert Witnesses and Ancient Mysteries in a Colorado Courtroom," *Lingua Franca*, vol. 6, no 6 (September/October), pp. 34–46.

Merrill, Thomas W. 2015, "Possession as a Natural Right," *N.Y.U. Journal of Law & Liberty*, vol. 9, pp. 345–74.

Miller, Lisa 2011, "Justice Scalia Speaks for Himself on Death Penalty, Not Catholic Church," *Washington Post*, October 27.

Miller, Perry 1865, *The Life of the Mind in America*, New York: Harcourt, Brace & World.

Mitgang, Herbert 1987, "Handwritten Draft of a Bill of Rights Found," *New York Times*, July 29.

Mohler, R. Albert Jr. 2003, "Standing Together, Standing Apart: Cultural Co-belligerence without Theological Compromise," *Touchstone*, v. 16, no. 6 (July/August). www.touchstonemag.com/archives/article.php?id=16-06-070-f (accessed January 5, 2017).

Moody, Chris 2014, "Clarence Thomas: Society is Overly Sensitive about Race," *Yahoo News*, February 11.

Murphy, Bruce Allen 2015, *Scalia: A Court of One*, New York: Simon and Schuster.

Murray, John Courtnay 2005 [1960], *We Hold These Truths: Catholic Reflections on the American Proposition*, Lanham, MD: Rowman & Littlefield.

Nelson, Craig 2007, *Thomas Paine: Enlightenment, Revolution, and the Birth of Modern Nations*, New York: Penguin.

Neuhaus, Richard John and Charles W. Colson 1994, "Evangelicals and Catholics Together: The Christian Mission in the Third Millennium," *First Things*, no. 43 (May), pp. 15–22.

Noonan, John T. Jr. 2009, "Conscience and the Constitution," in H. Jefferson Powell and James Boyd White (eds.), *Law and Democracy in the Empire of Force*, Ann Arbor: University of Michigan Press, pp. 238–49.

Norton, Anne 2004, *Leo Strauss and the Politics of American Empire*, New Haven, CT: Yale University Press.

Note 1990, "Justice Scalia's Use of Sources in Statutory and Constitutional Interpretation: How Congress Always Loses," 1990 *Duke Law Journal* 160.

Oppenheimer, Mark 2010, "Marco Rubio: Catholic or Protestant?" *New York Times*, November 26.

Posner, Richard A. 2004, "Comments on Citing Foreign Courts," Leiter Reports: A Philosophy Blog. http://leiterreports.typepad.com/blog/2004/12/response_to_com_1.html (accessed January 5, 2017).

——— 2008, *How Judges Think*, Cambridge, MA: Harvard University Press.

——— 2016, "The Supreme Court is a Political Court: Republicans' Actions are Proof," *Washington Post*, March 9.

Pryor, William H. 2006, "The Religious Faith and Judicial Duty of an American Catholic Judge," 24 *Yale Law and Policy Review*, vol. 24, pp. 347–62.

Renteln, Alison Dundes 2004, *The Cultural Defense*, Oxford: Oxford University Press.

Ring, Kevin A., ed. 2004, *Scalia Dissents*, Washington, DC: Regnery Publishing, Inc.

Rogers, Eugene F. Jr. 2013, *Aquinas and the Supreme Court: Biblical Narratives of Jews, Gentiles, and Gender*, New York: Wiley-Blackwell.

Rosen, Jeffrey 2000, "One Man's Justice," *New York Times Book Review*, December 17, p. 26.

——— 2010, "Radical Constitutionalism," *New York Times Magazine*, November 28, pp. 34–36.

Rosen, Lawrence 1988, "Continuing the Conversation: Creationism, the Religion Clauses, and the Politics of Culture," in Philip B. Kurland, Gerhard Casper, and Dennis J. Hutchinson, eds., *The Supreme Court Review 1988*, Chicago, IL: University of Chicago Press, 1988, pp. 61–86.

——— 2006, *Law as Culture*, Princeton, NJ: Princeton University Press.

Rosen, Michael 2012, *Dignity: Its History and Meaning*, Cambridge, MA: Harvard University Press.

Sahlins, Marshall 2008, *The Western Illusion of Human Nature*, Chicago, IL: Paradigm Press.

Sandefur, Timothy 2013, *The Conscience of the Constitution: The Declaration of Independence and the Right to Liberty*, Cato Institute.

Santorum, Rick 2006, *It Takes a Family*, Wilmington: Intercollegiate Studies Institute.

Scalia, Antonin 2002, "God's Justice and Ours," *First Things*, May. www.firstthings.com/article/2002/05/gods-justice-and-ours (accessed January 5, 2017).

——— 2011, "The Originalist," *California Lawyer*, vol. 31, no. 1 (January 2011), p. 33.

——— and Bryan A. Garner 2012, *Reading Law: The Interpretation of Legal Texts*, St. Paul, MN: West.

Seagrave, S. Adam 2014, *The Foundations of Natural Morality: On the Compatibility of Natural Rights and the Natural Law*, Chicago, IL: University of Chicago Press.

Shklar, Judith N. 1964, *Legalism*, Cambridge, MA: Harvard University Press.

Shorto, Russell 2010, "How Christian Were the Founders?" *New York Times*, February 14.

Singer, Barbara A. 1983, "The Reason of the Common Law," *University of Miami Law Review*, vol. 37, pp. 797–823.

Skinner, Quentin 1978, *Foundations of Modern Political Thought*, vol. 2, Cambridge: Cambridge University Press.

Soper, Philip 1992, "Natural Confusions about Natural Law," *Michigan Law Review*, vol. 90, pp. 2393–2423.

Stone, Geoffrey 2009, "Justice Sotomayor, Justice Scalia and Our Six Catholic Justices," *Huffington Post*, September 28. www.huffingtonpost.com/geoffrey-r-stone/justice-sotomayor-justice_b_271229.html (accessed January 5, 2017).

——— 2016, "Tough, Brilliant, and Kind: The Antonin Scalia I Knew," *The Daily Beast*, February 14.

Strauss, David A. 1991, "Tradition, Precedent, and Justice Scalia," *Cardozo Law Review*, vol. 12, pp. 1699.

Strauss, Leo 1999 [1953], *Natural Right and History*, Chicago, IL: University of Chicago Press.

Sunstein, Cass 2007–8, "Due Process Traditionalism," *Michigan Law Review*, vol. 106, pp. 1543–70.

Teles, Steven M. 2010, *The Rise of the Conservative Legal Movement: The Battle for Control of the Law*, Princeton, NJ: Princeton University Press.

Thomas, Clarence 1987, "Affirmative Action: Cure or Contradiction?" *Center Magazine*, November/December.

—— 1998, "Civility," *Race and Ethnic Ancestry Law Journal*, vol. 4 (Spring), pp. 1–6.

Tierney, Brian 2014, *Liberty and Law: The Idea of Permissive Natural law, 1100–1800*, Washington, DC: Catholic University Press of America.

Toobin, Jeffrey 2007, *Nine: Inside the Secret World of the Supreme Court*, New York: Anchor Books.

—— 2009, "No More Mr. Nice Guy: The Supreme Court's Stealth Hard-Liner," *The New Yorker*, May 25.

Weber, Max 1968, "Natural Law," reprinted in S. N. Eisenstadt, ed., *Max Weber on Charisma and Institution Building*, Chicago, IL: University of Chicago Press.

Weinreb, Lloyd L. 1990, *Natural Law and Justice*, Cambridge, MA: Harvard University Press.

Wiecek, William 2001, "Felix Frankfurter, Incorporation and the Willie Francis Case," *Journal of Supreme Court History*, vol. 26, no. 1 (March), pp. 53–66.

Wilentz, Sean and Laurence H. Tribe 2002, *Jurist: Legal Intelligence Forum*. www.jurist. org/forum/forumnew60.htm (accessed January 5, 2017).

Will, George F. 2014, "Progressives are Wrong about the Essence of the Constitution," *The Washington Post*, April 16.

Wills, Gary 2005, "Fringe Government," *New York Review of Books*, vol. 52, no. 15 (October 6), pp. 46–50.

Wolfe, Christopher 1994, *The Rise of Modern Judicial Review*, rev. ed., New York: Rowman and Littlefield.

Wollheim, Richard 1967, "Natural Law," in Paul Edwards, ed., *The Encyclopedia of Philosophy*, vol. 5, New York: Macmillan, pp. 450–54.

Wolterstorff, Nicholas 2008, *Justice: Rights and Wrongs*, Princeton, NJ: Princeton University Press.

Wood, Gordon S. 2014, "A Different Reading of Our Declaration," *New York Review of Books*, August 14.

Worthen, Molly 2012, "The First Principles of Rick Santorum," *New York Times*, February 9.

Wright, R. George 1994–95, "Is Natural Law Theory of Any Use in Constitutional Interpretation?" *Southern California Interdisciplinary Law Journal*, vol. 4, pp. 463–87.

Yoo, John 2016, "The Constitution of Clarence Thomas," *National Review*, July 11, pp. 18–21.

Ziolkowski, Theodore 1997, *The Mirror of Justice: Literary Reflections of Legal Crises*, Princeton, NJ: Princeton University Press.

Zuckert, Michael P. 1997, *The Natural Rights Republic: Studies in the Foundation of the American Political Tradition*, Notre Dame, IN: University of Notre Dame Press.

Cases cited

Barnes v. Glen Theatre, Inc., 501 U.S. 560, 111 S. Ct. 2456 (1991).

Baskin v. Bogan, 766 F. 3d 648 (7th Cir. 2014).

Bowers v. Hardwick, 478 U.S. 186 (1986).

Bradwell v. Illinois, 83 U.S. (Wall.) 130 (1872).

Bush v. Gore, 531 U.S. 98 (2000).

Callins v. Collins, 510 U.S. 1141 (1994).

Christian Legal Society v. Martinez, 561 U.S. 661,130 S. Ct. 2971–3020 (2010).

Church of the Holy Trinity v. U.S., 145 U.S. 457 (1892).

City of Boerne v. Flores, 521 U.S. 507 (1997).

Commonwealth v. Perry, 155 Mass. 117, 28 N.E. 1126 (Sup. Ct. of Mass., 1891).

Davis v. Beason, 133 U.S. 333 (1890).

District of Columbia v. Heller, 554 U.S. 570 (2008).

Edwards v. Aguillard, 482 U.S. 578 (1987).

Employment Division v. Smith, 494 U.S. 872 (1990).

Erie v. Pap's AM, 529 U.S. 277 (2000).

Furman v. Georgia, 408 U.S. 238 (1972).

Golinski v. Office of Personnel Management, 824 F.Supp.2d 968, (N.D. CA 2012).

Griswold v. Connecticut, 381 U.S. 479 (1965).

Harris v. Runnels, 53 U.S. 79, 12 How. 79, 13 L. Ed. 901 (1851).

Jones v. Randall, Court of King's Bench, 1 Cowp. 37 (1774).

Kardo Co. v. Adams, 231 F. 950 (6th Cir. 1916).

Lawrence v. Texas, 539 U.S. 558 (2003).

Louisiana ex rel. Francis v. Resweber, 329 U.S. 459 (1947).

McCreary County, KY v. American Civil Liberties Union, 545 U.S. 844 (2005).

McDonald v. Chicago, 561 U.S. 3025, 130 S. Ct. 3020 (2010).

McLean v. Arkansas Board of Education, 529 F. Supp. 1255 (E.D. Ark. 1982).

Meachum v. Fano, 427 U.S. 215 (1976).

Michael H. v. Gerald D., 491 U.S. 110 (1989).

Obergefell v. Hodges, 576 U.S.___ (2015).

Palko v. Connecticut, 302 U.S. 319 (1937).

Perry v. Schwarzenegger, No C 09-2292 VRW (August 4, 2010).

Romer v. Evans, 517 U.S. 620 (1996).

Rutan v. Republican Party of Illinois, 497 U.S. 62 (1990).

Singh v. Singh, 213 Conn 637, 569 A.2d 1112 (1990).

Snyder v. Massachusetts, 291 U.S. 97 (1934).

Texas v. Johnson, 491 U.S. 397 (1989).

Troxel v. Granville, 530 U.S. 57 (2000).

United States v. Virginia, 518 U.S. 515 (1996).

United States v. Windsor, 570 U.S. 12, 133 S. Ct. 2675, 186 L. Ed. 2d 808 (2013).

Zablocki v. Redhail, 434 U.S. 374 (1978).

PART III

Reaching out

7

MEDICALIZING THE LAW

The debate over male circumcision

Sometimes the law catches up with the culture, sometimes the culture catches up with the law, and sometimes—whether by chance or design—they arrive at a common destination simultaneously. In the case of same-sex marriage in the U.S., it may have been a bit of each; by comparison, in the case of the abortion decision, Roe v. Wade, *the question of who got where when has itself become an integral part of the issue.[1] When it comes to the relation of law and culture, male circumcision is, in this regard, an unusual example. Male circumcision dates back at least to ancient Egypt and is not only linked for some to religious practice but has, in more recent times, been justified as medically advised. Whether one sees it as a remnant of rituals of inclusion and sacrifice or as a means of avoiding disease, the clash of values and rationales would seem to pit religion against state authority, doctor against doctor, parent against child.*

More to the present purpose, circumcision not only forces us to decide what is good and what is bad—or what to do if faced with the more difficult task of deciding between one good and another—but when and how to defer to our cultural orientations. Indeed, how does the law affect the decisions that others will have to make in this regard? If disputants rely on personal faith or questionable medical views, what if any credence should the law give to children's rights or 'the traditions of our people'? Indeed, is any compromise practicable or proper for courts? And if culture is being sneaked in through the side door—whether under the rubric of 'liberty' or 'tradition' or 'due process'—is the choice of language crucial to the way public debate may go forward? In the following discussion of circumcision, all of these factors come into play, even if they may not always be explicitly stated by those most involved.

★ ★ ★

In 2010, following a six-month relationship, an unmarried Florida couple with the Latinate-sounding names of Heather Hironimus and Dennis Nebus had a son. They entered into a parenting agreement that provided for the boy, Chase, to be circumcised. Neither parent had a religious reason for seeking the procedure. Subsequently, the mother changed her mind, ran off with the child, and took refuge in a women's crisis shelter. She said the boy was afraid of the procedure and that she was terrified by the possible consequences of the child being subjected to a general anesthesia. A judge ordered that the circumcision agreement be honored, stating, without specification, that there was a 'medical condition' warranting the procedure and that male circumcision was "just the normal thing to do."[2] The mother's attorneys filed a civil rights suit against the father, the judge, and the enforcing sheriff asserting, among other grounds, that male circumcision was unnecessary—indeed physically and emotionally harmful—and that the court should recognize the child's right not to be harmed. It took until the child was 4 years old, and Judge Jeffery Dana Gillen's order that "She is going to sign the paperwork authorizing Chase's circumcision or she's going to sit behind bars until she does" for a tearful and handcuffed Heather to sign a document indicating that she would abide by the terms of the original agreement. In the interim, anti-circumcision advocacy groups picketed against forced circumcision, doctors expressed divergent views, and the entire question of male circumcision was placed in contention (Figures 7.1 and 7.2).

This was hardly the first occasion in recent times when the procedure has been contested. Not only do people disagree as to the benefits of circumcision or the reasons potential harm ought to negate parental rights in favor of consent by the individual, but doctors and nurses, politicians and professors, municipalities, hospitals, and religious leaders have all been caught up in the debate.[3] For example, in the 1990s some nurses in New Mexico refused to participate any longer in the practice, regarding it as child abuse. In San Francisco, opponents of the procedure sought to place on the ballot a referendum barring male circumcision and rendering its practice before the boy turns eighteen a crime. In response to the initiative, California's Governor Jerry Brown signed an order preventing

FIGURE 7.1 Heather Hironimus signing agreement (Amy Beth Bennett/TNS/ZUMA).

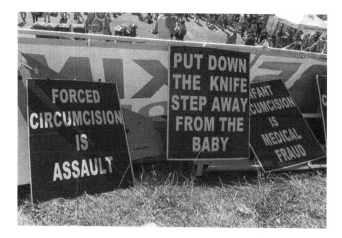

FIGURE 7.2 Circumcision protest placards (public domain).

localities from banning the procedure. Other countries have experienced equally contentious debates on the issue. In several European countries, for example, it has been suggested that if female circumcision is barred then equality demands a similar ban on male circumcision. That position appears to be supported by a non-binding resolution emanating from the Parliamentary Assembly of the Council of Europe, whose members said they were "particularly worried about a category of violation of the physical integrity of children" and included in this category "circumcision of young boys for religious reasons." Following the decision by a court in Cologne that male circumcision constituted the infliction of bodily harm, Chancellor Angela Merkel expressed her opposition to any such ban: "Amid warnings from the chancellor that Germany could become a 'laughing stock' if it outlawed such a basic religious rite, the federal legislature passed a law to protect the practice, as long as parents were informed about the slight risks" (Anonymous 2013).[4] French President François Hollande expressed a similar opinion when he said, "France totally rejects the assimilation [into a single category] of the excision practised on young girls and the ritual circumcision of boys. An unacceptable form of mutilation with heavy physical and psychological consequences for the women who are subjected to it cannot be compared to a ritual practice which is widespread across the world and sometimes encouraged by the medical profession" (Anonymous 2013).

Over time, the nature of the debate has changed as the rationales for male circumcision have reflected alterations in the social, religious, and medical contexts. Most recently, the debate has been fueled by the presence of immigrants who engage in female circumcision, a practice that is almost universally condemned by Westerners yet raises the question whether the rationales for circumcising boys are not equally worthy of condemnation. Opponents of both practices would, therefore, prefer that the term 'genital mutilation' be applied to the male procedure no less than the female. As one surveys the history of circumcision one is necessarily, then, surveying much of the connected cultural history of the periods.

Prior to the nineteenth century, male circumcision was relatively rare in Europe and the United States. After all, few people in the Christian West wanted their son mistaken for a Jew or a Muslim. A number of Medieval and Renaissance-era paintings depict the circumcision of Jesus—an event still celebrated in some churches—as one aspect of his claim to be the Messiah in the line of the house of David, while other art works, perhaps as a way of representing Christianity's divergence from its Jewish origins, show the Virgin Mary with the baby Jesus seated on her lap, his uncircumcised penis visible and even indicated by his blessed mother.[5] Indeed, penile circumcision was replaced by St. Paul's use of the metaphor (Romans 2:29) of the 'circumcision of the heart,' by which the outward sign on a man's body, which can lead him to believe he has actually achieved purity, is replaced by the true sign of one's acceptance of God and His only son, the inward change being rendered by the Holy Spirit to the heart as the metaphoric seat of sincerity (Figure 7.3).

It was not until the Victorian period that circumcision became more acceptable in Britain and the United States due to the growing tendency to medicalize a wide range of practices. In particular, the adoption of circumcision in this period was largely connected with an anti-masturbation campaign, it being thought that a young boy, by rubbing the foreskin of his penis in the crib, might come to enjoy the sensation at the risk of going blind, becoming insane, or suffering other ailments. The best way to address the problem, it was thought, was, therefore, to remove the foreskin altogether. This style of reasoning was part of a much larger medicalization of numerous aspects of a person's overall well-being

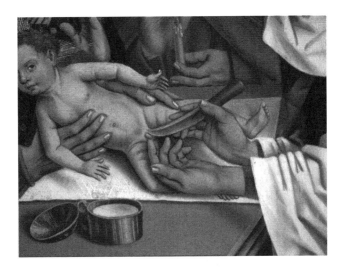

FIGURE 7.3 Christ child's circumcision (detail of *Circumcision of Christ* by Friedrich Herlin, 1466; public domain).

taking place at this time. Lobotomies for mental illness, female circumcision for hysteria, and electric shock for depression were far more common practices than most people realize.[6] More recently, equally questionable medicalized studies claim that if a woman places a newborn on her tummy they will 'bond' with one another, such that the mother need not feel guilty if she then spends much of her time away from the child pursuing a career.[7]

A particularly revealing example of the medicalization phenomenon is provided by the problem of kleptomania. In the late nineteenth century, middle-class women began to be more responsible for shopping for daily household needs. But a woman of this class should not simply be out walking the streets. Hence the invention of the department store, an indoor place where such a woman could do her shopping, perhaps take tea in full view of others, and not be mistaken for a 'streetwalker.' The problem was that some of these ladies were stealing things. To avoid having to characterize them as ordinary thieves—and consistent with the medicalization of all sorts of behavior in this era—it was said that these women were suffering from a physical ailment. Moreover, because it was also a characteristic of this mode of explanation, the problem needed to be attributable to some localized part of the body. In this case, women were said to have a problem with their womb—indeed to suffer from "womb disease mania," also called "uterine insanity."[8] Men, lacking wombs, could not be kleptomaniacs. That no doubt explains why, until the most recent editions, the *Diagnostic and Statistical Manual of Mental Disorders* (DSM) indicated that kleptomania is a problem virtually limited to women.[9]

As in these other instances, changes in the social context of male circumcision also played into the shift to hygienic rationales. Not only was circumcision claimed as a cure for ailments ranging from prevention of masturbation and epilepsy to spinal paralysis and the rape of white women by black men, but once women started going to hospitals to give birth they became much more susceptible to medical professionals who indicated the necessity of the operation. The same orientation has persisted even as the conditions to be treated by a therapeutic/prophylactic circumcision have varied. Thus, it has been said that penile uncleanliness and urinary tract infections could also be avoided by the procedure. Others have claimed that penile cancer is much less likely to occur if the child is circumcised, even though the incidence of such cancer is very low and the correlation is negligible. As the fear of HIV/AIDS has displaced penile cancer, the purported benefit of circumcision has shifted to arguments favoring the operation as a way of preventing that ailment.[10] Each instance, of course, appears totally plausible to its age and highly questionable when the explanation of the moment has been superseded. As psychology critic Thomas Szasz has quipped about the changeable nature of such rationales: Whereas in the nineteenth century masturbation was viewed as a disease, now it is seen as the cure.[11]

Notwithstanding new medical claims replacing older ones the rate of male circumcision has been declining in most Western nations. Although sources for statistics vary a good deal, the rates appear to have peaked in the U.S. in the

1980s at 75–85 percent or more and fallen off to around 60–65 percent since the 1990s. Rates have long been much lower, though quite variable, in Western Europe and Great Britain.[12] In each instance, the rationales affecting rates over time have varied. Proponents claim that women prefer the appearance of a circumcised penis, that the operation is essential for those whose religious identity and birthright are connected with the practice, that sexual pleasure is actually increased, and that circumcision even constitutes a useful form of pain for a child to endure.[13] By contrast, the opponents cite the practice as one that reproduces patriarchy, perpetuates unwarranted gender differentiation, and relies solely on tradition rather than science. The medical profession has not come to a shared resolution of these issues. While some organizations have indicated that they see no necessary medical benefits to the procedure, others have stated that the risks are minimal or undetermined.[14] If there is a later change of mind, plastic surgery can restore the foreskin in some cases, and a number of men have sought medical assistance to do so.[15]

The legal situation is no less resolved than the medical.[16] Although a number of commenters equate male circumcision with child abuse there is no clear judicial precedent in the U.S. or most other countries supporting that claim.[17] Instead, cases that raise the issue of circumcision are commonly those that seek damages following a botched procedure.[18] Indeed, the safety of the procedure is debatable, especially in the light of some notorious cases of malpractice. In one such instance, following a procedure that went tragically wrong, doctors convinced the parents to turn the little boy into a girl, only for the child, upon reaching adolescence, to learn what happened and to suffer considerable psychological trauma before reestablishing his male identity.[19]

Since any judicial consideration of circumcision must address potential harm, the fact that there is disagreement as to the actual risks hampers any clear-cut approach to the matter. Infections are not infrequent, and some deaths have been reported. Brigman (1984–5: 340) cites a 1979 article by one doctor who calculated that 229 infants were dying each year from the procedure. Studies that address such neonatal deaths do not indicate how many are due to incompetency on the part of those performing the operation. Many doctors are unfamiliar with the procedure and make mistakes. That may be why, when Queen Elizabeth had Prince Charles circumcised, she called in a Jewish *mohel* to perform the operation.[20] Traditionally, at the end of the Orthodox Jewish ceremony (in a practice called *metzitzah b'peh*) the ritual circumciser, holding a sip of wine in his mouth, will suck on the bleeding wound three times. In more recent times, this ritual act has been justified in medical terms. However, in the nineteenth century, concerns about the transmission of tuberculosis led to some countries barring the practice: France, for example, outlawed it in 1845. Recently, cases have been reported in which herpes was transmitted in this fashion. As a result, calls were issued in New York for the legal elimination of the practice. In September 2013, the New York City Board of Health passed a regulation requiring Jewish ritual circumcisers to obtain informed consent from the parents about the risk of a potentially fatal herpes infection linked to the ritual of oral suction of the penis following circumcision (Stempel 2013). Subsequently, it was agreed that informed consent would not be required but that a circumciser who transmitted the disease—which has resulted in several infant deaths—could be barred from future practice (Wulfhorst 2015). Such disputes, however, may only compound the potential conflict between opposition to circumcision and religious freedom.[21]

The courts and legislatures of various countries have taken different approaches to the entire issue of male circumcision. A British family court in 1999, faced with a non-practicing Muslim father who sought the procedure and a non-practicing Christian mother who opposed it, blocked the circumcision of their five-year-old boy as contrary to the child's best interests. However, the court indicated that in the hypothetical instance of a Jewish child born after the couple separated, the judges might well reject the argument of an opposing husband and find in favor of a mother who wishes to have the son look like his older brothers.[22] Ordinarily in the U.S. one would have to show criminal intent to convict a parent who chose to have the child circumcised, a difficult standard to achieve when the parent believes he or she is doing what is best for the infant. Constitutional challenges fall on both sides. Privacy rulings would seem to favor barring the practice (with analogies drawn to Supreme Court decisions on contraception or interracial marriage) while a combination of parental rights and freedom of religion (with analogies drawn to rulings on religious objections to extended schooling, corporal punishment, or medical decisions made by parents) would seem to weigh in favor of the practice. Arguments on both sides have invoked issues of personal security, due process, equal protection, privacy, the availability of less intrusive measures, unfair and deceptive practices by physicians, insurance coverage for the operation, and even whether foreskins may be sold to pharmaceutical companies for their research programs.[23] A bill that failed in Congress would have effectively protected a parent's right to make the final decision.[24] Moreover, some states in the U.S. have carved out an exception for certain groups, such as Christian Scientists, who practice faith healing and whose withholding of medical attention might otherwise subject them to charges of parental abuse, thus suggesting that pressures on state authorities (as in Governor Brown's action in California) could effectively create an exception to an otherwise generally applicable statute. Even a civil suit against the parents would have to demonstrate negligence, knowledge that damage was 'substantially certain to follow,' and that the procedure is without value. At trial proponents would undoubtedly testify to circumcision's professed benefits while opponents (in the words of pediatrician Dr. Paul M. Fleiss) would argue that, "One of the social functions of medicine is to free humankind from harmful and useless customs."[25]

Compromises are also hard to come by. An interesting example is afforded by the attempt by a hospital in Seattle to make an arrangement with members of the local Somali community who practice female circumcision. The hospital proposed that the girl be brought to the hospital where a surgeon would barely and harmlessly nick the clitoris. Somali leaders agreed to the suggestion. But when the arrangement became public the outcry against any intrusion whatsoever on a girl's body was so great that the parties had to call off the deal. The proposed compromise also went national. As Adler notes: "The American Academy of Pediatrics briefly recommended that its physicians perform a ritual pinprick of a girl's genitals if that might prevent more harmful genital cutting, even though this would have violated federal law. This ignited a storm of protest, and the policy was quickly retired. Thus, even a pinprick of girls' genitals is a federal crime."[26] In the case of male circumcision, it is hard to imagine what sort of ceremony or minimalist invasion would satisfy both sides and public opinion.

As we have seen throughout this volume, much depends on the metaphors and analogies through which culture is brought into the law and vice versa. If we envision male circumcision as an issue of control over one's own body, then any operation should be postponed until the child is of age; if it is a matter of a parent guiding the child's spiritual, social, or medical well-being then it is a question of who takes precedence, the parent or the state; and if it is predominantly a medical issue, courts and legislators would have to weigh evolving science against ever-shifting social attitudes. We know that each approach implies certain elements of leeway and certain bounds. To say 'my body is a temple' suggests the issues are so personal as to be sacrosanct; to wish, as a Native American might, to hang from the pole with hooks through one's flesh as a ritual of purification might be regarded as going beyond the category of the sacred to a level of impermissible self-abuse. The choice of comparisons will greatly affect how the debate will go forward. Two issues that will figure prominently in any such debate are worth considering in a bit more detail.

Laws concerning control of one's body have fluctuated a good deal over the years. Assisted suicide is a good example of categories currently in contention. While most jurisdictions in the U.S. continue to regard suicide as a crime—at least for purposes of holding the individual for appropriate disposition—several states have passed assisted suicide statutes, notwithstanding the U.S. Supreme Court ruling that there is no constitutional right to such assistance.[27] By comparison, for the most part one is free to acquire tattoos. But would it be permitted if, like the wearing of a face veil, the tattoos totally obscured one's features? Or will face recognition software, already used for a variety of identity papers issued by the state, be so intrusive as to fall under the category of constitutionally protected privacy?

A related set of issues concerns the commodification of one's body. Leaving aside such issues as prostitution and wage legislation, the line between a gift and a sale has moved significantly in recent years, sometimes in response to changing cultural practices, sometimes in response to technological possibilities. So, for example, well into the 1960s one could donate blood but not sell it, only for both law and acceptable custom subsequently to include blood within the realm of the body parts convertible to cash.[28] Once it became technologically possible for a woman to carry to term the fetus formed by the egg and sperm of other parties the question arose as to which category would govern. If her effort is viewed as a gift can expenses be paid; if it is like other services or commercial items, what contractual terms will pass legal scrutiny? In divorce, the question became whether a wife's household services were capable of being valued or whether, like sexual 'favors,' they were to be regarded as something that loses value when commodified. And, though one can donate organs upon death, what cultural alterations should a court of law attend to when deciding which organs and recipients qualify while the donor is still alive? If, building on one or another of these analogies, the foreskin is seen as having no place in the world of things, then the commercial interests of the medical profession in promoting a procedure of limited value may be regarded as a matter that needs to be taken entirely out of the realm of the marketplace and only controlled by the individual affected. Once again, in the law the contest over analogies may ultimately prove decisive.

* * *

The temptation is to say that male circumcision is at once deeply embedded in the personal life of those who choose it for their sons and of only minimal and fleeting concern for most people most of the time. As a result, even the more egregious incidents of malpractice garner little notice, and groups that picket or protest are unlikely to convince the general public of the pressing need to change the law. It is also tempting to say that the practice touches so closely on the religious and/or personal lives of those involved—perhaps most forcefully on fathers who have themselves been circumcised—that it is difficult to turn circumcision into a major political issue. It is, of course, possible that, as with same-sex marriage and abortion, circumcision could become a more dominant concern, and if it were also to become a vehicle for questioning state power, medical dominance, and the limits of parental rights, interest might shift dramatically. Denial of insurance coverage for a botched procedure or a case involving the offspring of a major celebrity could also change the nature of the debate.[29] But William E. Brigman's (1984–5: 356) statement about circumcision and the criminal law applies to the practice more generally, for it is likely to remain true that "it will be extremely difficult to get a conviction, since circumcision is not culturally acknowledged as child abuse at the present time." Similarly, he is still undoubtedly correct when he says, apropos of the difficulty of bringing civil actions, that "negligence, like crime, is grounded in societally determined assumptions and expectations" (Id.: 357).

Redirecting the conversation away from medical rationales and towards human rights—and more particularly the rights of children—trenches on many other issues, ranging from education to poverty to sexual trafficking. Courts, legislatures, and political leaders can be instrumental in shifting the categories by which a given issue is connected to other practices. Surely, it was a factor of no small import in the U.S. when same-sex marriage was moved from being a question of acceptable unions to one of civil rights. So, too, equating male and female circumcision, or equating both with the universal rights of children, can change the conversation and hence the outcome. But there is something that may be more distinctive about the case of circumcision, something that makes it a different kind of relation between law and cultural assumptions.

Circumcision may be one of those instances in which the law simply cannot buck the culture. It is, quite frankly, difficult to see male circumcision as so clearly beneficial as to trump the child's interests—indeed it is hard not to see it as potentially harmful and hence best delayed until the individual can make his own choice. But the cultural forces—some religious, others medicalized—continue to be so well entrenched within the broader culture that courts and legislatures are loath to intervene. In some respects that seems to make it much like same-sex marriage: One must wait until the culture catches up with what the courts would like to do—or be forced to do—before remedial action can be taken. (Justice Ruth Bader Ginsberg, for example, expressed reluctance to decide same-sex marriage, as she recalled how the Supreme Court got out ahead of other social issues, mainly abortion, only to encounter great opposition to the implementation of their rulings and hence jeopardize their own legitimacy. Only when the lower appeals courts split on the issue was the Supreme Court forced to address the matter.[30]) Here, though, the cultural direction is unclear. Rates of circumcision are declining such that only religious groups may care strongly about the matter. Courts can either defer to the medical profession or hold back and wait for greater clarity from science and medicine. So far the result is that the courts are avoiding this issue and letting the cultural forces do their work. In an odd sort of way, as deeply cultural an issue as male circumcision may be, in this instance and at this moment it may represent an example less of the incorporation of cultural assumptions into the law than of constructing legal blinders in the hope that individual choice or social alterations will keep the law from having to involve itself.

The usual rule—that one ignores cultural assumptions and expectations at the risk of not comprehending the course of events even when they are taking place right in front of us—may, in the present debate over circumcision, be displaced by a kind of legal fiction, in which the usual approaches are set aside until greater cultural consensus or medical information points in a clear direction. Not for the last time are the courts and legislatures hoping that culture will handle the problem before the law finds itself no longer able to ignore the issue.

Notes

1 See generally, Greenhouse and Siegel (2010).
2 The 'condition' in question may have been phimosis, where the foreskin is too tightly attached to the glans of the penis to retract, a condition some regard as normal and others believe should be treated by circumcision. See Glenn (2015b). Subsequently, the child developed leukemia. The father sought to bar access to the child by the mother, but the court allowed her visitation rights. Freeman (2015).
3 See, e.g., Glenn (2015a,c). See generally, Silva (2016). Among the anti-circumcision websites are www.intactamerica.org; and www.bloodstainedmen.com

4 Following broad consultation and in the face of contradictory local court rulings, the German parliament on December 12, 2012, passed legislation permitting non-therapeutic circumcision performed under regulated medical conditions. See generally, Munzer (2015).

5 See, e.g., Starr (2014). See also, Abramson and Hannon (2003) and Steinberg (1996).

6 On female circumcision in U.S. history, see Rodriguez (2008). Clitoridectomy was covered by Blue Cross-Blue Shield insurance in the U.S. until 1977. For an example dating from 1947 in the American Midwest, see Bergstrom (2016). See generally, Gruenbaum (2000).

7 Eyer (1992). Fathers, too, could bond instantly with the child, thanks to a male nursing bra that held two baby bottles.

8 See, Abelson (1989). An intriguing work about the department store and the middle-class woman may be found in a novel by Emile Zola (1995) [1883].The medicalization continues to this day: see Martin (1992).

9 Other sources continue to suggest that kleptomania is mainly a feminine disorder by indicating, for example, that there is a 65% correlation between kleptomania and bulimia.

10 For a history of the different medical claims associated with circumcision, see Glick (2005: 179–214). For the argument that circumcision does not prevent HIV/AIDS, see Circumcision Resource Center, "Circumcision and HIV: Harm Outweighs 'Benefit'." www.circumcision.org/hiv.htm (accessed January 5, 2017).

11 See generally, Szasz (2007: 80–89).

12 Figures for the early 1980s, when the rate was peaking in the U.S., have been reported at 6% in the UK and virtually zero in Scandinavia. See citations at Brigman (1984–5: 341). For a comparison to Japan, see Castro-Vázquez (2015).

13 On the claim that circumcision increases sexual pleasure, see Frisch 2011. For one study that claims men who have not been circumcised have a slightly higher rate of sexual dysfunction, see Laumann (1997: 1054).

14 See, e.g., American Academy of Pediatrics (2012): ("[I]t is difficult, if not impossible, to adequately assess the total impact of complications, because the data are scant and inconsistent regarding the severity of complications.") The statement was updated November 21, 2015 (American Academy of Pediatrics 2015). See also, Glick (2005: 210–13). By contrast, an organization called Doctors Opposed to Circumcision (2016) is highly critical of the Academy's statement. Already in 1999 the Academy had, however, recommended that all circumcisions be conducted under a general anesthetic. For an overview of the medical benefits and detriments revealed by various studies, see the assessment by a professor of pediatrics at Carroll (2016).

15 See, Collier (2011) and Hyfler (2011).

16 For additional legal analyses see, Miller (2002) and Chessler (1997). See generally, Denniston (1999).

17 The terms used by opponents of the law permitting male circumcision vary quite a bit: *Compare* Brigman (1984–85: 337) ("cultural astigmatism...prevents contemporary Americans from perceiving or acknowledging the most widespread form of child abuse in society today: mutilation through routine neonatal circumcision of males.") *with* Glick (2005: 281) ("When all is said and done, I believe we face a single inescapable question: Are we now prepared to accept the principle that, from the moment of birth, every child has all the human rights of any other person—including the inviolable right to freedom from nonconsensual, nontherapeutic bodily alteration?"); *and* Adler (2013: 446, 448, 482, and 483) ("Circumcision harms all boys and the men they will become...[B]oys, like girls and adults, have absolute rights under the common law to personal security and bodily integrity, and to freedom or the autonomy to make important and irreversible decisions... for themselves....[U]nder any analysis, circumcision is illegal.").

18 For a number of cases, mostly involving malpractice, see Attorneys for the Rights of the Child 2015. See also, "Boy Turned Girl Turned Boy" 2013. There have even been cases in which a circumcision was performed by a hospital accidentally: see Tasker (2010).

19 Colapinto (2006). Others who have suffered from a circumcision gone awry include at least one Olympic athlete.

20 See, Wallop (2015) and Levitt (2013).

21 For a video debate during the 2013 campaign among New York mayoral candidates on the issue, see Buxton (2013). On other legal challenges to religious circumcision, see Rassbach (2016). Orthodox Judaism also calls for circumcision even for a child who dies before being circumcised. The circumcision takes place at the graveside without a benediction, but the infant is given a name so he may be included among the resurrected dead and can recognize his parents.

22 *Re J (Child's Religious Upbringing and Circumcision).* Compare this position with one involving a 12-year-old boy, *In re Marriage of Boldt* (2008: 393–4) ("Although the parties and amici have presented extensive material regarding circumcision, we do not need to decide in this case which side has presented a more persuasive case regarding the medical risks or benefits of male circumcision. We conclude that, although circumcision is an invasive medical procedure that results in permanent physical alteration of a body part and has attendant medical risks, the decision to have a male child circumcised for medical or religious reasons is one that is commonly and historically made by parents in the United States.")

23 These and similar arguments are rehearsed in Adler (2013): passim. On the sale of foreskins, see Id., p. 479.

24 Religious and Parental Rights Defense Act of 2011, H.R. 2400, 112th Cong. (2011) (proposed law prohibiting states from adopting any statute or regulation restricting a parent's right to circumcise their male children).

25 Quoted in Glick (2005: 203).

26 Adler (2013: 465). Federal law forbids female circumcision. See, Female Genital Mutilation 18 U.S.C. § 116 (2006).

27 See the 1997 cases of *Vacco v. Quill* and *Washington v. Glucksberg* as discussed in *Gonzalez v. Oregon* (2006).

28 Titmuss (1997). See generally, the argument on 'incomplete commodification' in Radin (1996). A series of cases has set the terms and limits of the sale of body parts, including *Moore v. Regents of the University of California* (one does not have property rights to body parts, so there can be no sale of them; body parts are valuable, but not in commerce); *Hecht v. Superior Court of Los Angeles City* (the settlement between the mistress and family of a deceased man for dividing vials of sperm is not valid, because body parts are not consideration for an agreement); *Cryolife v. Santa Cruz Superior Court* (in suit by plaintiff against a tissue bank for a defective, infected tendon, held: No suit can be brought, because the tendon is not property—a service was paid for, not a product). See generally, Phillips (2013) and Hardcastle (2009).

29 The British, for example, stopped paying for male circumcision through the National Health Service in the 1950s. The rate at which the operation was performed then dropped to 5–6%. Szasz (2007).

30 See, Bazelon (2015).

References

Abelson, Elaine S. 1989, *When Ladies Go a-Thieving: Middle-Class Shoppers in the Victorian Department Store*, Oxford: Oxford University Press.

Abramson, Henry and Carrie Hannon 2003, "Depicting the Ambiguous Wound: Circumcision in Medieval Art," in Elizabeth Wyner Mark, ed., *The Covenant of*

Circumcision, Hanover, NH: Brandeis University Press/University Press of New England, 2003, pp. 98–113.

Adler, Peter W. 2013, "Is Circumcision Legal?" *Richmond Journal of Law and Public Interest*, vol. 16, no. 3, pp. 439–83.

American Academy of Pediatrics 2012, "Male Circumcision," *Pediatrics*, vol. 130, no. 3, pp. 585–86. http://pediatrics.aappublications.org/content/130/3/e756 (accessed January 5, 2017).

——— 2015, "Where We Stand: Circumcision," www.healthychildren.org/English/ages-stages/prenatal/decisions-to-make/Pages/Where-We-Stand-Circumcision.aspx (accessed January 5, 2017)

Anonymous 2013, "Circumcision and the Law: A Clash of Entitlements," *The Economist*, November 14.

Attorneys for the Rights of the Child 2015, "List of Court Settlements and Legal Victories Proving Harm of Circumcision." http://arclaw.org/resources/settlements (accessed January 5, 2017).

Bazelon, Emily 2015, "Backlash Whiplash," *Slate*, May 14. www.slate.com/articles/news_and_politics/jurisprudence/2013/05/justice_ginsburg_and_roe_v_wade_caution_for_gay_marriage.html (accessed January 5, 2017).

Bergstrom, Dr. A. Renee 2016, "'FGM Happened to Me in White, Midwest America'," *The Guardian*, December 3.

"Boy Turned Girl Turned Boy," 2013. April 20. http://alfre.dk/boy-turned-girl-turned-boy/ (accessed January 5, 2017).

Brigman, William E. 1984–5, "Circumcision as Child Abuse: The Legal and Constitutional Issues," *Journal of Family Law*, vol. 23, no. 3, pp. 337–57.

Buxton, Ryan 2013, "Metzitzah B'peh, Blood-Sucking Jewish Circumcision Ritual, Debated by NYC Mayoral Candidates," *The Huffington Post*, May 30. www.huffingtonpost.com/2013/05/30/metzitzah-bpeh-blood-sucking-jewish-circumcision-ritual-debated-by-nyc-mayoral-candidates-video_n_3360526.html (accessed January 5, 2017).

Carroll, Aaron E. 2016. "Should You Circumcise Your Child?" *New York Times*, May 9.

Castro-Vázquez, Genaro 2015, *Male Circumcision in Japan*, New York: Palgrave Macmillan.

Chessler, Abbie J. 1997, "Justifying the Unjustifiable: Rite v. Wrong," *Buffalo Law Review*, vol. 45, pp. 555–613.

Colapinto, John 2006, *As Nature Made Him: The Boy Who Was Raised as a Girl*, New York: Harper Perennial.

Collier, Roger 2011, "Whole Again: The Practice of Foreskin Restoration," *Canadian Medical Association Journal* (CMAJ), vol. 183, no. 18, pp. 2092–3. www.cmaj.ca/content/183/18/2092 (accessed January 5, 2017).

Denniston, George C. 1999, *Male and Female Circumcision: Medical, Legal, and Ethical Considerations in Pediatric Practice*, New York: Kluwer Academic/Plenum.

Doctors Opposing Circumcision 2016, "Medical Organization Statements on Circumcision," www.doctorsopposingcircumcision.org/for-professionals/medical-organization-statements/ (accessed January 5, 2017).

Eyer, Diane E. 1992, *Mother-Infant Bonding: A Scientific Fiction*, New Haven, CT: Yale University Press.

Freeman, Marc 2015, "Mom in Failed Circumcision Fight Can Visit Sick Son, Judge Rules," *Sun Sentinel* [Florida], December 24. www.sun-sentinel.com/local/palm-beach/fl-circumcision-parents-court-ruling-20151224-story.html (accessed January 5, 2017).

Frisch, Morten, et al. 2011, "Male Circumcision and Sexual Function in Men and Women: A Survey-Based, Cross-Sectional Study in Denmark," *International Journal of Epidemiology*, vol. 40, pp. 1–15.

Glenn, Amy Wright 2015a, "Failure is Impossible: The Significance of the Hironimus vs. Nebus Circumcision Case for America," *Philly Voice*, May 23. www.phillyvoice.com/hironimus-vs-nebus-chase-circumcision-america/ (accessed January 5, 2017).

———— 2015b, "One Boy Slumbers while Another Suffers: A Mother Reflects on Hironimus v. Nebus," *Philly Voice*, June 8. www.phillyvoice.com/mother-reflects-on-hironimus-nebus-circumcision/ (accessed January 5, 2017).

———— 2015c, "Ending Circumcision, Part One: The Case for Extending Legal Protections to America's Boys," *Philly Voice*, September 26. www.phillyvoice.com/ending-circumcision-part-one-the-case-for-extend/ (accessed January 5, 2017).

Glick, Leonard B. 2005, *Marked in Your Flesh: Circumcision from Ancient Judea to Modern America*, Oxford: Oxford University Press.

Greenhouse, Linda and Reva Siegel 2010, *Before Roe v. Wade: Voices that Shaped the Debate before the Supreme Court's Ruling*, New York: Kaplan Publishing.

Gruenbaum, Ellen 2000, *The Female Circumcision Controversy: An Anthropological Perspective*, Philadelphia: University of Pennsylvania Press.

Hardcastle, Rohan 2009, *Law and the Human Body: Property Rights, Ownership and Control*, Oxford: Hart Publishing.

Hyfler, Richard 2011, "Circumcision: You Can't Have It Both Ways," *Forbes*, May 26. http://news.yahoo.com/circumcision-cant-both-ways-021711316.html;_ylt=A0LEV77rMFpWoAQAU04nnIlQ;_ylu=X3oDMTEzMWU1bGVwBGNvbG8DYmYxBHBvcwM4BHZ0aWQDRkZSVkJLXzEEc2VjA3Ny (accessed January 5, 2017).

Laumann, Edward O., et al. 1997, "Circumcision in the United States: Prevalence, Prophylactic Effects, and Sexual Practice," *Journal of the American Medical Association*, vol. 277, no. 13, pp. 1052–57.

Levitt, Jonathan 2013, "Britain Wonders if Baby Prince Will Be Circumcised; Prince Charles Snipped by Royal Mohel," *The Algemeiner* [Brooklyn, NY], July 24.

Martin, Emily 1992, *The Woman in the Body: A Cultural Analysis of Reproduction*, Boston, MA: Beacon Press.

Miller, Geoffrey P. 2002, "Circumcision: Cultural-Legal Analysis," *Virginia Journal of Social Policy and the Law*, vol. 9, pp. 497–585.

Munzer, Stephen R. 2015, "Secularization, Anti-minority Sentiment, and Cultural Norms in the German Circumcision Controversy," *University of Pennsylvania Journal of International Law*, vol. 37, pp. 503–81.

Phillips, Anne 2013, *Our Bodies, Whose Property?* Princeton, NJ: Princeton University Press.

Radin, Margaret Jane 1996, *Contested Commodities*, Cambridge, MA: Harvard University Press.

Rodriguez, Sarah W. 2008, "Rethinking the History of Female Circumcision and Clitoridectomy: American Medicine and Female Sexuality in the Late Nineteenth Century," *Journal of the History of Medicine and Allied Sciences*, vol. 63, no. 3, pp. 323–47.

Silva, Chris 2016, "To Circumcise or Not to Circumcise: A New Father's Question," *New York Times*, March 1.

Starr, Bernard 2014, "The Cut That Divided Jews and Christians—and the Mystery of the Missing Circumcision in Artworks," *Huffington Post*, March 3.

Steinberg, Leo 1996, *The Sexuality of Christ in Renaissance Art and in Modern Oblivion*, (2nd edition), Chicago, IL: University of Chicago Press.

Stempel, Jonathan 2013, "New York City Circumcision Law: Judge Won't Block Ritual Regulation," *Huffington Post*, March 12. www.huffingtonpost.com/2013/01/10/new-york-city-circumcision-law-judge-wont-block-ritual-regulation_n_2452024.html (accessed January 5, 2017).

Szasz, Thomas 2007, *The Medicalization of Everyday Life*, Syracuse: Syracuse University Press.

Tasker, Fred 2010, "South Miami Hospital Faces Lawsuit after Accidental Circumcision," *Miami Herald Sun Sentinel*, September 16.

Titmuss, Richard Morris 1997, *The Gift Relationship: From Human Blood to Social Policy*, New York: The New Press.

Wallop, Harry 2015, "'Circumcision is One of the Oddities of the Royal Family'," *The Telegraph* [London], March 31.

Wulfhorst, Ellen 2015, "NYC, Orthodox Jews Reach Deal on Circumcision Ritual," *Huffington Post*, April 26. www.huffingtonpost.com/2015/02/24/nyc-jews-circumcision_n_6748188.html (accessed January 5, 2017).

Zola, Emile 1995 [1883], *The Ladies' Paradise* [*Au Bonheur des Dames*], Oxford: Oxford University Press.

Cases cited

Cryolife v. Santa Cruz Superior Court, 2 Calif. Rep. 2d 296 (Cal. App. 2003).

Gonzalez v. Oregon, 546 US 243 (2006).

Hecht v. Superior Court of Los Angeles City, 16 Cal. App.4th 836, 20 Cal. Rptr.2d 275 (Cal. App. 1993).

In re Marriage of Boldt, 344 Or. 1, 176 P.3d 388.

Moore v. Regents of the University of California, 51 Cal.3d 120, 271 Cal. Rptr. 146, 793 P.2d 479 (CA 1990).

Re J (Child's Religious Upbringing and Circumcision), Family Division (Wall, J.) (1999). www.cirp.org/library/legal/Re_J/ (accessed January 5, 2017), *aff'd.* 1 Family Court Reports 307–314 [2000]. (cited as *Re J* [2000] 1 FCR 307). www.cirp.org/library/legal/Re_J/2000.html (accessed January 5, 2017).

8

THE INCORPORATION OF CUSTOM

The case of the flashing headlights

[H]e is a barbarian, and thinks that the customs of his tribe and island are the laws of nature.

—George Bernard Shaw, *Caesar and Cleopatra*

Something about it just sounds old-fashioned. When was the last time you thought about custom as a source of the law? Perhaps in the Middle Ages it mattered; perhaps even now in some commercial dealings. But our legal systems have, one imagines, long since come to depend on statutes, case law, and administrative decisions rather than reaching out to understand the practices by which people arrange their relationships or orient their actions towards others without recourse to legislation or adjudication. Indeed, if one wants to implement "an action or way of behaving that is usual and traditional among the people in a particular group or place" (to borrow the dictionary definition of custom) one can go to an agreed-upon conciliator, a religious court, or some form of arbitration or mediation. These less formal mechanisms may allow greater scope for the particular relations among members of a more restricted group or the use of enforcement mechanisms that are structured into their communities.

And yet custom does enter the law both formally and, as with so much of culture, almost by osmosis. For as courts read between the lines of the statutes or the facts that have been adduced they may, directly or indirectly, look to the scope and duration of a practice, favoring regularization and predictability so long as no clear state-sponsored proposition has been violated or cannot be rationalized as superseded. Thus in the U.S. we have notions of custom formally acknowledged in the Uniform Commercial Code's provision for introducing evidence of 'custom and usage in the trade' but we also have the far less formal acknowledgment of standards of acceptable conduct as informing due care, moral blameworthiness, pornography, or the moral conscience of the jury. In the example that will set up the issues that follow, we can see an instance that may be familiar to many people—that of a driving custom that may even be contrary to the formal law. The question will be whether and how

a court imports such custom and its attendant cultural assumptions into its thinking, and
if so how one is to address the problem of the stranger, the problem of knowledge, and the
problem of change.

★ ★ ★

While driving along a slightly narrow road you notice that the car coming towards you flashes his headlights. What does it mean? Does it indicate that the
driver is warning you not to proceed because he is coming ahead? Or does it
mean that he wants you to go first? There are, of course, other possibilities. He
could be warning you of a danger in the roadway (like a pothole or flooding),
alerting you to some fault in your car (such as a burned-out headlight), signaling
his appreciation of something you have already done, testing his own lights,
chasing an animal out of the way, or warning you that there is a policeman ahead
and you should slow down. Of course, he might just be an aggressive driver
in the throes of road rage or seeking your attention because of some personal
emergency. He may even be engaging in a celebratory event or political protest.[1]

How can you resolve the uncertainty? You could, perhaps, quickly consult the
Highway Code to see if it tells you what is permissible or forbidden in such an instance, hoping that the other driver is an equally well-informed and law-abiding
citizen. Or you could try to communicate with him through other means in an
effort to elicit a less ambiguous response. You may also choose to err on the
side of safety or hope to avoid any liability by stopping or pulling out of the way
altogether. Even if you do not know the precise statutory rule, you might have
some sense, at least from the popular media, of how the law has viewed such
matters when confusion has led to an accident. Indeed, if you feel any inkling of
uncertainty in the situation—unlike, say, when you encounter a stop sign or hear
a siren—it might suggest that some form of local knowledge could be at work.
However, if you are an outsider you may regard it as unfair to expect that you
could easily obtain such information.

Similar situations have yielded different rules and practices. Roundabouts,
which are common in the UK and Europe and are becoming more so in the
U.S., are said to help prevent accidents and speed up traffic.[2] The usual rule in
Europe is that one yields to the person on one's right; the usual rule in America
is that one yields to the person already in the circle. However, custom may
modify this practice. At one such roundabout by my university, for example, the
custom quickly developed—despite the sign indicating one yields to the person
in the circle—of taking turns from the several roads that lead into the circle, the
rationale perhaps having developed that since the main road is very crowded
at rush hour people in the secondary road servicing a major parking lot might
otherwise be stuck there for a long time. Alternatively, simple courtesy or the
experience of having oneself been trapped in that service road may have yielded
this informal, turn-taking way of handling the problem. But if one defers to

this 'custom'—which is neither universally applied nor of long vintage, and is in direct contravention of the formal rule—will not the 'law' have been completely vitiated? Or do the people who regularly use the circle get to establish the practice, even for the unknowing visitor? And does the occasional practice of flashing one's headlights combine with the developing custom to signal that the other should go first? (Figure 8.1).

At least until they are clarified—and certainly after they are codified—practices and rationales related to the flashing of headlights vary quite widely within and among countries. In the UK, drivers have been fined for flashing their lights to warn others about speed traps, whereas in the U.S. a number of state courts have held such an act to be protected speech under the First Amendment, even if it risks warning an escaping felon.[3] Laws as well as norms can be confusing. In some American states it is permissible to flash your headlights to indicate an intention to pass another vehicle, but not if it is a multi-lane highway. On the European continent, one would be regarded as patently ignorant not to know that the left lane on the superhighway is for fast cars whose drivers signal their annoyance at any interference with lights or horn, often accompanied by coming up close from behind. In Qatar, flashing one's lights means the car close ahead should speed up.[4] And custom must play some role in Yemen where, we learn, "on multi-lane roads it's acceptable for cars to use the far right lane to travel in the reverse direction if making a U-turn is too inconvenient. And yet the roads are not full of smoldering wreckage" (Ceglowski 2015).

FIGURE 8.1 Law—Yield to Left *versus* Custom—Take Turns.
Source: Photo by author.

Similar questions are raised by the practice in many parts of the United States in which, having cleared a public parking space of a great amount of snow and having placed a chair or similar object at the site an individual claims to be able to exclude others from using the spot (Figure 8.2). Most cities do not legally recognize such claims. Some (like Boston) do not enforce a ban on reserving such spots for the first 48 hours after a declared snow emergency; others (like Pittsburgh) tend to respect the markers without giving them legal sanction, but may forcibly remove chairs and other objects as abandoned furniture. Regardless of the formal law, it is common for people to regard their cleared spots as validated by local custom. In at least one case a judge acknowledged that, in an altercation with police concerning such a practice, custom effectively takes precedence over misdemeanor charges. In Boston and Chicago the practice has occasioned heated disputes as those who have invested a great deal of effort to clear the snow assert custom and a kind of Lockean right to exclusive use during bad weather, while local officials face stringent opposition after having passed laws forbidding the practice.[5]

In the process of making any decision concerning the role custom should play in state-controlled law, several classical approaches will probably be replicated. To many commenters, custom forms a poor basis for direct application of expectations and sanctions. Two problems in particular arise: how widespread the knowledge has to be to qualify for recognition and how long it has to be prevalent to be regarded as binding. In some respects, these two criteria are intermingled. For if you think that generalized knowledge comes only after long persistence—if you think that everyone can or should be expected to know the custom because of its duration and expanse—then time and social awareness may depend on certain shared assumptions. If, on the other hand, you see many

FIGURE 8.2 Claiming cleared parking space.
Source: Photo by author.

so-called customs as only the beliefs of a segment of the overall population—whether divided by gender, power, descent, or profession—the claim of custom may only be a claim by and for a limited part of society. Moreover, ascertaining a custom is far from unproblematic. Does one conduct a survey or set of observations and base recognition on statistical prevalence? Does one rely for guidance or judgment on the opinion of elders or other authorities?[6] Does one engage in legal fictions, claiming that a custom must date from 'time immemorial'—only for the courts or legislature to mark the time at but a few years—thus sustaining both the illusion of long-term legitimacy and the ability to respond to rapid change?[7] Or are concepts like 'for as long as the present generation can remember' or until the memory 'disappears into the darkness of the past,' historically aimed at limiting the power of monarch or state to institute rules against the desires of the people, thus constituting purposely vague formulations that its proponents see as having the advantage of limiting and dispersing power? As one of the architects of American political conservatism stated, in his list of conservative canons (Kirk 1953): "Custom, convention, and old prescription are checks both upon man's anarchic impulse and upon the innovator's lust for power."

The relation of custom to statutory or precedent-setting case law is also crucial. Common law has often been seen as open (in Justice Oliver Wendell Holmes' words) to "the actual feelings and demands of the community" and "the exigencies and usages of the country."[8] Courts have even said that criminal culpability may apply when "acts, which being highly indecent, are *contra bonos mores*" or when "the feelings and natural sentiments of the public would be outraged."[9] Statutes and contracts generally trump custom, but not always. For example, in some American labor cases the Supreme Court has said: "The collective bargaining agreement states the rights and duties of the parties. It is more than a contract; it is a generalized code to govern a myriad of cases which the draftsmen cannot wholly anticipate....The labor arbitrator's source of law is not confined to the express provisions of the contract, as the industrial common law—the practices of the industry and the shop—is equally a part of the collective bargaining agreement although not expressed in it" (*United Steelworkers of America v. Warrior & Gulf Navigation Co*).

If placed under the heading of custom, common law courts usually require that the specific custom be proved. In doing so, however, one eliminates the use of analogy or logic thereby rendering custom immune to a significant aspect of common law legal reasoning. Discussing the practice in India, Jain (1994: 66), noting that customs cannot be built upon by logical reasoning or analogy, writes: "One custom cannot be adduced from another. As the Supreme Court has stated: 'Theory and custom are antithesis; custom cannot be a matter of mere theory but must always be a matter of fact...' [A] custom has to be established by evidence and not by *a priori* methods." It can also be argued that practices based on *other* practices (in such areas as international customary law) are not to be regarded as a custom: "...to the extent an argument is based not upon pure custom but upon an extension of custom, the argument has changed the basis of its authority because it no longer arises solely from widespread historical consent. One may fairly then ask: on what authority can it be based?" (Ramsey n.d.). Others have seen the matter differently: The Roman jurist Salvius Julianus (c. 110–c. 170), also known as Julian the Jurist, long ago argued that if custom is incomplete it can be supplemented by analogy (see Dawson 1968: 128).

The deference to custom will necessarily depend on the boundaries of the community a court chooses to recognize. In one such example an American court held that in a motion to dismiss a lawsuit, concerning pledged support to a synagogue, the trial judge must consider the Jewish custom that such cases should only be brought to a rabbinical court: "We have held the defense of custom or usage may be asserted. Custom may be binding if certain, definite, uniform, and notorious"—factors, it appears, that may be established, for example, by showing this had been the practice for centuries, that other donors had a similar understanding, and that those arguing for the custom are knowledgeable experts on such matters (*Congregation B'nai Sholom v. Martin*).

In theory, as cases like *Martin* would seem to suggest, attending to custom works better the smaller, more uniform, and more exclusive the group, the greater the internal pressures for conformity, or the greater the forces that quell one's doubts about the wisdom of the collectivity.[10] Thus a bounded group of merchants, craftsmen, or practitioners of a given occupation often succeed in gaining deference by the state to the custom and usage in their trade, quite aside from conducing members to use forums exclusive to their group. In the leading case of *Ghen v. Rich*, the Massachusetts court in 1881 held that the custom governing the ownership of a mortally wounded whale turned on the recognition of "a custom which embraced an entire business, and had been concurred in for a long time by everyone engaged in the trade....Unless it is sustained, this branch of industry must necessarily cease, for no person would engage in it if the fruits of his labor could be appropriated by any chance finder."[11] Like others, the court emphasized the societal value of the activity and the "general acquiescence of a whole community" in supporting the practice.

Alternatively, one may defer to the argument of Jeremy Bentham that custom is far too uncertain and ambiguous to ever form a solid basis for law. Instead, statutes should incorporate any customs worth preserving and in doing so completely displace evidence of a practice that has not been so codified. While this may appear to solve some of the evidentiary problems posed by the recognition of custom, it nevertheless leaves open other issues: Can legislatures really be expected to respond expeditiously to all changing social practices and technological advances? If only the code sets the law, does that mean no space is left for equity or exceptional circumstance? Recognition—and indeed deference—to custom is sometimes enshrined in codes, as in the provisions on custom and usage in the trade in Article 2 of the Uniform Commercial Code. Under the Code, courts can look to the course of dealing, performance, and usage to fill in the gaps of contractual agreements.[12] Interestingly, the Code, in its official note, states that, unless carefully negated, evidence of usage is admissible to supplement any written agreement. Thus, a contract to provide horsemeat with a specified proportion of protein is to be read against the customary and rather different standard of the industry.[13] In other instances, courts and commenters have raised cautions when utilizing custom as a basis for deciding cases involving intellectual property. Jennifer Rothman (2007: 1981), referring specifically to cases of intellectual property (IP), thus writes: "When a custom is certain, representative, aspirational, and applied against in-group members for a positive proposition, it is at its peak value. When a custom is pragmatic, unrepresentative, uncertain, and likely to foreclose any use without explicit permission or permit all uses of another's IP, it should be dismissed."

The custom and usage in a given trade are often thought to be best implemented by calling on experts, reciting industry codes, or relying on statistical evidence. However, Lisa Bernstein's survey of cases suggests that so much time is needed to understand the requirements of a trade that the testimony of employers and employees, rather than of outside experts, is most commonly acknowledged. The result, she suggests, is that having to sustain the costs of incorporating trade information constitutes a serious flaw in what may have been expected by the authors of the code (Bernstein 2015, 2016).[14] Others would argue that where custom may be involved it is always better to defer to the common law approach of the courts who can consider cases one at a time, developing concepts of broad applicability as real-life situations may suggest. Indeed, by the use of juries or even elected judges the results may partake of popular legitimacy. What constitutes evidence of custom to the trier of fact will still pose significant issues, but to the extent that one places confidence in this type of common law development—either because one believes adversarial advocacy yields greater truth or because of one's confidence in some Tocquevillian or Jeffersonian theory of democratic involvement—custom will not be closed off by statute or ignored as too equivocal to be credited by the law.

American courts acknowledge custom in a variety of instances, often subordinating it, however, to other precepts. In the United States the classic statement where personal injuries are involved is that of Supreme Court Justice Oliver Wendell Holmes in *Texas & Pacific Railway Co. v. Behymer* (1903: 470): "What usually is done may be evidence of what ought to be done, but what ought to be done is fixed by a standard of reasonable prudence, whether it is complied with or not." Thus while evidence of a custom may be introduced as an indication that someone had operated with reasonable care, the courts will still ask whether the average reasonable person would have acted this way under the prevailing circumstances.[15] In one leading case, *Trimarco v. Klein*, the plaintiff tenant sued when he fell through the glass door enclosing his bathtub. He argued that the custom among builders was to use shatterproof glass. The court said that part of the standard to be applied is whether it was general practice for such contractors to use safety glass, part whether the harm that occurred was reasonably foreseeable, and part whether not following that custom was tantamount to a failure to use reasonable care. Other courts and commenters have stressed the issue of cost versus benefit, whether following the custom really would have made all the difference, whether materials needed are readily available, whether a previous standard was displaced by a new one, and whether the safeguard is so important that even if it has never been used the potential harm is so great that it should have been available.

If, then, one is to rely on custom in whatever degree in a legal proceeding it would appear that, despite codification or case law standards, a series of cultural assumptions play some role in these types of cases: the notion of reasonableness and the reasonable person, the basis for assuming knowledge is shared and 'informal' sanctions effective, the relation of expert knowledge to that of the ordinary person, the ways in which factors may be quantified and how such incommensurables as money and harm are to be equilibrated, the nature of time such that sufficient passage may convert an incident into a custom, and the presumptions concerning truth and consequence employed in the face of the doubtful, the improbable, and the indeterminable.

Even though many of the cultural assumptions found when custom is an issue pervade multiple domains, certain cultural notions do appear to be cast up with special note. Indeed, more than in a number of other domains of the law, it is in the approaches toward custom that many of American cultural ambiguities are on full display. Among these often-contradictory cultural assumptions the following might be included:

1. *The maintenance of impersonal time.* More than other realms of law—with the possible exception of constitutional law—cases that deal with custom preserve the appearance of being validated by impersonal time rather than momentary accommodation. Not only do the criteria for establishing legally cognizable customs include collective acceptance of a proposition, but even when 'time immemorial' is clearly not required the image of long duration is important to the legitimacy of custom's inclusion. This may no longer be due to attempts to limit the power of the state—though deference to popular opinion and non-state associations may yet influence the acceptance of custom. Nevertheless, time is conceived as simultaneously the revelation of historic movement in a progressive direction and as seeming to slow down sufficiently to allow predictable and stable relationships. This dual quality of the temporal partakes deeply of the image of time in multiple domains of American culture. For Americans not only see time as directional—'time flies like an arrow': you cannot, as Woody Allen once quipped, say that 'time flies like a banana'—but unlike many other cultures Americans are reluctant to think of time as cyclical, static, or repetitive. Whether it is in religion, where Christ fulfills the past and points to the future, in politics, where one could hardly call on the electorate to 'follow me as we back into the future,' or in biography, where time reveals the truth of character, the vision of time and custom is one of movement and restraint, alteration and tradition operating simultaneously. It is these cultural contradictions that account for the

often-incongruous ways in which change and custom are grasped within the legal realm proper.

2. *Consensus confronts individuality.* American law, as we shall see in more detail in the next chapter, has never settled on a proper place for the collective versus the individual. Since at least the Revolutionary era, the individual has taken pride of place over the collective, particularly in the law. At the same time, Americans have a certain romantic vision of community. In its approach to custom, the contradictions thus encountered manifest themselves in the awkward ascertainment of what constitutes the collective will and, more to the point, why the collective should ever take precedence over the individual. One result has been to allow contracts to trump custom, but with such key—and potentially contradictory—provisos that the contractual terms must not contravene public policy and that custom must not embrace the immoral. Moreover, custom gives the appearance of social solidarity, even when that may come at the cost of change. Once again, American ambivalence about the collective and the personal yields some degree of strain and vagueness whenever custom is allowed to play a role.

3. *Deference to associations.* One way to resolve some of these contradictions is to grant a certain amount of deference to non-governmental collectives, particularly, but by no means exclusively, in the realm of commerce. Thus, the custom and usage of a trade will be acknowledged whereas (as we shall see in our discussion of community in the next chapter) unusual voluntary associations (e.g., hippie communes) will have a difficult time gaining legal recognition. The deference to commercial groupings takes place within the context of a free will vision of contract, such that not only does opting-out remain a key component of contract theory but so does recognizing as a vital aspect of American culture various images of freedom of movement, association, and the fashioning of a persona unregulated by the group. Indeed, there are those who argue that, whereas game theory ostensibly demonstrates that people who interact with one another frequently forge new customs, the state should encourage the formation of such groupings as a means of developing those customs that would be more readily accepted than laws imposed from above.[16]

4. *Left alone, custom follows a natural course.* Custom, it is often suggested, works best if at all when groups are small, stable, transparent, and involve repeat players, massively scaling up custom being difficult if not impossible. Both features fit nicely with American cultural and economic conceptions—and both are highly questionable. Cultural concepts can be very widespread and need not be confined to small groups, yet it serves the American self-image to think of the country as a congeries of such groupings notwithstanding the scope of many people's cultural assumptions to the contrary. Moreover, some of the favorite examples prove to be dubious. Thus, as Emily Kadens (2012) argues, the medieval law merchant did not arise from some small-scale grouping in an almost natural fashion. To the contrary, she argues,

contractual forms, not custom, developed in that context. And while one might question whether shared contractual forms are not themselves an expression of custom the image of the spontaneous effervescence of these particular commercial customs is, she suggests, mythical. Indeed, such a myth fits with the American romance of community that will be of concern in the following chapter. For present purposes, the issue is not whether cultural concepts become normalized through practices that can inform both special sectors and large gatherings but that the assumption that custom emanates 'naturally' from small groups is deeply writ in the way Americans interpret history and imagine our institutions. Custom, as the product of natural forces, will, in this view, yield the utility and efficiency the law should not hinder.[17]

5. *Custom as morality.* American law claims not to be implementing morality directly, yet it is clear that, in various guises and under various rubrics, morality enters with considerable frequency. It may be in the dubious form of claiming, as Lon Fuller and others did, that the common law being rational and evil being irrational the good always wins out through the inherently logical style of common law legal reasoning. H. L. A. Hart, on the other hand, argued that norms of behavior, including moral norms, may not be a sufficient basis for recognition as applicable custom, a 'critical reflective attitude' by which particular values are internalized being an indispensable accompaniment. But just as Lucretius said you can throw nature out the door but it will come rushing back in through the window, American law also tends to let morality into its accommodation with custom by claiming that the law may not violate public policy or be patently in furtherance of an immoral precept. In a number of former British colonial territories, the check on custom was a clause in the law stating that no ruling may be repugnant to 'justice, equity, or good conscience.' (Mustafa 1971). Although U.S. law contains no such repugnancy clause, it is clear that courts can find a similar foundation under such rubrics as 'public policy,' *'contra bonos mores,'* or 'the conscience and traditions of our people.' In short, it is a distinctive part of American culture to believe that law filters out the truly iniquitous, that (in the words of Dr. Martin Luther King) "the arc of the moral universe is long, but it bends towards justice." By concurrently allowing what the plurality do and limiting such practices to what appears to those on the bench as not in contravention of moral principles, American law maintains its curiously anti-centralist, pro-moral tone through the mechanism of culturally informed discretion.

6. *Custom fosters peace.* It is commonly assumed that if most people recognize a custom as valid they will conduct themselves in accordance with it and be less likely to use non-legal means to effect their ends. One of the few studies that seeks to document this proposition is that of cattle ranchers in Shasta County, California, by Robert Ellickson (1994). He found that disputes about wandering cattle were more effectively handled by local custom

than by government mandate. It may be generally true, as David Bederman (2010) notes, that such practices work to the detriment of outsiders and perpetuate antiquated norms. But the belief in such localism is part of the American romance of community, a factor that undoubtedly contributes to the assumption that locals are better able to handle matters than nonresidents. With over 3000 counties in the United States and over 7000 local governments in the state of Illinois alone, the American assumption that democracy works best at the local level is, in part, made manifest by the legal style of addressing customary law.

★ ★ ★

Relying on custom may be seen as a shorthand way for allowing change to come from the bottom up, for making it appear that the state is not really controlling matters, and for allowing an open texture into which assumptions of human nature can be drawn differently by various parties. Proponents of statutory codification may imagine they have eliminated custom. But as H. R. Hahlo (1967: 249, 251) has suggested, "the immediate effect of the introduction of a code is to create a lengthy period of increased legal uncertainty" as codes, opening up new disputes, become "buried under a heap of subsequent enactments and judiciary law."[18] Nor is a common law approach any less ambiguous. Bentham had said that by replacing custom with statutes all that would be lost are those customary laws that "depend upon the want of amplitude and discrimination, the indeterminateness, contradiction, tautology, ambiguity, and obscurity" that statutes would remove. But, as Jeremy Waldron points out, "those were the very aspects of customary law that were likely to be highlighted not diminished by the common law's insidious advances."[19] Questions that date far back in history still confront us: "For what does it matter whether the people declares its will by vote or by circumstances and conduct," asked an early commenter.[20] And might it actually be true, as François Gény (1861–1959) asserted, that 'laws have propelled the formation of custom' and not just the other way around? Mechanisms and rationales for addressing custom thus remain vigorous, notwithstanding that many such customs may seem antiquated. In parts of Scandinavia, for example, custom continues to play a role in fishing and other property disputes, while in South Africa courts have had to face the difficult question whether perpetuating Apartheid-era laws is worse than revitalizing customary laws that often discriminate against women.[21]

People still drive around the traffic circle by my university allowing others on the trunk road to go ahead despite the sign and statute to the contrary. Occasionally, too, they flash their lights urging—ah, what?—courtesy or caution, deference or right. So far, I know of no accidents that have occurred. But if there is one, should the court defer to a custom that is only discoverable by experience and only legible from the acts of others? Is failure to note the behavior of locals a form of negligence, or is unbending assertion of one's statutory right to proceed lack of due care? Should everyone, local or outsider, simply be held to 'the law'? Or is this a case of 'the people' engaging in a quiet form of protest against the formal law, a subtle if ironic form of what the British humorist Alan Bennett meant when, tongue firmly in cheek, he remarked, "We started off trying to set up a small anarchist community, but people wouldn't obey the rules." However you decide, what you assume about people and relationships will, as always, intercede—and would you, or could you, have it any other way?

Notes

1 There was even a film, appropriately called *Urban Legend*, that played on the rumor that a gang member had to drive with his headlights off and when another car flashed its headlights at him the gang member could only complete his initiation by assaulting or killing the other driver. See, Mikkelson (2010).

2 See, Taub (2015).

3 A number of the instances mentioned here, not all of which could be separately confirmed, are derived from the Wikipedia (2016) article. See also *People v. Rose* (just flashing one's headlights from a distance is not grounds for a policeman stopping a vehicle), and *State of New Jersey v. Luptak* ("[statute] is not violated when a motorist flashes his or her high beams to warn oncoming motorists of radar").

4 For Qatar, see Jaybird (2015); for India, Blaise and Mukherjee (1977: 33).

5 See, e.g., Weiss (2014), Klinger (2011), and Baker (2015).

6 On the determination of custom in the African experience, see Woodman (1969) and Allott (1957); for New Guinea, Demian (2003) and Larcom (2015). See also Kuruk (2007), Sheleff (1999), and Zion (1988). On surveying to establish custom, see Stewart 1998 (Zimbabwe high court erred in disallowing women inheritance rights, customary practice being far more varied and flexible than court found). On the problem of reifying culture when addressing customary law, see Fishbayn (1999).

7 Marc Bloch (1964: 113), speaking of the medieval period in Europe, said: "A custom…might seem especially to deserve condemnation when it was too new….The strange things is that this law in whose eyes any change seemed an evil, far from being unchangeable, was in fact one of the most flexible ever known." Similarly, Theodore F. T. Plucknett (1936: 272–3), discussing the same period in Britain, wrote that "the remarkable feature of custom is its flexibility and adaptability…. In an age when custom was an active living factor in the development of society there was much less insistence upon actual or fictitious antiquity. If we want the view of a lawyer who knew from experience what custom was, we can turn to Azo (died 1230): 'A custom can be called *long*,' he says, 'if it was introduced within ten or twenty years, *very long* if it dates from thirty years, and *ancient* if it dates from forty years.'" Such 'flexibility' may be due to the highly discretionary nature of its recognition. As one legal scholar (Ibertson 2008) has said: "It is rarely possible to know in advance whether a custom will in fact be recognized as law. How longstanding the practice must be is often indeterminate…Creating instant traditions is a phenomenon well known to anthropologists and historians." For example, short, belted kilts are thought by many to date from ancient times in Scotland whereas they were actually the invention of a Quaker, Thomas Rawlinson, in 1720. See generally, Hobsbawm (1992).

8 For a discussion of whether law can ever operate without some reliance on custom, see Murphy (2014). Two useful sets of essays on law and custom are Symposium (2012) and Symposium (2013).

9 Holmes and others are quoted in *State of Maine v. Frank E. Bradbury* (it is an outrage against public feelings and hence criminal to cut up and burn a dead body in a home incinerator).

10 See generally, Schauer (2007, 2013).

11 See also, *Brilliant Coal v. Barton*; and *Wilmington City Ry. Co. v. White*.
12 Few attorneys or law teachers know that this provision was written into the Uniform Commercial Code by its author, Karl Llewelyn, based on his experience studying the pre-contact laws of the Cheyenne Indians, who had a similar proposition Llewelyn believed would work well for commercial transactions in the United States.
13 *Hurst v. Lake and Co., Inc.* (although contract called for X proportion, custom in the trade holds that X really means a different number). See also the discussion of custom in *Provident Tradesmen's Bank and Trust co. v. Pemberton*.
14 On the decline of custom in American property law, see Smith (2013).
15 Thus, in *Wilmington City Ry. Co. v. White*, the court held that a local custom by which trolley cars stopped for funeral processions may and must be specifically pleaded, but the requirement of due care still applies: "What will constitute negligence or want of due care may depend upon the observance or nonobservance of a usage or practice known to exist under particular circumstances." See generally, Abraham (2009).
16 See, Druzin (2014). See also, Hetcher (1999, 2004).
17 "[C]ustom ought to be accepted more readily, once proved, than a typical overturning of existing case law because a group of persons engaged in the practice have demonstrated the convenience and utility" (Note 1955: 1204–5).
18 For a contrary view that law always arises from customs that are expressive of a 'communal moral context,' see Barden and Murphy (2010).
19 Waldron (1998: 114), quoting Jeremy Bentham's draft dedicatory letter for his *Of Laws in General*.
20 See, Dawson (1968).
21 On the Scandinavian situation see Obebech (2013). On South Africa's dilemma, see Bennett (2009).

References

Abraham, Kenneth S. 2009, "Custom, Noncustomary Practice, and Negligence," *Columbia Law Review*, vol. 109, pp. 1784–1822.

Allott, Anthony N. 1957, "The Judicial Ascertainment of Customary Law in British Africa," *Modern Law Review*, vol. 20, pp. 244–63.

Baker, Billy 2015, "Space-Saver 'Justice' Undercuts Ban in South End," *Boston Globe*, February 16.

Barden, Garrett and Timothy Murphy 2010, *Law and Justice in Community*, Oxford: Oxford University Press.

Bederman, David L. 2010, *Custom as a Source of Law*, Cambridge: Cambridge University Press.

Bennett, T. W. 2009, "Re-Introducing African Customary Law to the South African Legal System," *The American Journal of Comparative* Law, vol. 57, pp. 1–31.

Bernstein, Lisa 2015, "Custom in the Courts,"*Northwestern University Law Review*, vol. 110, pp. 63.

———— 2016, "Trade Usage in the Courts: The Flawed Conceptual and Evidentiary Basis of Article 2's Incorporation Strategy." www.law.uchicago.edu/files/file/669-452-lb-trade-2.pdf (accessed January 5, 2017).

Blaise, Clark and Bharati Mukherjee 1977, *Days and Nights in Calcutta*, New York: Doubleday.

Bloch, Marc 1964, *Feudal Society, Vol. 1*, Chicago, IL: University of Chicago Press.

Ceglowski, Maciej 2015, "Ta'izz," *Idle Words*, May 17.

Dawson, John P. 1968, *The Oracles of the Law*, Ann Arbor: The University of Michigan Press.

Demian, Melissa 2003, "Custom in the Courtroom, Law in the Village: Legal Transformations in Papua New Guinea," *Journal of the Royal Anthropological Institute, New Series*, vol. 9, pp. 97–115.

Druzin, Bryan H. 2014, *Planting Seeds of Order: How the State Can Create, Shape, and Use Customary Law*, April. http://works.bepress.com/bryan_druzin/13 (accessed January 5, 2017).

Ellickson, Robert 1994, *Order without Law: How Neighbors Settle Disputes*, Cambridge, MA: Harvard University Press.

Fishbayn, Lisa 1999, "Litigating the Right to Culture: Family Law in the New South Africa," *International Journal of Law, Policy and the Family*, vol. 13, pp. 147–73.

Hahlo, H. R. 1967, "Here Lies the Common Law; Rest in Peace,' *Modern Law Review*, vol. 30, pp. 241–59.

Hetcher, Steven A. 1999, "Creating Safe Social Norms in a Dangerous World," *Southern California Law Review*, vol. 73, pp. 1–82.

—— 2004, *Norms in a Wired World*, Cambridge: Cambridge University Press.

Hobsbawm, Eric A. 1992, *The Invention of Tradition*, Cambridge: Cambridge University Press, 1992.

Ibertson, David 2008, "Custom as a Source of Law," in Peter Cane and Joanne Conaghan, eds., *The New Oxford Companion to Law*, Oxford: Oxford University Press, p. 291.

Jain, M. P. 1994, "Custom as a Source of Law in India," reprinted from *Jaipur Law Journal*, vol. 3 (1963) pp. 96–130, in Alison Dundes Renteln and Alan Dundes, eds., *Folk Law, Volume I*, New York: Garland Publishing, 1994, pp. 49–82.

Jaybird 2015, "A Qatari Travelogue (And Conversion)," *Ordinary Times*, June 28. http://ordinary-gentlemen.com/blog/2015/06/28/a-qatari-travelogue-and-conversion/ (accessed January 5, 2017).

Kadens, Emily 2012, "The Myth of the Customary Law Merchant," *Texas Law Review*, vol. 90, pp. 1153–1206.

Kirk, Russell 1953, *The Conservative Mind from Burke to Santayana*, Chicago, IL: H. Regnery.

Klinger, Karen 2011, "'That's My (Shoveled-Out) Parking Spot!' A New Cambridge Trend?" Cambridge Community Television, January 28. www.cctvcambridge.org/node/71306 (accessed January 5, 2017).

Kuruk, Paul 2007, "The Role of Customary Law under Sui Generis Frameworks of Intellectual Property Rights in Traditional and Indigenous Knowledge," *Indiana International & Comparative Law Review*, vol. 17, pp. 67–118.

Larcom, Shaun 2015, *Legal Dissonance: The Interaction of Criminal Law and Customary Law in Papua New Guinea*, New York: Berghahn Books.

Mikkelson, Barbara 2010, "Lights Out." www.snopes.com/crime/gangs/lightsout.asp#! (accessed January 5, 2017).

Murphy, James Bernard 2014, *The Philosophy of Customary Law*, Oxford: Oxford University Press.

Mustafa, Zaki Dean 1971, *Common Law in the Sudan: An Account of the 'Justice, Equity and Good Conscience' Provision*, Oxford: Oxford University Press.

Note 1955, "Custom and Trade Usage," *Columbia Law Review*, vol. 55, pp. 1192–1209.

Obebech, Peter 2013, "Western Scandinavia: Exit *Birgerliches Gesetzbuch* – the Resurrection of Customary Laws," 48 *Texas International Law Journal* 405–33.

Plucknett, Theodore F. T. 1936, *A Concise History of the Common Law*, 2d edn., Rochester, NY: Lawyers Cooperative Publishing Co.

Ramsey, Michael D. n.d., "Two Forms of Argument from Custom." www.researchgate.net/publication/265520801_Two_Forms_of_Argument_from_Custom (accessed January 5, 2017).

Rothman, Jennifer E. 2007, "The Questionable Use of Custom in Intellectual Property," *Virginia Law Review*, vol. 93, pp. 1899–1982.

Schauer, Frederick 2007, "Pitfalls in the Interpretation of Customary Law," in Amanda Perreau-Saussine and James Bernard Murphy, eds., *The Nature of Customary Law*, Cambridge: Cambridge University Press, pp. 13–34.

———— 2013, "The Jurisprudence of Custom," *Texas International Law* Journal, vol. 48, pp. 523–34.

Sheleff, Leon 1999, *The Future of Tradition: Custom, Common Law and Legal Pluralism*, London: Frank Cass.

Smith, Henry E. 2013, "Custom in American Property Law: A Vanishing Act," *Texas International Law Journal*, vol. 48, pp. 507–21.

Stewart, Julie 1998, "Why I Can't Teach Customary Law," in John Eekelaar and Thandabantu Nhlapo, eds., *The Changing Family*, Oxford: Hart Publishing, pp. 217–30.

Symposium 2012, "Custom and Law," *Duke Law Journal*, vol. 62, pp. 529–855.

Symposium 2013, "Lessons from the History of Custom," *Texas International Law Journal*, vol. 48, pp. 349–534.

Taub, Eric A. 2015, "As Americans Figure Out the Roundabout, It Spreads across the U.S.," *New York Times*, July 30.

Vanderbilt, Tom 2008, *Traffic*, New York: Alfred A. Knopf.

Waldron, Jeremy 1998, "Custom Redeemed by Statute," in M. D. A. Freeman, ed., *Current Legal Problems 1998*, vol. 51, Oxford: Oxford University Press, pp. 93–114.

Weiss, Debra Cassens 2014, "Parking-Dibs Tradition becomes a Federal Case in Chicago," *American Bar Association Journal*, January 9.

Wikipedia 2016, "Headlight Flashing." https://en.wikipedia.org/wiki/Headlight_flashing (accessed January 5, 2017).

Woodman, Gordon R. 1969, "Some Realism about Customary Law—the West African Experience," *Wisconsin Law Review*, pp. 128–52.

Zion, James W. 1988, "Searching for Indian Common Law," in Bradford Moore and Gordon Woodman, eds., *Indigenous Law and the State*, Dordrecht, Holland: Foris Publications, pp. 121ff.

Cases cited

Brilliant Coal v. Barton, 203 Ala. 38 (Ala. 1919).

Congregation B'nai Sholom v. Martin, 382 Mich. 659, 173 N.W.2d 504 (MI 1969).

Ghen v. Rich, 8 F. 159 (D.C. Mass. 1881).

Hurst v. Lake and Co., Inc., 141 Or. 306, 16 P.2d 627 (1932).

People v. Rose, 67 A.3d 1447 (NY App. Div., 4th Dept. 2009).

Provident Tradesmen's Bank and Trust co. v. Pemberton, 24 Pa. D. & C.2d 720, 196 Pa.Super. 181, 173 A.2d 780 (Pa. Super. 1961).

State of Maine v. Frank E. Bradbury, 136 Me. 347 (1939).

State of New Jersey v. Luptak, Superior Court of New Jersey, Appellate Division A-6074–97T1 (July 29, 1999).

Texas & Pacific Railway Co. v. Behymer, 189 U.S. 468, 23 S. Ct. 622, 47 L. Ed. 905 (1903).

Trimarco v. Klein, 56 NYS2d 98, 436 NE2d 502 (Ct. of App., NY 1982).

United Steelworkers of America v. Warrior & Gulf Navigation Co., 363 U.S. 574, 80 S. Ct. 1347, 4 L.Ed.2d 1409 (1960).

Wilmington City Ry. Co. v. White, 6 Penne. 363, 66 Atl. 1009–13 (DE 1907).

9

IS THERE A PLACE FOR COMMUNITY?

The Amish and the American romance of community

The ultimate foundation of a free society is the binding tie of cohesive sentiment. Such a sentiment is fostered by all those agencies of the mind and spirit which may serve to gather up the traditions of a people, transmit them from generation to generation, and thereby create that continuity of a treasured common life which constitutes a civilization.

—Justice Felix Frankfurter
Minersville School Dist. v. Gobitis

Americans romanticize the idea of community. They see in it an ideal of the republican form of life and governance—yet they constructed a constitution that essentially allows no place in the law for such an entity. Associations, of course, take numerous forms—with the right of association itself protected by the Constitution. And there are contractual property regimes that involve provisions affecting everything from the age and income of residents to restrictions on renting, sale, and even the placement of exterior religious symbols. Indeed, twenty percent of all Americans (some 64 million people) now live in more than 300,000 condominiums, homeowners associations, or other common-interest communities.[1] But these groupings are not necessarily comprised of people with common backgrounds or interests beyond the terms of their contract. Lying somewhere between the state and the individual, and all but pushed out by those two categories, 'the community,' fraught with airy imprecision and imagined reality, lies in a legal limbo, either awaiting vindication in case law or remaining an idealized template from a world that never was.

And yet the image, the ideal persists. Indeed, it even gains occasional reality, sometimes in a zoning case where it is argued that the changes in building styles or road construction will destroy small community businesses, safe access to friends and relatives, or identity as an integrated neighborhood combating 'white flight.' Rarely, too, 'the community' shows up as a test of cultural ideas and ideals when a distinctive group wishes to pursue a way of life that requires a degree of separation from others yet appears to embody religious promptings that are imagined as central to the nation's identity. This may involve an Orthodox Jewish community that wants to string a line around the area within which it would be permissible to carry objects on the Sabbath as if in one's own home, the display of a Christmas Creche or the Ten Commandments on public property, or just a desire on the part of older people to set an age limit that would reduce the level of noise in their neighborhood. 'Community' may even figure at a constitutional level, as when the U.S. Supreme Court determined that the test for pornography would be "local community standards." For purposes of this chapter, however, we will concentrate on the case of the Amish.

The Amish, as we shall see, would appear to embody many of the ideals associated with America—agrarianism, peacefulness, religious commitment, and escape from discrimination and brutalization abroad. Whatever the reality, the case they present tests the idea of community in the American imaginary and the place of such an entity within the legal landscape. As such, it affords yet another variant instance of the law trying to deal with cultural concepts that, in this case, find resonance more outside of formal legal strictures than within. How the notion of community allows incorporation within the existing legal vocabulary depends in great part on how one tells the story of the Amish—and how one imagines that story ought to end.

★ ★ ★

From its very inception, the United States has had a romance with the idea of 'community.' Like any romance, it has had its ups and downs, and like any combination of emotion and relationship it has suffered—when it has not benefited— from imprecise definition and inexact application. Initially, a number of the American colonies were small faith-based collectivities with relatively homogeneous populations and, in a surprising number of cases, an established religion. Once the Federalists had won and the nation was set on the course of a consolidated union rather than a congeries of confessional entities, however, political units that were not mentioned in the Constitution—that were neither federal nor state (or derivative from one or the other)—lacked any clear legal status. And yet the image, the ideal, of the local community never quite died. At times it has cropped up under the rubric of 'civic republicanism'—though that is predominantly a notion applied either to the nation as a whole or to a politically bounded and politically interactive entity. More commonly, 'community' has been a vague ideal of something that may never have really existed but for which there is nevertheless some felt sense of loss.[2] It has been used for a variety of designations. It can refer to neighborhood enterprises ('community development' and 'community benefits agreements'), localized legal forums ('community courts' [e.g., Bernstein 2016; Goodmark 2015] and 'community conciliation boards'), places of sectarian gathering ('Jewish Community Center'), or distinctive work groups ('the academic community'). It has entered popular discourse as a way of legging up to the ideals of the collective—the intelligence 'community,' the gay-lesbian-bisexual-transgender 'community'—each usage conjuring an image of common interest and fellow-feeling. What is largely missing, however, is the legal standing of a grouping that is caught between that which can be analogized to a political grouping and that which can be analogized to the individual.

The question then arises whether courts, perhaps relying on this cultural ideal, have found ways in which the community can be likened to legislatively enumerated or judicially created entities with recognizable powers and protections. Voluntary associations, such as political parties, are not communities in this sense, nor are religious groupings, which may on occasion share a bounded living situation but may lack the distinct political recognition that other units possess. Non-governmental groups of various sorts have some legal protections: Constitutionally recognizable associations, for example, may refuse to divulge their membership lists and have the right to remain free from state-sponsored discrimination or stigmatization.

While the term 'community' may crop up in these cases it is, however, in more of a vernacular than strictly legal sense that it does so. Indeed, trying to press one category into the other—whether it is using 'community standards' to assess pornography or describing racial discrimination as yielding "a feeling of inferiority as to their status in the community"—always seems to lack precise legal fit.[3] The highest court in New York State may hold that "the carelessness required for criminal negligence is appreciably more serious than that for ordinary civil negligence, and that the carelessness must be such that its seriousness would be apparent to anyone who shares the community's general sense of right and wrong" (*People v. Conway* 2006: 872).[4] But other than regarding the jury as the voice of that community, the courts do not seek community input in any direct sense. Indeed, the courts have even limited appeals by counsel to the jury as the 'conscience of the community': "Our condemnation of a 'community conscience' argument is not limited to the use of those specific words; it extends to all impassioned and prejudicial pleas intended to evoke a sense of community loyalty, duty and expectation. Such appeals serve no proper purpose and carry the potential of substantial injustice when invoked against outsiders" (*Westbrook v. General Tire and Rubber Co.* 1985: 1239).

Thus, the definitions, much less the legal entailments, of a 'community' remain vague and contradictory, even when acknowledged on the occasional case-by-case basis. Several legal decisions may, however, be helpful in understanding the tensions, ambiguities, and cultural assumptions that suffuse this unusual yet revelatory domain in which aspects of a people's self-worth and self-image are expressed and entangled, yet not formally structured, within the country's legal system. To see how the law's concept of community plays out, there may be no better starting point than the Amish education case, *Wisconsin v. Yoder.*

In 1972, the United States Supreme Court held that the State of Wisconsin had violated the constitutional rights of the defendant Amish parents by requiring them to send their children, then ages fourteen and fifteen, to school beyond the eighth grade.[5] It was hardly the first time the Amish had encountered a state that sought to control the education of their children. During the Great

Depression, in an effort to reduce unemployment, the Roosevelt Administration allowed states to raise compulsory school attendance age. Amish and Mennonite parents had earlier been arrested and fined for not sending their children to public schools: Some children (like Native Americans) were forced to give up their traditional clothing and sent off to boarding schools. As late as the 1960s, Amish children were chased by truant officers through Iowa cornfields and then herded onto buses that took them to state-run schools.[6] Other states had made arrangements for alternative schooling within their Amish communities, but Wisconsin rejected plans similar to those in Indiana and Pennsylvania that were proposed to them by the state's Amish.[7] What might at first blush appear to have been a valid state interest in furthering the education of all its citizens turned out, in the *Yoder* case, to have been largely motivated by the desire of the Green County government, after the Amish opened their own elementary school and withdrew 37 students from the county school, to retain the $18,000 in tax revenues the school district received from the Amish children's attendance—a fact that was never mentioned by the U.S. Supreme Court (Quaqua n.d.). Jonas Yoder and the other Amish parents were charged with contributing to the truancy of the children, found guilty at trial, and fined five dollars each.[8] Appalled by the situation, a Lutheran minister, Rev. William C. Lindholm, enlisted the aid of a Catholic attorney, William Ball, who carried the appeal to the U.S. Supreme Court. Arguing that "only those interests of the highest order and those not otherwise served can overbalance legitimate claims to the free exercise of religion," the Court found that the Amish faith and their mode of life were so inseparable and interdependent that the social repercussions of compulsory high school attendance would necessarily infringe on the well-being of the community as a religious entity (*Wisconsin v. Yoder* 1972: 215). Because retention of that religious community was vital to any one member's ability to practice his or her religion, the Court found that the constitutionally protected freedom of religion of Mr. Yoder and his co-defendants was adversely affected. In reaching its decision, the Court made frequent reference to the testimony given at the trial court level by the anthropologist John A. Hostetler (Figures 9.1 and 9.2).

Hostetler was an intriguing witness. A professor of anthropology at Temple University, he had been raised in an Amish community, though he never engaged in the defining feature of membership, undergoing adult baptism. A number of his relatives had voluntarily left the community, but his own father was actually excommunicated. In an autobiographical statement, Hostetler (1992: 553) wrote, "When I was eleven years old, my father was excommunicated from the Amish church. He saw himself as a victim of a jealous member who took his complaints to the bishop." While Hostetler mentions that his father had "registered our herd of purebred milking cows," the foreword to one of his book says the father was actually removed "for taking too great a worldly pride in a herd of cows." Hostetler does not say if his father was 'shunned,' a penalty that usually requires that no one, including close family members, any longer talk to the person. Hostetler later expanded his essay, even acknowledging his own participation in the practice of

FIGURE 9.1 Amishmen sentenced for violation of state compulsory school attendance law, 1960.

Source: Photo by Edward G. Schneider, Reading Eagle Co.

FIGURE 9.2 John Hostetler.

Source: Courtesy of Temple University.

'bundling,' in which adolescent Amish 'visit' one another's beds in the night, where sexual relations may or may not take place (Hostetler and Miller 2005). He actually identifies himself as Mennonite: "My parents were very disappointed that I didn't stay to take over the farm, but I had a compelling feeling that I should prepare myself educationally. Therefore, when I became 18, I chose not to be baptized. Instead, I joined a Mennonite congregation that allowed high school and college. My two older sisters, Lizzie and Sylvia, are Amish. Two younger sisters, Barbara and Mary, are Mennonite, as are my wife, daughters and myself" (Clayton 1985). Like many Amish, he did not initially attend high school, only later developing an interest in continuing his education. Throughout his career (he died in 2001) Hostetler concentrated his academic work on various Amish, Mennonite, and Hutterite groups, his well-known book, *Amish Life*, having sold more than half a million copies during his lifetime (Anonymous 2002). His commitment to the legal rights of the Amish endured throughout his life: *Yoder* was only the most noteworthy of a number of cases in which he appeared on their behalf as an expert witness.[9]

At trial, Hostetler testified that "as a part of their way of salvation [the Amish] require a church community that is separate from the world" (*Wisconsin v. Yoder* 1970: 49). Requiring the children to go for the extra two years to a high school posed an existential threat to the Amish: "I think," he said, "that if the Amish youth are required to attend the value system of the high school as we know it today, the church-community cannot last long, it will be destroyed" (*Id.*: 51). In response to direct examination, he said that this is because "great psychological harm can be done to the children," as well as to the community, as a result of the alienation that can arise from a clash of values (*Id.*: 52). In a 1972 news release from Temple University following the Supreme Court decision, he is quoted as saying: "When culturally different children attend a school that teaches an unattainable identity, an identity that would demand the rejection of the values of the home, of parents, the tribe, or the street, and even the color of their skin, what can be expected but alienation and rebellion?" Hostetler (1992: 561) later wrote, "The word education as used in American society is regarded with suspicion by most Amish people. To them it signifies ego advancement, independence, and cutting the ties that bind one to the community of faith and work." He continued: "The role of the public school system is to facilitate uniformity and to provide preparation for those seeking to participate in mainstream American culture. ... Faith communities in America function as mediating structures in the pluralistic makeup of our society. ... These communities are an extension of familial love, informing us who we are, where we come from, and what is distinctive about us" (Id.: 562). In the Amish view, he testified, higher learning is regarded as "wisdom not responsible to the community" (*Wisconsin v. Yoder* 1970: 54A). The Amish, he asserted, train their children to be members of a self-sufficient community and do not place a burden on American society as a result of delinquency or welfare requirements.

On cross-examination, the state's attorney tried to bring out that the Amish do not object to sending their children to public school through the eighth grade and that Amish children come into contact with outsiders on their occasional trips to town. Hostetler reasserted, in the following testimony, that the prosecutor's approach was not without its own bias:

Q: Are you saying in effect, Professor, that to minority groups, which includes the Amish, that they should govern themselves as far as education; should minority groups, be it Amish or otherwise, would you say be permitted to set up their own rules as to whether they shall or shall not be educated?

A: I think we need to know a great deal more about how to teach the culturally different child, know the poverty children, and I think it is dangerous to put all children through the same type of value orientation.

Q: Isn't that the reason then, Professor, in the institutions of higher learning, high school and up, you will have elective courses so the children won't all have to take the same.

A: The trouble is it is still the same environment, it doesn't matter what courses they take.

Q: The principal purpose to attend school is to get education, is it not, isn't that the primary purpose?

A: Yes, but I think there is a great deal of difference what education means, education for what.

Q: To put it bluntly, education so the child can make his or her place in the world?

A: It depends which world.

Q: This one, the one we live in?

A: I think education—this is one of the myths in American society—all education is good; education must be tied to a culture that emotionally guides the child in the direction he knows he is going to live when he is an adult.

Q: Well in other words, Professor, you are saying that education should be tied in the sense to culture, is that right?

A: Yes. Anthropologists would say there isn't education without culture climate at all.

Q: So if I am in one culture and you another the education we receive should be different?

A: I would say if there is this difference in Amish society we should have a parallel culture in the society to know each other as common Americans but a different heritage.

(Wisconsin v. Yoder 1970: 67–68)

Finally, the state raised the issue of the effect of insufficient education on those who later choose to leave the community:

Q: Is it fair to say, Professor, that an adult who in his childhood might well be an Amish and now decided not to stay with the Amish is at a handicap because he did not receive the education he might have received were he not an Amish?

A: The conclusion is that the skills required to become an adult are such that if one doesn't have an adult high school education, well, normally people are always looking for people to do manual work. I don't believe any segment is deprived by not having education.

Q: Even those who later cease to become members of the Amish faith and find themselves having to compete in the worldly world?

A: No, I don't think they are deprived.

(Id.: 69)[10]

In deciding for the Amish, the U.S. Supreme Court adopted the reasoning, and indeed many of the phrases, contained in Hostetler's testimony. The Court (*Wisconsin v. Yoder* 1972: 235–36) summarized its position in the following terms:

> It cannot be overemphasized that we are not dealing with a way of life and mode of education by a group claiming to have recently discovered some "progressive" or more enlightened process for rearing children for modern life. Aided by a history of three centuries as an identifiable religious sect and a long history as a successful and self-sufficient segment of American society, the Amish in this case have convincingly demonstrated the sincerity of their religious beliefs, the interrelationship of belief with their mode of life, the vital role that belief and daily conduct play in the continued survival of Old Order Amish communities and their religious organization, and the hazards presented by the State's enforcement of a statute generally valid to others. Beyond this, they have carried the even more difficult burden of demonstrating the adequacy of their alternative mode of continuing informal vocational education in terms of precisely those overall interests that the State advances in support of its program of compulsory high school education.

Only Mr. Justice Douglas dissented in part from the majority opinion. He pointed out that attrition from Amish communities is often quite high.[11] He argued that, although the case involved criminal charges against the parents for violation of compulsory school attendance laws, the interests of the children should have been represented in the case. Douglas noted that one of the children had testified at trial that she did not want to attend the public school beyond the eighth grade, but he argued that all the other children should have been heard from as well. He also objected to granting an exception only to groups whose values had a religious, rather than philosophical, basis (*Wisconsin v. Yoder* 1972: 247–49).[12]

Leaving aside the wisdom of the Court's unprecedented decision to grant the Amish an exception from the requirements of a valid state statute because of their religious beliefs, the case raises important issues concerning expert anthropological testimony. The Court was correct when it noted that the state had presented no expert to contradict Hostetler's assessment of Amish life: Indeed the opinion noted the "uncontradicted testimony" of experts on religious history and education who appeared for the Amish, frequently citing Hostetler (to whom the Court referred as a historian rather than an anthropologist) and Prof. Donald A. Erickson (an associate professor of education at the University of Chicago) and tracking their very wording (*Wisconsin v. Yoder* 1972: 209). The Court especially picked up on Hostetler's assertion, repeated several times in Mr. Ball's oral argument to the Court, that to send the children to school beyond the eighth grade would lead to the destruction of the Amish community.[13] Nor did the state succeed in undermining Hostetler's contention that religious and social life are inseparable in Amish communities and that an attack on the one was necessarily an attack on the other.

And yet, from the testimony alone, it might appear that Hostetler's interpretation of Amish culture rests on an unstated and unchallenged theoretical assumption—namely, that Amish society is the sort of homeostatic, functionally integrated, organically constituted holistic entity that is best analyzed in terms of structural-functional theory. He had stated that, "When culturally different children attend a school that teaches an unattainable identity, an identity that would demand the rejection of the values of the home... what can be expected but alienation and rebellion?"[14]—an assertion that ignores the possibilities of growth, development, or change. Another expert, or another lawyer, might have pointed, as Mr. Justice Douglas did, to Hostetler's own findings concerning drinking patterns and social tensions among the Amish[15] and might have challenged the view that two years of additional education would have increased the attrition rate even though the Amish have clearly survived heavy losses in the past.

The case thus raises many questions for experts. Do they have a duty to express alternative theories even if counsel does not ask about them or is unaware of them? Should prospective assessments of the likely impact of a given practice be stated solely in terms of personal opinion or should the expert explain and evaluate alternative interpretations before voicing a professional opinion? What sort of conception of 'community' was the Court employing, and how did the expert anthropology testimony support that interpretation? A second set of issues concerns the expert's own affinity to the cause of those on whose behalf he appears. Hostetler, as has been noted, was himself raised as an Amishman and felt very close to the people. At one point in the testimony, he even referred to "*our* Amish culture."[16] The attorney for the Amish, on oral argument to the U.S. Supreme Court, effectively pointed to Hostetler as an example of someone who was indeed able to make his way in higher education after being raised in an Amish community (Kurland and Casper 1975: 816). But this background was not emphasized at the trial level. John Hostetler was clearly the most conscientious and thorough of scholars, and his deep concern and commitment to the Amish represented the finest in humanistic anthropology. Of what relevance should it be, then, that he was raised an Amishman, and what, if any, obligation for such disclosure should be imposed as a general rule on all experts?

There can be no doubt, too, that the Court's image of the Amish was melded into a larger vision—one might say a larger *nostalgic* vision—of America and its history. Chief Justice Warren Burger characterized the Amish as "odd," "even erratic," and "different,"[17] but then alluded to an idyllic American past, no doubt to reduce the potential threat of Amish differentness and its implication of civic confusion. Indeed, in an obvious attempt to reduce the sense of difference Burger said that Amish adult baptism is "not unlike the Bar Mitzvah of the Jews" and that Amish rules inform "the entire way of life, regulating it with the detail of Talmudic diet."[18] In addition to citing the experts for the proposition that the survival of Amish communities was under threat, Burger also stated: "A related feature of Old Order Amish communities is their devotion to a life in harmony with nature and the soil, as exemplified by the simple life of the early Christian era that continued in America during much of our early national life."[19] Through these analogies, as Sarat and Berkowitz (1994: 301) note, "The problem of disorder is overcome because it, like the difference with which it is associated, is dissolved into a nostalgic identity." And, as we have seen, the Court distinguished the Amish case from one that might involve "a way of life and mode of education by a group claiming to have recently discovered some 'progressive' or more enlightened process for rearing children for modern life" (*Wisconsin v. Yoder* 1972: 235).

Moreover, while referring to the Amish as a 'community,' the majority couched some of its argument as if such entities were but the individual writ large rather than units with collective rights of a distinguishable nature. Thus the majority argued that, "The Amish mode of life has thus come into conflict increasingly with requirements of contemporary society exerting a hydraulic insistence on conformity to majoritarian standards" and that, "Its members are productive and very law-abiding members of society; they reject public welfare in any of its usual modern forms" (*Wisconsin v. Yoder* 1972: 207).[20] Only Justice Douglas made reference in a footnote to Hostetler's own characterization of significant instances of alcoholism, suicide, and 'rowdyism' in Amish communities,[21] although it should be noted that at the trial level public officials testified that there were no arrests among the Green County Amish or any instances of social services being called upon to deal with cases of illegitimacy or alcoholism.

There is no mention, too, of the practice, called Rumspringa, during which Amish youth may take a leave of absence from the community, often engaging in drinking and sex, as they decide whether to undergo adult baptism and live by the rules of the community.[22] And while levels of crime do not always reach those of the outside communities, even later commenters on the case have often ignored demonstrated charges of drug trafficking and other criminal activities carried out by particular Amish.[23] On the question of attrition in the Amish community members of the court disagreed. The majority opinion by the chief justice said: "There is no specific evidence of the loss of Amish adherents by attrition. …" By contrast, Justice White cited Hostetler himself to the effect that attrition runs at the rate of "probably two-thirds" while Justice Douglas cited Hostetler for rates ranging from forty to eighty percent. From Hostetler's own functionalist perspective, one might have suggested that those less likely to adhere to the community's requirements drop out, thus preserving rather than threatening the integrity of the whole. One may, then, fairly ask whether Hostetler's functionalist view of Amish society—indeed his claim of potential destruction of the community if the children must go to school for one or two more years—does not constitute a theoretical orientation counsel or the court should have endeavored to question.

In sum, the Court treated the Amish as a valid exception to school attendance laws based on the Court's measurement of them against some generalized concept of community. By focusing frequently on the Anabaptist history of the Amish—hounded out of Europe, finding a home in religiously tolerant America—the Court makes clear that 'communities' must be of long duration, preferably have suffered religious discrimination, and, by exemplifying an aura few now embrace except in myth, partake (in this particular manifestation) of that vision of American yeomanry that has been integral to the nation's self-imaginary since at least the time of Thomas Jefferson.[24] At every juncture in the opinion that idyll was perpetuated by the Court's choice of language and analogies: They referred to the family farm as an "ancient tradition"; they spoke of the first years of education as taking place in a "nearby rural schoolhouse" as opposed to the rather cold-sounding later years at a "consolidated school, often remote from the student's home" and cultural sources (*Wisconsin v. Yoder* 1972: 229). They even noted that distinctive and separated religious groups not unlike the Amish preserved civilization through the Dark Ages (*Id.*: 217, 223). And, perhaps due to their acceptance of Hostetler's functionalist view, the majority was fearful that they would be the ones to destroy this community if they required the children to attend an alternative cultural environment. Yet all the features of religious persecution and pastoral peacefulness may be precisely the elements that ultimately rendered the Amish case unique. It is, therefore, noteworthy that no other grouping has since qualified for the same kind of exemption. In the words of the Sixth Circuit Court of Appeals: "*Yoder* rested on such a singular set of facts that we do not believe it can be held to announce a general rule that exposure without compulsion to act, believe, affirm or deny creates an unconstitutional burden.... As the [*Yoder*] Court noted, the requirement of school attendance to age 16 posed a 'very real threat of undermining the Amish community and religious practice as they exist today'" (*Mozert v. Hawkins County Board of Education*).[25]

Yoder is not, however, the only context in which the concept of community figures in legal decisions. *Santa Clara Pueblo v. Martinez* may appear to be such a case.[26] In *Martinez*, a woman who was a member of an American Indian pueblo married an outsider man. Under the rules of the tribe, her daughter was not considered a member whereas a child of a male member of the group who married an outsider woman would be so regarded. Julia Martinez sued, claiming that as an American citizen she and her daughter were being discriminated against on the basis of gender, in violation of the Indian Civil Rights Act of 1968. The U.S.

Supreme Court ruled that the right of a tribe to make and be governed by its own rules, especially concerning membership, takes precedence over Martinez's claim of gender discrimination. The case really turns more on the issue of tribal sovereignty, though, than community as such. More comparable may be the Canadian case of *Sandra Lovelace v. Canada*, where the facts were very similar. There, Ms. Lovelace and her child were denied the right to return to their tribal grouping, having moved away. Lovelace (who later became a Canadian senator) brought suit before the Human Rights Committee of the United Nations, whose judgments Canada had agreed to honor. In 1981 the Committee ruled in Lovelace's favor, stating that "in the opinion of the Committee the right of Sandra Lovelace to access to her native culture and language 'in community with the other members' of her group, has in fact been, and continues to be interfered with, because there is no place outside the Tobique Reserve where such a community exists." This may be as close as any court has come to recognizing a kind of right to one's community, though again this case may be distinctive for involving native peoples who constitute a political as well as a cultural unit.

Zoning cases raise the concept of community somewhat more directly. When, for example, a road is to be constructed that bisects a community—for example, that of the Arab-American community in Dearborn, Michigan—courts have recognized some interests possessed by the collectivity even if they are not a politically bounded unit. By contrast, in *Moore v. East Cleveland*, the U.S. Supreme Court ruled that zoning for single family dwellings could not, as the statute did, bar a woman from having more than one set of grandsons living in the same home with her.[27] While the Court stressed the importance of extended families, it was the city that, somewhat ironically, was trying through the statute to maintain a racially mixed community by limiting the size of households. The collective interest was lost, it would appear, because the parties were conceptualized in terms of political and individual entities rather through any recognition of the 'community' as a legally recognizable unit. However, it was not as a political entity but as some kind of 'community' that the city had, in fact, conceived of its zoning needs. Similarly, the notion of 'group defamation,' which is recognized in some European nations, has never gained traction in the United States.[28] Once again, the place of such a group-based unit would appear to have been squeezed out, the individual and the state having taken up the available conceptual space.

And yet the allure of 'community' persists. This is especially so in the case of pornography. After many attempts at setting a standard of review for such cases—whether the material appealed to prurient interest, whether it had some redeeming social merit, etc.—the U.S. Supreme Court, in *Miller v. California*, said that a key part of the test is whether "the average person, applying contemporary community standards" would find that the work, taken as a whole, appeals to the prurient interest.[29] But how is the community to be defined or bounded— by geography, sentiment, or self-identity—and what method (experts, surveys, juries) should be used to ascertain the local standard? Where, for example, is one's community when using the Internet? In time, the legal criteria fell back into the familiar categories of state-wide standards and individual free speech. Yet the fact that *somehow* it was, and still is, felt that 'community' either exists for many people or should do so contributes to a sense that there is a gap between law and self-view that ought to be bridged.

A number of legal scholars have tracked the history of American notions of community and suggested ways to recognize their rights as separate and distinct from any other category. Bruce H. Mann (1986: 1420), for example, traces an intriguing shift in actions for debt in the early years of the United States. Owing to "the intricate web of multilayered social relations that characterized early communities...debtors and creditors did not, indeed could not, limit their relations to single transactions." Debts were recorded in such a way that when disputes occurred the result was a broad inquiry into the totality of the parties' relationship rather than just the particular transaction that initiated the debt. The bounds of relevance were thus quite wide, reliance on community-based account books allowing procedures for resolving the dispute being quite flexible. Juries were the primary deciders and no doubt placed the dispute within a broad cultural context, as judges did not even instruct them as to any legal propositions concerning debt (Id.: 1425). By 1730, however, as communities grew larger, more secure, and more diverse, the interlocking relationships that supported extra-legal pressures to abide by arbitration or air a wide range of grievances of which the debt was but a part gave way to more formal legal strictures. "All of this," Mann concludes (1986: 1438–39), "is not to suggest that law became divorced from society, but rather that it became divorced from community." Yet that image of community lingered in the popular imaginary.

Indeed, we can see its imprint in much more recent times. Frank Michelman, for example, points to the case of a predominantly Polish neighborhood in Detroit, popularly called Poletown, where General Motors sought to use the municipality's right of eminent domain to compensate the property owners and then tear down much of the area in order to build a plant that would employ thousands in this economically stressed area. The Michigan Supreme Court held that eminent domain was appropriate in this instance, as the project would serve a public purpose.[30] Michelman (1981), however, argues that property rights are not simply matters of personal ownership but are political rights in the sense that "property may represent more than money because it may represent things that money itself can't buy – place, position, relationship, roots, community, solidarity, status...." Indeed, he argues, without envisioning property as integral to the constitutional right to participation in the life and decisions of the social world to which one belongs, the purpose of the constitutional clauses pertaining to property would not be served. Staughton Lynd (1987: 927), too, asks, in the context of steel manufacturers pulling out of several American cities, whether "some kind of community property right arises from the long-standing relation between a company and a community." A judge in one of the cases initially suggested such a community right might exist: "I think the law can recognize the property right to the extent that U.S. Steel cannot leave [the]...area in a state of waste, that it cannot completely abandon its obligation to that community, because certain vested rights have arisen out of this long relationship and institution" (Id.: 940). Yet in ultimately dismissing the property claim, the judge opined, "United States Steel should not be permitted to leave the Youngstown area devastated after drawing the life-blood of the community for so many years. Unfortunately, the mechanism to reach this ideal settlement, to recognize this new property right, is not now in existence in the code of laws of our nation" (Id.)

Property is not the only analogy that has been employed to assert group rights. Ronald Garet (1983), for example, suggests that collective rights, even though not incorporated in the Constitution, emanate from the right to live a moral life in concert with others.[31] What he calls 'communality' is thus a form of collective right that is distinct from individual and group rights. At this point, however, matters become quite vague as no specific rights are suggested, 'communality' being described as "the process of celebration or dynamic ritual activity that brings material and symbolic groups together in a common experience of groupness" (Id.: 1073). Garet may be right when he says (Id.: 1017 18) that, "As a matter of constitutional law, we already 'have' both individual rights and group rights; but we will only accept the latter in the same way that we accept the former when we become accustomed to referring rights to communality as we are to referring rights to personhood." But without some more solid touchstone on which to build analogies the basis for such claimed rights remains vague, however much it persists as part of the American cultural vocabulary.

Collective rights can, of course, be analogized to individual rights, whether they are based on the notion (as we saw in *Yoder*) that the ability to practice one's own religion may require the presence of a group of similarly oriented persons or (as we saw in *Lovelace*) because the tribe is the irreducible unit through which individual socialization and security can be perpetuated. To some the analogy works best when put in terms of psychology: Deprived of one's fellows great confusion and anxiety can result. Thus in the litigation arising out of the 1972 Buffalo Creek flood that destroyed a number of West Virginia settlements when a coal slurry dam burst, attorneys for the victims argued for both psychological harm and loss of community. The court was prepared to hear evidence under the heading of "psychic impairment" even for those who had suffered no physical injury but experienced a loss of community. However, the case was settled before trial so no clear precedent on the concept of loss of community was established (see Erikson 1978 and Stern 2008). In the extreme—as we know from the removal of Native Americans or Pacific islanders from their homes, or from the effects of natural or man-made disasters—even death can result from lost community (Lewis 1986). Yet once one starts from the base of the individual it is almost impossible not to be pulled back to that singular unit—to see communities as collections of persons or to characterize individuals by a single feature (race, gender, religion, sexual preference), an orientation that seems antithetical to the right not to be reduced to a category.

In each of these commenters' approaches, the question may be asked whether this is more an example of the American romance of community than an appropriate reading of the U.S. Constitution. Indeed, what is it that makes Poletown a 'community' that rises to the level of a unit the absence of which makes it impossible to exercise enumerated political rights? Note, too, that Michelman must build his analogy to property, there being no space for 'community' in the structure of the common law or the Constitution as such. Indeed, referring specifically to the *Poletown* case, Joseph L. Sax (1984: 500, original italics) notes the legal dilemma: "These particular instances reveal that there *is* a widespread sense that community is important, and a willingness exists to protect community interests, yet there is no principle or doctrine to which to turn in those cases where, for whatever reasons, the people afflicted are unable to generate the political support necessary to induce an act of grace." Sax (1984: 511) calls for the right of communities, such as those adjacent to national parks, not to have their distinctiveness adversely affected by state action where such communities "function as living organisms, with their life and lifestyle, whose vitality is itself important." In this, he once again voices that romantic vision of the community to which the law—except in its most nostalgic, romantic, fearful, or conflicted moments—has difficulty attending.

★ ★ ★

"Community is an elusive concept," says Richard Lewis, and then proves it: "By 'community' I mean a feeling, or a complex of feelings and beliefs, that has been described as 'not feeling lost' and as 'enjoying an established position in the world'... 'a web of public respect and trust, and a resource in time of personal or neighborhood need'."[32] Admittedly, 'community' is not some positivistic entity to be discovered but a construct of our own creation. Like many concepts, it benefits from being open-textured and essentially contested. Americans may rue the 'loss of community' and, with Alexis de Tocqueville (1969: 506, 508), feel that people have been led to "a passionate and exaggerated love of self" in which "each person may be shut up in the solitude of his own heart."[33] But Tocqueville was also aware of the ambivalent nature of 'democratic man,' for he not only said of such a person that democracy "constantly leads him back to himself alone" but, "I remarked a hundred times that, when needed, [Americans] almost never fail to lend faithful support to one another," that "Americans of all ages, all conditions, all minds constantly unite," that "they seek each other out," that "[i]n democratic countries the science of association is the mother science," and that in regards to the family "[d]emocracy loosens social bonds, but it tightens natural bonds. It brings relatives together at the same time that it separates citizens."[34] This ambivalence continues to manifest itself in the cultural assumptions that appear in a number of domains of the law.

As we have seen, the romance of community comes up against the romance of the individual, the latter having won out in the formulation of the nation's founding documents. Cases like *Yoder* test the limits of each concept, but can only reveal the tension between the person and the collective when the latter is rendered an idealized version of a national origin myth. In the absence of categories intermediate between the state and the individual, neither group defamation nor analogies drawn from property and tort law can gain purchase. Judicial rhetoric favors the notion of 'community,' but the cultural assumption that the cloying nature of the collective may inhibit the freedom of the individual almost always renders the references to community little more than dicta. Philosophers of law and students of jurisprudence have been no more successful in breaching the bounding categories of person and state.

Still, one could imagine arguments that, in some very particular cases, might still find a place within the existing conceptual space. For example, anthropologists have stressed the cross-cutting ties that are vital to many of the societies they have studied. Thus one may be simultaneously a neighbor, a member of a religious grouping, a kinsman, and a trading partner—and all of these affiliations cross-cutting one another such that one is less likely to press one's advantage in one role or context knowing that one will have obligations to many of the same people in another context. Marriage, redistributive networks, and ritual patterns all operate to service these interlocking ties. To sever one strand in this multiplex structure is to threaten unraveling many other strands. It is this view that may apply to the Amish or the people of Santa Clara Pueblo and perhaps to other groupings, and such interdigitating relationships may find legal support in that the individual cannot practice his or her culture if the full range of ties is undermined by state or private acts. Such an interpretation may still place emphasis on the individual's right to the society in which that right alone may be viable, but it does at least emphasize that for some people or for some relationships individuality and collective interests that are not co-extensive with political units are not necessarily mutually exclusive categories. And if that is a romance—well what are romances for if not that?

Notes

1 Boyack (2014: 770) (though ostensibly voluntary "freedom of contract is an inadequate justification for covenant enforcement in the context of privately governed communities. Such covenants do not necessarily represent voluntary owner assent to obligation and do not necessarily reflect neighborhood preferences").

2 See, e.g., Lee (2008: 563) (indicating that civic republicanism emphasizes "community, deliberation and the common good…*conceives of citizens as part of a larger political community* and stresses the potential of reaching…the common good through deliberation" (emphasis added). See also, Barden and Murphy (2010).

3 The quotation is from *Brown v. Board of Education* (1954: 494). See, Garet (1983: 1006). Community standards may also arise in other contexts: See, e.g., Neusel (2012).

4 See also, *People v. Cabrera.*

5 *Wisconsin v. Yoder.* See generally, French (1999).

6 See the video and photos of the Amish children being chased by truancy officers and its aftermath at Clayworth and White (2015). For other encounters with the law, see Hostetler (1984).

7 This point is made in the majority opinion of Chief Justice Burger (*Wisconsin v. Yoder* 1972: 237) and the concurring opinion of Justice White (*Id.*: 237, n. 2), both of whom urged the state to reach such an accommodation. On the relation of the Amish to the American legal system historically, see Kraybill (2003).

8 Mr. Yoder refused to pay the fine. On appeal, the Wisconsin appellate court sustained the trial court decision, but the Wisconsin Supreme Court reversed it, at which point the state appealed to the U.S. Supreme Court. Though each Amish community is small, it is worth noting that there are roughly 300,000 Amish in the United States.

9 In a letter written to the author dated September 10, 1976, Hostetler says: "I do not really expect to be [sic] expert witness again, nor to offer my name to a pool of experts who may be called upon. When asked to serve I would be duty bound to serve." See generally, Weaver-Zercher (2005).

10 In a personal communication to the author dated September 10, 1976 Hostetler wrote that he meant 'high school education' in this remark. He further emphasized this point in a personal interview conducted by the author at that year's meeting of the American Anthropological Association.

11 *Wisconsin v. Yoder* (1972: 245, n.2) (citing Hostetler's *Amish Society* 1963: 226). In the concurring opinion joined by Justices Brennan and Stewart, Justice White also noted: "There is evidence in the record that many children desert the Amish faith when they come of age" (*Wisconsin v. Yoder* 1972: 241, n.3).

12 On Thoreau's personal and philosophical objections to laws, see Burger's remarks at *Wisconsin v. Yoder* (1972: 216).

13 "[W]e're talking about—as will appear—the continued existence of the Amish faith community in the United states" (Irons and Guitton 1993: 97). "The Question before the Court, then, is whether the state may destroy—because that's what it will come to if these children are forced into high school—a peaceful, self-sustaining community, two hundred and fifty years on this soil..." (Id.: 99).

14 Temple University (1972).

15 Hostetler (1963: 281–3); *Wisconsin v. Yoder* (1972: 246–7).

16 Transcript of Testimony, p. 71 (emphasis added). It is not clear if the state's counsel realized Hostetler was raised Amish. Certainly, no one expected the U.S. Supreme Court to focus so heavily on the sociological information provided. Indeed, after the oral argument the attorney for the Amish, Mr. Ball, sent a note to his law partner, Joe Skelly, saying "We have LOST" (Quaqua, n.d., original caps).

17 *Wisconsin v. Yoder* (1972: 224).

18 *Id.*: 210 and 216.

19 *Id.*: 210. More recent studies show that forty percent of the Amish work in jobs unrelated to farming. See Rifkin (2009).

20 By statute, the Amish have been exempted from having to pay Social Security taxes. *Wisconsin v. Yoder* (1972: 222 and note).

21 "The observation of Justice Heffernan, dissenting below [i.e. at the Wisconsin Supreme Court], that the principal opinion in his court portrayed the Amish as leading a life of 'idyllic agrarianism,' is equally applicable to the majority opinion in this Court. So, too, is his observation that such a portrayal rests on a 'mythological basis.' Professor Hostetler (1963: 283) has noted that '[d]rinking among the youth is common in all the large Amish settlements.' Moreover, '[i]t would appear that, among the Amish, the rate of suicide is just as high, if not higher, than for the nation' (*Id.*: 300). He also notes an unfortunate Amish 'preoccupation with filthy stories,' (*Id.*: 282), as well as significant 'rowdyism and stress' (*Id.*: 281). These are not traits peculiar to the Amish, of course. The point is that the Amish are not people set apart and different" (*Wisconsin v. Yoder* 1972: 247, n.5).

22 See, Shachtman (2007).

23 See, Green (2014) and Hambright (2014).

24 Indeed, Jefferson was invoked several times in the opinions, e.g., for his view of America as based on an agrarian yeomanry of which the Amish are held out by the Court as exemplars (*Wisconsin v. Yoder* 1972: 221, 225).

25 For a case that did not extend Yoder to another religious group, see *State v. Kasuboski*. I have only found one unreported case that comes close. There, a trial court judge allowed a Seminole Indian father to keep his son from attending school up to the

mandatory age. The newspaper report of the opinion was ambiguous: The judge said the boy had all the education he needed to be a member of his community. But did that mean the limited education was enough for an Indian or that further state schooling would be contrary to the preservation of his community? And does the fact that this was a case involving a federally recognized tribe rather than a religious group make the difference?

26 See generally, Valencia-Weber (2010) and Struve (2009).
27 For background, see Davis (2008).
28 See, *Beauharnais v. Illinois*; Riesman 1942a, b, and c. Whether groups should have rights in some general sense is discussed in D'Amato 1995. For an example of the concept of community applied in a British case, see Demian (2010).
29 For an empirical test of perceptions of these factors in a sample of western Tennessee residents, see Linz et al. (1995).
30 *Poletown Neighborhood Council v. City of Detroit*. See generally, Wylie (1990) and *Kelo v. City of New London* (5–4 decision allowing seizure by state of private property to be used for a commercial venture). To date, the site has never been built upon: Somin (2015).
31 Garet cites Chief Justice Burger, in *Shad v. Borough of Mt. Ephraim* (1981: 87), saying: "Citizens should be free to choose the shape of their community so that it embodies their conception of the 'decent life'."
32 Lewis (1986: 365). See internal quotations at his notes 1–3.
33 On loss of community, see Bellah (1985) and Putnam (2001).
34 Tocqueville (2000: 404, 563, 492, 492 and 489) respectively. Among the popular works that alternately laud the renewal of 'community' and its loss are Putnam and Feldstein (2004) and Dunkelman (2014).

References

Anonymous 2002, "Obituary of John A. Hostetler," *Anthropology News*, vol. 43, no. 5 (May), p. 34.

Bellah, Robert N. et al. 1985, *Habits of the Heart*, New York: Harper and Row.

Bornstein, Avram et al. 2016, "Tell It to the Judge: Procedural Justice and a Community Court in Brooklyn," *POLAR: Political and Legal Anthropology Review*, vol. 39, no. 2 (November), pp. 206–25.

Boyack, Andrea J. 2014, "Common Interest Community Covenants and the Freedom of Contract Myth," *Journal of Law and Policy*, vol. 22, no. 2, pp. 767–844.

Clayton, Dawn 1985, "John Hostetler Bears Witness to Amish Culture and Calls the Movie Witness 'A Mockery'," *Archive*, vol. 23, no. 10, March 11. www.people.com/people/archive/article/0,,20090135,00.html (accessed January 5, 2017).

Clayworth, Jason and Rodney White 2015, "1965 Amish School Photo Started Rural Revolution," *USA Today*. www.usatoday.com/story/news/nation/2015/05/12/amish-lost-schools-iowa/27204767/ (accessed January 5, 2017).

D'Amato, Anthony 1995, "Should Groups Have Rights?" in his *International Law and Political Reality, Collected Papers, Volume One*, The Hague: Kluwer Law International, pp. 309–22.

Davis, Peggy Cooper 2008, "*Moore v. East Cleveland*: Constructing the Suburban Family," in Carol Sanger, ed., *Family Law Stories*, St. Paul, MN: Foundation Press, pp. 77–93.

Demian, Melissa 2010, "'Community' at the Expense of 'Kinship' in British Courts," *Journal of Legal Anthropology*, vol. 1, no. 2, pp. 230–46.

Dunkelman, Marc J. 2014, *The Vanishing Neighbor: The Transformation of American Community*, New York: W.W. Norton.

Erikson, Kai 1978, *Everything in Its Path: Destruction of Community in the Buffalo Creek Flood*, New York: Simon & Schuster.

French, Rebecca 1999, "From Yoder to Yoda: Traditional, Modern and Postmodern Models of Religion in U.S. Constitutional Law," *Arizona Law Review*, vol. 41, pp. 49–92.

Garet, Ronald R. 1983, "Communality and Existence: The Rights of Groups," *Southern California Law Review*, vol. 56, pp. 1001–75.

Goodmark, Leigh 2015, "'Law and Justice are Not Always the Same': Creating Community-based Justice Forums for People Subjected to Intimate Partner Abuse," *Florida State University Law Review*, vol. 42, pp. 707–63.

Green, Emma 2014, "Violence among the Amish," *The Atlantic*, September 2.

Hambright, Brett 2014, "Crimes are on the Rise in Amish Communities," *Lancaster Newspapers*, September 7.

Hostetler, John A. 1963, *Amish Society*, Baltimore, MD: Johns Hopkins Press.

——— 1984, "The Amish and the Law: A Religious Minority and Its Legal Encounters," *Washington and Lee Law Review*, vol. 41, pp. 33–47.

——— 1992, "An Amish Beginning," *The American Scholar*, pp. 552–62.

Hostetler, John A. and Susan Fisher Miller 2005, "An Amish Beginning," in David L. Weaver, ed., *Writing the Amish: The Worlds of John A. Hostetler*, University Park, PA: Penn State University Press, pp. 5–35.

Irons, Peter and Stephanie Guitton, eds., *May It Please the Court*, New York: The New Press, 1993.

Kraybill, Donald B. ed. 2003, *The Amish and the State*, Baltimore, MD: Johns Hopkins Press.

Kurland, Philp B. and Gerhard Casper, eds. 1975, *Landmark Briefs and Arguments of the Supreme Court of the United States: Constitutional Law, vol. 71*, Arlington, VA: University Publications of America, pp. 803–26.

Lee, Jin Hee 2008, "A Civic Republican View of Hospital Closures and Community Health Planning," *Fordham Urban Law Journal*, vol. 35, pp. 561–600.

Lewis, Richard 1986, "Destruction of Community," *Buffalo Law Review*, vol. 35, pp. 365–79.

Linz, Daniel et al. 1995, "Discrepancies between the Legal Code and Community Standards for Sex and Violence: An Empirical Challenge to Traditional Assumptions in Obscenity Law," *Law and Society Review*, vol. 29, no. 1, pp. 127–68.

Lynd, Staughton 1987, "The Genesis of the Idea of a Community Right to Industrial Property in Youngstown and Pittsburgh, 1977–1987," *The Journal of American History*, vol. 74, no. 3, pp. 926–958.

Mann, Bruce H. 1986, "Law, Legalism and Community before the American Revolution," *Michigan Law Review*, vol. 84, pp. 1415–39.

Michelman, Frank I. 1981, "Property as a Constitutional Right," *Washington and Lee Law Review*, vol. 38, pp. 1097–1114.

Neusel, Conor 2012, "Community Standards v. Teacher Rights: What is 'Immoral Conduct' under Missouri's Teacher Tenure Act? (Homa v. Carthage R–IX School District, 345 S.W.3d 266 (Mo. App. S. D. 2011))," *Missouri Law Review*, vol. 77, pp. 855–77.

Putnam, Robert D. 2001, *Bowling Alone: The Collapse and Revival of American Community*, New York: Simon and Schuster.

Putnam, Robert D. and Lewis Feldstein 2004, *Better Together: Restoring the American Community*, New York: Simon and Schuster.

Quaqua n.d., "Road to *Wisconsin v. Yoder*." www.quaqua.org/mennonites.htm (accessed January 5, 2017).

Riesman, David 1942a, "Democracy and Defamation: Control of Group Libel," *Columbia Law Review*, vol. 42, pp. 727–80.

——— 1942b, "Democracy and Defamation: Fair Game and Fair Comment, Part 1," *Columbia Law Review*, vol. 42, pp. 1085–1123.

———— 1942c, "Democracy and Defamation: Fair Game and Fair Comment, Part 2," *Columbia Law Review*, vol. 42, pp. 1282–1318.

Rifkin, Glenn 2009, "The Amish Flock to Small Businesses," *The New York Times*, January 7.

Sarat, Austin and Roger Berkowitz 1994, "Disorderly Differences: Recognition, Accommodation, and American Law," *Yale Journal of Law and the Humanities*, vol. 6, pp. 285–316.

Sax, Joseph L. 1984, "Do Communities Have Rights? The National Parks as a Laboratory of New Ideas," *University of Pittsburgh Law Review*, vol. 45, pp. 499–511.

Shachtman, Tom 2007, *Rumspinga: To Be or Not to Be Amish*, New York: North Point Press.

Somin, Ilya 2015, *The Grasping Hand: Kelo v. City of New London and the Limits of Eminent Domain*, Chicago, IL: University of Chicago Press.

Stern, Gerald 2008, *The Buffalo Creek Disaster: How the Survivors of One of the Worst Disasters in Coal-Mining History Brought Suit against the Coal Company—and Won*, revised edition, New York: Vintage.

Struve, Catherine T. 2009, "The Story of *Santa Clara Pueblo v Martinez*: Tribal Sovereignty, Sex Equality, and the Federal Courts," in Vicki C. Jackson and Judith Resnick eds., *Federal Court Stories*, St. Paul, MN. Foundation Press, pp. 301–28.

Temple University 1972, "John A. Hostetler," Temple University News Release.

Tocqueville, Alexis de 1969, *Democracy in America*, New York: Anchor.

———— 2000, *Democracy in America*, Chicago, IL: University of Chicago Press.

Valencia-Weber, Gloria 2010, "Three Stories in One: *Santa Clara Pueblo v. Martinez*," in Carole Goldberg and Kevin Washburn eds., *Indian Law Stories*, St. Paul, MN: Foundation Press, pp. 451–88.

Wisconsin v. Yoder 1970, Transcript of Testimony, Wisconsin Circuit Court, Green County, WI. Mimeographed.

Wylie, Jeanne 1990, *Poletown: Community Betrayed*, Urbana: University of Illinois Press.

Cases cited

Beauharnais v. Illinois, 343 U.S. 250 (1952).

Brown v. Board of Education, 347 U.S. 483 (1954).

Kelo v. City of New London, 545 U.S. 469 (2005).

Miller v California, 413 U.S. 15 (1973).

Minersville School Dist. v. Gobitis, 310 U.S. 586 (1940).

Moore v. East Cleveland, 431 U.S. 494 (1977).

Mozert v. Hawkins County Board of Education, 827 F.2d 1058 (6th Cir. 1987).

People v. Cabrera, 10 N.Y.3d 370 (2008).

People v. Conway, 6 N.Y.3d 869 (2006).

Poletown Neighborhood Council v. City of Detroit, 410 Mich. 616, 304 N.W.2d 455 (1981).

Santa Clara Pueblo v. Martinez, 436 U.S. 49 (1978).

Shad v. Borough of Mt. Ephraim, 452 U.S. 61 (1981).

State v. Kasuboski, 87 Wis.2d 407, 275 N.W.2d 101 (WI Ct. of App. 1978).

Westbrook v. General Tire and Rubber Co., 754 F.2d 1233 (5th Cir. 1985).

Wisconsin v. Yoder, 406 U.S. 205 (1972).

CONCLUSION

"Secreted in the interstices"

The "certainty" of law resides in the "uncertainty" of its basic concepts.
—Max Gluckman

There are, of course, two main avenues through which cultural assumptions are brought into the courts—by others or by the judges themselves. The former involves lawyers, witnesses, experts, the background knowledge of jurors, and the occasional fact-finding master appointed by the court. We have seen these agents at work most directly in the chapters that dealt with the cultural defense plea and the anthropologist as expert witness. Less accessible and less straightforward are those instances in which judges, knowingly or not, rely for their rulings, in whole or in part, on their own assumptions about people, events, history, and nature. Here the examples of incest, circumcision, and natural law have afforded some insight into the modes of expression that judges employ as they bring culture into the forum. At other times, as they try, for example, to fit the square peg of community into the round hole of the Constitution, they may only be able to justify their decisions by finding an overriding cultural norm. Alternatively, as in the case of circumcision, they may shift categories either to implement a decision under a new heading or duck the issue altogether. So, too, custom and the metaphors of a people's intellectual life may constitute an unavoidable avenue for conceptualization, the broader context of these features being at times welcome, at times unavoidable. Whether the cultural information arrives through outsiders or from the judge's own experience, in both types of inclusion procedural rules no doubt play a pivotal role.

Sir Henry Maine (1883: 389), speaking about an early period in the British common law, observed "that substantive law has at first the look of being gradually secreted in the interstices of procedure." This notion—that substantive propositions may be "secreted in the interstices of procedure"—also resonates in the case of importing cultural assumptions. Procedure shapes the process by which information comes before the trier of fact—through presumptions and exclusions, determinations of the weight of evidence and the process of cross-examination. Personal intuition can certainly play a key role. As Loevinger (1992: 343) notes: "Proof is a process, not a...revelation. Proof is the process of inference from evidence data, or assumptions to a conclusion. The validity of the conclusion depends on the validity of the process. ... In law, and most other disciplines, the process is only occasionally conducted according to formerly rigorous rules, and is often simply intuitive...." But cultural assumptions, too, may play a key role, whether overt or secreted in the interstices, cloistered in the gaps left by uncertainty. H. L. A. Hart once noted that for any legal judgment a twinned problem exists, what he characterized as "the uncertainty of fact and the indeterminacy of aim." Faced with these issues judges turn not only to procedure and precedent, statute and case law but to what they or others profess as commonsense assumptions drawn from their cultural background. Whether it is in the construction of procedural rules—which carry assumptions of probative value based on ideas about the relation of demeanor to credibility, psychological cause to social effect, or time to the construction of truth—or in the direct application of beliefs about the frailty of human nature, the accessibility of inner states, or the structure of familial relationships, cultural assumptions filter into the gaps of uncertain fact and inform the system's goals. If, out of the undifferentiated continuum of experience, the rules of procedure contribute to the skeletalization of facts so that a question may be posed for which a recognizable answer may be offered, then culture may be a not insignificant resource by which the bare-boned issues may be fleshed out with seeming fact.[1]

Indeed, the very uncertainty in the law demands the import of concepts that simultaneously validate shared assumptions and constitute one of the many domains in which they are challenged. A problem nevertheless remains. For many years, anthropologists (particularly those associated with the University of Chicago's department in the 1960s–80s) characterized culture through the notion of 'shared symbols.' Great attention was given to the idea of symbols—their structure and content, their manipulation and alteration—but very little attention was paid to the 'shared' part of the equation. In law, as in life, though, there must be sufficient sharing that one can orient oneself towards others: We have to be able to categorize their acts, divine their general import, and simply get on with things. But more than mere sharing of definitions is involved. As Ludwig Wittgenstein (1991 [1953], §§ 242, 241) said: "If language is to be a means of communication there must be agreement not only in definitions but also (queer as this may sound) in judgements ... [judgements that involve] not agreement in opinions but in form of life." Some connection is essential. As R. A. Duff notes: "[T]here must be a bridge, a bridge which is neither too long nor too far, which can take ordinary citizens from ordinary language into enough of the language of the law for them to be able to speak the relevant parts of that language in the first person"—although (as we saw in the discussion of the cultural defense plea)—"for some citizens that bridge is so long, or so steep, that the law cannot reasonably demand that they cross it."[2] To say that cultural concepts solve the dilemma posed for agreement would be to claim too much, particularly for those who are foreign to or unfamiliar with the law's habits. But it is also not too much to say that judges do try to cross that bridge—or at least to keep it intact—often relying on imported assumptions from the culture at large, however much they may avoid the attribution, clothe the importation in statutory or constitutional interpretation, or keep a careful (if seldom acknowledged) eye on public opinion.

Uncertainty itself, of course, takes a cultural form. In the American case, a significant part of that form is couched in terms of the quantifiable. In tort law we ask *how much* is a life worth, in criminal law *what length* of sentence equates with the deed, in patent law *what period* of exclusivity balances the act of creation. Even the intangible and inchoate must be reduced to numbers. We apply what has been called "unsegmented imponderables" to time as well as to love, and even when it smacks of the arbitrary we know in our hearts what the mathematician Nicole Oresme pointed out in the fourteenth century, that "although indivisible points, or lines, are non-existent, still it is necessary to feign them" (Crosby 1997: 71 and 110). And as in math, even if the sleight-of-hand proves unreal it does produce real results. Cultural notions, however well or poorly shared, make possible another step, another 'solution, ' another point on which the law, no less than in the operations of everyday life, can make whatever comes next seem possible, acceptable, and right enough.

It is here, too, that the legitimacy of the judicial system enters the picture. For judgments must appear to make sense not just as momentary solutions to uncertain situations; they must also preserve the sense of orderliness that is indispensable to a viable cultural system. As part of the culture, and not some disconnected aspect of it, the courts must represent their decisions in ways that tap into the assumptions that run through numerous other domains of life. Legal forums must be at once the arbiters of the propositions current in society and the repository of them. For all their grand theorizing, their arcane terminology, and their professional self-interest a common law legal system is deeply entwined in and indebted to the culture of which it is a part as its participants set about determining what is quite often indeterminable.

Commenters and court officials are not unmindful of the uncertainties with which they are faced. Recall Judge Learned Hand's confession to Justice Felix Frankfurter, following the judge's decision in the *Repouille* case, that: "I don't know how we are supposed to deal with such cases except by the best guess we have. ..." Law professors have spoken of 'incompletely theorized judgements' and the inability to monetize all that might be disputed as 'incomplete commodification.'[3] Such 'incompleteness' is the subject of many attempts to eradicate it. The temptations to comprehensive explanations drawn from the preeminent source of authority for contemporary Americans—science, or its nearest look-alike—always lurks near the courthouse door, offering an answer to uncertainty, balm to the nagging doubt. In the past, the offer was of determining character from the bumps on one's head or the commonsense of women's inability to reason, blacks' incapacity to usefully interbreed with whites, or native peoples' inability to govern themselves. If once Mr. Justice Holmes could assert that "The Fourteenth Amendment does not enact Mr. Herbert Spencer's Social Statics,"[4] courts have, in more recent years been told that the invisible hand of the market will see us through to the right decisions, that if only the psychiatrists are given free rein will criminal intent and insanity be pinned down once and for all, or that (given the predilection of the day) biology or neurology will relieve us of all uncertainties. Of late—and as a counter to the law and economics movement that has captured the terms of discussion in the U.S. for over a generation—we are offered behavioral psychology, complete with a Nobel Prize for its progenitor, Daniel Kahneman, to match that of its law and economics rival, Ronald Coase, with, as a final trump card, a brain scan at the end to prove where the light really lies. At their moment of dominance, each theory appears all-embracing, perhaps because our need for greater certainty is so pressing. And pressing it is in the law, where actual decisions of a binary nature—guilty or innocent, liable or not—render indecision unseemly and, worse, threaten the entire system's legitimacy.

Yet in each instance, it is the linkage of these claimed explanations to the many other domains of life that either succeeds or fails to render them integral parts of an overall cultural design. That the design is itself imperfect, emergent, and comprised of 'essentially contested concepts' is not, however, to say that it is without persuasive force. Ironically, it may be that it is because of its reliance on cultural concepts that are themselves open-textured that the law, dependent as it is on those concepts for its orientations and credence, is itself heir to a certain form of uncertainty. For it is, as we have suggested throughout, of the very essence of our species that we are category creating animals, governed not by instinct but endowed with the ability to fashion the categories of our own experience. And it is that capacity that will continue to inform the law as part of culture, albeit in constantly varying ways, so long as we confront a world to which we must make our assumptions feel innate, our structures immanent, and our decisions legitimized by the way they partake of the world as we have come to make it seem.

Notes

1 On skeletalizing in the law, see Geertz 1983: 167–234.
2 Duff (1998: 200 and 206). See also the case of an intra-tribal murder involving Australian aborigines described in Misner 1986.
3 The phrases come, respectively, from Sunstein (1996) and Radin (2001).
4 *Lochner v. New York* (1905: 75).

References

Crosby, Alfred 1997, *The Measure of Reality: Quantification and Western Society, 1250–1600*, Cambridge: Cambridge University Press.

Duff, R. A. 1998, "Law, Language and Community: Some Preconditions of Criminal Liability," *Oxford Journal of Legal Studies*, vol. 18, no. 2, pp. 189–206.

Geertz, Clifford 1983, *Local Knowledge: Further Essays in Interpretive Anthropology*, New York: Basic Books.

Loevinger, Lee 1992, "Standards of Proof in Science and Law," *Jurimetrics Journal*, vol. 32, pp. 323–60.

Maine, Henry S. 1883, *Dissertations on Early Law and Custom*, London: John Murray.

Misner, Robert L. 1986, "The Awkward Case of Henry Gibson," *Arizona State Law Review*, vol. 1986, pp. 691–725.

Radin, Margaret Jane 2001, *Contested Commodities*, Cambridge, MA: Harvard University Press.

Sunstein, Cass 1996, *Legal Reasoning and Political Conflict*, New York: Oxford University Press, 1996

Wittgenstein, Ludwig 1991 [1953], *Philosophical Investigations*, 3rd ed., New York: Wiley Blackwell.

Case cited

Lochner v. New York, 198 U.S. 45 (1905).

INDEX